Electronic Day Trading Made Easy

Revised and Expanded 2nd Edition

MISHA T. SARKOVICH, PH.D.

PRIMA MONEY
An Imprint of Prima Publishing
3000 Lava Ridge Court • Roseville, California 95661
(800) 632-8676 • www.primalifestyles.com

PRIMA MONEY and colophon are trademarks of Prima Communications Inc. PRIMA PUBLISHING and colophon are trademarks of Prima Communications Inc., registered with the United States Patent and Trademark Office.

Library of Congress Cataloging-in-Publication Data
Sarkovich, Misha T.
    Electronic day trading made easy: become a successful trader by learning how to
1. Execute trades. 2. Minimize risk. 3. Trade strategically. 4. Analyze technical data.
5. Evaluate level II screens / Misha T. Sarkovich.
Rev. and expanded 2nd ed.
    p. cm.
Includes index.
ISBN 0-7615-3098-3
    1. Electronic trading of securities. 2. Day trading (Securities) I. Title. II. Made easy series (Roseville, Calif.)

HG4515.95.S27   2000
332.64'0285—dc21   00-068820
                                              CIP

01 02 03 04 HH 10 9 8 7 6 5 4 3 2 1

Printed in the United States of America

How to Order

Single copies may be ordered from Prima Publishing, 3000 Lava Ridge Court, Roseville, CA 95661; telephone (800) 632-8676 ext. 4444. Quantity discounts are also available. On your letterhead, include information concerning the intended use of the books and the number of books you wish to purchase.

Visit us online at www.primapublishing.com

Contents

Section III
Introduction to Technical Analysis Tools

Section IV
Introduction to Order Executions

Section V
Day Trading Techniques

Section VI
Introduction to Day Trading Brokers

Appendixes

Acknowledgments

Just as I did the first edition, I dedicate this second edition to my family, especially my wife, Kimberly, and our sons, Stefan and Marco, whose ongoing support made this conceivable.

The last word of acknowledgment delightfully goes to Prima Publishing editor David Richardson, for his professional assistance and continuous faith in this work.

Disclaimer

Since this book covers the topic of securities day trading, the book naturally begins with disclaimers. The day trading business involves money (sometimes a lot of money), and we live in a litigious society. Disclaimers are an unfortunate part of the securities trading business.

➤ This book is designed as an introduction to day trading. It is intended only to give readers a general idea of how the day trading business works and how to get started if they desire to trade. The book could never be 100% complete, since the day trading business is continuously evolving.

➤ Much of the information provided in this book represents the author's own opinions. He encourages all readers to do their own research and verify the information presented in the book.

➤ Day trading is an inherently risky business. Day traders should be prepared to lose their trading capital. Since day traders open and trade margin accounts (where a part of the money put into play is borrowed), it is possible to sustain losses that are greater than one's initial trading capital. Do not trade money that you cannot afford to lose.

➤ Day traders must be responsible for their own actions. Each day trader is accountable for every completed trade, even if the trader did not intend to make a specific trade. Please, if you are a beginning trader, be careful when executing trades.

➤ The author does not recommend the purchase or sale of any particular security. Nor does he guarantee that any specific return can be achieved through day trading. Furthermore, the author does not guarantee the effectiveness of any particular trading strategy.

➤ Electronic day trading is on the cutting edge of technology, and day traders must accept all associated risks of computer equipment, network, and software failures.

Introduction

Over the past two decades, technology has revolutionized the way in which our securities market operates. Securities transactions that were once slow and costly, dependent on long paper trails and intensive human labor, have become instantaneous and inexpensive with the advent of computers. Today, with the click of a button, orders can be entered, executed, and confirmed within seconds.

Dr. Richard Lindsey
Director of Market Regulation
U.S. Securities and Exchange Commission
May 1997

THE DIGITAL INFORMATION REVOLUTION, AND PARTICULARLY THE INTERNET, has fundamentally changed Wall Street and the way Americans trade stocks. This new phenomenon of electronic stock trading is in fact one of the fastest growing segments of the U.S. securities market. Even after taking into account all of the hype, the reality is still spectacular, and it is difficult to find parallels to the explosive growth of electronic stock trading.

The explosion in online investing and trading and the emergence of deep-discount brokers—as well as the huge increase in the number of mutual funds and 401(k) retirement plans—have made the stock market more accessible to the average American than ever before. At the end of 1999, 48% of U.S. households owned stocks. Just four years earlier, that number was 41%, and ten years earlier, 32%. According to Forrester Research, 3.1 million households in the United States were trading online at the end of 1999, up from 2.2 million in 1998. That number is expected to grow to 6.7 million households by 2002 and to 9.7 million by 2003. In contrast, full-service brokers account for 40 million accounts. At the end of 1999, online trading transactions represented 17.8% of all equity exchanges in the United States.

For 2000, the Electronic Traders Association (ETA) estimates that electronic stock trading accounted for about 15% of The Nasdaq Stock Market's (NASDAQ, formerly known as the National Association of Securities Dealers Automated Quotation System) daily volume, up from a 10% share in 1997. This daily trading volume is generated by approximately 5,000 full-time electronic day traders. More than half of all limit orders—a trade order to buy or sell stock when a price is fixed—submitted to the NASDAQ come from those day traders. When the occasional or part-time day traders who trade electronically from their homes over the Internet are added into this equation, total daily volume attributed to electronic traders is closer to 25%.

One common concern about day trading is the success rate of people who actively trade. A study conducted by the North American Securities Administrators Association (NASAA) determined that 70% of day traders lose money and only 11.5% can make a living through day trading. Not surprisingly, the ETA immediately questioned the methodology and validity of the NASAA study. For instance, the ETA pointed out that only 17 day traders from a single firm were part of the NASAA study. It is difficult to take seriously the results from a sample of only 17 out of a population of 5,000 traders. What would be the confidence interval or the error term of the NASAA conclusions based on such a minuscule sample? Select another sample of 17 traders and you may obtain completely different results. This is clearly bad science. The ETA plans to commission its own study, which I hope will draw from a much bigger sample and thus have a larger confidence interval.

Trading Electronically

Since the advent of stock exchanges, individuals have been engaged in professional stock trading for their own accounts, with those individuals who could afford to do so holding seats on a stock exchange. Working on the exchange floor gave professional traders a substantial trading advantage, such as instantaneous quotes and order executions. In exchange for that privilege, a professional trader would pay many thousands of dollars for an exchange seat. However, with advances in computer and networking technology, as well as new Securities and Exchange Commission (SEC) regulations, the NASDAQ and New York Stock Exchange (NYSE) are now accessible to amateur traders.

It is now possible for novice and experienced amateur traders to do their own research over the Internet and execute their own trades electronically from their homes. Essentially, they can trade the way professional traders and money managers have been doing for decades. David Whitcomb, a Rutgers University finance professor, stated in a newspaper article that "most day trading firms see themselves as Wall Street's populists, allowing the little guy to bypass brokers and get the direct access to the market. It is the democratization of trading." Main Street has moved closer to Wall Street.

There are two ways to trade stocks electronically. The first is to trade through a discount broker over the Internet. The convenience of trading at home and the low commissions charged by online brokerages have opened up stock trading to the small player. More than 160 brokers offer online trading services, although a mere 15 companies made up 96% of the online brokerage market at the start of 2000. Because the electronic brokerage business has mushroomed in the United States during the past few years, it pays to research your online broker. E-commerce expert and evaluator Gómez *(www.gomez.com)* currently ranks 55 brokerage firms that offer online stock-trading brokerage services. Similarly, Internet Investing *(www.internetinvesting.com)* and Wall Street Online *(www.wallstonline.com)* provide reference lists of online brokers. Some of the firms are well-known names on Wall Street, such as Charles Schwab, E*Trade, Ameritrade, Fidelity, DLJ Direct, and American Express. Those brokerage firms sell more than electronic access to equities' traders. They also sell options, IRAs, mutual funds, and asset and cash management services.

The second method of electronic trading is working through one of the electronic day trading firms that has branch offices all over the United States. Day trading firms cater to professional day traders who demand instantaneous quotes and executions, and they specialize in electronic stock trading only. They tend to be small, new firms.

Not Without Risk

Day trading is not simply a "Get Rich Click" scheme, and it is not for everyone. Many have tried it, and quite a few have failed. But for those who succeed, day trading is a financially and intellectually rewarding way to make a living. In the financial world, a long-held axiom states that there is a positive correlation between risk and return: the higher the risk, the higher the return. This is clearly true for the business of electronic day trading.

There is only anecdotal evidence (media reports) about the profitability of day trading, and no scientific formal study has been completed that authoritatively documents day traders' income. The variance of income distribution among day traders is huge. Several magazine and newspaper articles have featured day traders who are making six- or seven-figure incomes. And in fact, a few experienced traders who have access to large trading capital can earn such high levels of income. Most day traders will not reach these levels. However, if properly trained and with enough experience and trading risk capital, a day trader can earn sufficient income to take this from a part-time endeavor to a full-time profession.

James Lee, president of the ETA *(www.electronic-traders.com)*, claims that after a six-month learning curve, a third of the players lose money, another third tread water, and the rest do well. Lee also noted that "day trading is trading and not investing, and people need to understand that. And though it is a very successful business long-term, it is very difficult to get started."

In summary, following are some caveats from the ETA regarding the risks of day trading:

➤ Day trading requires skill, discipline, and hard work.

➤ Successful traders regard day trading as a career and not a hobby.

➤ National securities markets are extremely efficient and competitive.

➤ New traders will compete against professional traders who have been trading for many years.

➤ Financial markets are very dynamic and competitive, and their conditions change. What may have been a successful trading strategy in the past might not work in the future.

➤ Only risk capital should be used for day trading. Do not trade money that you cannot afford to lose.

➤ The learning curve is steep. Most people who begin day trading sustain losses or produce only marginal profits during the first three to five months of day trading. Do not trade unless you are willing to sustain losses while gaining day trading experience.

➤ Individuals who are not highly disciplined should avoid day trading.

➤ The new trader should limit both the number of trades he or she makes and the size of the trades to limit losses during the learning process.

➤ In addition to the normal market risk (that is, price volatility), the day trader is exposed to occasional trading-execution risks. The entire electronic trading platform (the computer network) could fail due to factors beyond anyone's control.

➤ Market orders can be risky, since large price gaps can occur (for example, buying stock at a higher price or selling it at a lower price than anticipated). Sometimes limit orders cannot be executed.

Many individuals have opened trading accounts with electronic day trading firms or through online brokers without fully understanding the skills needed or the risks involved in being successful. The risk of loss in day trading is substantial: at best the day trader can only manage or control the risk; it can never be eliminated completely. Anyone considering day trading should evaluate their suitability and appropriateness in light of their financial resources and circumstances.

In January 1999, SEC Chairman Arthur Levitt stated,

> Investing in the stock market, however you do it and however easy it may be, will always entail risk. I would be very concerned if investors allowed the ease with which they can make trades to short-cut or bypass the three golden rules for all investors:
>
> > Know what you are buying.
> > Know the ground rules under which you buy and sell a stock.
> > Know the level of risk you are undertaking.
>
> Strategies such as day trading can be highly risky, and retail investors engaging in such activities should do so with funds they can afford to lose.

Well said.

Stock Market Essentials

Before we go any further, I would like to outline here a few of my views about the stock market and trading that underscore the ideas that permeate this book. I believe that most stock market participants would concur with my assessments.

1. The Stock Market Is Not a Zero-Sum Game.

Many people have called the stock market a "zero-sum game" in which for every winner there is also a loser. It's my belief that the stock market is anything but a zero-sum game; however, other markets, such as futures and options and so-called derivatives, certainly are. Unlike the derivatives market, the stock market does not have contracts with expiration dates that must have an equal number of winners and losers. Options and futures trading involve executing contracts between the sellers and the buyers that have stipulated expiration dates. When the contract expires, either the contract buyers or the contract sellers have made money. Options and futures trading are extremely competitive and efficient. It is my opinion that in this particular trading environment there is a transfer of wealth from the less experienced and knowledgeable options and futures amateur traders to the more experienced and knowledgeable options and futures professional traders. I believe that trading equities is easier than trading options and futures.

In the long run, the overall stock market has had a positive rate of return, or a positive long-term bias. Since 1926, the stock market has returned an average annual return of approximately 11%, which is a higher annual rate of return than the risk-free U.S. Treasury bond market's 5.2%. And the late 1990s have been even better. Stocks in the S&P 500 Index (which represents 80% of the overall market capitalization) increased in value 21% in 1999. In addition, the average annual returns for three-year, five-year, and ten-year periods were approximately 28%, 29%, and 18%. Where is the zero-sum game here?

The equities market has many diverse and heterogeneous participants. Investors, traders, mutual and pension funds, institutional holders—each has diverse objectives and holding periods that range from the extreme short-term period (day traders) to the extreme long-term period (pension funds). Different participants in the equities market have different price targets and time frames for their decisions. It is quite feasible for a trader to sell to an investor a stock at a price that is overvalued at that point in time (and the trader would make money on the trade), and for the long-term investor to make money on that stock many years later when the stock is finally sold. In other words, short-term traders can make money in the short run and long-term investors can make money in the long run.

Finally, the total amount of funds in the stock market is not fixed. There is a continuous inflow and outflow of funds from the bond or fixed income markets and from abroad. I perceive the stock market to be an alpine lake with an inflow and outflow. The water level of that lake is sometimes rising, and sometimes declining, but it never remains constant. For instance, if short-term interest rates drop, there will be an outflow of funds from the bond market into the stock market. If the Japanese yen appreciates in value against the U.S. dollar, the U.S. stock market will become cheaper for Japanese investors and there will be an inflow of funds from Japan. There might even be changes in U.S. tax laws, demographics, and savings patterns that will affect the flow of funds into the stock market.

2. The Stock Market Is Extremely Volatile in the Short Run.

Is this news to anyone? The stock market, and particularly the NASDAQ, is a roller coaster in the short run. On Friday, April 14, 2000, the NASDAQ plunged a record 355 points, or approximately 10%, which was the worst one-day drop in history. Consider also that on Tuesday, April 4, 2000, the NASDAQ initially plunged 574 points, or approximately 14%, in an intraday decline before rallying back to close down less than 100 points. Altogether, April 2000 brought unprecedented volatility for the technology-loaded NASDAQ, which declined 25% in value during one week of trading.

The surprising element is that investors took this volatility in stride, without any panic. Then, approximately one month later, the NASDAQ recorded the best week in its history. The NASDAQ Composite Index rose 608 points for the week beginning on May 29, 2000, which was an astounding 19% gain in one week. Then we observed another major market correction for NASDAQ stocks in September and October 2000, when the NASDAQ Composite Index declined more than one-quarter in value. Altogether, the NASDAQ Composite Index lost nearly half its value in ten months of trading since its all-time peak in March of 2000.

Perhaps you recall October 28, 1997, when the Dow Jones Industrial Average dropped 554 points, or 7.2% of its value, in a single day. And think back ten years earlier than that, to October 19, 1987, or Black Monday, when the Dow crashed 508 points in one day, an astonishing 22.6% decline. As an investment, bond markets are much calmer in terms of short-term price volatility because of their fixed income component structure.

Many Wall Street analysts are concerned that stock market price volatility has increased in the recent past, and they believe that the volatility results from increased speculation. The North American Securities Administrators Association (NASAA) reported that short-term volatility has indeed been high and continues to rise. For the 12-month period in 1999, more than 40% of the daily closing prices for the S&P 500 Index differed from the previous day's close by more than one percentage point. This level of price volatility has been surpassed only twice during the past 35 years.

Is this increased short-term volatility the result of stock speculation that comes with the practice of day trading or online stock trading? There is no clear answer to this question. However, I question the cause-and-effect relationship. Short-term traders are attracted to volatile stocks at the outset. Traders trade Internet stocks *because* those stocks are volatile. How would a stock that did not have any price movement be traded? The fact that traders are trading Internet stocks does not make Internet stocks volatile in themselves. The real reason Internet and other high-technology stocks are volatile is that the Internet and high-tech firms have expected corporate earnings streams that are uncertain and volatile.

3. Risk and Return Are Positively Correlated.

This statement is intuitively clear and should be no surprise to anyone. Yet I am always amazed to hear people compare stock trading with investing. Stock trading is not investing. A stock trader's objective is to earn a high income *now*, whereas the investor's objective is to receive a high-percentage rate of return in the future. To earn that high level of income, the short-term trader must increase her trading activity and thus command greater financial leverage. In other words, a trader will execute many trades with limited risk capital during the year and, as a result, will end up purchasing a large amount of stocks during that year.

If the trader is successful, the absolute dollar amount of income, when translated into percentage terms, represents an extremely high rate of return. The only way anyone can earn such a high rate of return on a limited investment is to assume higher risk and leverage. Therefore, you cannot compare returns between the stock trader and the investor, because the risk factors are dramatically different.

Likewise, you cannot compare the failure rate between stock traders and investors, because the risk–reward metrics between the two groups is dramatically different. So what if 100% of U.S. Treasury-bond investors made money (assuming the investor is holding the bond to maturity) if the annual rate of return is 5% or 6%? Short-term traders seek a 500% or 600% annual rate of return. Is it so surprising, given the higher assumed risk, that the majority of short-term traders will lose money?

4. In the Short Run, Stock Prices Are Determined by the Interplay of Many Market Forces. In the Long Run, the Most Important Market Variable Is Expected Corporate Earnings.

In the short run, a myriad of market variables, such as investors' sentiment, weather, or interest rates, can and do influence a stock's price. However, in the long run, earnings determine whether a company is a viable business enterprise. Investors buy a piece of paper (the company stock) because that paper represents an ownership claim on the company's future earnings. If the prospects for a company's future earnings are not there, there will be little demand for that paper. Consequently, investors and traders pay close attention to corporate earnings and earnings announcements or surprises.

5. Stock Trading Is Not Gambling.

Stock trading is not a game of chance. The only similarity between stock trading and gambling is the probability of loss. But unlike gamblers, stock traders have the opportunity to manage their risk. Because online traders have a wealth of financial information at their fingertips and more information on their monitors than the great majority of participants in the stock market, they are able to take educated and calculated risks. In addition, online traders can execute their orders relatively quickly, so they can get out quickly when they need to.

It is not realistic to expect that traders will be correct 100% of the time. Even if they are correct 50% of the time, which would be equivalent to a game of chance, stock traders can still be profitable if they minimize losses when they are wrong (get out quickly at a minimal loss) and allow profits to rise when they are right. To be successful in the long run, stock traders must minimize their losses and maximize their profits. Given the quantity and sophistication of the financial information presented to online traders in real time, the probability of being right should be higher than 50%. With trading experience (that is, at least six months of live trading), that probability should increase.

It is true that many stock traders have a gambling mentality: They enjoy the rush of adrenaline when they make the right trade. However, good traders do not gamble. A good trader will enter a position only when he receives a clear trading signal, such as those we will discuss in the chapters on technical analysis. My point is that good traders follow the signals from the trading system they use, and they do not gamble. Bad traders, or soon-to-be ex-traders, do not have a trading system; they gamble.

6. Stock Trading Is a Business That Is Not Suitable for Everyone.

Stock trading is hard work and not entertainment. Stock trading requires knowledge of trading, time to trade, adequate risk capital, and a great deal of self-discipline. I believe that stock traders are true entrepreneurs. They risk their own capital and they make all their own business (trading) decisions. If trading becomes a hobby, it becomes an expensive hobby.

To be successful in this emerging profession, stock traders must be disciplined, patient, and have the ability to assume risk. Successful traders patiently wait for a trading signal, and if they are wrong, they have the discipline to get out of the trade and minimize the loss.

Not all potential traders have the required personal characteristics to be successful traders. In addition to the key personal traits of self-discipline, patience, and the ability to assume risk, successful stock traders also tend to exhibit the following characteristics:

➤ *Intelligence*. Trading is an extremely competitive business. At any point in time, the trader is competing against professional market makers and other day traders. To survive in this business, traders must be smart.

➤ *Flexibility*. Market conditions are fluid and are always in a state of motion. The trader must be able to change and adapt with the changing trading environment. For instance, traders should be able to trade both long and short positions with relative ease.

➤ *Ability to work hard*. Trading is a business. People who succeed in this business have worked hard to get there, and they have paid their dues.

➤ *Willingness to learn*. Successful traders strive to learn something new during each trading day, if not during each trade. They know that there is always room for self-improvement.

➤ *Confidence*. Traders are not troubled by a series of bad trades during the week. They are confident that their trading discipline, risk management, and perseverance will ultimately translate into success.

➤ *Ability to react under stress*. This ability to react to trading losses or respond to information overload is important for traders to succeed. Traders should be able to make trading decisions without freezing up or panicking.

If you believe that you possess these characteristics, then you can certainly benefit from what this book has to offer. The book's purpose is to provide a complete, reliable, and responsibly written guide to stock trading for both future and current stock traders. The book does not profess to abolish the risk of stock trading, because that risk is always there, no matter how much you know. It only presents the tools of risk management and demystifies, in a step-by-step manner, the complex knowledge that is required today to trade stocks for maximum profit. Only then, with adequate knowledge, can you gain control of your trading.

Introduction to Day Trading

NO SINGLE BOOK CAN CREATE A SUCCESSFUL DAY TRADER. HOWEVER, READING this book is a step in the right direction. In section I, we start at square one and define, explain, and illustrate the basic day trading terms and concepts being used in the profession today.

➤ Section I starts with a description of the current day trading environment. The relative advantages of day trading, such as the speed and control of trading and going home "flat," are identified. Several important distinctions are made: the day trader versus the investor, the day trader versus the gambler, being reactive versus proactive, and using technical analysis versus fundamental analysis.

➤ The relative risks associated with short holding periods for day trading are described. The importance of continuous oversight and trading discipline is strongly emphasized. Finally, the benefits and drawbacks of paper (or simulation) trading are discussed.

➤ We also elaborate on the four essential qualities that day traders must possess: (1) knowledge and skill of stock trading, (2) adequate risk capital as well as potential sources of trading capital, (3) time to day trade, and (4) the ability to manage risk with a disciplined trading style.

➤ Finally, we briefly introduce the trading markets, such as The Nasdaq Stock Market (NASDAQ) and the New York Stock Exchange (NYSE).

1

What Is Day Trading?

Day trading consists of the direct opening and closing of stock positions on major stock exchanges. Day trading can be done by using a computer on the trading floor at a branch office of a day trading firm with a direct line to The Nasdaq Stock Market (NASDAQ) and New York Stock Exchange (NYSE) systems, or by using a home or business computer to access an Internet broker (like E*Trade or Charles Schwab). The key word in this definition is *direct*. In day trading, a trader has direct electronic access to NASDAQ market makers or NYSE specialists.

The market makers are National Association of Securities Dealers (NASD) brokers and dealers who either buy or sell NASDAQ stocks for the accounts of others or for their own proprietary accounts. In essence, the market makers are stock merchants. One NASDAQ stock will have many market makers who are continuously trading in that stock and thus *making a market* for that stock. On the other hand, one NYSE stock will have one assigned specialist. The role of the specialist is to maintain a fair and orderly market in that security. The specialist may act either as a broker and execute orders for other securities brokers or act as a dealer in a principal capacity when trading for his or her own account. The specialist will take on the role of a principal infrequently, in order to maintain stock marketability and counter temporary imbalances in the supply and demand of that security.

The day trader does not need a stockbroker. The trader does not use a telephone to call a stockbroker, nor does a broker relay that order to the brokerage firm's order desk, nor does a clerk route that order to the market maker. Day trading firms eliminate all that. Consequently, time delays and most of the expenses associated with having middlemen process trade orders are eliminated. The day traders are their own brokers, and their order executions are fast and affordable.

On a computer that runs specialized trade-execution software, the trader simply keys in the stock symbol, presses the appropriate function key or clicks the mouse, and buys or sells shares of stock on a major exchange. It is that simple. The software used by day trading firms for order execution is relatively user-friendly and provides an efficient interface between the stock exchanges and the day trader. Because access is direct, order executions and trade confirmations are fast. And with no middlemen involved, transaction costs are deeply discounted.

The New Trading Environment

Historically, stock trading has been the domain of professional traders. Wall Street firms have traditionally had access to better information and trade execution, which gave them a clear trading advantage. Day trading has changed that. For the first time, amateur traders have the tools—real-time quotes and order execution—to compete with the professionals. These tools are now available because of:

➤ Technological advancements in computer hardware;

➤ Technological improvements in networking science;

➤ Securities and Exchange Commission (SEC) regulations that mandated direct access to the NASDAQ market for small players;

➤ Low-cost commission structure; and

➤ Increasing intraday price volatility.

Technological improvements in computer hardware since the early 1990s have resulted in computers and servers that are extremely fast and have large amounts of memory (RAM). Consequently, these computers are capable of reliably processing a large quantity of real-time data flow. In addition, such computers are increasingly more affordable, and day trading firms and their branch offices can order relatively inexpensive and fast DSL, T1, or 56 Kbps communication lines, too. Computer networking advances since the early 1990s have made real-time financial data feed as well as trade-order execution feasible and affordable.

Another result of this technological leap is that small groups of investors can pool their financial resources and open branch offices of day trading firms in small towns anywhere in the United States, which levels the playing field for all participants. Technologically feasible and financially affordable electronic access to relative information and trading has made this possible.

The stock market crash of 1987 propelled the SEC to mandate NASDAQ market makers to provide individual investors with better access to trade execution. In October 1987, when stock prices were free-falling, some market makers simply refused to pick up their ringing phones and execute sell orders for panicked sellers. In other words, the market makers refused to buy stock that was continually declining in value. In 1987, the SEC mandated market maker participation in the NASDAQ Small Order Execution System (SOES). The SOES was implemented to ensure small customers and traders access to the posted market price, thus ensuring public confidence in the NASDAQ. The SOES initially was the dominant execution vehicle for day traders. Today, however, more and more day traders are using electronic communication networks (ECNs).

In May 1975, Wall Street firms ended the practice of charging fixed commissions. This deregulation resulted in the emergence of discount brokers. Then, technological advances in the 1990s brought the emergence of Internet brokers and electronic day trading firms. The new competition caused trading transaction costs to decrease even further. This low-cost commission structure makes daily in-and-out stock trading financially feasible. Day traders can make 50 or more trades a day, and their potential profits are not eaten up by commissions.

Most day trading firms tend to charge deeply discounted commissions that range from $10 to $25 per trade. Competition among day trading firms in large metropolitan areas can result in even lower commissions. Furthermore, established and profitable day traders are often able to negotiate even lower commission structures. As a general rule, Internet brokers offer the lowest commissions—$5 to $30 per trade for market orders. However, Internet brokers provide a different type of trading service, with somewhat slower quotes and order execution.

In the 1990s, the U.S. stock market became increasingly more volatile, a derivative of the dynamic, interdependent, and global U.S. economy. Intraday price volatility is here to stay, and is exactly what fuels day trading profit opportunities. The objective of an experienced day trader is to trade volatile stocks in large-share blocks and profit from their intraday price movement.

Speed Advantage

The key advantage of this style of trading is its speed. The technology is advanced enough to afford traders the ability to receive and observe real-time price quotes tick by tick and to send an electronic execution order directly to the NASDAQ market maker. The process of day trading is relatively simple: Day traders sit in front of computer monitors, observe real-time financial data that is packaged in advanced format by sophisticated software (for example, custom tickers and technical analysis charts), and attempt to identify a price trend or momentum. Once the trend is observed and recognized, the trader needs only to react and participate in that trend.

When an order is placed, electronic order execution is fast. With the stroke of a key, orders are sent directly to the NASDAQ market makers. Confirmations are received in seconds. Exiting trades is as easy and fast as entering the trade positions, although the submitted market orders might not receive the price that the day traders are hoping for. Sometimes, the holding period between the buy and sell order is only a few minutes, because a stock price can move up or down $\frac{1}{4}$ or $\frac{1}{2}$ point in such a short time. On 1,000 shares, that translates into $250 or $500 potential profit or loss. The speed of the received order execution and financial information gives the day trader a fighting chance to compete with the professional Wall Street players.

Control Advantage

The other key advantage of day trading is the control of trading. Day traders are always in control of their own trading. They are their own brokers. They examine the financial data, ascertain the trends, and make their own decisions to buy or sell. There are no stockbrokers involved to provide advice or recommendations on what and when to buy or sell. Day traders receive full credit or blame for the success or failure of their trading.

Since traders have access to real-time price quotes and order execution, there is no need to send *stop orders*—orders to buy or sell at a price above or below the current market price. Investors often use stop buy or stop sell orders to limit loss or to protect unrealized profits. Stop orders are activated if the market price of the stock hits the specified order price.

Some people in the securities industry believe that brokers have the ability to manipulate the short-term market price, and thus have the ability to activate the stop orders if the stop order price is set too close to the current market price. In such a case, the price could go up or down briefly regardless of the overall trend and activate the stop order. The broker could then execute the order and get the commission.

Day traders monitor their trading positions in real time, observing price movement and getting out of a position quickly if the market is moving against them. Day traders do not need to submit stop orders; that is, they do not need to advertise the price at which they are willing to get out of the trade. Day traders do not have to assume the risk of being "picked up" by the brokers who are "running the stops." In other words, they do not need to be irritated that the short-term stock prices were being manipulated by the brokers just to activate their trade orders.

Also, day traders do not have to worry about price *slippage*. They monitor market prices tick by tick. At any point during the trading day, the trader knows the stock's best BID—the price a market maker is willing to pay—and ASK—the price a stock holder is willing to sell—price. If the market is stable at that point in time, the day trader's buy or sell market order will be executed at the best BID or ASK price. The day trader would route or preference her buy or sell market order to the NASDAQ market maker who is posting the stock's best BID and ASK price. Thus, the day trader gets the best price at that time. In addition, day traders working in day trading offices can submit and receive an even better price. Those day traders can cut the *spread* between the BID and ASK prices by offering to buy or sell through private ECNs such as Island or Instinet.

Investors who are buying or selling stock through a broker over the phone do not have such a luxury. Most likely, such investors would not know what the actual best BID and ASK prices are at that point in time since they do not have access to real-time quotes. If the broker is also a market maker for that stock, the investors will receive the price that is advertised by that broker, which may not be the best price. Day traders are assured that they are receiving the best price because they control their own trades.

Going Home "Flat"

At the end of the trading day, day traders close all of their trade positions and go home *flat*. At 4:00 P.M. Eastern time (or 1:00 P.M. Pacific time), their jobs are done—no worries or stress. Without any open positions, day traders do not carry any overnight risk exposure. They do not need to worry about a *long* or *short position*—because they do not have overnight positions. The entire stock market could collapse overnight (which admittedly is a very unlikely scenario), and a day trader would not lose a penny.

A new day is truly a new beginning. It does not matter how the day trader performed the previous day; yesterday's performance has no impact on today's outcome. Each morning a day trader starts fresh. Each morning the day trader's computerized account manager will start again with a zero profit-and-loss balance.

Even if a trader has a winning long position at the end of the day and the trend is continuing, my advice would be still to go flat. A day trader's commission structure is low enough that it does not make sense to assume an overnight long position to save on a commission. If the trader is trading in 1,000-share increments, a long overnight position translates into substantial overnight risk exposure. A price *gap* (or difference between the previous day's stock closing price and today's opening price) of only 1 point would translate into $1,000 potential loss. Why risk $1,000 in order to save $20 on commission?

Many factors could lead into a situation in which the stock is opening with a price gap. Companies usually wait for market close before management announces bad news. The federal government usually announces economic news at 8:00 A.M. Eastern time, before the markets open. Large financial institutions continue to trade after the markets close through private markets such as Instinet, and thus the price at the market open could be dramatically different than at the previous day's close. Many things can happen to a stock price overnight, so price gaps occur frequently. By holding an overnight position, day traders essentially relinquish their advantage of being in control.

CHAPTER

2

Day Traders

T HE DAY TRADER'S ULTIMATE OBJECTIVE IS TO TRADE EXPENSIVE AND volatile stocks on the NASDAQ and NYSE in increments of 1,000 shares or more, and to profit from small intraday price movements. The trader may make many trades in a single day—sometimes 50 to 100—and hold onto stocks for only a few minutes or hours, but almost never overnight. Most day trading is confined to the NASDAQ market, which is better equipped for computerized trading and is laden with expensive and volatile high-technology and Internet stocks. Day traders are short-term price speculators. They are not investors, and they are not gamblers.

Day Trader Versus Investor

Day trading is not investing. The day trader's time frame of analysis is short: one day. The only intent is to exploit a stock's intraday price swings or daily price volatility. Unlike stock investors, day traders do not seek long-term value appreciation. If the stock value is going up at that point in time, day traders will take a long position—that is, purchase the stock. The day trader would purchase the stock at a low price and hope to sell it in a few minutes or hours at a higher price.

If the stock value is going down, the day trader will take a short position—that is, sell the stock first after borrowing it from the brokerage firm. At that time, the day trader would sell short a stock at the high price and buy it a few minutes or hours later at a lower price. If the stock values are stable, the day trader will sit on the sideline and simply not trade. Good day traders can play both short and long positions and thus not care whether the market is moving up or down, as long as it is not going sideways, which indicates stable prices.

Stock volatility is generally a rule of the market rather than an exception. Most stock prices move up or down in any given day due to a variety of external factors. Even if the market is relatively calm, there are always individual stocks that are volatile. Day traders seek to identify a stock that has a trend, either up or down, and then go with that trend. "Trend is a friend" is a common motto among day traders. They seek to pick up a relatively small stock movement, $\frac{1}{8}$ or more on a particular stock. If a day trader is trading a large block of shares—that is, 1,000 shares or more per trade—then he will profit $125 from a $\frac{1}{8}$ price movement. Conversely, if a day trader acquired 1,000 shares and was wrong—the stock price goes in the opposite direction, down—then he will lose $125 from a $\frac{1}{8}$ price movement. Volatility is a double-edged sword.

For expensive stocks that trade for $100 or more, a $\frac{1}{8}$ or 12.5 cents movement is a small relative price change that happens all the time. Consequently, there are plenty of day trading opportunities. It is not uncommon to see a day trader executing many, sometimes as many as 100 trades, in a single day. On the other hand, an investor's time frame is much longer. Investors seek a much larger price movement than $\frac{1}{8}$ (they look for 2 or 3 points or higher) to earn their desired rate of return. That takes time. In short, day traders seek to extract an income from intraday price volatility by trading the stock frequently, while investors seek long-term capital appreciation.

Day Trader's Objective Versus Investor's Objective

There is a clear divergence of objectives between the investor and day trader. The objective of an investor is to earn long-term capital appreciation or long-term return on investment with limited risk. Consequently, investors are not concerned with short-term market price fluctuations, since they are in the stock market for the long haul. They do not care if their trade orders are executed in ten seconds or ten minutes. They do not mind if the received price for the purchased stock is 12.5 cents or 25 cents higher than anticipated. One eighth or $\frac{1}{4}$ point in the stock price will not make a difference in the long run when the objective is to wait for capital appreciation of several points. The expectations are much more modest. At best investors hope to double their investments in five years.

On the other hand, day traders seek to double their trading capital every few months. Consequently, the objective is not the long-term return on the investment but earning short-term income. To earn that substantial short-term income, and thus possibly double trading capital every few months, day traders are willing to absorb an inordinate amount of risk. Not surprisingly, high income potential is associated with high risk. Day traders are willing to place $20,000 or $50,000 at risk and lose it all in order to double that same amount in a few months of trading.

Since day traders are affected by short-term market volatility, they care whether their trade orders are executed in ten seconds or ten minutes. Even a ten-second wait for a trade confirmation seems to be a long time for many day traders. Since day traders are exploiting small and short-term price fluctuations, they demand from brokerage firms almost instantaneous trade executions, and they notice if the received price for the purchased stock is only 6 cents higher than anticipated, since $\frac{1}{16}$ of a point in the price could make a difference between breaking even or losing money on a trade.

Day Trader's Risk Tolerance
Versus Investor's Risk Tolerance

It is unrealistic and unfair to compare an investor's risk with a day trader's risk. The risk associated with the potential to earn a 20% annual rate of return on investment is substantially smaller than the risk that corresponds with a 200% increase in trading capital after six months of day trading. This trade-off between financial risk and return is well documented in financial literature. Since day traders are pursuing high short-term income from trading, they automatically and willingly accept high risk. Unfortunately, such high risk translates automatically into a high rate of failure. The majority of day traders simply fail, and lose some, if not all, of their trading capital. It is a fact of life for many novice day traders. If you do not want to lose your money, do not trade stocks—*invest* your money.

Second, investors are risk-averse individuals, while day traders are clearly risk takers. The day trader's tolerance for financial risk is substantially higher than that of the investor. It is redundant to remind day traders that they could lose their money day trading. If an individual seeks financial safety and security, she can purchase U.S. Treasury bonds and earn a 5% annual rate of return. However, the day trader's objective is on the other side of the financial risk–return spectrum: an unsafe and insecure financial environment that provides a potential to earn a 500% annual rate of return.

Proactive Versus Reactive

To become a proficient trader, one need not anticipate the future price movement of a particular stock. Traders do not need to be proactive. They need only be reactive. Their objective is to identify the existing price momentum and go with that trend. In my opinion, it is much easier to observe the present short-term movement than to read and anticipate long-term future prices.

Day traders do not need the knowledge of *fundamental analysis* that investors do. They do not need to know the story behind the stock or the reasons why the stock has been increasing in value. In fact, traders do not need to know anything about the company, or the price history, or the future price targets, or whether the stock is overvalued or undervalued compared to some industry standards. Before making a single day trading-style trade, there is no reason to research any of the stocks' fundamentals.

All day traders need to do is identify a trend or price momentum. All they need to know is that the stock is moving. The underlying cause of that price movement is irrelevant to the day traders. Also, they do not need to enter the trade at the bottom of that price trend or exit the trade at the top of the swing, since it is impossible to ascertain the price turning points exactly.

Fundamental Analysis Versus Technical Analysis

On the other hand, investors must anticipate the long-term price trend. They have to research stock fundamentals to determine whether, over the long haul, the stock will go up in price. Therefore, investors need to understand the history of the company, its products, its management, and its competitors. Investors will pay close attention to the fundamental analysis indicators that measure the company's overall performance, such as the company's *price/earnings ratio*, its *earnings per share*, *dividends* per share, *market capitalization,* and *yield.* None of these fundamental analysis indicators are of interest to day traders, who focus on short-term price movement and rely strictly on technical analysis.

Consequently, the majority of trading software packages offer a large number of technical analysis indicators that provide valuable insights about stock prices. The focus of technical analysis is almost always the price of a stock. The technical indicators utilize information on the stock price at that point in time, the daily closing or opening stock prices, and the highest or lowest price in the selected time period. Furthermore, a technical analyst will also evaluate and incorporate the stock trading volume into the analysis.

For instance, investors using fundamental analysis indicators need to develop their own well-defined investment strategies and decide if they want to own small capitalization (small cap) stocks with a high three-month price gain or large capitalization stocks with a high dividend yield and a low price/earnings ratio. Of course, each investment strategy has different risk factors and different return potential. Which investment strategy should the investor follow? Financial literature is crowded with investment advice, and informed investors spend hours reading and researching the fundamentals of a company prior to actually purchasing a stock.

Holding Periods and Risk

The level of *risk* for day traders and investors is dramatically different. An investor's stock-holding period is much longer than a trader's holding period. If the investor makes a wrong investment decision and the position is losing money, the investor can simply hold onto the position and sell the stock when it recovers. Time is on the investor's side.

Day traders do not have the luxury of waiting for long-term equity appreciation. They cannot afford to tie up limited capital in a losing position and wait it out. A good day trader will most likely close losing positions and seek other trading opportunities. Time is not the trader's ally.

The day trader's most important resources are acquired trading knowledge, trading capital, and the time to trade during the market hours. If the day trader ties up her capital in a long-term position that is a losing trade, she will be unable to utilize her resources effectively.

Oversight and Discipline

The level of oversight required by day trading and investing is dramatically different. Since investors seek long-term capital appreciation, they should not be as concerned with daily stock market gyrations as day traders should be. Investors can afford to enter a stock position and walk away from any kind of monitoring, particularly real-time monitoring. On the other hand, day trading is work.

Undisciplined day traders often become investors by mistake. They take a long stock position, anticipating that the price increase will continue. Unfortunately for the day trader, the market could suddenly reverse the trend. A good, disciplined trader would get out of a reversing position immediately, and thus minimize the loss. However, some traders refuse to take a loss, even an initially small loss. An undisciplined trader will hold a position and hope that the stock will turn around and go up; if that does not happen that day, the trader will hold the position overnight, becoming an investor. If the declining trend continues the next day, the day trader might become a long-term investor. With each passing day, a small loss becomes a larger loss. If the trader has limited trading capital, all of that capital might be tied up in that long and losing position.

Table 2.1 summarizes the differences between the stock day trader and investor.

Comparison Between Day Trading and Investing

Table 2.2 provides an example of how an individual could potentially make $125,000 per year by investing or day trading. The hypothetical goal of $125,000 was selected because it is a round number and is, in my opinion, a reasonable and feasible goal. Please note that I do not mean to imply that anyone who starts trading stocks will make $125,000 annually. Many terms used in Table 2.2 are explained in great detail in later chapters.

Table 2.1   *Electronic Traders Are Not Investors*

Investor	Electronic Trader
Risk-averse individual	Risk-tolerant individual
Proactive stand, anticipates trends	Reactive stand, observes trends
Performs fundamental analysis	Performs technical analysis
Long-term holding period	Short-term holding period (less than one day)
Few buy and sell activities in a week	Many buy and sell orders in one day
Seeks long-term capital appreciation	Seeks short-term ordinary trading income
Delayed price quotes acceptable	Real-time price quote system is a must
Real-time order execution is unimportant	Real-time order execution is a must
Passive stock performance oversight	Active stock performance monitoring

When creating the example in Table 2.2, I made the assumption that both of the stock market players have the same annual goal—a $125,000 profit. The investor's time frame is one year, whereas the day trader has a much shorter time frame of one day. Let us focus for a moment on how each of the two players approaches that goal of $125,000, starting with the day trader.

The Day Trading Analysis

Assuming that there are 250 trading days in a year (in reality the number is closer to 240 days), a day trader must net $500 per day to reach the goal of $125,000. The day trader's objective is to make many trades every day to exploit the intraday price volatility and profit from small intraday price movements. In other words, the day trader's goal is to earn a small incremental profit, such as $\frac{1}{8}$ or 12.5 cents, on each share traded. However, the day trader is trading in increments of 1,000 shares, so 12.5 cents translates into a $125 gain.

Like an investor, the day trader will make trades that lose money as well as those that result in profits. So let us assume that 60% of all trades were winning trades. This is a conservative estimate; a knowledgeable

Table 2.2 *A Hypothetical Case for Grossing $125,000 Annually in the Stock Market*

	Day Trader	Investor
Annual goal	$125,000	$125,000
Typical holding period	One day	One year
Number of trading periods per year	Approx. 250 trading days in a year	One in a year
Net goal per trading period	$500 per day	$125,000 per year
Number of trades per trading period	12 round-trip trades per day	Three per year
Number of trades per year	3,000 per year	Three per year
Commission per round-trip trade	$32	$128
Typical trade increments	1,000 shares	10,000 shares
Typical goal per trade per share	$\frac{1}{8}$ or $0.125	7 points or $7.00
Gross gain (assuming 60% of all trades were winning trades)	$900 per day	$126,000 per year
Gross annual profit	$225,000	$126,000
Total commission cost	$96,000	$385
Net annual profit	$129,000	$125,615
Total annual value purchased (assuming $50 average stock)	$150,000,000	$1,500,000
Purchasing power per trade (assuming $50 average stock)	$50,000	$500,000
Trading capital requirement (assuming a margin account)	$25,000	$250,000
Return on investment	500%	50%

and experienced trader with the appropriate trading tools and information (that is, professional trading software with real-time financial data feed) can reach a much higher winning percentage. After all, having a 50% winning trade record would be similar to flipping a coin or a similarly random method of choosing stocks.

To earn $500 per day, a typical day trader must complete 12 round-trip trades, which is one buy trade or ticket and one sell trade or ticket, at $16 per each trade or ticket. That translates into 3,000 round-trip trades per year. This number of trades results in $96,000 in commission expenses. That means that even though the day trader generated $225,000 in gross revenue, after paying commissions, his net profit is $129,000. If the day trader is trading in increments of 1,000 shares and the average stock price is $50, his purchasing power is only $50,000. He can acquire that by opening a margin account with $25,000. A return of $129,000 on the trader's $25,000 up front translates into an approximately 500% return.

During the market turmoil that occurred in the spring and fall of 2000, much attention was focused on the dangers of trading on margin. These dangers will be discussed within the chapters on risk management and margin accounts *(see chapter 22)*. For now we need only focus on the fact that the true day trader would close all of the positions at the end of the day, and thus the true day trader would not be subject to any margin calls.

If the average stock price were $50 during the year, making 3,500 trades would mean that the day trader bought and sold an incredible sum of $150 million worth of stocks. The $150 million in shares that a day trader might control illustrates the enormous leverage he commands—even if only for a few minutes or hours at a time—with a $25,000 investment. The point here is that a high level of activity and a high amount of leverage can translate into a hypothetical high annual return of 500%.

The Investing Analysis

Let us compare the day trading style to the other extreme—investing. The investor's time frame in this example is one year, although many investors have much longer investment horizons. The investor must earn $125,000 during that year. Her objective is to make a few trades in a year and profit from the price movement throughout the year. Because the investor has time to wait for price movement, it is reasonable to expect that she could earn an average of 7 points in a year on a stock that is priced on average at $50.

We also assume that our investor will be successful on 60% of all trades. To earn $125,000 in a year, our hypothetical investor completes three round-trip trades with 10,000-block shares at $128 commission cost per trade. Commission expenses are higher for the investor due to the large size of the trade order. This generates $385 in commission expenses, which is a minuscule expense compared with the day trader's commission expense. That means that after commission, the investor's profit is $125,000. If the investor is trading in increments of 10,000 shares and the average stock price is $50, then the required purchasing power is $500,000. This must be accomplished by opening a margin account with $250,000, which is more money than many of us have to invest.

A return of $125,000 on a $250,000 investment translates into a 50% return. If the average stock price were $50 during the year, then three trades in blocks of 10,000 would translate into the investor having bought and sold only $1.5 million worth of stocks. This is in stark contrast to the day trader's high financial leverage of $150 million. Compared with the day trader, the investor utilizes lower leverage throughout the trading year, because the investor controls only $1.5 million worth of stocks with a $250,000 investment. The point here is that low activity and low leverage translate into an annual return of 50%, which is much lower than the day trader's 500% return.

The Style Comparison

The lower trading activity and lower leverage commanded by the investor translates into a lower annual return compared with that of the day trader (50% versus 500%). Trading $150 million worth of stocks and completing 3,000 trades in one year creates a lot of work and stress for the day trader. In contrast, the investor's task is dramatically simpler. Our hypothetical investor makes, on average, three trades per year and trades $1.5 million worth of stock. Because the investor makes fewer trades and completes lower dollar amounts of trading, the level of risk of investing is lower than the risk associated with day trading.

Table 2.3 *Stock Trading Styles*

	Investing	Day Trading
Leverage size	Low	High
Trading activity	Low	High
Trading account size	High	Low
Total trading commission cost	Low	High
Trading risk level	Low	High
Trading oversight	Low	High

A typical day trader practices what I call "precision trading," which requires a great deal of trading skill. Day traders must have sharp eyes, minds, and execution skills to pick up small price movements frequently and accurately. There is very little room for error. If the day trader is wrong and the price goes against him by only $\frac{1}{4}$ of a point—a common and minor price gyration—a good day trader would have no choice but to exit the trade, take the small loss, and move on to the next trade. There is no opportunity for second chances. Time is not on the day trader's side.

The investor, however, can afford to weather the small and common price gyrations because the holding period is much longer. Assuming that the stock analysis is correct, the investor can wait for the price reversal. The investor's stop-loss limit is much higher than the day trader's loss tolerance. (The topic of stop-loss limits will be discussed in chapter 22, "Risk Management.") The stop-loss limit is not as tight and precise as the day trader's are. In other words, the investor could be wrong initially and lose a point when entering the trade. But in the long run, the investor could be right and end up with a profitable trade. Time could be on the investor's side. Table 2.3 summarizes the differences between the two styles.

3

Do You Want to Be a Day Trader?

DAY TRADING IS A NEW TRADING STYLE, SO IT IS NOT SURPRISING THAT most day traders are young. They tend to be male, computer literate, well-educated individuals. They are savvy stock market participants who are accustomed to taking risks. Before becoming traders, they usually have opened accounts already with discount brokers or Internet brokers. They are attracted to day trading because of its potential for high returns.

To be a successful day trader, a person must meet four essential requirements:

1. Knowledge and skill of stock trading;
2. Adequate risk capital;
3. Time to trade; and
4. Ability to manage risk with a disciplined trading style.

Requirement 1: Knowledge and Skill of Stock Trading

The first and foremost characteristic that day traders need is trading knowledge and skill. Knowledge is power! Anyone trading stocks should read as much as possible about stock trading in general. (Listed at the back of this book are some general resources.) A new day trader competes against experienced professionals such as the NASDAQ market makers, NYSE specialists, and other day traders. New day traders must have knowledge of the NASDAQ and NYSE securities markets and their trading rules to be able to survive. Acquiring those skills is time-consuming and often expensive; yet they do not guarantee to make anyone a good trader.

If your town has a day trading firm, visit the office and see what kinds of trading education they offer. Day trading firms often have free seminars and classes. Sometimes firms charge a training fee, which can be nominal or substantial. Ask if you can talk with others who have taken the training class. Find out who is presenting it and if the training is well-organized. Talk to the other traders. Ask them how they trade. Ask them if they are profitable. Pay close attention to the actions (executions) of the profitable traders. Dedicate a few weeks to paper trading.

Paper Trading

Day trading firms use sophisticated financial software for order execution and display of real-time financial data. The software will most likely have a training module (demo or simulation mode) that will provide real-time data flow and somewhat realistic simulated execution. New traders can sit in front of the computer monitor during market hours, view real-time quotes and charts, and paper trade. *Paper trading* means that buy and sell orders are not actually executed, but only processed and confirmed by a trader's computer. The computer will keep track of trading activities and update trading statistics. New traders are much better off making mistakes in a demo mode than in a live mode. Mistakes committed in a demo mode are much cheaper: Any losses are only paper losses! Paper trading is an easy and comfortable way to become familiar with the trading software and the NASDAQ and NYSE markets. New traders should practice paper trading for several weeks before beginning to trade live.

As well, before a new trader graduates from paper trading to live trading, he should consistently make, day after day, at least $1,000 in paper trading profit every day for several weeks. Consistency is crucial. The new trader should then discount the paper trading profit by at least one-half. We suggest this because live trading is dramatically different from paper trading. All paper trading market or *limit orders*—orders to buy or sell at a specified price or at a better price—are filled automatically at the requested limit price or posted market price. In reality, that does not happen very often. Traders will learn quickly that live market orders are not filled at the expected price, and limit orders are often not filled at all.

For example, a trader is watching real-time quotes on the screen; there is one market maker with the best-posted selling price (ASK), and the trader submits a buy market order for a NASDAQ stock. That order goes into a computerized queue. A *market order* is defined as an order to buy or sell a security at the most advantageous price obtainable at that moment in time. If the trader is first in line, the order will be executed; however, it is rare that a trader is first in line. One of two things could then happen. The trader's order could be executed at the same price if the market maker elects, at her discretion, to refresh the same selling ASK price. However, if the price is moving up fast, then the market maker will not refresh the same ASK price, but will back away and post a higher ASK price. The trader's market order would then be executed at a price higher than expected. If the market is moving up very fast, the trader might end up with a substantially higher price than anticipated.

Similarly, when a trader electronically submits a buy limit order for a NASDAQ stock, this order might never get executed at the specified price. If the price trend is up, the market maker will increase the ASK price. That would mean the limit order would never get executed at the lower price. In other words, the stock price may be moving too quickly and could simply pass over the limit order before it is executed. (More information on order executions will be provided in section IV.)

Finally, paper trading does not involve real money, and thus there is no real risk. Without the genuine risk of losing money, the trader's emotions are not involved. Fear, greed, panic, and hope do not interfere with trading judgments, so it is easier to be a disciplined trader. However, there is no substitute for real-life experience. Simulated or paper trading is not a realistic predictor of future trading results.

The most expensive and reckless trading education is to start live trading without undertaking an adequate and sufficiently long training program. New traders will make mistakes. Some mistakes will simply be the wrong trades—that is, buying a stock when market is going down. Some of those mistakes will be execution errors—that is, pressing the wrong key. Trading software used by day trading firms is sophisticated and complex, and it takes time to master it. It takes time to learn about the NASDAQ and NYSE markets and their trading rules. That is simply part of the learning curve.

Requirement 2: Adequate Risk Capital

Day traders must have access to adequate trading capital, which will clearly always be at risk. They should be able to sustain losing that capital, although that, of course, is not a trading objective. A day trader should never trade money that she cannot afford to lose. I do not advocate obtaining a second mortgage to raise risk capital or using retirement funds or credit card advances.

Most day trading firms generally require a minimum capital of $20,000, although several established day trading firms require at least $50,000 to open an account. All of these accounts are margin accounts. In a *margin account*, the National Association of Securities Dealers (NASD) broker is extending credit to a customer who is purchasing stocks on "margin"—in essence, a credit issued to finance securities transactions. Under the Federal Reserve Board regulation (Regulation T) that governs the amount of credit that can be extended, the maximum amount that brokers can advance is 50%. That means that a trader's deposit of $20,000 will result in an additional $20,000 credit (advance or loan) from the broker, and the trader will have $40,000 purchasing power. Every brokerage firm has a margin department that provides oversight and supervision of the extension of credit. Internet brokers cater to investors who might purchase stocks in increments of 100 shares, and thus their minimum account is dramatically less than the minimum of $20,000 needed to open a trading account and trade stocks in increments of 1,000 shares.

Adequacy of Trading Capital

If a trader does not have adequate capital to purchase 1,000 shares of expensive and volatile technology stocks, then the trader is already somewhat handicapped. If a trader opens a margin account with the minimum requirement of $20,000, the trader can afford to purchase only 400 shares of expensive stock (that is, stock priced at $100 or more per share) for his $40,000. If a trader makes a correct buy and a stock goes up $\frac{1}{8}$ point, then he would earn $50, which would only cover the trader's buy and sell order commission costs. Commission cost is commonly $15 or $20 per ticket; in this case the trader's round-trip commission cost will range from $30 to $40.

With $40,000 purchasing power, traders have two options: (1) Trade stocks listed for $40 or less in increments of 1,000 shares, or (2) Trade the expensive stocks in increments substantially fewer than 500 shares. Both strategies have drawbacks.

Consider the first option. If the day trader (with $40,000 purchasing power) were trading a less expensive stock (that is, $40 or less per share) in increments of 1,000 shares, then the stock would need to increase in value 1 point for the trader to earn $1,000. But stocks do not usually go up 2.5% that easily, especially within a single day. Something must drive that stock up 2.5%, such as positive news (for example, higher than estimated earnings, a merger, a projected stock split), and that does not happen very often. Traders need to be patient and spend time monitoring the inexpensive stocks for a 2.5% price movement that earns $1,000. If a trader wants to earn only $125 on a trade, the stock needs to move $\frac{1}{8}$. But that is $\frac{1}{3}$ of a 1% increase in value for a stock that is priced at $40. Again, it takes time for this to happen.

Consider the second option. If a day trader (with $40,000 purchasing power) is trading expensive ($100) stock in increments of 400 shares, then the stock would need to increase in value 2.5 points for the trader to earn $1,000. Again, this does not happen very often. If a trader wants to earn only $125 on a trade, the stock needs to move $\frac{5}{16}$. This, too, may not happen quickly.

Either way, the trader is handicapped. The best long-term scenario is to trade expensive and volatile stocks in increments of 1,000 shares and profit from the small (1% or less) price movement. This happens frequently. But to do that, one needs an adequate amount of trading capital.

Please, do not misunderstand this point: New day traders should not begin by trading expensive, volatile stocks in increments of 1,000 shares. That is the domain of the experienced day trader. Even if adequate trading capital is available, the novice trader should start slowly by trading inexpensive stocks that do not move very fast. As a rule of thumb, he should start trading with 100 shares, and increase the size of the shares traded with gained experience, increasing the trading block by 100 shares every week until he reaches the block of 1,000 shares. It is unrealistic to expect that new traders will start making money immediately. Trading is a skill that takes time to develop.

Sources of Trading Capital

The best source of funds for new day traders is the traders' own capital. However, day trading tends to attract young individuals who often do not have access to large sums of money. One method, which I do not advocate, is for young traders to raise money for their trading account by putting up a limited risk capital ($10,000 or less) and then borrowing additional money ($40,000 or less) from their friends, relatives, or other day traders. This would give a trader a sizable deposit of $50,000. With a margin account, the purchasing power is $100,000. Now the day trader has a sufficient trading account to trade expensive and volatile NASDAQ stocks in increments of 1,000 shares and profit from small price movements.

Hypothetically, the loan money is never at risk, with all of the trading losses coming from the trader's own initial risk capital. Friends, relatives, or other day traders who provided the loan would monitor the risk by asking for and receiving the trader's daily trading statements. This is an arrangement between private individuals, and requires daily monitoring and trust. If the risk capital is depleted, then the loan will probably be called immediately.

The key word in the preceding text is *hypothetically*. The loan money is always at risk. So what happens if the new day trader loses more than his own $10,000, which is a distinct possibility? First of all, it is very difficult to monitor this type of lending arrangement. At best, a lender would learn of the balance in the trading account only after the market close, which might be too late for the lender. Day trading is an extremely active and volatile business activity, and the deposited trader's initial risk money could be wiped out in a single day. Most important, who will control the trading account? If the account is in the trader's name only, what is the guarantee that the account will be closed and the loan money refunded on demand? Again, I do not advocate this approach.

The other method for securing trading funds is to create a partnership account with a private investor who believes in the trader's future trading potential and is willing to assume a significant risk of loss. Again, that private investor is most likely to be a friend, relative, or other day trader. This is workable if the relatively new day trader has some experience, track record, or potential to succeed but lacks the funds. The partnership agreement would specify how the profits, if any, are split between the trader and investor, though usually it is a 50–50 split. Again, this is an arrangement between private individuals, and most brokerage firms would not want to have any part in it.

Requirement 3: Time to Trade

The third element that future day traders must have is time. Stock exchanges open at 9:30 A.M. Eastern time (or 6:30 A.M. Pacific time), and at that time, serious day traders are at their trading stations waiting for the market to open. This is the most active and volatile time of day on the stock exchange. Many different market participants are placing buy and sell orders: the amateurs (individual investors) and the professionals (mutual and pension funds managers, institutional investors, and other traders). Day traders monitor the activity and try to ascertain trends. If the day trader sees momentum, he will jump in and go with the trend.

Once a day trader takes a position, she is glued to the monitor, watching the stock performance tick by tick. With open positions, traders are reluctant even to go to the bathroom. In the few minutes the trader might be gone, a profitable trading position can turn into a loss, or a small loss can turn into a much larger loss. The bottom line is that day trading is a job and requires time and effort. The market closes at 4:00 P.M. Eastern time (or 1:00 P.M. Pacific time). A serious day trader will be in front of the monitor from the opening to the closing bell.

It is, however, possible to be a part-time day trader, particularly if one lives on the west coast. One can trade from 6:30 to 8:30 A.M. Pacific time, when the stock market is most active and volatile. After closing all positions, traders often go to their "day jobs." Some part-time traders return to trade for the market closing, which is the second most active and volatile trading period. And on the west coast, market closing conveniently coincides with the lunch hour. Thus it is possible to engage in day trading and keep one's day job.

After-Hours Trading

Another alternative is to trade after the NASDAQ, NYSE, or AMEX exchanges have closed, in what is commonly known as "after-hours trading." However, my word of advice to both novice and experienced traders is, don't trade after hours. Before I explain why, let's define *after-hours trading*.

The aftermarket hours are different for each electronic communication network (ECN) that provides this service. Island (*www.island.com*) offers after-hours trading between (all times to follow Eastern) 7:00 A.M. and 9:30 A.M. as well as from 4:00 P.M. to 8:00 P.M. Instinet (*www.instinet.com*) is open 24 hours a day, every day. The NASDAQ's Select-Net offers after-hours trading from 4:00 P.M. to 6:30 P.M., and 9:00 A.M. to 9:30 A.M. The MarketXT *(www.marketXT.com)* is open from 4:00 P.M. to 8:00 P.M., and 6:00 A.M. to 9:00 A.M. The Archipelago *(www.tradearca.com)* runs from 8:00 A.M. to 8:00 P.M. The NYSE is actively considering after-hours trading. As you can see, different ECNs offer different, and thus confusing, trading hours. Finally, only limit orders are accepted.

In my opinion, after-hours trading is literally "trading in the dark." For the following reasons, after-hours trading is treacherous and unpredictable for both the novice and experienced traders:

1. *Market fragmentation.* After-hours trading occurs through ECNs, which means that you are trading with only a few traders who are trading *at that particular ECN* at that point in time. Unlike the national markets, such as the NASDAQ or NYSE, where the equilibrium price is determined simultaneously by many buyers and sellers from all national, regional exchanges, and ECNs combined and posted nationally and immediately by the exchanges, the aftermarket environment is dramatically different. For instance, with the low volume and number of players on any particular ECN, it takes only a limited number of traders who post a few limit orders for shares of Dell, for example, to determine Dell's price at that point of the night on that ECN. That price may be much different than another ECN's posted price for Dell at the same point in time. In other words, the national stock market during normal trading hours has become fragmented into several smaller private markets during the after-hours trading, and thus it is difficult to determine one national equilibrium price for a stock at a particular point in time.

2. *Low liquidity.* Simply stated, markets are thin or there is small trading volume. For instance, on average, 40 to 50 million NASDAQ shares exchange hands during after-hours trading, which is a fraction of the 1 billion shares commonly traded during traditional trading hours. Because

of low trading volume, it is difficult to get the trades executed at the desired price, and since there are no market makers present during after-hours trading, there is no guarantee that there will be someone else on the other side of the market. All submitted orders are limit orders, and there is no guarantee that any other traders are willing to fill this order at that stipulated price. In addition, even if the price is met, there is a distinct possibility that your order will be only partially filled.

3. *Huge short-term absolute price volatility.* In other words, given the low liquidity and fragmented ECN markets, the interaction among a few traders determines the stock price in one ECN market, which can jump all over the map as the traders enter and exit the thinly traded market for that stock.

4. *Huge spread between the BID and ASK prices.* Due to low trading liquidity and high price volatility, the trading risk increases and thus the spread escalates. In other words, trading becomes more expensive.

5. *Few price observations.* Because the market is so thin, there are few price data points or there are huge gaps in the price data, and it is very difficult to ascertain any price pattern using technical analysis tools. Because after-hours price data is scarce, choppy, discontinuous, or contains large gaps, technical analysis indicators are less reliable and accurate.

6. *Poor oversight.* After-hours trading is truly the reincarnation of the Wild West. The SEC and NASD regulators, along with the financial market media reporters and the public companies' officials whose stocks were being traded, are literally asleep during after-hours trading. This is a perfect environment for "pump-and-dump" schemes. Unscrupulous individuals can deliberately spread false rumors throughout Internet chat rooms, and there is not single person available to refute the bogus announcements.

7. *Specialized brokers.* You must have specialized brokers who provide direct access to many different ECNs in order to achieve best price execution during after-hours trades. For instance, CyBerCorp *(www .cybercorp.com)* provides multiple-ECN access, while other online brokers, such as Datek *(www.datek.com)* or E*Trade *(www.etrade.com)* provide access to only one ECN, which might not provide the best price execution.

If you still wish to trade in the after-hours market despite these warnings and want to learn more about aftermarket trading, there are several

Internet sites devoted exclusively to this topic. The two most popular sites are *www.afterhourstrading.com* and *www.afterhourstrades.com*.

Requirement 4: Ability to Manage Risk with a Disciplined Trading Style

Last but not least, day traders must have the skill to manage risk using a disciplined trading style. Since winning trades take care of themselves, the focus of risk management is on managing the losing trades. The trader must be disciplined enough to accept the fact that her trading decisions can be wrong, to recognize this quickly, and to get out with a minimal loss. This is not as easy as it seems.

Traders are often reluctant to admit they've made an error and are unwilling to take a small loss and move on to other trading opportunities. Instead, undisciplined traders start hoping that their losing stock position will reverse its trend. That is when small losses turn into large losses. A $\frac{1}{8}$ or $\frac{1}{4}$ point loss could quickly turn into a $\frac{1}{2}$ to 1 point loss. Instead of losing $125 on 1,000 shares, traders wait too long and the trade results in a much larger loss.

Day traders have a motto: "Do not fight the tape." The stock market is always right. If the trader has a long position and the price of the stock is declining with each tick, then the market is giving the trader a clear signal: Get out of that trade. Disciplined traders will quickly recognize that message and will get out immediately. Furthermore, the disciplined day trader waits patiently for a clear trading signal to buy or sell a stock. Without that signal, the trader will not enter the trade; without it, trading becomes gambling. Finally, a good day trader does not let a winning trade turn into a losing trade. A day trader takes profits regardless of how small they are. A day trader does not go broke taking profits.

CHAPTER
4

Trading Places

W<small>HEN</small> W<small>ILLIAM</small> B<small>ATTEN</small>, <small>FORMER CHAIRMAN AND</small> CEO <small>OF THE</small> N<small>EW</small> York Stock Exchange (NYSE), was asked what stock exchanges do, he eloquently replied, "We produce the price." This is very true. In a nutshell, a stock exchange is a marketplace that determines a stock's price. However, different exchanges have different ways of determining the price for a particular stock at any point in time. The NYSE is an established and centralized auction-type exchange with a string of intermediaries. It is very different from The Nasdaq Stock Market (NASDAQ), which is a negotiated, decentralized electronic exchange that relies on a computerized network of several hundred stock merchants. And both the NASDAQ and NYSE are dramatically different from the privately held electronic communication networks (ECNs), which are the new players on the block.

All three types of trading environments determine stock prices, but with different levels of efficiency, cost, and fairness. A day trader may choose to trade on a variety of exchanges or ECNs, so it's important to understand how each works. It is worth mentioning that day traders largely use the NASDAQ and ECNs because they offer detailed books or schedules on the buy and sell trade order flows at different price levels *(see chapter 6).*

The NASDAQ

The NASDAQ system was created in 1971 as a true electronic securities exchange. The NASDAQ market is a negotiated and decentralized marketplace. There is no centralized meeting place or trading floor. Transactions are conducted through a computer network that connects the National Association of Securities Dealers (NASD) broker/dealers, who never see each other face to face. The NASD regulates the NASDAQ market.

NASD members include securities brokers and dealers who are authorized by the NASD to transact securities business in the United States. A NASD *broker* is defined as any individual, corporation, partnership, association, or other legal entity engaged in transacting securities business for the accounts of others. A NASD *dealer* is any individual, corporation, partnership, association, or other legal entity engaged in the business of buying and selling securities for its own account. Most national and regional retail brokerages are broker/dealers, which means they can trade stocks both on your behalf and on their own behalf.

A trading transaction on a NASDAQ-listed stock is initiated when a trader places an order with a NASD broker. The NASD broker completes an order ticket, which is then routed electronically to the NASD dealer who carries that security in his inventory. The NASD dealer is required to provide continuous bids (BID is the price at which the NASD dealer is willing to buy the security) and offers (ASK is the price at which the NASD dealer is willing to sell the security). The NASD dealer is said to "make a market" in that security. Thus, the NASD dealer is called a "market maker."

NASDAQ market makers (and NYSE specialists) are the sanctioned securities merchants. The market maker and the specialist have two distinct roles. They are the brokers who transact securities business for the accounts of others, and at the same time, they are dealers engaged in trading securities for their own proprietary accounts. It is important that traders understand this dual nature of the "market-making" business.

In essence, there are two ways that the market makers and specialists can make money. The first is to earn the spread, which is accomplished by buying the stock from the public at the lower BID price and selling it to the public at the higher ASK price. Suppose, for instance, that the best BID and ASK prices for Cisco Systems Inc. (CSCO) are 50.50 and 50.563, respectively. (Because this is a NASDAQ stock, I focus on the market makers, although the same principle applies for the NYSE listed stocks.) That means that the market makers are buying low (50.50), selling high (50.56), and earning the spread of $\frac{1}{16}$, or 6.25 cents. In this case, the market makers are acting as the agents for the public that desires to buy or sell that stock. Keep in mind that when market makers buy and sell stock, they are either adding shares or extracting them from their own portfolios.

If one market maker buys 1,000 shares from the public at the BID price and sells the same 1,000 shares a few seconds later at the ASK price, a $1/16$ spread translates into a $62.50 profit. If the spread remains at the average of 6.25 cents during the day, and if Cisco's average daily trading volume over 52 weeks remains at 61 million shares, then market makers as a collective group would earn $3.8 million on that stock alone.

A brief look at the daily trading volume at the NASDAQ and NYSE reveals the scope of the market-making business. NASDAQ's daily average trading volume over 52 weeks is approximately 1 billion shares (ranging from 775 million to 1.2 billion shares). Collectively, market makers could earn $66 million in one day if the average spread is only $1/16$. Similarly, the NYSE's daily trading average volume during 1999 was approximately 809 million shares. Collectively, NYSE specialists could earn $50 million in one day. Obviously, the market-making business is quite lucrative.

The other way that market makers make money is to trade stocks for their own proprietary accounts. The only way to make money trading is to buy low and sell high. In other words, all market makers and specialists want to accumulate shares when the price is low, and then sell the stock from inventory when the price is higher. When the market makers or the specialists anticipate that the price will go up, they become buyers of that stock. When they anticipate that the price will decline, they become sellers of that stock. At that time, the market makers or specialists start selling the stock and depleting their inventory.

There are approximately 500 market-making firms providing liquidity for the more than 5,000 actively traded stocks on the NASDAQ National Market System. All market makers have a four-letter identification code that is displayed on the Level II screen *(see chapter 6)*. Because there is competition among the market makers on the NASDAQ, it is important to know who is who among the market makers. Some market makers are large, established Wall Street institutional firms that have access to enormous capital and employ the most experienced professional traders. Those firms are 800-pound gorillas capable of stopping the price momentum at any time.

Because the large firms have a vast capital base, they have a huge inventory of stocks. In addition, they can borrow stock from other Wall Street firms. Those market makers are capable of "sitting" at the top of the BID and ASK quote and continuously buying or selling a particular stock at that price level. In other words, through the continuous buying, those market makers are capable of stopping any short-term price decline. Conversely, the same large market makers are capable of stopping any short-term price increase by continuously selling the stock. These key market makers are often referred to in the trading industry as the *axes*. It is important to know who the ax is for a particular stock. (A list of the 50 most influential market makers is included in appendix 5 of this book.) Each market maker has a symbol, and traders using a Level II screen can therefore recognize when a dominant market maker places an offer to buy or sell shares.

The most important ax market makers are large investment banks with sizable amounts of trading capital and equally large corporate cultures, such as Goldman Sachs & Co. (GSCO), Morgan Stanley (MSCO), Lehman Brothers (LEHM), and Salomon Brothers (SALB). The other important market makers are the large full-service retail brokerage firms such as Merrill Lynch & Co. (MLCO), Dean Witter Reynolds (DEAN), Paine Webber (PAIN), Prudential (PRUD), and Smith Barney Shearson (SBSH), because they have a huge order flow from their client base. In addition, Wall Street has a few wholesalers that do not transact any retail business but represent the securities discount retailers (for example, Charles Schwab) and Internet brokers (for example, E*Trade). Those Wall Street firms are Mayer & Schweitzer (MASH), Herzog Heine Geduld (HRZG), Knight (NITE), and Sherwood (SHWD).

The NYSE

The NYSE is a much different animal. A NYSE member is a firm that employs one of 1,366 individuals, usually as an officer or partner, who owns a seat on the exchange. Only a member of the NYSE may transact business on the floor of the exchange. Every listed stock that trades on the NYSE floor is assigned a specialist. The role of the specialist is similar to that of a market maker—to maintain a fair and orderly market in his specific security. The specialist must maintain a continuous market by standing ready to buy when there are no bidders (buyers) or sell when there are no offerers (sellers) at the trading post. Unlike the NASDAQ, there is no competition among different Wall Street firms to provide the liquidity for the listed stock. A specialist has a monopoly.

Like NASDAQ market makers, the NYSE's specialists also make money trading the stocks in their own proprietary accounts. Keep in mind that this activity is much less pronounced on the NYSE than on the NASDAQ, because the specialist is a monopolist who is regulated by the exchange. The NASDAQ market, however, is much more market-oriented and competitive, and thus stock dealing is prevalent.

Super DOT

The NYSE uses a system called designated order turnaround (DOT) to route the trade orders directly to specialists. The DOT system allows orders to be entered by traders from the day trading firm's floor directly into the NYSE computer-execution system. The order bypasses the floor broker and goes directly to the NYSE specialist for execution. In addition, even if other regional exchanges have better prices than do the NYSE—which is not a very likely scenario—it is impossible to route that order electronically to different exchanges.

DOT is an efficient way to execute trade orders on the NYSE. For example, if there is an exact price match between Lucent (LU) buyers and sellers, the DOT will match those orders quickly, and both the buyers and sellers will receive the trade confirmation in a few seconds. The specialist need only approve the trade by pressing a key in the Super DOT system. A great majority of trades on the NYSE fit this scenario. The specialist, using Super DOT, will pair or match the stock buyers with the stock sellers and collect a small commission. In only about 30% of all executions would the specialist step in and provide the other side of the trade, thereby playing the role of the market maker and providing the liquidity for that stock.

It is my opinion that it is somewhat safer and easier to trade NYSE stocks than NASDAQ stocks. NYSE stocks are "slow" stocks. Trading is conservative or slow compared with the volatile NASDAQ stocks. NYSE stock prices tend to move in a somewhat smoother fashion; there are fewer sharp price turns.

There are several reasons for the relatively higher intraday price stability at the NYSE. First, the stocks listed on the NYSE tend to be large and established industrial corporations. The NASDAQ, however, is laden with technology companies pursuing long-term growth strategies. Consequently, growth stocks attract stock speculators, who tend to be short-term investors who are always chasing hot stocks and jumping in and out.

Second, the NYSE companies are simply too large and established to be very volatile. Large blue-chip companies seldom issue news that can send stock prices skyrocketing up or down. Whereas it is a rare event for a NYSE stock to lose 50% of its capitalization value in a few days, that happens often on the NASDAQ. NASDAQ companies are relatively young companies; a single bad corporate announcement can send the stock price into a major decline.

Finally, intraday price volatility is lower with NYSE stocks because there is only one specialist who controls the price for each stock. The specialist can act to absorb and soften sharp price movements. Because the specialist controls the order flow, she knows the exact depth of the market (supply and demand) at any time. There is little chance that the specialist will overreact.

The NASDAQ market makers, however, compete against each other and against traders. The market makers do not know the complete order flow for a stock. They know what is in their individual order book, but they do not know the order flow of other market makers. Like any other traders, market makers can see on the Level II screen the required minimum size of the BID and ASK made by the other market makers, but not the actual orders. With such uncertainty and lack of comprehensive information, market makers might overreact and send a stock deeper in either price direction. Consequently, the average *Beta* value (which measures the relative price volatility compared with the industry average) is higher for NASDAQ stocks than for NYSE stocks.

Because NYSE stocks do not move very fast in either direction, traders have time to react. They can see prices going up or down. They are not easily whipsawed by sharp and sudden price reversals. As there is no true Level II information available, the traders must devote more attention to technical stock analysis. Charting becomes an important component of their trading style.

In addition, the competition is much different on the NYSE, where there are fewer traders and more long-term investors. It is my opinion that one is better off trading against NYSE investors than NASDAQ market makers and other traders. However, the momentum-trading opportunities are much fewer and smaller at the NYSE. And, unfortunately, smaller risk brings smaller return. Successful and experienced traders can potentially earn seven-figure incomes trading volatile NASDAQ stocks with a relatively small trading account of $100,000. Because the NASDAQ is so volatile, there are plenty of opportunities to make money.

The AMEX

The American Stock Exchange (AMEX) is the nation's second largest floor-based or auction-type exchange. However, the AMEX is well behind the NYSE in terms of trading volume and number of listed stocks. Nevertheless, it has a significant presence in index shares and equity-derivative securities such as options trading. Similar to the NYSE, AMEX trading is conducted through an advanced centralized specialist system, which combines the speed of computer-routed trade orders with the liquidity of customer-driven markets. AMEX members represent a cross section of the nation's largest brokerage firms, including 661 regular members who transact business in equities and options, and 203 options principal members who execute transactions in options only. An interesting development is the NASDAQ's acquisition of the AMEX. Some Wall Street observers anticipate that the AMEX will ultimately evolve into a derivatives exchange, whereas the AMEX common-stock listings will be moved to the NASDAQ.

Electronic Communication Networks

The SEC defines electronic communication networks (ECNs) as "automated mechanisms that widely disseminate market-maker orders to third parties and permit such orders to be executed through the NASDAQ system." In essence, ECNs are proprietary electronic execution systems that broadcast orders entered by traders and market makers. Online brokers advertise and extol ECNs as a way to improve the price and speed of trade executions as well as a way to trade outside regular market hours. Keep in mind that ECNs are an alternative and viable trading environment for actively traded NASDAQ stocks only.

For now, the NYSE and AMEX rules prevent the ECNs from gaining access to these trading environments. However, due to the increasing popularity of ECNs among active traders, the NYSE and AMEX are gradually changing their rules.

ECNs came about in January 1997, as a result of new SEC order-handling rules, which required market makers to display customer limit orders that were priced at or better than the market makers' current quote. If not immediately executed, the limit orders could be routed to an eligible ECN, where they would be displayed to the market. The new SEC rules created the opportunity for ECNs to interact directly with the NASDAQ market makers and to become an integral part of the NASDAQ system.

Subsequently, the volume of the ECNs exploded and a new industry was born. Deregulation and competition in the securities trading industry resulted in incredible growth of the ECNs, which remain in a constant state of motion. Two large ECNs, Island and Archipelago, have filed to become fully recognized exchanges by the SEC. The future will most likely bring consolidation or mergers among the smaller ECNs. Table 4.1 lists all ECNs and their relative market share of NASDAQ trades at the end of 1999.

Like Internet auction houses such as eBay, the ECNs are also the computerized "marketplaces" in which stock buyers and sellers meet. The ECNs electronically match stock buyers with stock sellers through sophisticated computerized networks that link thousands of market participants through the hundreds of NASD brokers who subscribe to the ECN service. The ECN system allows two traders to meet and trade directly with one another without any intermediary. Because all trade executions are done electronically, the ECNs are extremely fast and cost-effective. The cost savings are substantial because ECNs do not need to maintain large numbers of traders, floor brokers, and other fixed costs associated with operating an exchange.

A recent SEC analysis of stock trading activities produced evidence of the existence of a two-tiered securities market. The NASDAQ market makers routinely trade stocks at one price with their retail customers and at better prices with institutional clients through the ECNs. For example, a great majority of all the BID and ASK prices displayed through an ECN such as Instinet were posted at better prices than those posted publicly on the NASDAQ.

Table 4.1 *ECNs and NASDAQ Trades*

ECN	Owner(s)	Location	% of NASDAQ Trades	ECN Market Share
Island (ISLD)	Datek Online Holding	Iselin, NJ	11.7	41.9
Instinet (INCA)	Reuters Group	New York	11.0	39.4
Redibook (REDI)	Spear, Leeds & Kellogg	New York	1.3	4.6
Tradebook (BTRD)	Bloomberg, Bank of New York	New York	1.2	4.3
Archipelago (ARCA)	Terra Nova Trading, E*Trade Group, Goldman Sachs & Co.	Chicago	1.0	3.6
Brass Utility (BRUT)	Automated Securities Clearance (also Merrill Lynch, Morgan Stanley, Dean Witter Reynolds, Knight/Trimark Group)	Weehawken, NJ	1.5	5.4
Strike (STRK)	Strike Technologies (Bear Stearns, DLJ, Salomon, Smith Barney, Herzog Heine Geduld, PaineWebber)	New York	0.2	0.7
Attain (ATTN)	All-Tech Investment Group	Montvale, NJ	0.0	0.0
NexTrade (NTRD)	PIM Global Equities/ Pro Trade	Clearwater, FL	0.0	0.0

The advantages of ECNs are summarized in the following:

➤ *Low price.* ECNs typically charge a small fee for trade executions.

➤ *Speed.* Direct electronic access and avoidance of any mediators make the ECN trade-execution system extremely fast.

➤ *Liquidity.* Given the popularity of the few large ECNs, it is relatively easy to get trade orders filled.

➤ *Price transparency.* At any time, a trader can open an ECN book, such as the Island book, and determine the supply-and-demand flow of limit orders for any stock.

➤ *Order tracking.* A trader can see her order displayed on the Level II screen immediately.

➤ *Better price.* Only limit price orders are accepted and executed, and it is possible to cut the market makers' BID and ASK spread.

➤ *No spreads.* One trader sells and the other trader buys the same stock at the same price.

➤ *Reliability.* The ECNs are very robust and reliable because they tend to use the latest computer networking technology.

➤ *Open software architecture.* The trading platform is open and accessible, so it is relatively easy for the NASD brokers to subscribe to an ECN service.

Not surprisingly, the ECNs have certain disadvantages, too:

➤ *Low liquidity*

➤ *Partial order fills*

➤ *Difficult fills* with low-volume stocks

➤ *No guarantee of getting the best price* (unless you compare the ECN order book with a Level II screen)

➤ *After-hours prices are not reflective of the opening* and can result in high volatility and enlarged spreads

Island

Island (ISLD) is an ECN that was developed in 1996 and is owned by Datek Online Holding. It is the fastest-growing ECN, and its sole purpose is to match bids and offers electronically. In essence, Island is an electronic central auction market that automatically matches buy and sell orders. When an order is received for a particular stock, the Island limit order book is instantaneously scanned to determine if there is a matching order. If there is a matching order, the trade order is executed immediately. However, if there is no matching order, the order is displayed on the Island limit order book until a matching order is received or until the order is canceled. In addition, the top orders are represented in the NASDAQ Level II screen display. All Island orders are anonymous and are matched based on strict price-time priority without regard to the number of shares.

Retail customers cannot send orders directly to Island. Instead, Island provides execution services to brokerage firms that, in turn, offer those services to their customers. The Internet-based brokers and day trading firms allow their customers to send limit orders instantly into the Island system. Orders that are not matched immediately in the Island book are displayed on Level II screens if the order is more than 100 shares and inside the BID and ASK. Unlike Small Order Execution System (SOES) orders *(see chapter 17),* Island orders do not have tier size limits; all orders are left as day orders. Island is open every day that the stock exchanges are open for trading. In general, Island accepts orders between 7:00 A.M. and 8:00 P.M. Eastern time, although liquidity is dramatically lower during after-hours trading.

The Island trade-order execution system is rather simple: A trader places a limit order, either buy or sell, with the NASD broker who subscribes to and has the Island ECN servers. The broker immediately forwards the limit order to Island for processing. Island searches its order book for that stock and looks for a match. For example, brokerage firm AAAA representing trader A places an order to "buy 500 CSCO at 50." Almost at the same time, brokerage firm BBBB representing trader B places an order to "sell 1,000 CSCO at 50." These two orders match electronically, and the orders are executed against each other. Trader A will end up buying 500 shares of CSCO from trader B, and trader B will continue posting for sale the remaining 500 shares of CSCO. If no match is found at that price, the order will be placed and displayed on the Island book.

When a trade order is entered into Island, assuming that a trader is using a high-powered trading software package such as CyberTrader or TradeCast, the Island system directs the order first to an Island server for order matching and then to the NASDAQ SelectNet system. Traders can place trades by accessing Island directly or through the SelectNet execution system. Placing Island orders directly to Island is the faster of the two routes. Most day trading firms have an Island server that routes Island orders directly to the Island system. This should be an important consideration for the new trader who is looking to open an account with a day trading firm.

One of the positive aspects of Island fills is that they are quick and relatively inexpensive. Island trades usually cost $1 more than NASDAQ SOES orders. If the Island system has a better BID or ASK price available than the trader's submitted BID or ASK price, Island will fill the order at that better price. However, the trader should not use "fill or kill" orders through Island, as it is likely that the orders will not get filled. The main negative aspect of Island orders is partial fills.

The Island execution system displays the trader's Island order on the Level II screen only if the trader has entered the highest BID or the lowest ASK and only if the orders are greater than 100 shares. If several traders enter multiple Island orders at the same BID or ASK price, the Island system will simply total the share sizes to reflect all submitted orders. Using the Island execution system is crucial for a successful trading business. Island provides traders with additional liquidity and the opportunity to obtain a better price. In chapter 18, I will explain how traders obtain better prices when executing trades on Island.

Instinet

Instinet (INCA) is the largest ECN in terms of total combined NASDAQ, NYSE, and AMEX volume. It is a private corporation, headquartered in New York City and owned by the Reuters Group PLC. Instinet Corporation is registered with the SEC as a NASD broker/dealer; it is a member of all U.S. stock exchanges and other major international stock exchanges. It was created in 1969 to furnish equity transaction services specifically to an international base of institutional investors (that is, fund managers).

Instinet does not buy or sell securities for its own account. Its only business is to provide 24-hour access to securities brokerage services for the benefit of its institutional customers. The trader can execute an Instinet order by accessing INCA through the NASDAQ SelectNet. Many day trading brokerage firms have a stand-alone Instinet order-execution computer on the trading floor. However, Instinet is important not only as a vehicle that executes trade orders with large financial institutions. Instinet transactions also represent the activities of large financial institutions, and traders therefore pay attention to Instinet transactions because those transactions can provide insight into the activities of the Wall Street professionals.

There are a few proprietary software packages that track or filter trading activities on Instinet. The software tracks the volume of shares being bid and offered through Instinet by financial institutions. The software also tracks prices that are bid and offered by the financial institutions. Most important, the software keeps a record if and when there is a price differential between the stock prices on the public exchange (that is, on the NASDAQ) and on the private exchange (that is, on Instinet). This information can provide the trader with insights about whether there is the potential for a particular stock price to go up or down.

Archipelago

Archipelago (ARCA) was approved in January 1997 by the SEC. In August 1999, Archipelago filed with the SEC to become a national securities exchange that would offer an electronic trading system. To ensure its chances of SEC approval, Archipelago and the Pacific Stock Exchange (PCX) announced, in March 2000, that they were jointly creating this new electronic stock exchange. Today, as an ECN, Archipelago offers an anonymous order entry (that is, an order will show only as ARCA) and execution capabilities that give the customers access to all other ECNs.

ARCA is a unique order-execution system with a built-in set of formulas or algorithms that will optimally route the trade order for the best execution. In other words, ARCA provides an advanced electronic order-entry and -execution system for NASDAQ and NYSE stocks. For instance, ARCA will look at stocks trading on other ECNs at that specified price to fill the order. If there is no ECN at that price, ARCA will search for the most active market makers at the inside quote if it is a NASDAQ stock. Using the NASDAQ SelectNet system, ARCA would then access that particular market maker.

The beauty of using ARCA is that the system does all of the thinking and processing of the trade orders for you. Consequently, ARCA provides novice traders with an automatic pilot for optimum order execution. The only problem is that ARCA orders cannot be canceled in 30 seconds. While ARCA processes the order for the optimal price, a trader must wait for the order confirmation. If a trader is trading slow-moving or less volatile stocks, then the 30-second wait is acceptable. However, in a fast-moving market, a lot can happen in 30 seconds. As is the case with any ECN, individual traders cannot send orders directly to ARCA; rather their brokerage firms must route orders to Archipelago. Unlike ISLD, ARCA also accepts both limit and market orders.

Future Trading Environments

I believe that ECNs have a bright future. Today, they are on the cutting edge of NASDAQ stock trading. They are the young firms in the industry that are pushing the envelope and bringing vibrancy and technological innovation into this field. For instance, Island and Archipelago ECNs have already created an extended trading-hours platform. Now traders in the United States can trade whenever they choose, around the clock, using ECNs. The volume is extremely small or thin, but that is not surprising for any pioneering process. With time, there should be greater liquidity.

NASDAQ is also going international. In Japan, the NASDAQ has partnered with the Osaka Stock Exchange to bring the NASDAQ model of stock exchange to Asia. Similarly, the NASDAQ plans to open NASDAQ Europe and compete head to head with the London and Frankfurt stock exchanges. With each building block, NASDAQ is creating a global trading network, which might soon emerge as "Planet NASDAQ." Internationalization of the NASDAQ will bring more traders from abroad, who would gain access to the NASDAQ and thus increase the liquidity.

Finally, Internet service providers (ISPs) are moving to provide the necessary broadband needed to increase the speed of their service. Stock trading from your home via the Internet will be much easier and more reliable once cable modems and DSL lines become the norm. In addition, the emerging wireless trading technologies will make trading even more accessible and convenient *(see chapter 5)*. ECNs promote more active trading and thus the standard T+3 (trade date plus three days) settlement cycle will no longer be the industry norm. For instance, all traders use the specialized clearing firms that settle their trades on the very same day. Why not have the same one-day trade settlements for the rest of the general public?

Introduction to Day Trading Tools

THE OBJECTIVE OF THIS SECTION IS TO ESTABLISH A FOUNDATION FOR developing day trading skills and techniques. Before we can progress to more advanced topics of day trading, you should learn and master these basic concepts and tools.

➤ In this section we explain in detail Level I screen data, in particular the concepts of the highest BID and lowest ASK prices, the spread between the BID and ASK prices, the BID to ASK ratio, intraday trading volume, intraday high and low prices, close and open prices, and change for the day.

➤ We continue by building on our knowledge of the NASDAQ market makers and Level I screens by covering basic Level II screen information, such as the inside BID and ASK and the outside BID and ASK markets, and the depth of the inside market.

➤ Also covered are the ways that market forces of supply and demand generate the equilibrium price for a stock and how the Level II screen displays that information, with price increases and decreases.

➤ We discuss monitoring and alert tools used by day traders, such as the Time and Sales window, market ticker, Top Advances and Declines window, and 52-week or daily high and low.

➤ In this section we also examine the significance of longer-term trade alerts such as earnings reports, cash dividends, stock splits, mergers and acquisitions, and several seasonal events.

➤ Finally, we cover the trade alerts that are particularly relevant to IPOs, such as the first trading day, the end of the quiet and the lockup periods.

The Level I Screen

Most stock market participants are familiar with Level I stock quotes. They are ubiquitous in the stock market and are truly the starting point of any stock analysis. The Level I quotes are readily disseminated and provided in real time free of charge on CNBC, CNNfn, Bloomberg, and through other Internet streaming stock data providers, such as *www.freerealtime.com*. In addition, the Internet-based brokers usually provide free real-time Level I quotes to their customers.

The Level I stock quote simply shows a stock's price information as of the last trade. In other words, a Level I quote displays the current *inside market* or the best BID and ASK prices for the stock.

Understanding the Level I Screen

The Level I screen is a dynamic window, and during market hours the best BID and ASK information is continuously updated in real time. Day trading firms subscribe to data feed service providers that supply real-time stock quotes via satellite dish or dedicated T1 communication lines. However, if a trader is using an Internet-based broker, Level I quotes could be delayed by several seconds or several minutes. Also, many Level I stock quote providers use Java Script programs to "refresh" the screen every few seconds, and thus do not display true tick-by-tick data feed. This can sometimes lead to inaccurate stock quotes, especially when the stock market is moving quickly.

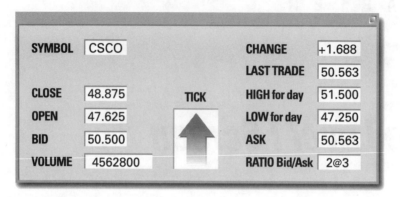

Figure 5.1 *Level I Screen Information*

It is difficult to ascertain a trend based on Level I information alone. Nevertheless, much information can be ascertained from the Level I screen. It is a logical place to begin illustrating the topic of day trading tools.

BID and ASK

The Level I quote features the stock symbol, an abbreviation for the name of the stock. In Figure 5.1, Cisco (CSCO) is used for illustration purposes. A Level I quote states that at this point in time, the best BID price for CSCO is 50.50, and the best ASK price is 50.563. Traders and investors buy stocks at the ASK price and sell them at the BID price. In this example, the trader or investor can purchase CSCO stock from the market makers at 50.56 and sell it to them for a lower price of 50.50. The best ASK price is often called the *inside offer.*

On the other hand, market makers who are providing a market (liquidity) for CSCO are buying the stock from traders and investors at the BID price of 50.50 and selling it to traders and investors at the ASK price of 50.56. Market makers are buying low (50.50) and selling high (50.56) and earning the spread, as discussed in chapter 4. In this case the spread is $\frac{1}{16}$ or 6.25 cents.

Spread

The *spread,* which is the difference between the BID and ASK prices, can vary. For well-traded stocks with large daily trading volume, such as

CSCO, the spread is small—$\frac{1}{16}$ or 6.25 cents—or even smaller at $\frac{1}{32}$ (3.12 cents). Sometimes during trading, the spread can widen to $\frac{1}{8}$ or 12.5 cents or even more. Market forces—that is, supply and demand for CSCO—will determine the size of the spread. For thinly (or infrequently) traded stocks the spread is larger.

When the trader purchases stock at the ASK price, she is already in the hole (out of money) by $\frac{1}{16}$. The day trader could immediately turn around and sell the stock at the inside BID price and thus lose the spread. If the trader is trading in increments of 1,000 shares, she is starting $62.50 in the hole. CSCO will have to go up $\frac{1}{16}$ point for the trader just to break even. In other words, both the BID and ASK price for CSCO will have to move up $\frac{1}{16}$ point (or 0.0625), so the BID price becomes 50.563. *Cutting the spread* becomes an important task for the trader. It would be ideal if the trader can purchase CSCO at the BID price (50.50) rather than purchasing at the ASK price.

Close and Open

Another piece of information that is provided on the Level I screen is the *close* price from yesterday and the *open* price for today. In Figure 5.1, CSCO closed yesterday on 48.875 and opened today at 47.625, or with the gap down 1.25 points. There are many reasons why stocks open with the gap up or down (mostly down). For example, companies will wait for the market to close before announcing any news (for example, earnings or dividends). Institutional investors continue to trade after market hours through Instinet. Market forces, and thus prices, do not stop at the close of the market.

In the example shown in Figure 5.1, CSCO opened with a large gap down. If the day trader had 1,000 shares of CSCO in the overnight long position, he would start that day with a $1,250 loss. This $\frac{1}{4}$ gap down is seemingly a large gap for a $50 stock. But the gap could be a lot worse. Something seemingly unrelated to CSCO could happen overnight in Asia, or anywhere else in the world, that could cause CSCO to open several points lower, resulting in a loss of several thousand dollars. The experienced day trader will seldom, if ever, carry an overnight position; that is simply good risk management. Seeing the price differential between close and open prices on Level I screens has reinforced my belief that day traders should go flat at the end of the trading day.

Volume

In Figure 5.1, the trading *volume* at that point of time for CSCO is over 4.5 million shares, implying that CSCO is a well-traded stock This snapshot is most likely from the early morning of the trading day. The trader must trade liquid stocks where daily trading volume is at least 500,000 shares. Liquidity is crucial in order to assure that there will be a seller to close the long position at the end of the trading. It is very risky to accumulate a large share block of thinly traded stocks. Imagine holding 10,000 shares of a stock trading in the $10 range with a daily volume of 100,000 shares. If the price starts to decline, it would be difficult to unload (sell) 10% of the daily volume quickly without driving the price further down.

Change

Change on the day is available on the upper right corner of the Level I screen. In this example, CSCO went up $1^{11}/_{16}$ from yesterday's closing price. Most trading software packages also have a symbol for the last price tick. In Figure 5.1 the symbol for the last price change is the arrow. And it is an up-tick. Other software packages have "+" or "−" symbols. Some software packages use green or red color-coded BID and ASK prices. A red BID would mean that the last BID was a down-tick. The tick symbol is a very useful visual tool.

High and Low

The Level I screen also displays the *high* and *low prices for the day*. In this example, the high ASK price for the day was 51.50, and the low ASK price for the day was 47.25. That means that CSCO had substantial intraday price volatility. In this example, it is 4.25 points. Day traders should focus on and trade stocks that have at least 2 points intraday price movement, so this range is good. It provides ample opportunity to day trade this stock.

A quick way to ascertain intraday price volatility is to look for the difference between the high and low prices for the day. That differential between the daily high and low prices is the proxy measure for intraday price volatility. If that price differential is small, then the stock is not moving in either direction, and the day trader will avoid it. There is no point in day trading a stock that is not moving.

To be a successful day trader, the trader needs to trade stocks that are more volatile relative to the overall Standard & Poor's 500 (S&P 500) price index average. (The S&P 500 Index is a composite price index consisting of 500 of the largest companies in the United States.) The day trader should search for stocks that have high daily trading volume and relatively high *Beta* value. The Beta coefficient is a statistical measure of the price volatility of a particular stock in relation to the entire stock market's (that is, the S&P 500's) volatility. The Beta coefficient is a common part of fundamental analysis and can be found in many financial search engines on the Internet (*Yahoo!, dailystocks.com*).

If the stock has a Beta value greater than 1, then that stock is more volatile relative to the entire stock market. A Beta of 2 would mean that stock went up (or down) on average 10% while the overall market went up (or down) 5% during a certain period of time (for example, 52 weeks). Appendix 4 contains a list of the 100 NASDAQ and NYSE stocks with the highest Beta values (Beta greater than 1.5) and average daily trading volume greater than 500,000 shares. My recommendation to day traders is to trade stocks that are volatile and liquid.

BID to ASK Ratio

The Level I screen shows how many market makers are buying CSCO and how many market makers are selling CSCO at this point in time, or how many market makers are on the BID and the ASK sides. In Figure 5.1, the ratio of BID to ASK is 2 @ 3 (see lower right corner of the Level I screen). It means that there are two buyers and three sellers. This ratio can be expressed in terms of BID and ASK volume as well. The bullish sign would be a BID to ASK ratio of 5 @ 1, which means that five market makers are buying and only one market maker is selling.

The ratio does not really show the depth of the market because it does not show how many shares each market maker is selling or buying. The ratio simply states that there are more buyers than sellers. If the single selling market maker is a large, established Wall Street firm that is selling a large block of shares for an institutional investor, then a 5 @ 1 ratio may lead a new trader to think that the market is moving up, when in fact, one seller can freeze the ASK price.

Scanning the Level I Information

A quick glance at the Level I screen at market close would reveal whether that stock is a good day trading stock or not. Figure 5.2 depicts a recent snapshot of IVI Checkmate Inc. (CMIV).

CMIV—developer of electronic payment hardware and software—is not a good day trading stock. BID and ASK prices are 2.594 and 2.719. The spread is small in absolute dollar terms ($0.125), which is good, but it is relatively high compared to the low stock price (4.8% of stock price), which is bad. In other words, the stock must move up 4.8% just to break even if you are buying at the ASK price and selling at the BID price. Most important, the trading volume for that day is 108,200 shares. Furthermore, CMIV average daily trading volume for the last 52 weeks is only 76,000 shares. Day traders should trade stocks that have at least 500,000 shares daily trading volume, so CMIV does not have the liquidity to be suitable for day trading. Also, CMIV does not have daily price volatility. The day's price range is 2.50 and 2.938, which relates to a price change of 43 cents. This 43 cents might be a high relative price change (17%) for an inexpensive stock such as CMIV, but 43 cents is a small absolute change. Day traders need to capitalize on high absolute price change since they are attempting to make a lot of money each and every day. It would be difficult to make money day trading CMIV stock if the maximum profit potential is only 43 cents per share.

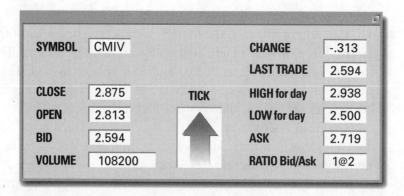

Figure 5.2 *Example of a Poor Day Trading Stock*

CHAPTER
6

The NASDAQ Level II Screen

T<small>HE</small> L<small>EVEL</small> II <small>SCREEN IS ONE OF THE DAY TRADER'S MOST EFFECTIVE</small> trading tools. In contrast to its limited availability in the past, NASDAQ Level II information is now available to the general public through several data feed providers. Figure 6.1 displays Level I and II screens together.

Inside and Outside Markets

In addition to posting the inside market's BID and ASK price quotations for all market makers, the Level II screen posts, in real time, BID and ASK prices that are outside the market. *Inside market* is the best (the highest) BID price at which the stock can be sold in the market and the best (the lowest) ASK price at which the stock can be bought in the market at a given point of time. In the hypothetical example in Figure 6.1, CSCO has five market makers on the inside BID and ASK prices; thus the current ratio of BID to ASK is 5 @ 5, as displayed by the Level I screen. But this time we see also which market makers are buying and selling, as well as the share size of their activities.

In this example, J. P. Morgan Securities (JPMS), Lehman Brothers (LEHM), Mayer & Schweitzer (MASH), Montgomery Securities (MONT), and Herzog Heine Geduld (HRZG) are selling 1,000 shares of CSCO each at 50.563. In other words, the public (traders and investors) is buying CSCO at the quoted ASK price of 50.56 per share from the five

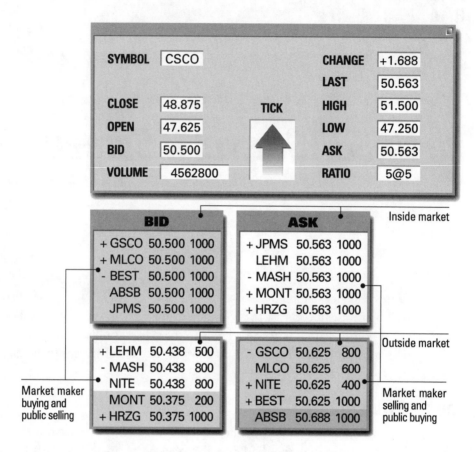

Figure 6.1 *Level I and II Screen Information*

market makers. Clearly 50.563 is the lowest buying price. A trader could buy 1,000 shares of CSCO from Merrill Lynch & Co. (MLCO) at 50.62 per share, but that is more expensive than the best ASK price of 50.563. MLCO is away from the market or in the *outside market*. In short, MLCO is not a seller of the stock.

Conversely, Goldman Sachs & Co. (GSCO), Merrill Lynch & Co. (MLCO), Bear Stearns & Co. (BEST), Alex Brown & Sons (ABSB), and J. P. Morgan Securities (JPMS) are buying 1,000 shares of CSCO each at 50.50. Public traders and investors are selling CSCO at the quoted BID price of 50.50 from the five market makers. Obviously, 50.50 is the highest selling price. The trader could sell 1,000 shares of CSCO to Montgomery Securities (MONT) at 50.375, but that is clearly less than the best BID price of 50.50. MONT is away from the market or in the outside market. MONT is not a buyer of the stock.

For easy reference, each price level on the Level II screen is a different color. In this example, there are five market makers on the BID side who are posting the best selling price, and they are all the same color. There are five market makers on the ASK side who are posting the best buying price; they are also the same color. Both BID and ASK sides have four distinct columns. The first column has "+" and "−" signs that indicate whether the market maker has increased or decreased the BID or ASK price. If there are no "+" or "−" signs, the market maker has refreshed the same BID or ASK price. The second column is the market maker's four-letter identification code. The third column is the market makers' BID and ASK price. And the last column is the number (size) of shares offered by the market makers at that BID or ASK price.

Figure 6.1 shows only ten market makers represented on the Level II screen. In reality, CSCO has many more market makers on both the BID and ASK sides. For a variety of reasons, some market makers may not be active in market-making activities but are required to post both BID and ASK prices. These market makers would deliberately back away from the best BID and ASK prices. They would post their BID and ASK prices at the bottom of the Level II screen.

The Level II screen has two distinct BID and ASK sides, with market makers required to post simultaneously on both sides. The position of the market maker on the BID and ASK side reveals whether that market maker is a buyer or seller. The market maker's relative position would reveal whether he is bullish or bearish on that stock. Figure 6.2 illustrates this point.

Figure 6.2 reveals that MLCO and GSCO are buyers. They are at the top of the BID side, buying the stock at 50.50. MLCO and GSCO have joined the BID, and they are in the inside market. Since both MLCO and GSCO are required to be on both sides of the market, GSCO and MLCO have posted a relatively high ASK price of 50.875, which is not a competitive price. These two market makers are buyers and not sellers. One could argue that GSCO and MLCO are bullish on that particular stock. GSCO and MLCO are buying stock at the low

Figure 6.2 *GSCO and MLCO Are Buyers*

price (50.50), and anticipating that stock will go up in value, so they could sell it at the higher price (50.875).

Why would a rational investor buy the stock from GSCO and MLCO at 50.875 when the lowest posted ASK price is 50.563 from JPMS and LEHM? If the investor does not have access to real-time data feed and Level II screen information, he would not know what the best ASK price (the lowest buying price) is. For example, an investor who has an account with Merrill Lynch & Co. and who is buying that stock through Merrill Lynch would most likely pay 50.875. However, day traders monitoring the stock would know the difference. One of the advantages of day trading your own account is the ability to view live Level II screen information and know that you are paying the best available price.

Conversely, Figure 6.3 reveals that MLCO and GSCO are sellers. They are at the top of the ASK side, selling the stock at 50.563. They have joined the ASK, and they are in the inside market. Since MLCO and GSCO are required to be on both sides of the market simultaneously, GSCO and MLCO have posted a relatively low BID price of 50.25, which is not a competitive price. GSCO and MLCO are sellers and not buyers. Figure 6.3 reveals that GSCO and MLCO are bearish on that particular stock. They are trying to sell that stock and deplete the inventory, anticipating that the stock will go down in value in the future: GSCO and MLCO are selling stock at the best ASK price (50.563) and anticipating that the stock will drop in value, at which time they can buy it at the lower price (50.25).

Figure 6.3 *GSCO and MLCO Are Sellers*

Again, why would a rational investor sell the stock to GSCO and MLCO at 50.25 when the highest posted BID price is 50.50 from WEAT and COWN? The investor who has an account with Merrill Lynch & Co. and who is selling that stock would most likely receive 50.25, MLCO's buying price. How would the investor know what the best BID price (the highest selling price) is if he does not have access to real-time data feed and Level II screen information? A day trader, because of his access to live Level II screen information, knows he is getting the best price.

Stock with No Price Depth

Thinly traded NASDAQ stocks have only a few market makers who provide liquidity. Most likely, if a stock is thinly traded, there would be only a few or one market maker at any price level. Figure 6.4 depicts a stock with no price depth. This would be a stock to avoid trading.

In this example, there are only five market makers providing liquidity for the stock. The trader has an opportunity to buy the stock at 50.563 from JPMS and BEST. The spread between BID and ASK is $\frac{1}{16}$ (0.063), which means the price would have to go up $\frac{1}{16}$ just to break even. However, there is only one market maker who is selling the stock at 50.50. If GSCO leaves the inside BID, the price would drop to 50.375. Then the spread between BID and ASK would be $\frac{3}{16}$ (0.188), which would mean that price would have to go up approximately 19

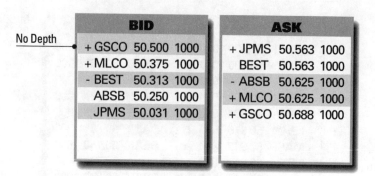

Figure 6.4 *Stock with No Price Depth*

cents per share just to break even. If the market turns quickly in the opposite (lower) direction, MLCO could leave the BID of 50.375, and the selling price would become 50.313.

It is very risky to trade thinly traded stocks with little depth. A stock should have several market makers on both sides of BID and ASK at one price level. Even actively traded stocks with many market makers could, during the trading day, end up in the situation depicted in Figure 6.4. The information in Figure 6.4 tells the trader that there is very little room for mistakes: The day trader may not be able to liquidate a position at the desired price level when there is very little liquidity. If only one market maker leaves the inside market, the price of the stock will change.

7

Stock Prices

THE FOCUS OF ANALYSIS FOR ANY DAY TRADER IS THE STOCK'S PRICE. THE price is the most important, and sometimes, the only variable under consideration. Day traders spend hours glued to their computer screens monitoring short-term stock price fluctuations.

And what determines the price of the stock? Economists would reply in unison, which is a rare event, two words: *supply* and *demand*. The interaction between supply and demand determines the price of anything: goods, services, commodities, and securities. Supply and demand are like a pair of scissors. To cut anything—that is, to establish a price— one needs both halves of the pair of scissors. In this chapter, we link Level II information with the market forces of supply and demand.

Supply and Demand

Anyone can be an economist. The two most important words you must learn to say are *supply* and *demand*. The best way to explain the stock-pricing mechanism is to define supply and demand and to graphically present the interaction between them. The following information may be tough going at first, but will make more sense as we go along.

On a chart, supply is a schedule or a line showing the quantity of a good, commodity, or a stock that sellers would sell at each price level, with other things being equal (*ceteris paribus*; Latin for "everything else being constant"). Figure 7.1 displays a positively sloped supply line. If

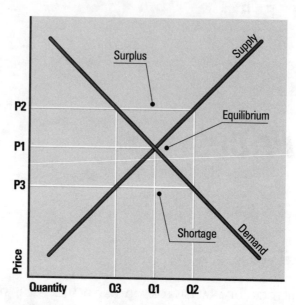

Figure 7.1 *Supply, Demand, and Equilibrium Price*

everything else remains the same, the supply line states that at the high price, many sellers would be willing to sell that stock, while at the lower price, few sellers would be willing to sell that stock.

Demand is a schedule or a line showing the quantity of a good, commodity, or a stock that buyers would purchase at each price level, ceteris paribus. Figure 7.1 also displays a negatively sloped demand line. If everything else remains the same, the demand line states that at the high price, few people would be willing to purchase that stock, while at the lower price, more people would be willing to purchase that stock.

Equilibrium Price

In Figure 7.1, if the stock price is high at P2, then Q2 is the quantity of the stock that sellers are willing to sell and Q3 is the quantity of the stock that buyers are willing to buy at that price. Since the quantity of the stock supplied (Q2) exceeds the quantity demanded (Q3), we have a condition of *surplus*. With surplus, there is a natural pressure for prices to drop. As long as there is a surplus, prices will continue to decline.

Conversely, at a lower price level such as the P3, Q3 is the quantity of the stock that sellers are willing to sell and Q2 is the quantity of the stock that buyers are willing to purchase. Since the quantity of the stock demanded (Q2) exceeds the quantity supplied (Q3), we have a condition of *shortage*. With shortage, there is a natural pressure for prices to increase, and as long as there is a shortage, prices will continue to increase.

At price level P1, the quantity of the stock that sellers are willing to sell will be equal to the quantity of the stock that buyers are willing to purchase, and we have a condition of *equilibrium*. Equilibrium is a state of balance, so there is no pressure or tendency for the price to change. At the equilibrium price P1, there is no surplus or shortage. The price will remain stable at level P1 as long as there is no change (shift) in demand or supply. As long as "everything else remains equal," the equilibrium price will remain at P1.

The next step is to link the supply and demand market forces to the NASDAQ Level II screen information. Figure 7.2 displays this information. There are five market makers on the BID and ASK side: five buyers and five sellers for that stock. The BID side represents the demand schedule, while the ASK side represents the supply schedule for this particular stock at this point in time. The equilibrium price at this time is 50.50 and 50.563.

Ceteris paribus is the crucial assumption here. Nothing in life remains constant, particularly in the stock market. Thus demand and supply lines are always shifting or moving. Whenever something happens in the market (either good news or bad news), it will change

Figure 7.2 *Level II and Supply and Demand Forces*

stock market participants' perceptions about that stock. If the news is good, more buyers will enter the market, and the demand will increase; the demand schedule will shift to the right. If the news is bad, buyers will exit the market, and demand for the stock will decrease. In this situation, the demand schedule will shift to the left.

Conversely, if news is good, then more stock sellers will exit the market and the stock supply will decrease—the supply schedule shifts to the left. If the news is bad, stock sellers will enter the market and the supply will increase; the supply schedule shifts to the right. Since the world of the stock market is dynamic, demand and supply are always moving; there is always an increase or a decrease in demand or supply.

Price Increase

Let us start with the good news. Good news results in increased demand for the stock from additional investors or traders. Also, good news restrains the stockholders from selling the stock because they anticipate getting a higher price in the future, thus there would be fewer sellers on the market. Increased demand and reduced supply would result in a new and higher equilibrium price. Figure 7.3 depicts that interplay between reduced supply and increased demand.

Increased demand is depicted with the demand line being shifted to the right. Reduced supply is illustrated with the supply line being shifted to the left. The interplay between the new increased demand and reduced supply will result in a new equilibrium point (E2) and a new equilibrium price (P2). The level of the price increase (from P1 to P2) and the quantity of the stock exchanged would depend on the magnitude of the shift in the supply and demand. In this example, the volume of stock trading remained the same.

Level II Screen and Price Increase

This basic economic concept of reduced supply and increased demand for a stock can be illustrated on the Level II screen as well. The Level II screen is updated dynamically (continuously). Market makers continuously enter different BID and ASK prices, or join or leave the inside BID and ASK prices. Consequently, Level II screen information is always moving. This is particularly true for fast-trading technology stocks.

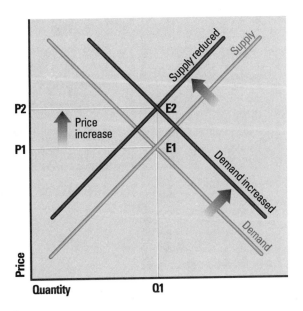

Figure 7.3 *Price Increase*

Because of this movement, it is difficult to link supply and demand market forces to the Level II screen. Figure 7.4 attempts to provide that link. The starting point is Figure 7.2. In that example, there were five market makers on the BID and ASK sides: five buyers and five sellers for a stock who were bidding and offering the same amount of shares on each side. The equilibrium price at this point in time was 50.50 and 50.563. Again, suppose that the stock had good news, and there had been a reduction in supply and an increase in demand for that stock. Imagine that we have frozen the Level II screen at that moment. Figure 7.4 depicts that change.

This time, there are only two market makers selling the stock on the ASK side, which translates to a reduction in supply of that stock. The color-coded inside ASK side has shrunk from five to two market makers. This is represented in Figure 7.4 by the up arrow on the ASK side, which shows that the color of the inside ASK is shrinking and moving up. On the other hand, there are eight market makers buying the stock on the BID side. The color-coded inside BID side has been enlarged from five to eight market makers. This is represented in Figure 7.4 by the down arrow on the BID side, which shows that the color of the inside BID is increasing and moving down.

Figure 7.4 *Level II Screen Information with Reduced Supply and Increased Demand*

The best BID and ASK prices are still 50.50 and 50.563. But this price will not last very long. There is a distinct possibility that the two remaining market makers (JPMS and LEHM) will eventually leave the ASK side. Even the large market makers with deep pockets, such as JPMS and LEHM, cannot supply the stock to the entire nation for an indefinite period at the ASK price of 50.563. Eventually, JPMS and LEHM will deplete their stock inventory and stop supplying the stock at that price (i.e., leave the ASK). At that time the ASK price will increase to 50.625.

On the other hand, there are eight market makers competing to buy that stock. One of the eight market makers might eventually increase the BID price. At that time the BID price would increase to 50.563. This development is depicted in Figure 7.5 by the following "freeze frame" picture of the Level II screen.

The two market makers (JPMS and LEHM) increased their ASK price from 50.563 to 50.625, and the color representing 50.563 "moved up" and disappeared from the ASK side. Two market makers (MLCO and GSCO) increased their BID price from 50.50 to 50.563. The color-coded price of 50.563 would move in counterclockwise motion from the ASK side to the BID side. The dynamic Level II screen shows this counterclockwise motion whenever there is a price increase.

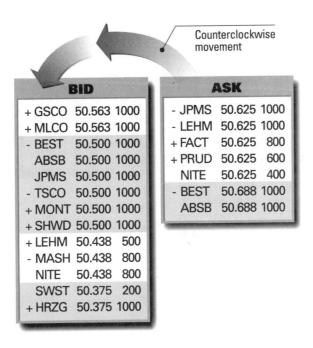

Figure 7.5 *Level II and Price Increase*

If the price increase momentum continued, there would be more market makers entering the BID side (that is, buying the stock). At the same time there would be more market makers leaving the ASK side. Figure 7.6 depicts that continued price increase movement.

The number of market makers on the inside ASK price has been reduced from five to two. The color-coded price block of 50.625 on the inside ASK price has shrunk and moved up. On the other side, the number of market makers on the inside BID price has increased from two to five. There are now more market makers on the inside BID price. The color-coded price block of 50.563 on the inside BID has been enlarged and moved down. The counterclockwise motion on the Level II screen would thus continue. In short, the color-coded block of the inside BID increases in size, and conversely the color-coded block of the inside ASK decreases in size.

For the time being, the best BID and ASK sides have remained the same, at 50.563 and 50.625. The day trader who has access to a live Level II screen would receive a visual confirmation that price increase momentum is there. She, in essence, has a preview of the future. If the

BID			ASK		
+ GSCO	50.563	1000	JPMS	50.625	1000
+ MLCO	50.563	1000	LEHM	50.625	1000
+ BEST	50.563	1000	+ FACT	50.688	800
+ ABSB	50.563	1000	+ PRUD	50.688	600
+ JPMS	50.563	1000	+ NITE	50.688	400
MASH	50.500	1000	BEST	50.688	1000
TSCO	50.500	1000	ABSB	50.688	1000
COWN	50.500	1000			
+ LEHM	50.438	500			
+ MHMY	50.438	800			
NITE	50.438	800			
MONT	50.375	200			
+ HRZG	50.375	1000			

Figure 7.6 *Level II Screen and Continued Price Increase Momentum*

price momentum continues in this counterclockwise motion on the Level II screen, the trader could expect new and higher BID and ASK prices of 50.625 and 50.688. The counterclockwise motion on the Level II screen would then constitute a BUY signal.

Day traders can observe that the counterclockwise motion on the Level II screen slows down and stops. This would mean that the price increase momentum is losing its steam. Other investors and traders who do not have the Level II screen could not preview this slowdown in the price increase momentum. The inflow of money is slowing down, and the demand for the stock has ceased to increase. There are no new market makers entering the inside BID, and the stock supply has stabilized and ceased to decrease. The market makers are not leaving the inside ASK price. All of this would tell the day trader that the momentum is shifting. Now is a good time to exit the long position, or sell the stock. The slowdown in the momentum is a signal to sell the stock.

It is always easier to sell stock on the up-tick. When the price momentum changes its direction, the price can quickly drop. If the day trader waits too long, then he would be selling on the weakness of the stock. It is always easier to obtain a better price and quicker execution if the day trader sells on price strength (when prices are still going up).

Price Decrease

Generally, what goes up must come down, and stock prices do not go up continuously. Eventually all price increases will end, and prices will start to decline. There are many reasons for this. Some are rational economic reasons, and some involve irrational human behavior. Obviously, bad news can drive stock prices down. So, let us deal with the bad news.

Bad news results in an increased (higher) supply of the stock from existing shareholders. Shareholders are now willing to "dump" the stock at the current price (anticipating a lower price in the future); thus there are more sellers on the market. Also, bad news restrains investors from buying the stock at the current price (they would anticipate a lower price in the future), and there are fewer buyers on the market.

Increased supply and reduced demand have resulted in a new and lower equilibrium price. Figure 7.7 depicts the interplay between reduced demand and increased supply. The level of the price decrease (from P1 to P3) and the quantity of the stock exchanged would depend on the magnitude of the shift in the supply and demand. Again, in this example the volume of the stock trading remained the same.

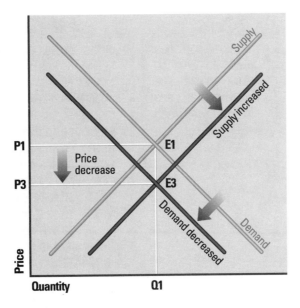

Figure 7.7 *Price Decrease*

This basic economics concept of reduced demand and increased supply for the stock can be illustrated on the Level II screen as well. Figure 7.8 attempts to provide that link. The starting point is again Figure 7.2. In that example, there were five market makers on the BID and ASK side: five buyers and five sellers for that stock. The equilibrium price at this point of time was 50.50 and 50.563.

Suppose that stock had bad news, and there has been a reduction in demand and an increase in supply for that stock. Imagine that we have frozen the Level II screen for that moment. Figure 7.8 depicts that change.

Now there are only two market makers buying the stock on the BID side; this would translate into a reduction in demand for that stock. The color-coded inside BID side has shrunk from five to two market makers. This is represented in Figure 7.8 by the up arrow on the BID side, which shows that the color-coded inside BID is shrinking and moving up. On the other hand, there are eight market makers selling the stock on the ASK side. The color-coded inside ASK side has been enlarged from five to eight market makers. This is represented in Figure 7.8 by the down arrow on the ASK side, which indicates that the color-coded inside ASK is increasing and moving down.

Figure 7.8 *Level II Screen Information with Increased Supply and Reduced Demand*

The best BID and ASK prices are still 50.50 and 50.563. But these prices will not last very long. The two remaining market makers (ABSB and JPMS) may eventually leave the inside BID side. At that time the BID price will decrease to 50.438.

On the other hand, there are eight market makers competing to sell that stock. Now, there is a distinct possibility that one or more of the eight market makers (or new market makers who are not currently on the inside ASK) will eventually decrease the ASK price. At that time the ASK price would decrease to 50.50. This development is depicted in Figure 7.9 by a freeze-frame picture of the Level II screen.

The two market makers (JPMS and LEHM) decreased their BID price from 50.50 to 50.438. One market maker (LEHM) refreshed the same price of 50.438 and thus LEHM joined the inside BID. The color representing 50.50 moved up and disappeared from the BID side. Four market makers (JPMS, LEHM, MASH, and MONT) lowered their ASK price from 50.563 to 50.50. This is shown as a new color-coded price and will show up on the ASK side. The color-coded price of 50.50 would

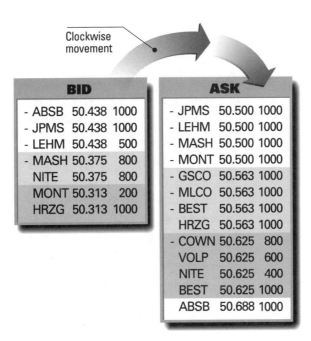

Figure 7.9 *Level II and Price Decrease*

move clockwise from the BID side to the ASK side. The dynamic Level II screen shows this clockwise motion whenever there is a price decrease.

This price decrease momentum would continue, and more market makers would enter the ASK side (that is, sell the stock) and at the same time leave the BID side. Figure 7.10 depicts that continued price decrease movement. The number of market makers on the inside BID price has been reduced from three to one. However, there are now altogether six market makers on the inside ASK price, and the color-coded price block of 50.50 has moved down. The clockwise motion on the Level II screen continues. The inside BID color-coded block would decrease in size, and conversely the inside ASK color-coded block would increase in size.

For the time being, the best BID and ASK side has remained the same at 50.438 and 50.50. The day trader who has access to a live Level II screen would receive a visual confirmation that the price decrease momentum is there. He has something of a preview of the future, and could expect that the best BID and ASK prices will eventually decrease to 50.375 and 50.438. If the price decrease momentum continues in this clockwise motion on the Level II screen, the trader should short sell the stock.

Furthermore, day traders can observe when the clockwise motion on the Level II screen slows down and stops. This would mean that price decrease momentum is losing its steam. Other investors and traders who

Figure 7.10 *Level II Screen and Continued Price Decrease Momentum*

do not have access to the Level II screen would not be able to preview this slowdown in the price decrease momentum. The outflow of money is slowing down, and the stock supply has ceased to increase. There are no new market makers entering the inside ASK, and some market makers may be refreshing at a higher ASK. The demand for the stock has stabilized, and it is no longer decreasing. Market makers are not leaving the inside BID price; this tells the day trader that the momentum is shifting. Now would probably be a good time to exit the short position. In other words, buy the stock and close the short position.

Short-Term Trading Alerts

THE DICTIONARY DEFINES THE NOUN *ALERT* AS "AN ALARM OF DANGER." In the stock market, an alert is an alarm of opportunity. A savvy stock trader or investor is continuously watchful and prompt in greeting the opportunity an increasingly volatile stock market brings. Traders use trading alerts to prompt them to take a closer view of a particular stock when the price momentum is changing. That alone can make the difference between being successful or unsuccessful in the market.

That said, in my opinion, an alert is *not* a signal to buy or sell stocks. An alert should only prompt you to take a closer look. No one should jump in and buy or short sell a stock just because the stock symbol pops up in one of the computer alert windows. After being alerted that the stock has the potential to move up or down in price in the near future, the trader should conduct some form of technical analysis. The trading signals would confirm or reject the trader's hypothesis that the stock has the probability to move in the desired price direction.

The shortest-term alert and the most important day trading alert tool is the NASDAQ Level II screen. As we learned in chapter 6, the NASDAQ Level II screen provides insight into the activities of many competing market makers who are dealing in the same stock. There are several trading software products that package Level II screen information in formats that are relatively easy to track. It takes time for a new trader to become familiar with the Level II format and to interpret such information as trading alerts.

In my opinion, in addition to the NASDAQ Level I and II screens, the three most important trading tools are the Time and Sales window, the market ticker, and the Top Advances and Declines report. Day traders use these tools as alerts, which remind the traders to take a closer view of a particular stock or as a signal that the price momentum is shifting.

Time and Sales Window

One of the most important trading tools is the Time and Sales window. This window is a standard feature of any trading software package and appears on the trader's computer screen. This tool shows tick by tick what is actually being traded. The Time and Sales window displays "prints" of the actual price and size of the buying and selling activities on a stock, which reveal whether the public is buying or selling the stock. The window also reveals the actual size (shares) and the respective prices of all buying and selling transactions.

This information is not available on the NASDAQ Level II screen. The Time and Sales window complements the Level II information by telling traders not only what the market makers are willing to do, but what is actually being executed right now in terms of price and size. Some traders need only a Level II screen with a Time and Sales window in order to trade proficiently.

Figure 8.1 displays the Time and Sales window. In this example, the inside ASK price is 50.563, which represents the price at which the public is buying that stock. All trades that were executed at the ASK price of 50.563 represent stock purchases. If the day trader is considering taking a long position, it would be reassuring to see the public buying that stock as well. A preponderance of buying transactions in the Time and Sales window can be translated as a bullish signal.

One way that the stock goes up in value is if the public continues to buy it. Not only does the day trader need to see purchases executed at the ASK price (50.563), she needs also to pay close attention to the size of the purchase. It would be reassuring to see the public buying that stock in increments of 500 or 1,000 shares. Small lots of 100 or 200 shares do not really move the market.

Figure 8.2 represents a Time and Sales window with a preponderance of sales. A preponderance of selling transactions in the Time and Sales window can be interpreted as a bearish signal. In that example, the

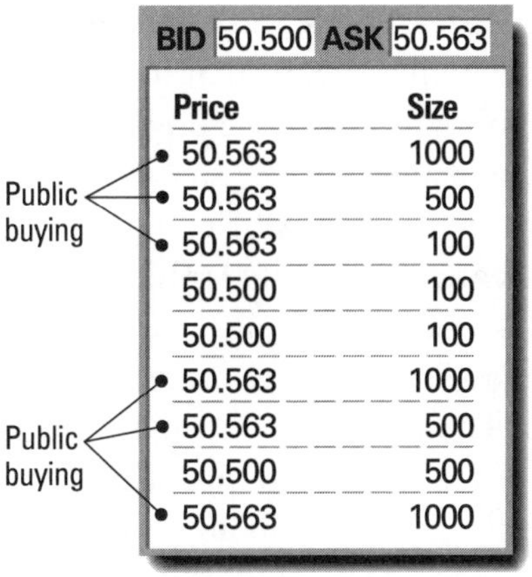

Figure 8.1 *Time and Sales Window with Buying Trades*

Figure 8.2 *Time and Sales Window with Selling Trades*

inside BID price is 50.50, which represents the price at which the public is selling the stock. All trades that were executed at 50.50 represent stock sales. If the day trader is considering taking a short position (selling the stock first in anticipation of a price decline), it would be a positive sign to see the public selling that stock as well.

Continuous selling of a stock is one way that the stock would decline in value. The day trader who is considering taking a short position would like to see in the Time and Sales window that trades are being executed at the BID price. Again, the day trader needs to pay close attention to the size of the sales. It would be reassuring to see the public selling the stock in increments of 500 or 1,000 shares, since small lots of 100 shares do not push the price down.

For liquid or actively traded stocks such as Dell Computers (DELL), Intel (INTC), or Microsoft (MSFT), buy and sell trades are continuously being executed, and the executed trades are continuously running on the Time and Sales window. For instance, all trades displayed in the Time and Sales window in Figure 8.1 occurred at that moment. However, less liquid stocks need to have a stamped time next to each trade, so that the trader can ascertain a momentum. If the Time and Sales window does not show activity, there is no point in trading that stock.

In addition, the Time and Sales window might display prints of trading activities in which the executed price was between the BID and ASK prices. That indicates that market makers either purchased the stock from the public for a price higher than the posted BID price or sold the stock to the public for a price lower than the posted ASK price. Most likely, these trading transactions were completed through an electronic communication network (ECN) such as SelectNet. Finally, some displayed prices in the Time and Sales window are simply not accurate at that point in time. They might be old prices that have been submitted late.

Market Ticker

The market ticker is another alert tool. It reports on inside BID and ASK quote changes for any stock. It can be set up to track price changes for the entire universe of NASDAQ or NYSE stocks, or it can be customized to follow only a select group of stocks. Market tickers are often used to track a group of commonly traded large-volume, volatile stocks and also to spot the price momentum. The day trader can individually select particular stocks to be tracked.

For example, the day trader might have a list of 10 or 20 stocks that meet his trading criteria. The trader would enter the stock symbols of that list into his personal ticker. From that point on, the ticker would highlight all changes in the inside BID and ASK prices for those stocks. In the event that the day trader does not have such a personalized list of stocks, the ticker can be programmed to track all NASDAQ or NYSE stocks that meet certain trading criteria. For example, a trading criteria could be "stocks greater than $20 per share, with the spread less than $\frac{1}{8}$

and daily trading volume over 500,000 shares."

Ticker reports can have two distinctly different formats. The first option is to customize the ticker to report only the actual changes in the inside BID and ASK prices. This type of ticker format reports on changes in the Level I price information. If the trader monitors only 20 stocks, this type of ticker would not move very fast and would report only when the actual price had changed. Therefore it is easier to follow.

Figure 8.3 represents such a Level I ticker. The ticker report is color-coded for easy reference. All stocks with the last up-tick or increase in price are reported in green. Stocks with the last down-tick or decrease in price are reported in red. Since Figure 8.3 here is not colored, all "green" up-ticks are displayed in black, and all "red" down-ticks are shaded. The most recent inside BID and ASK price change is reported at the top of the ticker page.

Usually, the trader would position a ticker report so it is prominently visible on the monitoring screen, and the trader would notice that DELL was reported twice. Initially the best BID and ASK prices for DELL were 50.50 and 50.563. The ASK price was increased to 50.563 as indicated by the green (black) ASK color. The next DELL was also green. On this occasion both the BID and ASK prices were increased.

This development would alert the trader that DELL is moving up; the ticker report would be used as a stock alert tool. At that time, the

MARKET TICKER			
DELL	50.563	50.625	+1.125
CIEN	27.250	27.313	+1.250
SUNW	101.063	101.125	–.313
AMZN	110.875	110.938	+1.063
INTC	130.375	110.438	+.875
INWO	26.938	27	–.625
DELL	50.500	50.563	+1.063
CSCO	99.875	99.938	+.875
WCOM	83.938	83.875	+1.313
YHOO	150	150.125	+2.250

Figure 8.3 *Market Ticker (Level I Information)*

trader would open the Level I and II screens for DELL, along with the Time and Sales window. Then the trader would open a chart of DELL that contains some technical charting analysis. The technical charting analysis window might be already on the monitoring screen and loaded with two exponential moving averages, a type of technical analysis.

The second format for ticker reports is to customize the ticker to report all the changes within the inside BID and ASK made by all market makers or ECNs. This is the Level II information limited to the inside BID and ASK quotes. Whenever one market maker enters into the inside BID and ASK quote, this action would be reported by the ticker. The best BID and ASK price has remained the same, but nevertheless, the entrance of that market maker into the inside BID and ASK quote would be shown to the day trader. Since commonly traded, large-volume, volatile stocks have many market makers, this type of ticker reporting tends to be very active and busy. Sometimes this ticker report moves very fast and is difficult to follow.

Figure 8.4 displays this type of the market ticker format. The best BID and ASK price for DELL went up only once from 50.50 and 50.563 to 50.563 and 50.625. However, DELL showed up six times on that ticker. Consequently, it is not easy to monitor this type of the market ticker.

MARKET TICKER				
DELL	[MONT]	50.563	50.625	+1.125
CIEN	[MLCO]	27.250	27.313	+1.250
DELL	[TUCK]	50.500	50.625	+1.125
AMZN	[GSCO]	110.875	110.938	+1.063
DELL	[NEED]	50.500	50.625	+1.125
DELL	[HRZG]	50.500	50.625	+1.125
DELL	[PRUD]	50.500	50.563	+1.063
CSCO	[NAWE]	99.875	99.938	+.875
DELL	[RAGN]	50.500	50.563	+1.063
YHOO	[ABSA]	150	150.125	+2.250

Figure 8.4 *Market Ticker with Market Makers (Level II Information)*

Top Advances and Declines

The Top Advances and Declines report is another commonly used alert tool. It shows the top ten stocks in terms of volume and largest dollar advance and decline for that point in time on that day. Figure 8.5 displays such a report. The report is updated dynamically in real time, so it is always current. Most trading software packages provide this alert feature for the NASDAQ and NYSE stocks.

A day trader would most likely focus on the top ten advances and declines. The volume indicator does not really change much. For the NASDAQ stocks, it is always the same large capitalization technology companies such as Microsoft, Dell, Intel, and Cisco. However, the top ten advances and declines are a different story. Different stocks will populate this window each day. The Top Advances and Declines report is also biased toward the expensive and volatile technology stocks.

Since the report is ranked in absolute dollar terms, expensive stocks usually are listed first. Some expensive Internet stocks with high intraday volatility are commonly on the Top Advances and Declines list. For those expensive and volatile stocks, a $10 absolute price change is still a small relative percentage change. At one point in time, Amazon.com (AMZN) and Yahoo (YHOO) were trading at the range of $200-plus per share. A $10 price change would constitute a 5% relative price change, which was quite a common occurrence.

NASDAQ VOLUME		NASDAQ TOP ADVANCES		NASDAQ TOP DECLINES	
MSFT	9,852,700	ASDV	+4.313	CPWR	–2.875
DELL	8,752,300	NETA	+4.250	PSQL	–2.625
INTC	5,653,000	SDTI	+3.875	MICA	–2.250
WCOM	4,823,500	AMZN	+3.375	DCTM	–2
CSCO	4,230,200	CIEN	+2.250	PLAT	–1.938
COMS	3,860,400	SEBL	+2.188	AMAT	–1.875
ORCL	3,243,100	HYSL	+2.125	SYBS	–1.625
AMZN	3,105,500	LGTO	+2.063	JDEC	–1.438
YHOO	3,025,820	CTXS	+2	BMCS	–1.313

Figure 8.5 *Top Advances and Declines Report*

Some NASDAQ stocks that show up in the Top Advances and Declines window are not good stocks to day trade. They tend to be small companies that have low daily trading volume. It is difficult to get buy and sell orders filled at the price the day trader wants. Also, they show up suddenly after some specific or particular bad (or good) news. The volatility is then short-lived. The stock price tends to stay at that level. Subsequently, the day traders can't really specialize and follow these stocks.

52-Week or Daily High and Low

The 52-Week or Daily High and Low are two additional alert tools available to day traders. This window is available in most trading software packages for NASDAQ and NYSE stocks. It shows the top ten stocks that hit the new intraday or 52-week high and low prices. Some software packages have a price filter so the day trader can exclude stocks that are inexpensive. The report is updated dynamically in real time. Figure 8.6 displays a 52-Week Highs and Lows report for NASDAQ stocks. A similar report can be displayed for the NYSE stocks.

The objective of this 52-week high is to focus on the price breakouts. A *breakout* is a movement of a stock price out of an established price trading range. The 52-week high price would be translated as a stock price breakout above the long-term price resistance level. *Resistance* is the upper boundary of the trading range, where selling pressure tends to

NASDAQ 52-WEEK HIGH		NASDAQ 52-WEEK LOW	
AMGEN	78	JDEC	13.938
BMET	44.500	BPAO	7.750
CHANF	10	ADSC	4
CPWM	28.875	CDEN	6.031
CPTL	16.500	CMDL	6.250
CSTR	17.688	DTLN	18.375
KIDE	38.875	DYMX	2.250
JAKK	18.875	INPR	3.750
WCOM	93.750	LKFNP	10.063

Figure 8.6 *52-Week High and Low*

keep the price below the established range. When a new stock symbol is displayed on the Day Highs report, the day trader could interpret this event as a stock price breakout above the intraday price resistance level.

If the price breaks out of the 52-week high price, the day trader would expect that stock price momentum to continue. At that time, the day trader would start to monitor the stock by pooling the stock into the market ticker. If the stock keeps showing up in the market ticker as a green up-tick, the day trader would open the Level I and II screens and technical analysis charts for that stock. The key point here is that the day trader was alerted about that stock.

The 52-week low price would be translated as a stock price breakout below the long-term support level. *Support* is the lower boundary of the trading range, where buying pressure tends to keep the price from decreasing below that established range. If a price breaks below the 52-week low price, the day trader would expect the stock price to continue to decline. Again, the key is that the day trader was alerted about the possibility to short sell that stock. Just as some day traders rely on the Level II screen and the Time and Sales window, others trade profitably day in and day out by simply buying the 52-week high stocks and short selling the 52-week low stocks.

9

Other Trading Alerts

I T IS NAIVE TO EXPECT THAT ALL ALERTS WILL OCCUR SIMULTANEOUSLY AND give the day trader a clear indication of whether to buy or sell a stock. However, the universe does not have to be lined up perfectly for a trader to obtain a clear signal that there is a price momentum shift. It is only important that he recognize the great majority of the alerts discussed in this chapter so that he can examine and analyze closely one particular stock. Furthermore, the alerts discussed in this chapter are longer-term alerts that have lasting or prolonged price impacts and are commonly used by short-term investors.

Earnings Reports

A company's quarterly earnings reports are by far the most important fundamental analysis alert. Just as location, location, location is the mantra of real estate professionals, earnings, earnings, earnings is the new hymn for stock market investors and traders. There have been several academic studies designed to measure the impact and price reaction of corporate quarterly earnings reports. The most often-quoted study is the work by Rendleman, Jones, and Latane, which was published in November 1982 in the *Journal of Financial Economics*. In that study the authors compared the firm's actual quarterly earnings numbers to the financial analysts' estimates of corporate earnings. The authors ranked all of the firms' positive and negative earnings surprises into ten possible categories, ranging from 10, the comparative highest positive earnings surprises, to 1, the comparative highest negative earnings surprises.

The extremely high positive earnings surprises are listed at the top of the list. For instance, category 10 represents the great earnings surprises of firms whose actual quarterly earnings were greater than two standard deviations from the analysts' consensus earnings estimates. Category 9 represents firms whose actual quarterly earnings were higher than expected but by a smaller margin than those in category 10.

Category 5, in the middle, represents firms that reported the same earnings as were estimated by financial analysts. The standard deviation between the actual and estimated earnings was close to zero. This group can be labeled as the "no earnings surprises" group.

The extremely negative earnings surprises were grouped into the bottom category 1, which is labeled "very bad earning surprises." This category includes firms whose actual quarterly earnings were less than two standard deviations from the analysts' consensus earnings estimates. The higher category 2 represents firms whose actual quarterly earnings were lower than expected but by a smaller margin than those in category 1.

Figure 9.1 depicts this relationship between price reaction and quarterly earnings reports. The authors measured on a horizontal axis the time in days before and after the quarterly earnings reports were issued. On the vertical axis, the authors measured the cumulative average excess return above or below the average stock market return.

Please note that stock prices began to react several days before the actual date of the announcement. The stock prices of the companies that would have positive earnings surprises were going up dramatically in value two to three days before the actual earnings reports were issued. Conversely, the stock prices of the companies that would have an announcement of negative earnings surprises were going down in value continuously and substantially 20 days before the actual earnings reports were issued. This is most likely the result of information leakage by company insiders.

After the issuance of the earnings report, the stocks that could be labeled as positive earnings surprises continued to increase in price. The pace of the price increase is dramatically smaller, but there is a positive price momentum. Conversely, the stocks labeled as negative earnings surprises continued to decrease in price after the earnings report was issued. The rate of the price decline is dramatically smaller than what

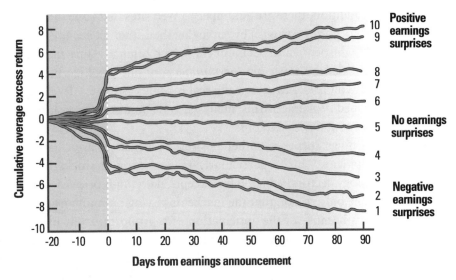

Figure 9.1 *Price Reaction and Quarterly Earnings Reports*

was experienced before the earnings report, but the negative price momentum exists. Companies who did not have any positive or negative earnings surprises continued to perform comparable to the stock market average.

The point of the study is that public information, such as corporate quarterly earnings reports, continues to have an impact on prices long after the announcement is made. Most of the price change was incorporated before the quarterly earnings reports were made public. This study supports the claim that the stock market is less than efficient in response to the announcement of quarterly earnings reports. My recommendation to investors and traders is to closely monitor quarterly earnings reports.

The ability to eavesdrop on earnings conference calls through the Internet and the deliberate practice by companies of understating earnings estimates prior to the announcement to achieve a positive surprise have greatly complicated the use of earnings announcements as a viable tool for traders. There are several Internet sites, such as *www.vcall.com, www.bestcalls.com, www.streetevents.com,* and *www.streetfusion.com,* that provide live-audio public access to earnings conference calls between corporate executives and Wall Street professionals. Keep in mind that these conference calls tend to be long and provide a mountain of financial fundamental analysis data that can be difficult to interpret.

In addition, there are a number of Web sites that issue their own forecast of corporate earnings by surveying their Internet site users. These so-called "whisper" earnings numbers, which often are amazingly accurate, are provided by *www.whispernumber.com* and *www.earningswhispers.com*. If you prefer to review the real earnings estimates developed by the established brokerage firms' analysts, your best bet is to visit *www.street IQ.com* or *www.zacks.com*.

Earnings surprises, either positive or negative, are clearly a major development. This is particularly true of growth stocks in the high-technology sectors, which have exceptionally high price/earnings multiples. The only reason that the market is paying premium prices for these stocks is because of the anticipation of a proportionately high earnings growth. When earnings do not materialize, many growth investors feel cheated, and there is a mass exodus from the market. Analysts' stock recommendation upgrades, and particularly downgrades, are relevant because a few analysts who are employed by large retail brokerage firms are influential and have substantial followings.

Cash Dividends

Although dividend-paying stocks tend to be less price volatile and from more established "old economy" companies, these stocks are nevertheless still viable trading stocks. Declaration of higher cash dividends serves as a bullish trading alert because it is interpreted as a sign of management's confidence in continued prospects of higher future earnings.

The board of directors commonly declares cash dividends on a quarterly basis on a date that is known as the *dividend declaration date*. The declared dividends are paid out of corporate net earnings and are most likely in the same magnitude as the previously declared quarterly dividends. The board is authorized to announce dividends of any size, even larger than the current corporate earnings. The board will also establish the *date of record* for the cash dividend, which means that the cash dividend is paid only to current shareholders of record on this specified date.

To simplify the process and answer the commonly asked question of who is entitled to the declared cash dividends, the brokers have created the *ex-dividend date*. The ex-dividend date takes into account the time required to clear the trading transaction between the stock buyer and seller. The *settlement date* is the date when a buyer pays for the security and a seller delivers the security and receives the proceeds of the sale. The standard settlement date is three business days after the trade day, or as the brokers call it, "T + 3." The transactions carried out on a cash basis settle on the same day as the trade.

Therefore, in order to receive a cash dividend, the investor must be identified as the shareholder of record at the date specified by the board to be the date of record. Because the standard settlement takes three business days, the investor needs to purchase the stock before the ex-dividend day, which is two days prior to the date of record. In addition, the board will also pick an arbitrary date when the dividend checks are physically mailed or electronically deposited into an investor's brokerage account. This "simplified" process is summarized and explained in Figure 9.2.

Declaration of increased cash dividends has a tangible economic meaning. The higher cash dividend goes directly into the shareholders' pockets. It boosts the future stream of income to the shareholders, which will automatically increase the net present value of that investment. In other words, higher declared dividends add additional value for the shareholders.

In addition, higher declared dividends translate into a clear market signal that company management is confident about continued prospects of higher future corporate earnings. Management is reluctant to cut dividends because that action will translate into public acknowledgment that the company expects declining future earnings. Because of this, management will cut cash dividends only as an absolute last resort. Conversely, management will increase cash dividends only if it is absolutely convinced that there has been a permanent increase in corporate profitability and thus there is a clear prospect of higher future earnings. The increased cash dividends serve as a clear signal from corporate insiders that the corporate earnings capabilities are lastingly enhanced.

The February 1969 paper by Fama, Fisher, Jensen, and Roll, published in the *International Economic Review,* attempted to examine the

June 15	→	July 12	→	July 13	→	July 15	→	Aug 20
Declaration date		Trade date		Ex-dividend date		Date of record		Payment date

Figure 9.2 *Settlement Dates*

nature of stock market reaction to announcements of higher cash dividends. The authors looked at several stocks' excess investment returns as compared to the average S&P 500 Index return in the time before and after of the declaration. They concluded that the price behavior of common stocks following the declaration of a cash dividend increase deviates significantly from the average returns of all other stocks.

The study revealed that the stocks had begun to increase in price prior to the higher cash dividend announcement. That makes sense. Corporate earnings went up, so the stock prices went up, and thus the stocks' return exceeded the market average. The increase in price is substantial, and it occurred many days or weeks prior to the declaration of the higher cash dividend. A relatively high corporate earnings is the leading force or cause that directs a company's management to declare a higher cash dividend.

After the higher cash dividend announcement date, the stock's prices, and thus the stock returns, continued to increase somewhat compared to the overall stock market return. The market has received a clear confirmation that corporate earnings are permanently enhanced, and the higher cash dividend resulted in continued higher prices or higher returns after the announcement date.

Stock Splits and Stock Dividends

A *stock split* does not impact any corporate revenues or expenses, and it does not change the firm's total market capitalization. The stock split only changes proportionately the size of the stock units in which the ownership is bought and sold. For instance, when a corporation announces a stock split of 2 for 1, the corporate pie is still the same, except there are now two smaller pieces instead of one large piece. Instead of having one ownership share bought or sold at $100, we now have two shares traded at $50 each.

It is often argued that all stock market participants respond favorably to stock splits because the split brings the stock price into a more affordable trading range. After the stock split, the lower stock price might have stronger appeal to investors, and thus increase demand for the stock. There are several Internet sites that provide stock split alerts for a nominal monthly fee from $10 to $50, such as *www.stocksplits.com, www.splitmaster.com, www.splittrader.com, www.rightline.com,* and *www.investmenthouse.com.*

Some market participants believe that a stock split acts as a leading indicator for a future increase in dividends. They claim that a stock split is often followed by a corporate announcement of increased dividends. However, other market analysts believe that a preponderance of many stock-split announcements is an early indication of an overvalued stock market. When corporate stocks are expensive, the board of directors might announce the stock split just to keep the stock prices in a reasonable trading range. In addition, some analysts believe that too many stock splits indicate that a general price correction might be forthcoming.

Several academic studies were undertaken to examine the nature of stock market reaction to the announcements of stock splits. The most often quoted result is the February 1969 research paper by Fama, Fisher, Jensen, and Roll that was published in the *International Economic Review*. The authors looked at stocks whose returns exceeded the average S&P 500 Index return in the vicinity of an event. They concluded that the price behavior of common stocks following the declaration of stock splits does not deviate significantly from the average returns of all other stocks.

The study revealed that the stocks had begun to increase in price prior to the stock-split announcement. This makes sense. Most likely, corporate earnings have increased, stock prices are going up, and thus the stocks' returns exceed the market average. The increase in price is substantial, and it occurred during many days or weeks prior to the declaration of the stock splits, so it cannot be attributed to insider trading. In fact, the relatively high stock price is the leading force or cause that directed the company to declare a stock split.

However, after the stock-split announcement date, the stocks' prices and returns remained flat and steady compared to the overall stock market return. In other words, the stock split did not result in continued higher prices or higher returns after the stock-split announcement date.

In contrast, reverse stock splits create a smaller number of outstanding shares. The reverse split results in an upward stock price adjustment. For instance, a 1-for-4 stock split would increase the stock price by four times and decrease the number of outstanding shares by four times as well. Corporate management will authorize a reverse split to raise the price of the stock. The exchanges usually require that a stock's price remain higher than a certain threshold in order for the firm to remain listed on the exchange. (The minimum stock price is only one of several exchange listing requirements.) The reverse stock split is the easiest way to keep the price over that level.

The relationship between the stock price reaction to reverse stock splits is diametrically opposite from the reaction to stock splits. Most likely, corporate earnings were already declining, and stock prices were therefore going down. Thus the stock's return was already below the market average. The price decrease most likely occurred during many days or weeks prior to the declaration of the reverse stock split. Indeed, the relatively low stock price caused the company to declare the reverse stock split. After the reverse-stock-split announcement, the stock returns remained low and steady compared to the overall market return. In other words, a reverse stock split by itself does not result in continued lower prices or lower returns after the its announcement. The company's stock prices are declining due to adverse economics and are not the result of a reverse stock-split announcement.

Stock dividends are very similar to stock splits and are fairly rare, especially among the technology stocks preferred by traders. The firm's board of directors has the discretion to declare or "pay" stock dividends to the company's shareholders. For instance, a 10% stock dividend means that a shareholder of record who owns 100 shares will receive 10 additional shares of the stock. It must be noted that the price of the stock will also be adjusted accordingly downward by 10%. The stock dividend only changes proportionately the size of the stock units in which the ownership is bought and sold.

News

News is an important factor that drives stock prices in the short run. Under the "news" heading, I do not include news about corporate earnings, declaration of cash dividends, or stock splits. *News* is narrowly defined here as reports of recent business events, such as mergers, acquisitions, changes in management, new products, and new accounts, all of which have the potential to impact a stock's price.

This type of news has the potential to quickly influence the opinions of many stock buyers and sellers, and thus it can dramatically shift up or down the supply and demand for the stock. In the short run, the stock price can jolt out of equilibrium and quickly go up or down. There are several free Internet sites that specialize in stock news coverage, with the most influential being *www.TheStreet.com, www.Bloomberg.com, www.CBS.MarketWatch.com, www.CNBC.com,* and *www.CNNfn .com.* If you are looking for real-time news coverage provided via the Internet, then you will end up paying a lot to different wire services, such as Dow Jones *(www.DJ.com)* or Reuters *(www.Reuters.com).* The other alternative is to sign up with a direct-access broker who bundles the real-time news feature into its brokerage service.

For the long-term investor, such news is less important. The good and bad news and its impact are only blips on the price chart or in normal short-term price fluctuations. All companies, including the strong blue-chip companies (the established and mature companies in their industries), have occasional bad news. Strong companies eventually overcome their short-term business difficulties and the stock rebounds. Time is on the side of long-term investors. However, traders do not have the benefit of time to weather the storm and wait for the stock to rebound. If their capital is tied up in that stock, they are out of business. Short-term traders cannot afford to ignore news about the company.

Important news is quickly disseminated throughout the stock market. The individual traders or short-term investors are not the first recipients of such news. It's likely that any important news was already leaked to the large shareholders and the press before it was publicly announced. The stock market has, in all probability, already reacted to such news before the public announcement. With the shift in the stock's supply-and-demand schedule, the stock price would change. If the news is perceived by a majority of market participants to be favorable news, the stock price would increase. That increase in price would already be displayed in one of the earlier price alerts, such as the real-time Level II screen, the Time and Sales window, the market ticker, and the daily high and low.

For instance, the traders or short-term investors who are monitoring Cisco (CSCO) stock, as an example, would already notice and observe the positive price momentum on the Level II screen, in the Time and Sales window, on the market ticker, or in the Daily High and Low window. They would have already seen Cisco's green symbol on the market ticker, its counterclockwise movement on the Level II screen, and large buy orders going off at the ASK price in the Time and Sales window. Depending on the relative importance of the news, the traders and short-term investors would see the Cisco symbol popping up in the Daily High or even the 52-Week High window. They would see positive price movement, but they would not know why the stock was moving up. Only the public announcement of the news would provide confirmation and explanation and the underlying reasons for such a price increase.

The traders or investors who are not monitoring Cisco stock right then will most likely receive the alert about Cisco's good fortunes from the electronic news reports, such as CNBC or Bloomberg. At that point in time, astute traders or investors must assimilate and quickly interpret the news about Cisco and quickly decide whether such news will have a lasting impact on Cisco stock. Although they are not the first individuals in the stock market to receive such news, they are not the last investors or traders to receive it, either.

It takes time for news to reach most market participants. There are many investors, particularly long-term investors, who will read about such news in the newspaper on the next business day. Again, the key to trading on news is to assimilate the news quickly and interpret the relative importance of the news on Cisco's future earnings potential. If your analysis concluded that Cisco's corporate earnings will improve in the future, then higher earnings will attract more buyers and fewer sellers of Cisco stock. At that time, the demand schedule for Cisco stock would increase, and the supply schedule would decline. The ultimate result is a stock price increase.

The trader then needs to act quickly, before the new information is fully appreciated by most of the market participants and thus fully reflected in the new equilibrium price. Act quickly, because the probability is high that you are not the only one who interpreted such news as being important and as potentially having a lasting positive impact on corporate earnings. Other investors and traders are already buying the stock and driving the price up.

It is self-evident that any news that deals with a company's core business is important. For instance, if the company is in the high-technology sector, then anything that impacts the firm's proprietary technology is important. Does the news mean that the firm is losing its technological advantage? Is there a new firm with a "killer application" software product that will make the firm's product technologically obsolete?

Finally, trading on news does not mean blindly buying or selling stocks just because the stocks were mentioned favorably on CNBC or through another media outlet. Favorable or unfavorable company news only serves as an alert to the trader to take a closer look at one particular stock. There is no substitute for thorough analysis. Examine one or two technical analysis charts, such as the *Moving Averages* (MA) crossover for asserting the price trend, and the *Bollinger bands* for determining the price supports and resistance. Look for market makers' movement on the Level II screen. Research a few fundamental analysis ratios. But do not blindly chase the media's hot stocks of the day or the week, because such a strategy can be extremely costly. You might simply end up buying the stock at the top.

Mergers and Acquisitions

News about mergers and acquisitions has a lasting impact on stock prices. As a general rule, when a publicly held firm is acquired, its stock price will inevitably go up. The reasoning is straightforward: To be acquired, the company demands and receives a stock price that is a premium over its current price. Why would the company's board of directors agree that the firm could be acquired if the price is not right?

The opposite is true for the acquirer or the new parent firm. The acquirer firm will most likely end up paying for the acquisition with its own stock. That simply means stock ownership dilution. After the merger or acquisition, there will be proportionately more shareholders having an ownership claim on the corporate earnings. Most likely, the corporate parent earnings would not increase proportionately after the merger or acquisition. The merger or acquisition is a costly endeavor that will reflect on the company's bottom line, and will also disrupt business operations for both firms. Since it will take some time for the new management to complete the merger or acquisition, it is normally anticipated that the acquirer firm (the new parent firm) will experience a stock price decline in the short run.

The monster merger between the Internet pioneer America Online (AOL) and media and entertainment giant Time-Warner (TWX) is a good example of the merger-and-acquisition effect on stock prices. After the merger announcement, the stock price of the firm to be acquired, Time-Warner, skyrocketed 39% in one day, whereas the shares of the acquirer (the new parent firm) AOL, declined approximately 2%.

In addition, AOL shares kept declining in the following days of trading, and the merger deal became less and less attractive for the Time-Warner shareholders, who were paid with AOL shares. As the AOL shares started declining in value in the following trading days, so did the shares of Time-Warner.

Rumors

Keep in mind that all news is not created equal. The media has a vested interest in hyping up the story and making a lot of noise. "Noisy" investment headlines sell papers and grab our attention. Investment noise is always a part of stock market news. The individual trader or investor must learn to filter out the noise and concentrate only on important news about the company.

However, day traders could elect to pay attention to stock rumors and trade based on rumors. Stock rumors are defined as widely disseminated opinions without any credible or discernible source. Trading on rumors is a dangerous strategy, particularly if you do not follow the particular stock and the stock is purchased at the price resistance levels, such as the upper Bollinger band or daily or weekly high price. There are several Internet sites that follow and track stock rumors, such as *www.stockrumors.com, www.stockselector.com, www.sixer.com, www.flyonthewall.com,* and *www.JAGfn.com.*

Another variation on the rumor-based trading is to purchase a stock of any company that is featured on CNBC or the like. For instance, a day trader would jump in and purchase a stock of XYZ the moment a trader would hear on CNBC that the CEO of XYZ is being interviewed or the CNBC analyst will feature the company in the next CNBC segment. The probability is such that the friendly analysis or CEO interview will result in a positive news spin, which might generate a buying interest. In fact, CNBC posts on the Internet the list of the upcoming guests, so traders have advanced notice.

Macroeconomic News

Traders can afford to pay less attention to macroeconomic news such as the performance of general economic indicators. This is true because there is a buffer between the individual stock impact and general economic developments. It will take time for general macroeconomic news to trickle down through the market and impact an individual stock, because the news is not directly related to an individual company. Several Web sites, such as *www.StockAndNews.com* and Dismal Scientist *(www.dismal.com),* provide free and straightforward macroeconomic analysis information to investors and traders.

Unfortunately, even though the traders are somewhat insulated from the macroeconomic events in the short run, that time frame doesn't last forever. For example, changes in the Federal Reserve's monetary policy will have a quick impact on interest-rate sensitive stocks, such as bank stocks. Likewise, the the chairman of the Federal Reserve's comments before a congressional committee can result in a substantial and general sell-off or acquisition and greatly impact the traders' stock positions.

In my opinion, traders should pose the following questions regarding the announcement of macroeconomic news:

1. What is the direction of the stock's supply-and-demand shift as the result of the economic news? Will the news bring more or fewer buyers and sellers for that stock? In other words, will this economic news indicate an increase or decrease in future corporate earnings?

2. What is the magnitude of the shift in the stock's supply-and-demand schedule? If the news is important, or perceived to be important by many stock market participants, then many stock buyers and sellers will simultaneously enter or exit the market for that stock, and the stock will quickly and dramatically adjust to a new equilibrium. With that in mind, ask yourself, What is the magnitude of the economic news impact on future corporate earnings?

Seasonal Events

Mark Twain once observed a simple and universal stock market seasonal rule that was true a century ago and is still true today. He wrote, "October is one of the dangerous months to speculate in stocks. The other months are July, January, April, September, November, May, March, June, December, August, and February."

All truisms aside, seasonal indicators are difficult to defend. If the seasonal rules are true and effective, then all market participants would eventually use the rules and thus all of us would be on the same side of the market exchange during that part of the year. And, it must also be noted that the seasonal effects do not appear to be substantial. The magnitude of these events is relatively small, so no one will become rich by simply implementing the seasonal trading "rules."

If you're a buyer and are adhering to the conventions of seasonal effects, you should buy before they kick in. In this way, the seasonal effect can be captured and the stocks purchased at a lower price. If you're a seller, you should sell after the seasonal effects kick in to capture the effect and to sell the stocks at a higher price. It must be noted that seasonal stock market effects tend to have a larger price impact on smaller-capitalization firms than they do on large-cap stocks.

The most common stock market seasonal effects are summarized as follows:

1. The summer doldrums effect

2. The January effect

3. The pre-holiday effect

4. The month-end effect

5. The day-of-the-week effect

An old Wall Street adage is "Sell in May, then go away." There is a lot of truth to this. Simply stated, investors and traders are less active in the summer months because they go away on vacation. Trading volume drops dramatically in the summer, creating the *summer doldrums*. For instance, the monthly change in NYSE trading volume from the previous month average drops significantly in June, July, August, and September. With the trading volume down in summer months, the price volatility is up. On the other hand, the beginning months in a year, such as January, February, and March, exhibit substantially larger average trading volume.

Also, it is not surprising that both the S&P 500 and NASDAQ Composite Indices have underperformed in the summer months as compared to the rest of the year. With a lower trading volume in the summer months, stock prices on average tend to decline as well. Since 1982, the S&P 500 Index monthly percentage gain for the months of August, September, and October was less than 0.5%. Beginning and end of the year months seem to generate the largest monthly gains for the S&P 500 Index. For instance, February has produced on average more than 2% monthly gain since 1982, followed closely by January, March, November, and December, which recorded on average more than 1.5% monthly gains.

The *January effect* exists because investors tend to oversell stocks during the previous December for tax purposes. Investors shed (sell) the "dogs" from their investment portfolio to minimize their tax liability for that year, and the subsequent selling surge results in lower stock prices for the month of December. Professional fund managers also tend to sell underperforming stocks in December to avoid having these stocks appear on year-end reports.

In the next year there is a resurgence of buying interest. Investors and mutual funds have cash to invest, and some stocks look like bargains now. Subsequently, the market tends to rebound in the first several trading days of the following month, and thus we see the January effect. Indeed, the average return in January tends to be approximately 3% higher than the average return for the other months in the year.

The 1988 "Incredible January Effect" study by Haugen and Lakonishok estimates that a large percentage of all average differences between the rates of return for small and large capitalization firms comes in the first five trading days in January. The first five trading days in January account for approximately 27% of the annual differences between the returns of small and large firms during the period between 1963 and 1979. Table 9.1 depicts this January impact.

The *pre-holiday effect* means that stock prices tend to go up each trading day before the holiday market close. There are ten holidays on which the major stock exchanges close: Martin Luther King, Jr., Day, Presidents' Day, Good Friday, Memorial Day, Independence Day, Labor Day, Election Day, Thanksgiving, Christmas, and New Year's Day. The only logical explanation for this effect is that short sellers tend to close their short positions before the holidays because they may fear that the companies might announce some good news while the market is closed.

The *month-end effect* basically derives from the propensity for stock prices to increase during the last day of every month and the first four days at the beginning of the month. In essence, the five continuous

Table 9.1 *Annual Extra Difference by Trading Day*

First trading day in January	10
Second trading day in January	6
Third trading day in January	4
Fourth trading day in January	4
Fifth trading day in January	3
All other trading days in the year	73

trading days tend to be good for investors with long positions. The following are the reasons for this:

> ➤ Mutual funds investment of monthly proceeds from monthly stock purchase plans;

> ➤ Mutual funds investment of monthly proceeds from the monthly 401(k) deferred compensation plans;

> ➤ Month-end portfolio adjustments by financial institutions

The *day-of-the-week effect* states that there are some differences in the expected percentage changes in stock prices depending on which day of the week trading is conducted. Review of the historical records between 1962 and 1978 revealed that the S&P 500 had a propensity to decline in value on Monday, whereas Wednesday, Thursday, and Friday tended to exhibit higher prices. The financial analysts refer to the observation that Mondays exhibit negative returns as the *weekend effect*. Most of the price decline on Monday occurs within the first hour of opening. Finally, Tuesday tended to have positive returns but with a much lower price increase than Wednesday, Thursday, and Friday. Figure 9.3 depicts this effect. Please keep in mind that the results reflect stock market data from the 1960s and 1970s, and that a study of the present stock market environment might generate a different outcome.

In addition, there is one more general and commonly accepted effect—the *presidential election effect*. The presidential election effect is not really a seasonal effect because, thankfully, we do not have annual

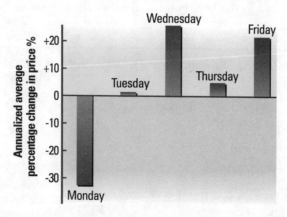

Figure 9.3 *Days-of-the-Week Effect*

presidential elections. Nevertheless, the presidential elections have a pervasive impact on the overall U.S. economy and subsequently on the U.S. stock market.

The logic behind the presidential election effect is straightforward. White House incumbents tend to sponsor expansionary fiscal and monetary policies in order to ensure a booming economy during the election year to assure the president's reelection or to help his party win the election. Market data supports this hypothesis. There is a strong positive correlation between the presidential election and the S&P 500's performance. The S&P 500 has increased in 11 out of 13 presidential elections since 1952, with the exception of the 1960 and 2000 elections. The average annual increase in the S&P 500 during the 13 elections was approximately 10%.

Stock Screening

Stock screening is essentially the process of data mining for stocks that meet a specified screening criteria within the universe of all stocks in the database. The Microsoft Network's MoneyCental Investor section *(www.MoneyCentral.MSN.com)* and Yahoo Finance *(www.Quote .Yahoo.com)* are the two most commonly used Internet-based stock search engines.

These two stock search engines have a pull-down menu of different predefined and common investment criteria. The price-momentum trader could specify the following stock screening criteria:

1. Market capitalization greater than 500 million
2. Average daily trading volume in the last year greater than 500,000 shares
3. Percent price change in the last week greater than 10%
4. Percent price change in the last month greater than 20%
5. Percent price change, by rank, in the last quarter high as possible

The result is a list of the large and midcap companies with plenty of trading liquidity (that is, the average trading volume is greater than 500,000 shares). Most important, the current stock prices of the companies on the list are changing at a faster pace than the rest of the market. If the screening match list is too large, the next step would be to increase the weekly and monthly percentage price change criteria from

10 and 20% to 20 and 30%, which narrows the list to fewer stocks. The result of the stock screening is only the first alert. It is up to the investor or trader to take a closer look at the stock to determine whether the stock deserves additional consideration.

Insider Trading

Insiders are any officers or directors of the company, any person who owns 10% of the company stock, or anyone with nonpublic information about the company. The SEC stipulates that it is illegal for anyone to trade a security on an organized exchange if the person has taken advantage of material inside information that is not disclosed to the general public. This statement begs the question: What constitutes material inside information? The answer is rather vague. Material inside information can be any information of which public dissemination can affect the market price of that security.

The SEC requires that all insiders report to the SEC within ten days of the following month any trading transactions they have made in the company's shares. The SEC will summarize and publish this information monthly in the *Official Summary of Insider Transactions*. The SEC information is then analyzed, repackaged, and published by several financial information services companies. One such service is the Vickers Stock Research Corporation of New Jersey, which publishes the *Weekly Insider Report*. In addition, Value Line Inc. *(www.valueline.com)* issues an index of the insiders' decisions. Another source is the Insider Trader *(www.insidertrader.com),* which publishes weekly a free listing of the select companies that filed the SEC insider activity reports. Another resource is Thomson Financial *(www.thomsoninvest.com),* which also chronicles insider activities.

It seems intuitively clear that a large selling volume by company insiders would indicate a bearish sign, whereas a large buying volume would constitute a bullish signal. However, interpretation of the limited insider trading data that is available is not that simple. First of all, the data on insider trading is published rather late. By the time the SEC receives the insider trading form (within 10 days of the following month) and issues the report (*Official Summary of Insider Transactions*), the market has most likely already reacted to the company news that prompted the initial insider trading in the first place. My point here is that it is probably too late for the general public to take advantage of the information about insider trading, because the market already made the price correction on that stock.

In addition, the SEC prohibits corporate insiders from short selling their stock. That means that there is no clear bearish signal derived from the insiders' actions. Also, insiders do not have any incentive to engage in short-term trading in the company stock. The SEC rule stipulates that any short-term trading profit made by the company insiders (where the short term is anything less than six months) must be returned to the company treasury. Consequently, insiders may only take long-term stock positions. Because company insiders are not active traders, there are only a few trading signals at hand.

Most important, insiders buy and sell the company's shares for many different and personal reasons that have little to do with the company's business performance. Sometimes the senior executive managers are buying the company's shares in order to exercise a stock option, which was most likely granted by the board of directors several years ago. Often, the insiders are selling the company's shares in order to raise money to buy or build new homes or finance other large purchases. Frequently, insiders are selling their shares simply to diversify their investment portfolios. Some are simply cashing out in order to retire. None of these sell orders indicate any potential for an adverse price trend. Indeed, there are plenty of circumstances in which a few insiders sell company shares, whereas other insiders are buying shares.

Some insiders, such as the company founders, are prohibited from selling the company's shares for several years after the initial public offering (IPO). Others, such as the executive managers, are fully vested with the stock only after waiting a few years following the IPO. These conditions were inserted in the IPO documentation to promote the long-term tenure of the initial ownership and management structure. In other words, the company founders and senior executives have a vested financial interest in remaining with the company for at least a few years following the IPO. After a few years, these insiders are free to sell their shares, which they generally do. Thus, the consequent selling activities do not provide any additional insight about the future of the company.

Some insiders sell some company shares every year for tax purposes. Tax accountants call this selling activity *tax planning*, and the objective is to minimize long-term tax liability. In addition, SEC rule No. 144

provides restrictions on the sale of the so-called control stocks, which are the stocks owned by the company insiders. The SEC restrictions stipulate how many and how often the insiders can sell the company's shares on the open exchange. For listed stocks, a company insider cannot sell more than 1% of the total shares outstanding, or the average weekly volume within one quarter. Subsequently, the insiders tend to sell some shares every year when they are allowed to sell, and thus this action does not represent a selling signal.

Finally, insiders are afraid of potential liability of trading the company stock. They do not want to be caught up in a legal quagmire and be charged by the federal government with insider trading. The insiders cannot trade during any of the four months in a year when the company's quarterly earnings are announced. If they do, they are trading based on inside information that has not yet been disclosed publicly. During other times of the year, insiders may have information about some new material developments, such as the potential for a merger, acquisition, or new account, or anything that can be construed or misconstrued by our litigious society as material inside information. Consequently, insiders are often advised by their legal counsel to simply avoid trading the company's shares.

It is my opinion that tracking insider trading activities is a time-consuming endeavor that seldom provides any meaningful information. The information that the general public receives about insider trading is always late—several days after the insiders have already bought or sold the stock. Most important, it is extremely difficult to interpret such information precisely and accurately. Company insiders buy or sell company shares for many different reasons. If you do not know the factors behind the insider trading, then you should not trade on such information.

10

Initial Public Offering Alerts

Many Wall Street players allege that the acronym for initial public offering—IPO—stands for "Immediate Profit Opportunity." An IPO is clearly an opportunity for profit if you are one of the privileged few who are able to obtain shares of the new issues. The hot IPO market has been driven mostly by enormous retail demand for new issues of start-up Internet companies. Hot IPOs are often oversubscribed by a huge factor. If there are only 2 million IPO shares available and there is demand for 10 million shares at the public offering price, then it is not surprising that the new issue will open up in the aftermarket with a huge gap up. Underwriters, such as Goldman Sachs & Co., Morgan Stanley Dean Witter, or Merrill Lynch & Co., also indirectly benefit from the big price jump upward in the first day of trading because such news will create additional excitement for the stock and for the underwriting business as well. As the stock price continues to increase, the underwriter will have an easier time selling her next IPO to the public. All she has to do is point to the previous IPO's performance.

However, IPOs are not a license to print money. More-skeptical IPO market observers point out that in many cases, IPO stands for "It's Probably Overpriced." That statement is even more true during years when the IPO market is not as hot as it was in 1999, such as in 2000. Even then, a number of IPOs performed poorly on the first day of trading. For instance, MotherNature.com lost 21% in value after the first day of trading. Even in the hot 1999 IPO market, approximately 26%

of IPOs issued that year fell below their offer prices by the end of the trading day.

In the long run, the IPO picture is not very bright. Most companies turn out not to be the next Microsoft or Dell. As the IPO luster fades, the IPO stock prices return to Earth. A few scant years later, many IPOs are no longer listed on an exchange because they were bought out by a competitor or they were out of business. In fact, 17% of all 1998 and 1999 dot-com IPOs are now penny stocks that trade for $5 or less.

An academic study by Jay Ritter, published in the *Journal of Finance* in 1991, revealed that the three-year return on IPOs was approximately 34%, whereas a broad sample of existing companies in the same industry generated an approximately 62% return. This is not to say that IPOs are not a profitable long-term investment, because they are. Rather, equity investments in more mature or seasoned companies provide a higher rate of return with a lower risk.

However, as you will discover later in this chapter, the volatility of IPO stock performances can make them risky but rewarding stocks for traders. Before getting to that, we first need to discuss the process by which IPOs are disseminated to the public.

Underwriters

A new issue is normally sold through a syndicate of investment bankers referred to as an *underwriting syndicate*. The issuer appoints a syndicate manager or a group of investment bankers as co-managers. The underwriters play by far the most important role in the IPO show. The IPO underwriter or the investment banker determines the price of the offering and helps draft the prospectus and other SEC filing documents. In addition to many federal laws, underwriters must navigate through the myriad of state laws that regulate IPOs. The state laws are called *blue-sky laws* because the judge in a nineteenth-century court case referred to an IPO sale as someone "selling the blue sky." Finally and most important, the underwriter must sell the new issue to the investment community. The lead underwriter has sole discretion regarding the pricing and timing of the new issue.

The importance of the underwriters cannot be overstated. Very often the underwriters themselves can mean the difference between the success and failure of the IPO. Therefore, IPO traders should make sure they know what banking firms are underwriting any IPO they are considering buying. There are approximately 410 listed investment banking firms in the United States today. These investment bankers can be grouped into three general types of IPO underwriters:

1. *Large global investment banks,* which have a huge capital base, experienced investment bankers, and many thousands of brokers across the world. A short and incomplete list of the largest would include Goldman Sachs & Co., Credit Suisse First Boston, Morgan Stanley Dean Witter, and Merrill Lynch & Co. These four investment banks were the lead underwriters for 61% of all new issues in 1999. These banks underwrite the highest-quality IPOs that have institutional support and perhaps the best chance of a positive long-term return on the investment.

2. *Medium-sized national investment banks,* which have a smaller capital base and fewer brokers than the international investment banks, and who are based mostly in the United States. A short and incomplete list would include Prudential Securities, Warburg Dillon Read, US Bancorp Piper Jaffray, Dain Rauscher Corporation, and Thomas Weisel Partners.

3. *Small, regional boutique investment banks,* which have a much smaller capital base and a few brokers, and which are based in a specific region in the United States. A sample list would include Blue Stone Capital, Capital West Securities, Chatfield Dean, Cleary Gull Reiland & McDevitt, and Dakin Securities.

From an investor's point of view, having a large global investment bank such as Morgan Stanley Dean Witter as the managing underwriter for an IPO is a step in the right direction. Analysts will most likely continue to monitor the stock in the secondary market, which indirectly promotes the stock in the long run and attracts attention from the broad investment community. Keep in mind, though, that stock market analysts are employees of the brokerage firm and its investment banking department. It is highly unlikely that the analysts will issue "sell" or even "hold" recommendations for an IPO firm in the secondary market if that deal was underwritten by the same brokerage firm. As a rule of thumb, research opinions from the "not so independent" analysts will invariably come out positive following the public offering.

Let's suppose, for example, that Morgan Stanley Dean Witter, as the lead underwriter, sells a large block of new issues to institutional investors. This is always a good sign (large institutional ownership is an

Table 10.1 *Investment Banks and IPOs in 1999*

Lead Underwriter	Proceeds	Market Share (%) ($ million)	Number of Issues
Goldman Sachs & Co.	14,638	21.2	54
Morgan Stanley Dean Witter	13,967	20.2	49
Merrill Lynch & Co.	7,843	11.3	42
Credit Suisse First Boston	5,913	8.5	59
Donaldson, Lufkin & Jenrette	3,892	5.6	39
Lehman Brothers	2,905	4.2	32
J. P. Morgan & Co.	2,785	4	10
Fleet Boston Corp.	2,695	3.9	45
Salomon Smith Barney	2,587	3.7	23
Deutche Banc Alex Brown	2,087	3	27
Bear Stearns	2,086	3	26
Chase Manhattan Corp.	1,317	1.9	23
Warburg Dillon Read	1,249	1.8	7
Mediobanca	611	0.9	2
Banc of America Securities	518	0.8	8
Prudential Securities Inc.	356	0.5	9
CIBC World Markets	352	0.5	8
US Bancorp Piper Jaffray	326	0.5	8
Thomas Weisel Partners	264	0.4	6
Dain Rauscher Corp.	244	0.4	4
Total	69,207	100	546

important predictor of the IPO's long-term success). With luck, Morgan Stanley Dean Witter's army of stockbrokers will then continue to recommend the stock to their clients in the secondary market, and thus generate a built-in demand for the stock. Table 10.1 lists lead underwriters and some of their IPO statistics.

Trading IPOs

When a hot IPO is released to the market, it is almost impossible for an outsider or a trader to purchase it at the inside price (that is, the public offering price). That is simply a fact of the underwriting distribution process. Because the lead underwriter sets the initial IPO price and determines the timing of the IPO, the most likely net result is oversubscription. Because the demand for the new issue exceeds the supply, it is almost impossible to acquire an IPO at the offering price.

The largest allotment of IPO shares goes immediately to the large institutional investors who are the investment banks' most important clients. They are always first in line because their support is crucial for the success of this particular IPO as well as for the next round of IPOs. Then there is an allotment of 5% to 10% for "friends and family" that goes literally to the issuer's pool of business friends and family members.

Then there is the practice of *spinning*. Spinning is the *quid pro quo* practice whereby the investment bank distributes shares of hot IPOs to its important clients, such as venture capital firms' executives, in anticipation of receiving their underwriting business in the future. This practice is strongly discouraged by the SEC, and a few investment banks claim that they no longer do this.

Finally, the remaining shares are then divided among the underwriting syndicate members, who individually distribute small IPO share allotments to their best brokers. However, only a few brokers have any clout with their employers (that is, the syndicate members) when it comes to receiving an IPO allotment. Once they receive their allotments, the lucky few brokers can call their best retail clients and offer tiny portions of the IPO for sale.

For a retail client to be on a broker's to-call list, the client should have the following asset: A large and actively traded account worth millions of dollars with an established stockbroker who works for a brokerage firm that has a large and established investment banking practice. In short, your best shot at getting an IPO at the inside price is to be very wealthy and have an account with Morgan Stanley Dean Witter, Merrill Lynch & Co., or Salomon Smith Barney. These large national brokerage firms accept individual accounts and also have active underwriting departments.

Your second option is to have an individual account with a regional underwriter, such as Raymond James or William Blair, although their underwriting volume is substantially smaller than that of the aforementioned. Still, you must satisfy the requirements of the first condition, which is always to be a wealthy investor. If you are not wealthy and do not have an account with any of these brokerage firms, you are at the bottom of the IPO food chain. It is not surprising that a great majority of investors in America do not buy IPOs at the public offering price.

I look at IPO distributions as a reward system. The retail client or the trader receives a few shares of an IPO as a reward for having a large account and doing a good business (generating a lot of commissions) with that brokerage house. The stockbroker receives an allotment because he is successful in generating a high volume of commission income for the brokerage house. The brokerage house receives the IPO allotment as a reward for having a successful investment banking department.

Some online brokers have tried to democratize the IPO distribution system by offering the IPO at the public offering price on a first-come, first-served basis. One online broker, the investment bank Donaldson, Lufkin & Jenrette, owns DLJ Direct, with whom a relatively small and actively traded account of $100,000 qualifies one for an IPO distribution. In addition, Charles Schwab & Co., E*Trade, and Fidelity have established a corresponding relationship with several underwriters. For instance, E*Trade has an alliance with Robertson Stephens and Goldman Sachs & Co. Schwab has corresponding relationships with Credit Suisse First Boston, J. P. Morgan, and Chase Manhattan Hambrecht & Quist. However, both Schwab and Fidelity require a $500,000 account balance in order for one to obtain IPOs.

Unfortunately, the IPO allotment given to online brokers has been extremely small, ranging from 10% to 1%. This is particularly true for the hot IPOs—online brokers often receive as little as 1% of the new issue. It appears that the online brokerage firms use and advertise this potential of purchasing the IPOs at the offering price as an enticement to open an account with their firm. The likelihood remains extremely small that the online investor would receive any shares of the hot IPO.

Finally, I need to mention the practice of IPO "flipping". *Flipping* IPOs is a lucrative practice whereby investors immediately sell IPO shares after the start of trading in order to make a quick profit. The underwriters do not want to see anything in the aftermarket that exerts heavy selling pressure on the stock at the beginning of the IPO trading.

All brokerage firms that offer IPO shares at the public offering price to their elite clients try to discourage the practice of flipping. The brokers condition a sale of an IPO to their clients with the requirement that prohibits sale of the IPO in the next 30 to 60 days. If the retail client sells the IPO within the 30-day time frame, most likely that investor's name will be deleted from the broker's IPO to-call list.

Spin-Offs

Spin-offs are a safer way to play the IPOs. A spin-off refers to a parent company selling a portion or all of a corporate division to the public in the form of an IPO. The bottom line is that spin-offs tend to increase shareholder value. The following are a few reasons for a spin-off:

1. The parent company wants to raise capital because the company may be highly leveraged and wants to pay off some debt. In essence, the parent company is selling a corporate asset to the public to pay off debt.

2. The company might be restructuring its corporate operations by selling off a non-core business.

3. The parent company might be an old industrial corporation whereas the corporate division to be sold might be a new-technology business. Many potential investors will not be aware of this new-technology division as long as it is buried in the parent's corporate structure. AT&T and Lucent Technologies are a prime example of this. The stock of Lucent simply took off after the spin-off.

4. The parent company might elect to spin off a division in order to raise the stock price of the parent by selling a poorly performing corporate division. The parent might even transfer some of the corporate debt to the new spin-off company. In essence, the parent is unloading unproductive assets to the public at the high IPO-level price.

The spin-offs can have two distinct formats:

➤ Traditional spin-offs, in which the parent company will end up owning 100% of the new company. In essence, the parent company divides its corporate assets into two businesses, and the parent company's existing shareholders will own 100% of both companies.

➤ Spin-offs with an 80–20 split equity cut up. In other words, the parent company will retain 80% ownership of the new company, and 20% will be distributed to the public at the IPO offering price. The 80–20 equity split is standard, because the 20% equity cut is a tax-free transaction. If the equity split is 75–25, then the transaction is taxable.

Spin-offs are attractive because the new company was in business as a separate corporate division for many years and has a performance history and most likely a track record of profitability, so investors are buying a known quantity. Experienced corporate management is already in place. The market share is already there, so spin-offs are considered to be less risky. Finally, spin-offs can be a very large new issue.

IPO Trading Resources

Because the probability is great that the average trader will not get an IPO in the primary market at the inside price, the only alternative is to get the new issue in the secondary market. Day traders armed with the latest IPO information, courtesy of the Internet, made their presence felt in 1999 IPO aftermarket trading.

Trading IPO stocks is a risky business, because some IPO stocks are thinly traded. As day traders move quickly in and out of an IPO stock—almost all of them at the same time—price volatility is substantial. If there is a massive panic sell, it is difficult to get out of that stock at a reasonable price when there are only a few traders or investors on the other side of the market. In other words, if the stock is thinly traded, the price drop can be sharp and substantial. My recommendation is to trade IPO stocks in the secondary market only if there is substantial trading volume—at least 500,000 shares traded daily.

The first day of trading of a new company's IPO is always tumultuous. The trader's first objective is to find out when the new issue will hit the market. There are a number of IPO Internet sites that provide a calendar of upcoming new issues. Some of the Internet sites are free, whereas other sites charge a monthly subscription fee.

The most popular free sites are Hoover's IPO Central *(www.IPOcentral.com),* Renaissance Capital *(www.IPOhome.com),* IPO.com *(www.IPO.com),* IPO Maven *(www.IPOmaven.com),* and

Direct IPO *(www.directIPO.com)*. Other popular sites that charge a monthly subscription fee include the Alert-IPO! *(www.ostman .com/alert-ipo)*, IPO Monitor *(www.IPOmonitor.com)*, IPO Spotlight *(www.IPOspotlight.com)*, and IPO Data System *(www.ipodata.com)*. Most Internet financial directories, such as Yahoo! *(www.Yahoo.com)* and Silicon Investor *(www.siliconinvestor.com)*, provide coverage on domestic IPOs.

The IPO industry even has its own magazine that covers primarily the high-tech IPOs and is called, appropriately, the *Red Herring* (the name comes from the color of the initial or preliminary IPO prospectus that new companies distribute). *Red Herring* magazine also publishes an online version *(www.herring.com)*.

There are some sources of IPO information that nobody deserves or wants. First of all, stay away from cold-call recommendations. Something must be wrong with the IPO if you receive a cold call from a broker offering you a "deal." You do not want that deal. Brokers are going through a large phone list looking and dialing for your dollars. I must repeat here the old Wall Street adage that states that if you are a small investor and can buy an IPO at the public offering price, you do not want that issue.

Next, beware of rumors distributed through the Internet chat rooms. Do not buy any IPO in the aftermarket based on rumor alone. Some of the new issues are thinly traded and are thus subject to stock manipulations. Do your own research before you buy an IPO. Also, stay away from unsolicited mail advertisements and e-mail messages that promote particular IPOs. Those could be the so-called pump-and-dump offerings, that are handled through small fly-by-night investment banks. Most of these pump-and-dump stocks are purchased by brokers who first hype the stock (pump) and drive up the price. They then solicit retail customers through unsolicited mail pieces or cold calls. When the brokers sell their allotment (dump), the marketing stops and demand for the stock simply disappears; and with that, the stock value disappears.

IPO Alerts: First Day

It is difficult to generalize the first-day trading pattern for any IPO. I do not think that there is a typical chart pattern that can be applied to all IPOs. Usually, there is a pop-up or price jump at the beginning of the trading. This is caused by investors who were unable to acquire shares at the offering price jumping immediately into the aftermarket. Because there initially is a huge imbalance between the supply and demand, the prices move up quickly. Also, there is large trading volume in the first 15 minutes of trading. If this is a hot IPO, prices will continue to go up after the initial pop-up. If this is a so-called broken IPO, prices will start to decline after the initial pop-up and will end up below the initial offering price at the end of the first trading day.

It is important to discuss the differences between the limit and market trade order executions for the IPOs. (More information on the different types of trade order executions can be found in chapter 17.) If the trader submits a limit order during the first half-hour of trading, there is a distinct possibility that the order will not get filled. Suppose that the price of the IPO is moving quickly, with small orders being filled in increments of 100 to 200 shares. This makes sense—the market makers can see that the prices are going up, so they are not willing to fill large orders. In order to display a continuous market and orderly price movement, the market makers are filling small orders and increasing the price rapidly by $\frac{1}{8}$. If the trader submits a market order, she might end up buying at the top of the pop. If this is a hot IPO, then all is well, and most likely the stock price will continue to go up. However, if this is a broken IPO, then the trader is in trouble.

Hot IPO: First Day

Figure 10.1 depicts the first day of trading for one hot IPO that trades at a substantial premium on the offering price. Selectica Inc. (SLTC) is a San Jose, California, software company *(www.selectica.com)*. It was founded in 1996, and at the time of its IPO, had 269 employees who created software for selling complex products on the Internet. The IPO's lead underwriter was CS First Boston, and the co-managers were Thomas Weisel Partners and US Bancorp Piper Jaffray. The size of the IPO was 4 million shares and it was offered on Thursday, March 9, 2000, at an offer price of $30. In the aftermarket on Friday, the stock opened at approximately $90. It quickly popped up to almost $150 in one hour of trading. After the first day of trading, the stock closed at $141.

On Monday, the next day of trading, the stock opened at approximately $115, which was a huge down gap. If a trader purchased 1,000 shares of SLTC at the first-day closing price and carried the position over the weekend, he would begin the week with a $26,000 loss. Figure 10.1 is based on five-minute *candlestick data* (*see chapter 12*), so it is worth noting the length of the candlestick wicks, which demonstrate the huge price difference between the high and low prices during five minutes of trading and how these orders were filled.

Figure 10.2 depicts the first day of trading for one hot IPO that closed below the opening price. RADVision Inc. (RVSN) is an Israeli software company *(www.radvision.com)*. It was founded in 1992, and at the time of the IPO, had 192 employees who created software that enabled voice and data packets to move on the Internet. The IPO's lead underwriter was Lehman Brothers and the co-managers were Salomon Smith Barney and US Bancorp Piper Jaffray. The size of the IPO was 3.8 million shares. RVSN was offered on Monday, March 13, 2000, at the offer price of $20. In the aftermarket on Monday, the stock opened at approximately $56. It quickly popped up to almost $65 in a few minutes

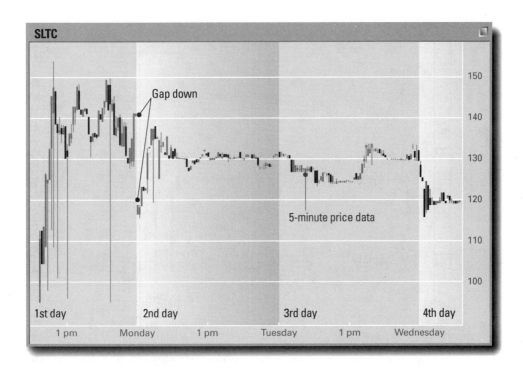

Figure 10.1 *Hot IPO: First Day of Trading for Selectica Inc.*

of trading and then dropped dramatically in one hour of trading to approximately $55. At the end of the first day of trading, the stock closed at $55.

If you were one of the lucky few investors who bought the stock at the offering price of $20, then the IPO was hot. Most likely, you would be one of the traders or investors who purchased this stock in the after-market. If that is the case, this IPO would not be hot, at least for the first day of trading.

The next day of trading, the stock opened with the large gap up of approximately $60. However, the stock prices immediately started to decline following the gap up. As you can see, IPOs are very volatile.

Broken IPO: First Day

Figure 10.3 depicts the first day of trading for a broken IPO, which trades at a substantial discount on the offering price. Netpliance Inc.

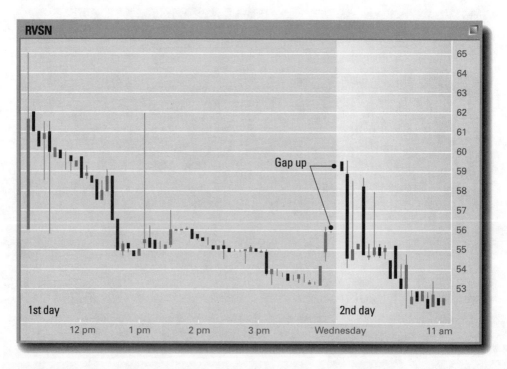

Figure 10.2 *Hot IPO: First Day of Trading for RADVision Inc.*

(NPLI) is an Austin, Texas, Internet company *(www.netpliance.com)*. It was founded in 1999, and at the time of the IPO, had 156 employees who provided appliances and portals for the Internet. The IPO's lead underwriter was Donaldson Lufkin Jenrette, and the co-managers were Chase Manhattan H&Q and Robertson Stephens. The size of the IPO was 8 million shares and was offered on Friday, March 16, 2000, at the offer price of $18. In the aftermarket on Friday, the stock opened at approximately $24. It quickly popped up to almost $26 in a few minutes of trading, and then the stock price started to decline. After the first day of trading, the stock closed at $22. The next day of trading, on Monday, the stock opened at approximately the same closing price of $22. The stock then quickly dropped to $18, which was the initial public offering price, and stayed in that price range for the rest of the day.

IPO Trading: The First Six Months

A broader look at the first six months of trading reveals that hot IPOs tend to go up continuously, whereas broken IPOs tend to decline

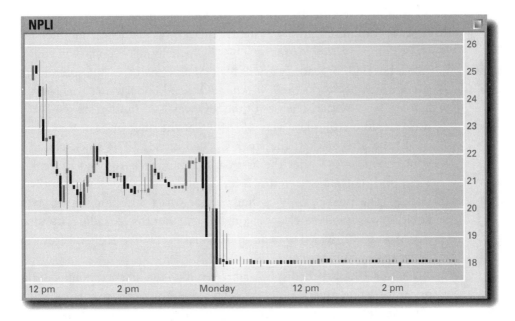

Figure 10.3   *Broken IPO: First Day of Trading for Netpliance Inc.*

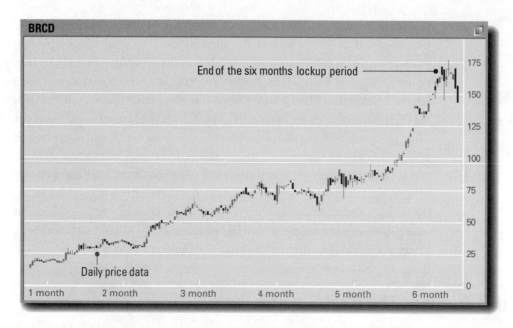

Figure 10.4 *Hot IPO: Six Months of Trading for Brocade*

continuously. Figure 10.4 depicts the first six months of IPO prices for Brocade Communications Systems (BRCD), a San Jose computer network company (*www.brocade.com*), which by all accounts is considered a hot IPO. Brocade provides fiber channel switches and software for storage area networks (SANs). The IPO's lead underwriter was Morgan Stanley Dean Witter. The size of the IPO was 3.25 million shares. BRCD was offered on Tuesday, May 25, 1999, at the offer price of $19.

In the aftermarket, the stock opened at $35. The stock closed at approximately $45 after the first day of trading. It reached its peak at $352 and had already had a 2-for-1 split after only three months of trading. The average daily trading volume was 1.5 million shares, so the liquidity was good. After approximately six months of trading, the stock closed at $340, which was an approximately 970% increase from the first day's opening price.

Figure 10.5 clearly displays a broken IPO: the first six months of IPO prices for Value America Inc. (VUSA). Value America is a Charlottesville, Virginia, Internet company *(www.valueamerica.com)* founded in 1996. At the time of the IPO, it had 227 employees who provided e-commerce

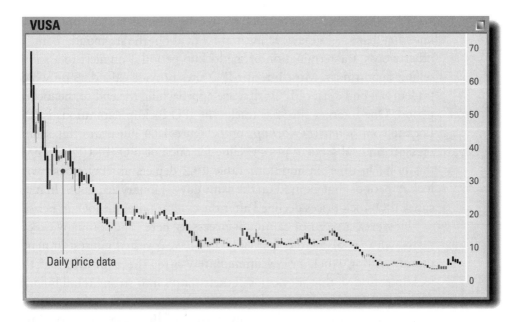

Figure 10.5 *Broken IPO: Six Months of Trading for Value America Inc.*

services on the Internet. The IPO's lead underwriter was Robertson Stephens, and the size of the IPO was 5.5 million shares. VUSA was offered on Friday, April 7, 1999, at the offer price of $23. In the aftermarket, the stock closed at $56 after the first day of trading. It reached $74 and was in a steady decline after that. After approximately six months of trading, the stock hit bottom at $3. It then inched up to about $6, which is an 89% decline from the peak price.

IPO Alerts: The Lockup Period

The lead underwriter restricts company insiders from selling their shares for a period of time, usually 180 days. An agreement between the company doing the IPO and the underwriters prohibits company executives and large shareholders from selling the stock during this *lockup period*. However, the lead underwriter has the discretion of lifting the lockup period at an earlier date. The objectives of the lockup are to limit selling pressures on the IPO and to stabilize prices.

Knowledgeable traders track the termination of the lockup periods, knowing that stocks may decline in price at about the six-month mark. In other words, the termination of the lockup period is an alert to a short-selling opportunity. Most Internet IPO sites provide calendars on which traders can find a list of IPOs that are approaching the end of the lockup period. One Internet site that tracks the IPO lockup expirations is IPO Lockup.com *(www.IPOlockup.com)*. Figure 10.4 illustrates this selling pressure and subsequent price decline for one hot IPO (BRCD) at about this point in time. In addition, Table 10.2 depicts all IPO stocks with lockup periods that expired on the same day—January 25, 2000. In most cases, IPO stock prices declined after the expiration of the lockup period.

However, a word of caution is necessary here. The company executives—who are also large shareholders—have a vested interest in maintaining strong stock prices immediately after the expiration of the lockup period so that they can sell their shares into strong retail buying. Thus, they would want to time any favorable news that the company might have to coincide with the expiration of the lockup period. Company executives might announce at that point in time a stock split or a new promising business deal or a new product line.

Table 10.2 *IPO Lockup Expirations and Closing Prices (IPO Priced on July 29, 1999, and IPO Lockup Expiration on January 25, 2000)*

IPO Stock Symbol	IPO Offering Price	Number of IPO Shares (Million)	% of IPO Shares	% of Lockup Shares	Price 1 Day Before	Price Lockup Expires	Price 1 Day After
BPUR	$12	3.5	16%	76%	$47.00	$36.44	$33.38
CNSW	$8	2.5	28%	72%	$15.88	$16.69	$16.06
DIGX	$17	10	17%	83%	$90.88	$90.38	$90.06
NTWO	$13	5.0	24%	73%	$18.19	$18.19	$16.50
NTOP	$15	5.4	11%	89%	$48.88	$46.06	$44.19
NTIA	$22	5.5	21%	63%	$21.38	$20.50	$22.13
NTIQ	$13	3.0	19%	15%	$69.00	$68.81	$62.75

Short Selling IPOs

The expiration of the lockup period corresponds with a large influx of IPO sellers and thus short-selling opportunities appear. When the IPO price-ascending movement stops and the price reverts in value, there is a sudden influx of sellers who are trying to get out of the stock quickly. Sellers rush to close their long positions in order to minimize losses or to protect profits. There is little movement, however, on the demand side. Buyers are waiting for a bargain. They are waiting for the price to decline further in value before stepping in and buying the stock. Because of these pressures, the IPO price tends to drop quickly.

As a review, *short selling* means that the trader is selling a stock that he does not own. In essence, the seller is "short" because he does not own the stock. The seller will borrow and deliver the shorted stock to the buyer at the settlement date, which is the "T + 3" date (or "trade plus three business days"). Because the seller has sold a stock which he does not own, the brokerage firm must first lend him the stock. In other words, the stock must be on the brokerage firm's short list of shortable stocks.

Both the NASDAQ and the listed exchanges, such as the NYSE, have a short sale rule that prohibits short selling on a down-tick. This short sale rule was developed to prevent speculative selling in NASDAQ or exchange-listed securities and accelerating a further decline in the price of that security. In essence, short selling can exert downward pressure on a stock's price and thus force the price to drop abruptly and significantly within a single trading day.

Listed exchanges such as the NYSE have a *tick test,* which states that the last reported sale price on the consolidated tape must be a plus tick. In essence, the SEC short-sale rule prohibits short sales of exchange-listed securities if the current price is below the previously reported last-sale price (that is, a minus tick or zero-minus tick). The last sale must be a plus tick before the trader can execute the short sale. The rule is simple and enforceable because the trade reports in most exchange-listed securities occur on a single exchange floor by a single specialist, who ensures the sequential trade reporting.

The NASDAQ market is a different matter. The trade reporting in NASDAQ securities involves different market makers for the same stock, who are reporting trades from different locations to the NASD via computer interface. NASD requires that all trades must be reported within 90 seconds after execution. That means that two sequential trades might not be reported to the NASD at the same time, and thus they would not appear on the NASDAQ tape in sequential order. Subsequently, the NASDAQ short sale rule was designed as a "BID test" rather than a tick test.

The NASD short-sale rule prohibits short sales if the new and current BID price is below the old BID price for a NASDAQ security. (More information on BID and ASK prices is available in chapter 18.) The trading software system automatically calculates if the current BID is an "up BID" or a "down BID" so that traders have that information at their fingertips when attempting to execute a short sale. The trader pays close attention to whether the current BID price tick arrow is up or down, or whether the current BID color is green or red. If the current BID color is green or the current BID tick arrow is up, then the short sale is legal. The trader can then short the stock.

The other short-selling requirement is that traders must open a type II account or a margin account. With a margin account, the purchase of a stock is partially financed, up to 50%, with borrowed money. The brokerage firm will issue a credit to the trader and charge interest so the trader can buy securities on credit and also borrow against the securities held in her account. The margin account will be in the name of the day trader and will carry her social security number as a tax-identification number.

Assume that the stock market is facing a major correction and that most stocks, particularly the hot IPOs, are declining in value. The only way the trader can make money in the down market is to short sell. Because stock prices tend to fall at a faster pace than they tend to increase, traders can earn substantial sums of money in a short period of time by taking short-sell positions. This is even truer for IPOs because they are more volatile (or speculative) than seasoned stocks. Keep in mind that NASD rules prohibit the short selling of IPOs within 30 days of the initial offering. Clearly, the expiration of the lockup period is one of the short-selling alerts, as illustrated in Table 10.2. This is not surprising, considering that a large percentage of IPO shares theoretically could be supplied in the market at that time.

It is important that traders are proficient and comfortable with the mechanics of short selling. Short selling is clearly the other half of the stock-trading equation. Traders cannot expect to go long on every single trade. There will be days when the overall market is declining, and at that time, traders need to go short. It is difficult to make money on long positions when overall market values are descending.

Short selling is also potentially very lucrative. Short sellers can make more money more quickly than the traders or investors who utilize mostly long positions. Prices tend to decline much faster than they tend to appreciate in value. A brief look at any price chart will generally reveal a gradual price increase followed by a sharp decline. The quick drop in value can be attributed to panic selling. Fear of losing money is a powerful motivator.

IPO Alerts: The Quiet Period

After the IPO is priced, the issuer and the underwriters face further restrictions on issuing any research on the IPO. The SEC considers this to be the "quiet period," which starts from the date of the IPO filing and lasts up to 25 days after the stock starts trading. The SEC wants to prevent any undue hype, and thus only information from the prospectus can be disseminated to the general public. At the end of the quiet period, the underwriters (that is, the brokerage firms) are free to issue their buy, hold, or sell recommendations. It is crucial for traders to know the Wall Street analysts' positions on the particular IPO at the end of the quiet period. The first recommendations will disclose if there is institutional support or backing for that particular stock.

In essence, first recommendations are the official Wall Street review for that stock. Traders can research the IPO calendars on any Internet IPO site and find a list of IPOs that are approaching the end of their quiet period. After the expiration of the quiet period, members of the selling syndicate and management of the new public company will most likely begin actively promoting or hyping the stock. Savvy traders anticipate a resurgence of public buying, and thus the expiration of the quiet period is commonly considered to be a bullish opportunity.

SECTION

III

Introduction to Technical Analysis Tools

SINCE THE CURRENT DYNAMIC FINANCIAL MARKET GENERATES A CONTINUOUS flow of financial information, technical analysis is essential for determining what is relevant in that sea of financial data. Technical analysis tools clarify and present that wealth of financial data in formats that can be easily reviewed and interpreted. These technical analysis tools are effective in reducing a great deal of the "noise" that is always present in the financial markets. In section III, we focus on the basic technical analysis tools and concepts that are used by professional day traders today.

➤ Section III starts with a description of the data formats of technical analysis, which is then followed by a clarification of the most common chart types, such as the tick-by-tick price charts, bar, line, and candlestick charts.

➤ After introducing the concepts of the Simple, Weighted, and Exponential Moving Averages, we describe how Fast and Slow Exponential Moving Averages and Moving Average Convergence/Divergence (MACD) tools are being used by day traders to generate buy and sell trading signals.

➤ Oscillator indicators that show whether a particular stock is overbought or oversold are then presented. Fast and slow stochastic oscillators, relative strength index, and momentum indicators are used as examples.

➤ The Bollinger bands concept is then introduced as a measure of intraday price support and resistance.

➤ Finally in section III, we cover how broad market index overlays and On-Balance Volume (OBV) indicators are used to gauge overall market and trading volume movements.

11

Introduction to Technical Analysis

Technical stock analysis sounds a lot more intimidating than it really is. It began in the 1900s, when Charles Dow, of Dow Jones publishing fame, became the first "technician" to plot and publish stock price trends in a consistent format. Today, technical analysis means different things to different people. On one end of the technical analysis spectrum there are chartists who continuously search for an emerging visual pattern of price fluctuations. At the other extreme are computerized stock market technicians who continuously crunch huge volumes of price and trading data to produce mathematical technical analysis indicators. We'll discuss both schools of thought in a moment. But first, let's explore the reasoning behind some of the harshest criticisms of technical analysis.

Perhaps the strongest criticisms are voiced by the man known as the father of fundamental stock analysis, Benjamin Graham, who wrote the following in his 1949 book, *The Intelligent Investor*: "In our own stock-market experience and observation, extending over 50 years, we have not known a single person who has consistently or lastingly made money by thus 'following the market' (i.e., technical analysis). We do not hesitate to declare that this approach is as fallacious as it is popular."

Another and more balanced criticism of technical analysis was delivered by author Burton Malkiel, who questioned in his 1973 book, *A Random Walk Down Wall Street,* whether technicians can predict price momentum over several time periods, such as minutes, days, or weeks.

"Stocks are likened to fullbacks who, once having gained some momentum, can be expected to carry on for a long gain. It turns out that this is simply not the case." Malkiel noted that sometimes one gets positive rising prices for several days in a row, but that sometimes when you flip a coin you also get a long string of heads in a row. This is what economists mean when they say that stock prices behave much like a random walk.

In addition, Malkiel argued that technical analysis does not automatically translate into better or superior results. According to Malkiel, when the buy-and-hold strategy is compared with the technical strategies, one sees that the technical schemes do often make profits for their users, but so does a buy-and-hold strategy. Only if technical schemes or systems produce better than average market returns can technical analysis be judged effective. Malkiel said that, to date, none has consistently passed the test.

It is my belief that technical stock analysis, in and of itself, is not the Holy Grail of stock trading. A technical stock analyst cannot forecast with certainty what a stock price will be in the future. Nobody can do that. Even if the recognized price pattern has any foundation in historical price data, there is no guarantee that history will repeat itself. However, although I believe that technical analysis does not guarantee success in stock trading, it can improve the probability of making more profitable trades. In other words, technical analysis helps traders time entry and exit points better and thus minimize risk and maximize return of their stock trading.

Charting Versus Mathematical Technical Analysis

The first broad area of technical analysis we'll discuss is *charting*. There is an old saying that holds, "There are no rich chartists on Wall Street." There is a good amount of truth to this adage. I personally do not believe that there is an exact science behind any of these descriptive charting patterns. The interpretation of the charting pattern is always subjective. Nevertheless, there is some benefit in attempting to visualize the price support and resistance levels by plotting and superimposing charting patterns over the price data. Plotting of price patterns is essentially a harmless activity, and it can only help to visualize the pattern.

In essence, charting is an art. Before computers and the Internet provided traders with real-time charts, adherents armed themselves with pencils, paper, and price data. A chartist might superimpose a pattern on the given paper price chart and visualize a pattern on the graph that would become a trading signal. Most often the chartist would draw a linear pattern on a given price chart and assign it a technical-sounding name. Charting patterns have an impressive array of esoteric names: triangles, head and shoulders, double bottoms or tops, saucers, flags, and other patterns. This book covers only the most basic and common chartist price patterns.

The Mathematical Approach

The advent of computerized technical analysis tools has provided more valuable insights about stock prices than charting patterns could. Computers can crunch huge volumes of price data quickly and efficiently and display instantaneously price patterns that are not immediately self-evident. The computer can help probe the price data much more deeply and much more precisely than the human eye. In addition, technical analysis software programs are increasingly the standard fare of any trading software package.

Using a computer to process huge volumes of price data mathematically is only half of the equation; understanding the output is the other half. Understanding and correctly interpreting the results of mathematical technical analysis is much more critical than being able to use technical analysis software.

Using the computer as a trading tool does not inherently give you an advantage. Author John Murphy eloquently wrote the following in his 1986 book *Technical Analysis of the Financial Markets:* "The amount of impressive technical data at one's fingertips sometimes fosters a false sense of security and competence. Traders mistakenly assume that they are automatically better simply because they have access to so much computer power."

All software stock trading packages contain a library of technical analysis indicators. This book focuses on those technical analysis indicators that use the current closing price as the basic unit of analysis. The current price and the last closing price are the most important stock market variables because they depict the balance of power between the buyers and sellers at that point in time and at the end of the game. In addition, there are other technical analysis indicators that utilize information on the stocks' opening prices, the highest or lowest stock prices in the selected time period, and trading volume.

Because the objective of the trader is to exploit present short-term price volatility, charting and analyzing historical prices is irrelevant. Do you really need to know such historical prices as the 60-day moving average for this time last year? This might be an issue only if you believe that the particular stock might have a strong seasonal trading pattern.

Instead, a day trader should chart and analyze intraday prices based on one-minute intervals. For their part, swing traders plan to hold stock positions for several days (or in some cases, a few weeks), and thus should chart and analyze the stock prices on a daily or one-hour interval basis. In either case, the objective of both the swing trader and the day trader is to exploit short-term price volatility. Nevertheless, it is always useful to look at the long-term price trend, as it provides information on long-term historical price support and resistance, such as the 52-week price support and resistance levels.

As a rule, I believe in keeping things as simple as possible, especially regarding technical analysis. There is so much financial data coming across the computer screen that it is easy to get bogged down in sophisticated and esoteric technical information. And thus I have narrowed the technical analysis discussion to basic price trend indicators and oscillators. For additional information, I recommend Steven Achelis's book, *Technical Analysis from A to Z*, which is the most complete reference guide on technical analysis.

Technical Analysis Formats

A picture is worth a thousand words. And a quick look at a price chart loaded with technical analysis data would immediately reveal the current status of the stock. Constructing technical analysis charts is not difficult. The software packages are relatively user friendly. Most of them are Microsoft Windows–based products with pull-down options menus. All you have to do is click with your mouse on the technical analysis indicator option, and the computer program will do all of the number crunching. Interpreting the results of the technical analysis study is an entirely different matter. It is much more difficult to understand the meaning of all these lines, bars, or histograms on the price chart. It takes time to become proficient in reading, interpreting, and understanding technical analysis tools.

A short-term trader can pack many technical analysis tools into a single price chart. A trader can decide to overlay simultaneously the stock price information on the chart with several technical analysis indicators. And each technical analysis indicator can subsequently be marked and color-coded for easy viewing and reference. Finally, the selected format determines only how the price data is displayed on the screen. The data format is not in itself the technical stock analysis.

Time Frame

All stock-trading software packages contain a technical analysis library, which includes many of the most commonly used technical indicators. These technical analysis indicators can be modified to suit any trading preferences by changing the format of the input values. For instance, a trader with an extremely short time frame would most likely elect to use the option of analyzing one-minute interval price data. A swing investor, however, with a longer time frame would likely use daily price data.

As a trader, selecting the time frame you use to view price data is an important decision. A graph of a stock at the same point in time can look dramatically different between short- and long-term time frames. Figures 11.1 and 11.2 illustrate this point for 3Com Corporation (COMS) stock. Both Figures also demonstrate tremendous price volatility at both the short- and long-term levels.

A day trader who has selected the one-minute price data could observe on the screen a short-term trend that indicates that the stock is increasing in value in the last few minutes. In the meantime, a swing investor who has selected the daily price data could observe on the screen a decrease in the last few days.

Given different time frames and trading objectives, it is possible that both the day trader and the swing investor are correct. A day trader could decide to open a long position on that stock for a few minutes or hours and have a profitable short-term trade. Meanwhile, a swing investor could decide to open a short position on that stock for a few days or a week and have a profitable longer-term trade as well. It is always a good idea to look at the same stock in different time frames. Sometimes, day traders are too close to the trees to see the forest. It is always good idea to pull back, open another chart on the same stock but with a longer time frame, and see the forest.

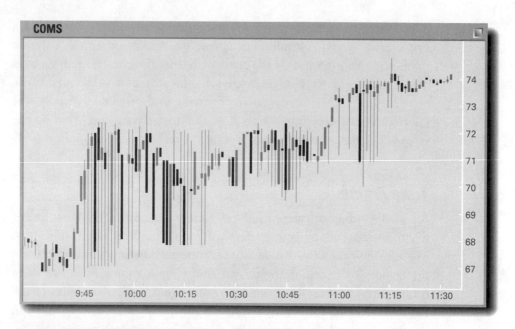

Figure 11.1 *Different Time Frames for the Same Stock at a Point in Time: One-Minute Data Compression for 3Com Corp.*

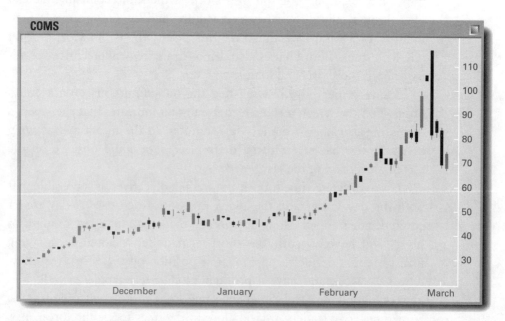

Figure 11.2 *Different Time Frames for the Same Stock at a Point in Time: Daily Data Compression for 3Com Corp.*

Tick-by-Tick Price

Many popular charting programs allow you to plot stock prices in real time, as each trade takes place. This is called *tick-by-tick data*. It is awfully difficult to perform any kind of formal technical analysis based on tick-by-tick prices. My advice is to use tick-by-tick charts only to visually follow the stock executions after the trade position has been taken. The graphical presentation of the tick-by-tick price chart is shown in Figure 11.3.

The tick-by-tick price chart displays a zigzag-pattern line chart. The current ASK price, which represents the market buying price, is at the top of the zigzag pattern. The current BID price, which represents the market selling price at that point in time, is at the bottom of the zigzag pattern. In other words, the buying price is always higher than the selling price at any point in time. The spread is the difference or distance between the top and bottom. Usually the spread is relatively constant (that is, $\frac{1}{16}$ or $\frac{1}{8}$, depending on the trading volume), so the distance is almost always the same. Sometimes, the spread narrows, and the gap between the top and bottom becomes smaller. Sometimes, the spread expands, and the gap between the top and bottom becomes larger.

As previously mentioned, a trader must decide what interval she will use to monitor price data: one-minute intervals or one-hour intervals. Following that, you have to decide on what component of price data

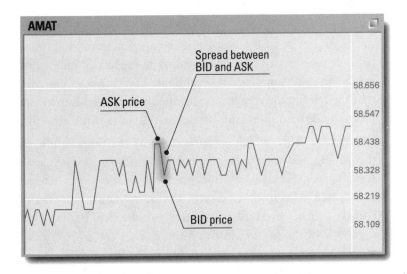

Figure 11.3 *Tick-By-Tick Price Chart*

you'll use within that time frame: the open BID, close BID, open ASK, close ASK, high BID, low BID, high ASK, or low ASK. My strong preference is to select the close ASK price for the input-format price. The close ASK price represents the last market buying price in that time interval. In other words, if you are entering a long stock position for the first time, then the close ASK price is the most important price.

Bar Charts

Now let's look at another—perhaps simpler—way to represent price data: the bar chart. The tick-by-tick price chart in Figure 11.3 contains a large amount of information that can be conveniently summarized into a bar chart. Bar charts are expressed as vertical lines, with left and right handles representing the opening and closing ASK prices for the selected period. Suppose that the entire Figure 11.3 graph represents price data collected during just one minute of trading. Note how Figure 11.4 summarizes all of the tick-by-tick price data into one vertical bar chart line.

As you can see, one simple bar chart line is packed with a lot of data. In our example, one minute of trading is summarized in a single bar chart. The same approach can easily be extended to one day's worth of price data. A daily bar chart would summarize data for the entire day of trading; it would show the following:

1. Opening ASK, which is represented by the left handle on the bar, is the buying price of the first trade in this time period. The opening ASK price at the start of the day's trading is especially important because it reveals the opening market sentiment. Looking again at the chart, note that the left handle represents the opening consensus price after all stock buyers had the opportunity to digest the market information overnight.

2. Closing ASK, which is represented by the right handle on the bar, is the buying price of the last trade in that time period. Again, the closing ASK has a great deal of importance when the bar chart represents the daily price data. In other words, the right handle represents the closing consensus price after all stock buyers and sellers had an opportunity to digest all of the market information during the entire trading day. The technical analysts pay close attention to the relationship between the daily open and close ASK prices. For instance, bullish traders would like to observe the closing ASK exceed the opening ASK.

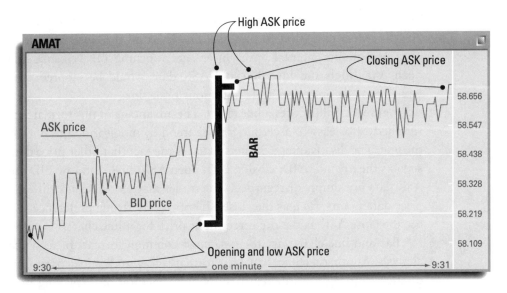

Figure 11.4   *Summarizing Tick-By-Tick Data into a One-Minute Bar Chart*

3. High ASK represents the highest ASK price for that period of trading. High ASK is represented at the top of the vertical bar chart, and it represents the highest price that buyers are willing to pay for the security during this time interval. If we are using daily price data, then high ASK represents the peak price for that day.

4. Low ASK represents the lowest ASK price for that period of trading. Low ASK is represented at the bottom of the vertical bar chart. In the case of the daily price data, it represents the lowest price that buyers paid for the security during this day-long interval. The size of the bar chart, or distance between the top and bottom of the bar, represents the trading range during this time frame. Often, the vertical distance of the bar chart is small, which indicates a narrow trading range or little price volatility. Conversely, if the vertical distance of the bar chart is large, then this would indicate a wide trading range or substantial price volatility during this time period, such as one day.

Line Charts

Stock price data can also be expressed visually as a line chart. However, line charts are not frequently used. They connect basically the same type of price information over time, such as the closing ASK price. For example, the trader can select to plot as a line chart all the close ASK prices on a one-minute interval basis. In essence, opening BID, closing BID, open ASK, high and low BID and ASK data would be ignored. This would provide one clean and continuous price line.

Figure 11.5 illustrates a line chart. The advantage of this format is its simplicity. It is easy to ascertain a price trend by monitoring the slope of the line. The disadvantage of this format is the fact that other price data, such as the opening BID, closing BID, open ASK, high and low BID and ASK data are simply disregarded. The trader may elect to track different price data points, such as the close BID price. My strong preference is to use the close ASK as the preferred input price for a line chart.

Bar and line charts are the two most common formats of technical analysis. Another technical analysis format is the candlestick chart. Candlestick charting is an increasingly popular method of displaying price data, and thus chapter 12 is devoted exclusively to this particular charting format.

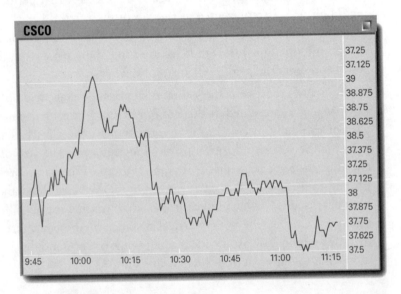

Figure 11.5 *Line Charts*

12

The Candlestick Charting Format

CANDLESTICK CHARTING ORIGINATED IN JAPAN IN THE 1600S AS A method of analyzing the price movement of rice contracts; thus it has certain mystical qualities. Some patterns still carry Japanese names, such as *doji* or *harami*, whereas other patterns have exotic-sounding translated names, such as *dark clouds, morning star,* or *evening star*. Many technical analysts like to use candlesticks because of that mystique.

I personally like to use candlesticks because they are very descriptive and easy on the eye. A candlestick chart displays the same information as a bar chart, but it brings an additional visual dimension. The colors of the several candlestick bodies illustrate bullish or bearish activity that is easy to visualize. Most important, candlesticks pack a lot of information about the relationship among the closing, opening, high, and low prices in the current and previous time periods. For additional information on candlestick charting, I strongly recommend the 1991 Steve Nison book, *Japanese Candlestick Charting Techniques*.

All popular charting software packages let you create candlestick charts by selecting the candlestick charting option. Instead of receiving price data displayed in the default format of bar charts, which is the most common approach, a trader can elect to choose candlestick charts. The candlesticks can be utilized on any time frame formats: one-minute, or hourly, daily, or weekly price data. Similar to bar charts, candlestick charts display the following price information, whether it is based on one-minute, hourly, daily, or weekly price data:

1. Opening ASK
2. Closing ASK
3. High ASK
4. Low ASK

If the market bulls beat the market bears in that period of time and the closing price is higher than the opening price, the candlestick body takes on a green shade. The green candlestick body is much easier to view than the position of small left and right handles that represent the opening and closing prices on the bar chart. Conversely, if the bears beat the bulls within the time period, and the closing price is lower than the opening price, the candlestick body becomes red.

Candlestick charts are plotted as vertical rectangular boxes that connect opening and closing prices for a defined time period. Vertical lines called *wicks* extend from the rectangles to denote extreme high and low prices for the period.

In this chapter, for easier visual identification, the color black was selected to identify a closing price that ends above the opening price. When the closing price for a time period finishes below the opening price, the rectangular box appears as gray. When the opening and closing price remain the same, no rectangular boxes representing the candle body are depicted. Figure 12.1 illustrates this point.

Candlestick Patterns

Candlestick charts make it easier to view a price trend, whether the stock makes an uptrend, downtrend, or lateral movement during the time period.

Using the candlestick format, the price uptrend can be generalized and defined as a series of the following:

1. Green candlesticks (shown as black)
2. Higher closing prices (or higher tops of green candlestick bodies)
3. Higher opening prices (or higher bottoms of green candlestick bodies)
4. Higher high prices (or higher tops of the candlestick wicks)

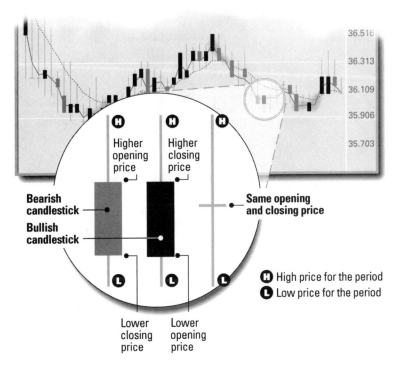

Figure 12.1 *Candlestick Chart*

5. Higher low prices (or higher bottoms of the candlestick wicks)

Figure 12.2 depicts this ideal price uptrend environment. Conversely, using the candlestick format, a price downtrend can be summarized as a series of the following:

1. Red candlesticks (shown as gray)

2. Lower closing prices (or lower tops of red candlestick bodies)

3. Lower opening prices (or lower bottoms of red candlestick bodies)

4. Lower high prices (or lower tops of the candlestick wicks)

5. Lower low prices (or lower bottoms of the candlestick wicks)

Figure 12.3 depicts an idealized price downtrend environment. Finally, using the candlestick format, a neutral or sideways market can be summarized with equal highs, lows, opening and closing prices, or continuous interchange between the same-sized green and red candlesticks

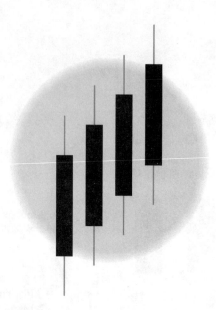

Figure 12.2 *Price Uptrend*

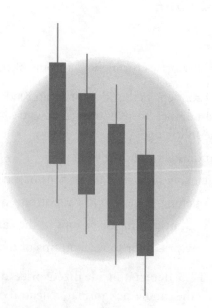

Figure 12.3 *Price Downtrend*

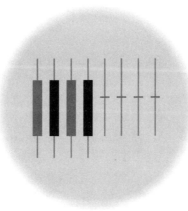

Figure 12.4 *Neutral Market*

(that is, one green candlestick followed immediately in the next period by a same-sized red candlestick). Figure 12.4 depicts this ideal sideways market environment.

Obviously, the three trend patterns shown here are oversimplifications of a real price trend. I wish that all trends could be that clear and obvious. The following illustrations present more realistic up, down, and neutral price trends expressed in candlestick format. Figure 12.5 depicts four bullish candlestick patterns. These patterns occur commonly enough to have names.

➤ *Hammer*. This pattern displays a significantly low price for the time interval (long lower shadow), which is substantially lower than the opening and closing price.

➤ *Piercing line*. This displays two candlestick lines. The first line is a bearish candlestick, where the first interval closing price is lower than the opening price. The second line is a bullish candlestick, where the second interval opening price is lower than the previous period closing price. However, the second interval closing price ended at a higher level than the second period opening price and the previous period closing price.

➤ *Bullish engulfing lines*. The first line is a small bearish candlestick. The second line is a strong bullish candlestick where the second interval opening price is lower than the previous period closing

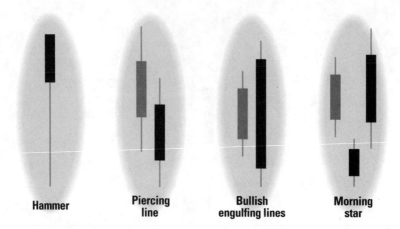

Figure 12.5 *Bullish Candlestick Patterns*

price, and the closing price is higher than the previous period opening price.

➤ *Morning star.* The first line is the bearish candlestick. The second line is the small bullish candlestick where the second interval opening and closing prices are lower than the previous period closing price. The third line is a large bullish candlestick where the third interval opening and closing prices are both higher than the second period closing price.

Figure 12.6 illustrates the four most common bearish candlestick patterns, which are summarized as the following:

➤ *Hanging man.* The pattern is similar to the hammer, except it occurs after a substantial price uptrend. It displays significantly low prices for both time intervals (long lower shadows), and a very small range between the opening and closing prices.

➤ *Dark cloud.* This displays two candlestick lines. The first line is a bullish candlestick in which the first interval closing price is higher than the opening price. However, the second line is a bearish candlestick in which the second interval closing price is lower than the previous period closing price, and lower than half of the first candlestick body.

➤ *Bearish engulfing lines.* The first line is the small bullish candlestick. The second line is the strong bearish candlestick because the

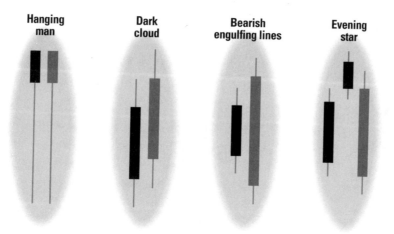

Figure 12.6 *Bearish Candlestick Patterns*

second interval opening price is higher than the previous period closing price, but the closing price is much lower than the previous period opening price. The bearish candlestick engulfed the small bullish candlestick.

➤ *Evening star.* The first line is the bullish candlestick; the second line is a smaller bullish candlestick. The second interval opening and closing prices are higher than the previous period closing price. However, the third line is a large bearish candlestick where the third interval opening and closing prices are both lower than the second period closing price.

Figure 12.7 shows the five most common neutral candlestick patterns, which are summarized as the following:

➤ *Spinning tops.* The pattern displays a relatively small range between the opening and closing prices and high and low prices for both time intervals.

➤ *Doji.* This pattern displays a line where the interval closing price is the same as the opening price. However, the second line is a bearish candlestick in which the second interval closing price is lower than the previous period closing price and lower than half of the first candlestick body.

➤ *Harami.* The first line is the large bullish candlestick. However, the second line is the small bearish candlestick, because the second

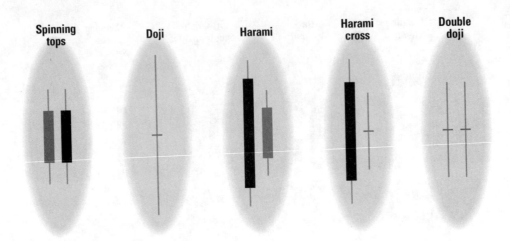

Figure 12.7 *Neutral Candlestick Patterns*

interval opening price is lower than the previous period closing price. The closing price is higher than the previous period opening price. In essence, the bullish candlestick engulfed the small bearish candlestick, which indicates a decrease in the positive price momentum.

➤ *Harami cross*. The first line is the bullish candlestick. However, the second line is the *doji* candlestick. In other words, the second interval opening and closing prices are the same, which depicts a decrease in the momentum.

➤ *Double doji*. The last candlestick pattern consists of two *doji* lines, which implies continuous indecision. That stock price will eventually break out in either direction.

Now that we have the three possible price trends presented in the most common candlestick patterns, I present for illustration purposes, a simplified buy signal using the hypothetical candlestick patterns. Swing or day traders can also use this simplified candlestick buy signal. The swing trader would examine the daily or hourly candlestick price chart, whereas the day trader would focus on one-minute or five-minute compressed price data in candlestick format. The buy signal pattern consists of three distinct stages:

1. An established downtrend pattern, which is depicted by a series of red (gray) candlesticks. In other words, the candlesticks display lower closing prices, lower opening prices, lower high prices, and lower low prices for three to five periods.

2. An established neutral trend, when prices are going sideways. This neutral position is depicted by the continuous interchange between same-sized green (black) and red (gray) candlesticks. This would symbolize the end of the price downtrend. It would also indicate that the trader is buying at the price support level.

3. After observing the two established downtrend and neutral-trend candlestick patterns, the trader should patiently wait for the beginning of a price uptrend. In other words, the emergence of the uptrend would constitute a buy signal. The first sign of the uptrend pattern can be any of the previously mentioned bullish candlestick patterns, such as the hammer, piercing line, bullish engulfing lines, or morning star.

Figure 12.8 illustrates the hypothetical buy signal using the bullish engulfing line as the sign of the uptrend.

Conversely, the following presents a simplified short-sell signal using candlestick patterns. This simplified candlestick buy signal can be used

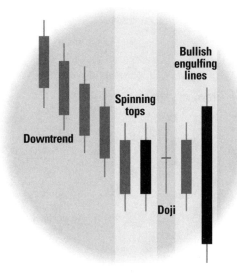

Figure 12.8 *Hypothetical Buy Signal*

both by swing and day traders. Again, the sell signal pattern consists of three distinct stages:

1. An established uptrend pattern, which is depicted by a series of green (black) or up-tick candlesticks. In other words, the candlesticks display higher closing prices, higher opening prices, higher high prices, and higher low prices for three to five periods.

2. An established neutral trend, when prices are going sideways. This neutral position is depicted by a continuous interchange between same-sized green (black) and red (gray) candlesticks. It symbolizes the end of the price uptrend. It would also indicate that the trader is short selling at the price resistance level.

3. After observing the two established uptrend and neutral-trend candlestick patterns, the trader would patiently wait for the beginning of a price downtrend. The emergence of the downtrend would constitute the short-sell signal. The first sign of the downtrend pattern can be any of the previously mentioned bearish candlestick patterns, such as the hanging man, dark cloud, bearish engulfing lines, or evening star.

Figure 12.9 illustrates the hypothetical short-sell signal using the bearish engulfing line as the sign of the price downtrend.

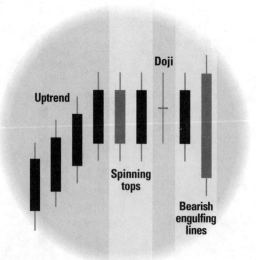

Figure 12.9 *Hypothetical Short-Sell Signal*

Because candlestick charts are a very visual tool, I use them as the standard charting format throughout this book. The next chapter will depict the most basic and common charting patterns, using the standard candlestick format.

13

Charting Patterns

Aℕ OLD WALL STREET ADAGE PROCLAIMS, "PRICE CHARTS DO NOT LIE."
This saying is true. Numbers do not lie, but chief executive officers or
chief financial officers of some companies have been known to do so.
Charts display a company's price history, thus eliminating any disagree-
ment about its past prices. A company's accountants, however, are capable of displaying even negative financial data in a favorable light, and its
CEOs and CFOs commonly put a favorable spin on the company's
financial documents.

For instance, declining company revenues may be presented as a
"new challenge," and mismanagement labeled as a "strategic paradigm
shift." All this suggests that fundamental analysis does not provide an
exact or precise representation of a company's financial position,
because the data are not perfect and because company management
often obfuscates the true financial situation.

However, there is another Wall Street adage, which states, "Price
charts have no memory." This is an important qualifier to the maxim
that price charts do not lie. The reasoning here is simple: Just because a
price exhibits the beginning of a certain pattern does not mean that the
price will continue in that pattern or that the pattern will automatically
result in a desired price movement. There is no scientific law explaining
why a stock price goes in a particular direction.

Rather, charting is a subjective art. There is no one best method for
visually representing the short-term trading range between price support

and resistance levels or for establishing an emerging price trend. Different traders can look at the same price chart and identify different patterns of price support or resistance levels.

It must be said that price charting is more appropriate for hourly and daily price data formats than for the one-minute data most often used by day traders. Day traders use the one-minute price data format because their focus and time frame of analysis are short. There is in the market a great deal of minute-by-minute price volatility, and it is very difficult to ascertain any clear charting pattern in short-term price movements. Because of this, charting patterns have more meaning for swing traders, who might be using hourly or daily price data, than for day traders.

In this chapter, my objective is to present those hourly or daily charting patterns most frequently used by traders. However, in chapter 14, which covers computerized technical analysis, I will return to the one-minute price data format.

Horizontal Lines of Price Support and Resistance

Trader and psychiatrist Alexander Elder, who wrote the classic trading book *Trading for a Living*, stated that support and resistance price patterns exist because people have memories. Traders and investors simply get used to buying and selling stocks within a certain price range. When a stock price drops to the lower edge of a trading range, it attracts buyers who perceive that the stock is undervalued. The lower price range becomes the *price support*. Conversely, when a stock jumps to the upper edge of a trading range, it attracts sellers who perceive an opportunity for profits. The stock selling at the upper price range creates the *price resistance*.

One easy, quick, and subjective method of identifying support and resistance levels within a trading range is to draw two horizontal price lines around the price congestion area. The *price congestion area* defines the trading range for a specific period of time. The top horizontal line, which spans the top edges of the price congestion area, is the price resistance level. The bottom horizontal line, which connects the bottom edges of the price congestion area, becomes the price support level. Figure 13.1 depicts the support and resistance levels for CMGI Inc. (CMGI) using daily price data.

The longer a price stays in the established trading range or the congestion area, the stronger are the price support and resistance levels. In

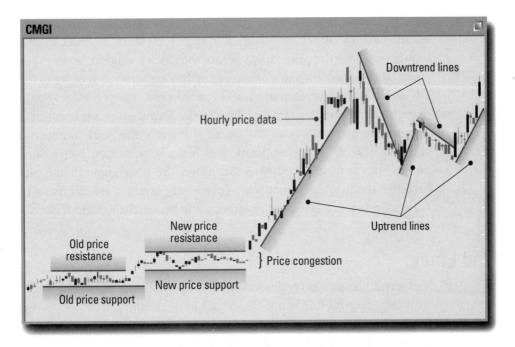

Figure 13.1 *Horizontal Price Support, Resistance, and Trend Lines*

addition, when the price range of the congestion area is relatively wide, the support and resistance levels are much stronger. Furthermore, traders pay attention to the level of trading volume in the price congestion area. If the trading volume is substantial, the price support and resistance levels are considered to be strong. Finally, the horizontal price support and resistance lines tend to have more meaning for the longer term than for the short term. For example, horizontal price support and resistance lines based on daily or hourly price data have more relevance than do lines based on one-minute price data.

The chartist's objective is to watch for the stock to break out of its congestion area. Sooner or later the stock price will penetrate the established horizontal lines of support and resistance. However, this alone does not mean that a new price trend will emerge. Experienced traders argue that stocks stay within the trading range more than in a newly established trend. Most breakouts are false breakouts, with the price quickly reverting to its usual price range. Experienced traders perceive this as an opportunity to take the opposite position.

For instance, if the price climbs above its resistance level, experienced traders look for a slowdown in the momentum, in order to short sell the stock. If the price drops below the stock's support level, experienced traders look for signs of increasing buying activity, in order to take a long position. Professional traders use the term *fading the breakout* to describe such a trading strategy. Fading the breakout means that traders observe the breakout, wait for the slowdown in the price momentum, and then take the opposite position. When a breakout does turn out to be real, in the case of a downward move, the price support line often becomes the new resistance line. Conversely, when a stock breaks out from its resistance level, the resistance line becomes the support line.

Trend Lines

The trend line points the direction of the price trend. However, the key feature of a trend line is not the direction of the line, which is obvious, but its slope or angle. The slope of the trend line reveals the relative market strength of the established price trend. A predominantly bullish market sentiment is displayed through steeper positive slope of the emerging trend line. If the trend line slope is positive but the angle of the slope is relatively small, then the bullish market sentiment is weak. Conversely, a predominantly bearish market sentiment is displayed by a steep negative trend line slope.

As a general rule, the longer the trend line, the stronger the trend. A long trend line occurs when there are more price-point observations to support the trend. Another factor that supports the emerging trend is trading volume. A relatively high trading volume confirms and supports an uptrend. Conversely, a declining trading volume confirms a downward price trend. Often the trend line breaks, which indicates that there is a change in the level of market sentiment. For instance, the trend line for a particular stock could still be positive, but the slope of the emerging trend line is diminished. This would indicate that the bullish market for this stock is losing its momentum. It might even indicate the potential for price reversal.

As was the case with support and resistance lines, there is a quick and easy way to identify the general trend line of an existing price trend. Simply draw the horizontal price line around the price congestion area at the bottom and the top. It's all right to leave out extreme price fluctuations and focus instead on the area of price congestion. Again, we can emphasize here that stock prices remain within a trading range between their support and resistance levels more often than they exhibit a trending pattern. Several continuous up-ticks do not constitute a price uptrend. Similarly, a few continuous down-ticks do not constitute a downtrend. The price could fluctuate between the established support and resistance levels for a prolonged period of time.

Gaps

Gap ups and downs are a common feature of today's stock market. The dictionary defines *gap* as an "unfilled space or a wide separation or break." For traders, a "gap" is an interruption in price continuity during a specific time interval. The reason we observe price gaps so frequently is that the stock market is highly dynamic. There are periods of market disequilibrium when either the demand or supply shifts suddenly and dramatically, leaving a temporary imbalance between the number of available buyers and sellers.

In the daily opening price data for a given stock, a gap up indicates that no trades transpired within the range between the highest price of the previous day and the lowest price of the present day. Likewise, a gap down indicates that no trades have occurred within the range between the lowest price of the previous day and the highest price of the present day. Figure 13.2 illustrates this point.

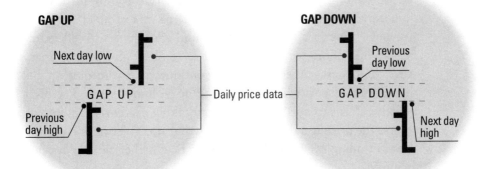

Figure 13.2 *Price Gaps*

Gaps occurring at market open have greater importance to short-term investors and traders than do gaps that occur during the trading day, simply because market-opening gaps are more frequent and more pronounced. Gaps at the opening indicate the overnight Wall Street reaction to news that most likely was announced after market close. If the news is positive and significant, the gap up in price can be substantial. Such gaps indicate that buy orders have accumulated before market opening. Market makers react to this increase in the stock's demand by adjusting the opening price above the previous day's closing price.

If positive news is announced during market hours and if traders are using short-term intervals such as the one-minute price data, the price gap up might be rather small. One would not expect that a preponderance of buy orders would reach the market makers all at the same minute. Rather, the continuous stock trading will display a gradual price increase.

Conversely, if the news is negative and significant, the gap down in the daily price chart will be even more pronounced than the gap up. Fear and panic selling generate a large preponderance of sell orders that reach the brokers before the market opening. The NASDAQ market makers and the NYSE specialist react to this increase in the stock's supply by adjusting the opening price much below the closing price from the previous day. However, if negative news is announced during market hours, the news will show only as a large trading range for that day in the daily charts.

In addition to gap ups and downs, there are other differences between the two basic types of price gaps:

1. *Common gaps.* Common gaps simply occur too frequently and seldom translate into a continued trend. Here's an example: Suppose positive news brings a disproportionate number of buyers to sellers into the market in a short period of time. The result is an opening price gap. After the opening, the stock price continues to go up quickly, but the momentum is short-lived. The trading volume is initially high but quickly returns to normal levels. Profit taking by short-term traders will reverse the price trend, and the price will drop. The prices revert back to the old trading range, and there are no new higher closing prices in the vicinity.

2. *Breakout gaps.* Breakout gaps are an infrequent occurrence. They result in a new and higher price trend. A continued high trading volume

characterizes breakout gaps. The positive price trend is confirmed by the sustained increase in trading volume. Any technical analysis trending indicator, such as the Moving Average, should likewise point to a new and higher price momentum trend.

It's difficult to trade using only daily price charts and price gap information. How do you know whether a price gap is a breakout or a common gap? It is my opinion that most price gaps are common gaps and that subsequent price reversals occur quickly. Most traders will look for short-selling trading opportunities after first observing the price gap up followed by the slowdown in the price increase. In trading jargon, the traders would *fade* the common price gaps: go against the gap after observing the price slowdown. When employing a fading-the-gaps trading strategy, a trader observes the gap up or gap down, waits for the slowdown in the price momentum, and then takes the opposite position.

Head and Shoulders

The most common and recognizable charting pattern is the *head and shoulders* pattern. This pattern will typically play itself out over a period of days or even weeks, and for that reason, it is especially relevant to swing traders. The name comes from the pattern's slight resemblance to a human head and shoulders, and it represents a bearish signal. By contrast, an *inverse head and shoulders* pattern is a bullish sign. Both patterns indicate price reversal.

The head and shoulders pattern indicates that the market bulls are running out of steam, and thus the peak of the second shoulder is lower than the peak of the head, pointing to a bearish price reversal. Chartists will pay close attention to the trading volume level that corresponds to the head and shoulders. A declining trading volume associated with the second shoulder is confirmation of future declining prices. The head and shoulders pattern also indicates potential for a price breakdown or the penetration of the established price support line. Figure 13.3 depicts the pattern using daily price data on Amazon.com stock.

Conversely, the inverse head and shoulders pattern points to the fact that market bears are slowing down; thus the bottom of the second shoulder is higher than the bottom of the head, pointing to a bullish price reversal. The increasing trading volume associated with the second shoul-

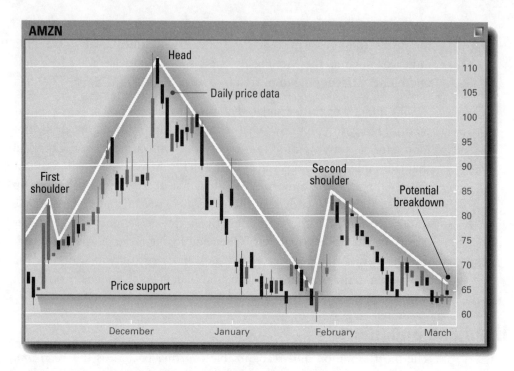

Figure 13.3 *Hypothetical Head and Shoulders Pattern*

der of the inverse head and shoulders pattern provides confirmation of an expected future price increase. The inverse pattern also indicates the potential for a price breakout or penetration of the established price resistance line. Figure 13.4 illustrates the inverse head and shoulders pattern using the daily Intel (INTC) stock price data.

Multiple Tops and Bottoms

Another common and recognizable charting pattern is *multiple tops and bottoms*. This pattern derives its name from its appearance—several higher and higher bottoms or lower and lower tops. The multiple tops send a bearish signal, whereas the multiple bottom pattern is bullish. Again, both patterns indicate a price reversal. You will see that the multiple tops and bottoms pattern is a variation on the head and shoulders pattern.

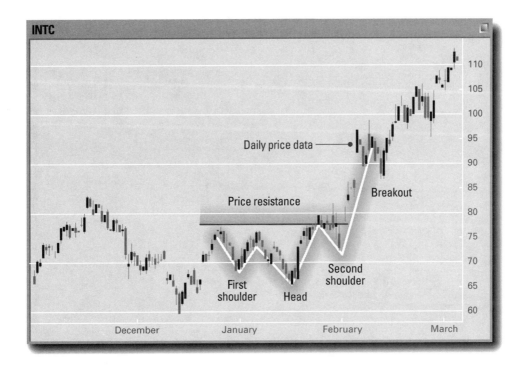

Figure 13.4   *Inverse Head and Shoulders Pattern*

Multiple bottoms indicate that the market bears are slowing and the floor price of the second or third bottom will be higher than the first bottom price—a bullish sign. Increasing trading volume associated with the higher second or third top is confirmation of an expected future price increase. Figure 13.5 illustrates the I2 Technologies' multiple bottoms chart that was based on the daily price data and relationship with respect to the price resistance level.

Conversely, the multiple tops pattern points to the fact that the market bulls are slowing, and the peak of the second or third top is lower than the first top. The multiple and lower tops point to a bearish price reversal. In addition, a chartist will pay close attention to the trading volume level that corresponds to multiple tops. The declining trading volume associated with the second or third lower top is confirmation of future declining prices.

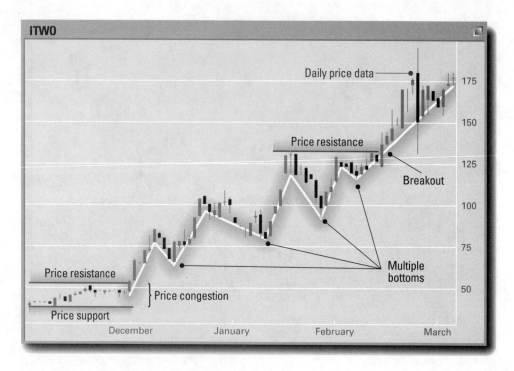

Figure 13.5 *Multiple Bottoms Pattern*

Triangles

Ascending or descending triangles are yet another common and recognizable chart pattern. Each triangle is defined by two converging lines. The upper line connects two or more period tops, and the lower line connects two or more bottoms. A descending triangle represents a bearish signal; an ascending triangle is bullish. Both patterns indicate price congestion that might result in a price breakout or breakdown. The ascending or descending triangles are similar to the horizontal lines of support and resistance.

The descending triangle pattern occurs when the upper boundary of the triangle is declining. The descending triangle shows that the market bulls are running out of steam, and the next period's high price is continuously lower than the previous period's high price. The continuously lower high prices point to a bearish price reversal.

Here again, chartists pay close attention to the trading volume level that corresponds to a descending triangle. The declining trading volume associated with the continuously lower high prices is confirmation of possible future declining prices. Finally, the descending triangle pattern indicates the possibility of a price breakdown or penetration of the established price support line. Figure 13.6 illustrates the hypothetical descending triangles pattern and relationship in respect to the price support level for Lucent Technologies (LU).

The ascending triangle pattern occurs when the lower boundary of the triangle is rising. The pattern also points out that the market bears are slowing, and the next period's low price is continuously higher than the previous period's low price. The continuously higher low prices in the period point to a bullish price reversal.

Increasing trading volume associated with continuously higher low prices is confirmation of possible future higher prices. The ascending

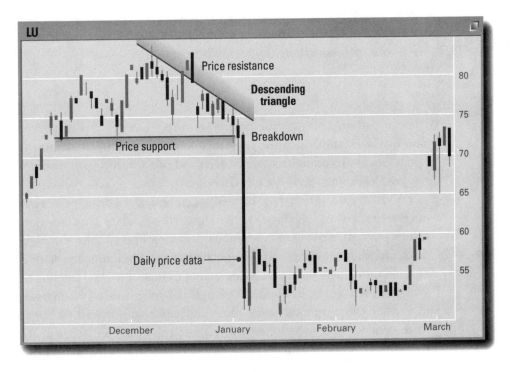

Figure 13.6 *Hypothetical Descending Triangle Pattern*

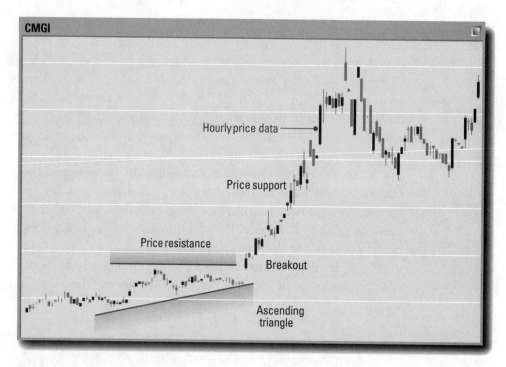

Figure 13.7 *Hypothetical Ascending Triangle Pattern*

triangle pattern indicates the possibility of price breakouts or penetration of the established price resistance line. Figure 13.7 illustrates the hypothetical ascending triangle pattern and relationship with respect to the price resistance level for CMGI stock.

A symmetrical triangle is defined when both the upper (price resistance) boundary and the lower (price support) boundary are converging. In other words, prices are continuously making lower highs and higher lows, and thus the congestion area is being narrowed. Imagine setting a descending triangle on top of an ascending triangle and thus creating one symmetrical triangle. Because the triangle is symmetrical, it is impossible to predict which market force (bulls or bears) will prevail out of the price congestion: the symmetrical triangle can result in either a price breakout or a price breakdown. Figure 13.8 illustrates the hypothetical symmetrical triangle pattern and relationship with respect to the price resistance level for Lycos (LCOS) stock.

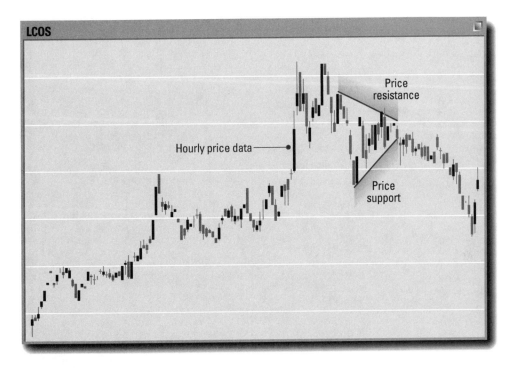

Figure 13.8 *Hypothetical Symmetrical Triangle Pattern*

Flags

The *flag* pattern is another consolidation or congestion pattern, so called because of the pattern's resemblance to an ascending or descending flag. Each flag is defined by two narrow parallel lines with an up or down slant. The upper flag line connects two or more period tops, whereas the lower flag line connects two or more bottoms. The ascending flag represents a bearish signal; the descending flag pattern is bullish. Both the upside and downside flag patterns indicate price congestion that might result in price breakdowns or breakouts. The ascending or descending flags are similar to the trend lines that represent price support and resistance levels.

The downside flag pattern is defined when the upper and lower boundaries of the flag are declining. The downside flag pattern represents a period of price congestion, which is supposedly followed by a breakout (or price increase). The appearance of the downside flag pat-

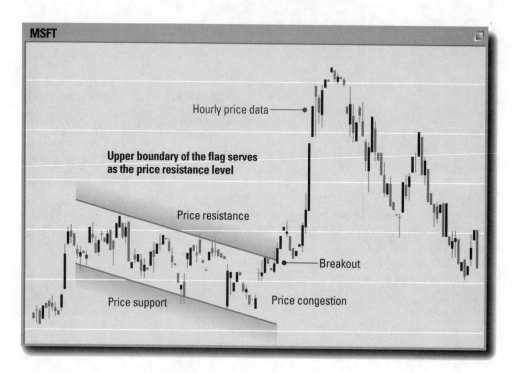

Figure 13.9 *Downside Flag Pattern*

tern is a bullish charting indicator. Figure 13.9 illustrates the downside flag pattern using Microsoft (MSFT) daily price data and its relationship to price support and price resistance levels.

Conversely, the upside flag pattern is defined when the upper and lower boundaries of the flag are increasing. The upside flag pattern represents a period of price congestion, which is supposedly followed by a breakdown (or the price decrease). The appearance of the upside flag pattern is a bearish charting indicator.

Charting price patterns are, in my opinion, of limited usefulness because they are too subjective. Nevertheless, they are always the starting point for anyone using technical analysis. There is, however, a better and more exact approach to technical analysis—the mathematical approach, which is presented in the following three chapters.

14

Moving Averages and Moving Average Convergence/Divergence

FOR THOSE TRADERS WHO USE COMPUTERIZED TECHNICAL ANALYSIS, THE most common indicator—and often the starting point—is the *Moving Average* (MA) indicator. There are many reasons that MA analysis is the most frequently used technical analysis tool. MA is a simple mathematical concept, and most people find it easy to understand. A primary benefit of the MA is the fact that it eliminates some of the market noise. Traders use MA indicators to filter out tick-by-tick price gyrations and to provide a view of a price trend. The MA line sometimes smooths out confusing price fluctuations. For that reason, it is a good tool for confirming a price trend. The MA line emphasizes the direction of a trend and confirms a trend reversal. However, the MA system does not work very well in a choppy market where there's no clear short-term trend. It does work well in a trending market where prices are clearly going up or down.

The MA is defined as the average price of a stock at a given point in time for a given number of periods. The technical analyst arbitrarily determines the number of periods for calculating an MA. And as you'll see shortly, it can range from 3 to 120 periods. In addition, the MA periods can be defined as part of any time interval, such as one-minute, fifteen-minute, hourly, or daily data. If you are a day trader, one-minute price data is the most appropriate time interval. If you are a swing trader with a longer time horizon for analysis, then hourly or daily price data is the most appropriate time interval.

The MA's most notable drawback is the fact that it's a lagging indicator: There is a time lag between the actual price line and the MA line, because the MA line is the average of the last several data observations. Thus, it always trails behind the most current actual price input. This lag limitation will be explained in detail shortly.

Simple, Weighted, and Exponential Moving Averages

A Moving Average is the sum of a selected number of previous price values divided by the total number of those values. In other words, a three-minute MA would be the sum of the prices of the previous three minutes divided by three. However, all three-minute segments are not created equally. The last or the most recent minute is more important than the previous minute or the first minute. Thus technical analysis differentiates between the *Simple Moving Average* (SMA), the *Weighted Moving Average* (WMA), and the *Exponential Moving Average* (EMA).

The Simple Moving Average (SMA) is the simplest, with every minute having equal weight. The last or the most recent minute has one-third weight, the previous minute also has one-third weight, and the first minute has one-third weight. But this is too simplistic.

Because all three minutes are not of equal importance, let us instead assign a weight to each minute interval. Since the last or the most recent minute is the most important observation, let us assign 50% weight to that price value. The previous minute would have 30% weight, and the first minute would have 20% weight. All together, the three minutes of price values would account for 100% of the MA value. This would constitute the Weighted Moving Average (WMA).

These assigned weights are purely arbitrary. Most technical analysts strictly use the Exponential Moving Average (EMA), which uses a mathematical method that automatically allocates the greater weight to the most recent price actions. I use the EMA exclusively in this book.

Figure 14.1 is a graphical presentation of a hypothetical exponential function that is used to assign a relative weight to each time period used to calculate a MA. If there are only three periods in the MA analysis, the

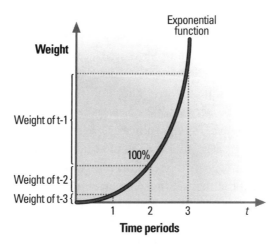

Figure 14.1 *Exponential Moving Averages*

relative weights are allocated by the exponential function. If there were nine periods in the MA analysis, the relative weights would be assigned automatically by the same exponential function.

Fast and Slow Exponential Moving Averages

Figure 14.2 presents two EMA lines. The first line is the Fast EMA of three periods of one-minute intervals. This EMA is called the *Fast EMA* because it will follow or hug the actual price movement very closely. There will be very little time lag between the three-minute Fast EMA and the actual price change. The Fast EMA will smooth out to some degree the actual price fluctuations, so it is easy to spot a trend in almost real-time terms. In essence, the Fast EMA will eliminate some of the market noise or brief gyrations.

The second line in Figure 14.2 is the *Slow EMA* of nine periods of one-minute intervals. A rule of thumb is that the period of the Slow EMA should be three times greater than the period for the Fast EMA. The trader could select any two periods of one-minute data intervals that have the 3-to-1 ratio—three-minute and nine-minute bars or five-minute and fifteen-minute bars. If the trader wants to reduce more of the market noise and obtain fewer trading signals, the trader would select longer time periods for the Fast and Slow EMA—nine-minute and 27-minute bars.

This EMA is called the Slow EMA because it does not follow the actual price movement very closely. There will be a substantial time lag between the nine-minute Slow EMA and the actual price change. The reason for that is simple. The nine-minute Slow EMA incorporates the stock price of nine minutes ago, and thus has to lag the current price. That lag can be very visible when there is a sharp change or movement in prices. Figure 14.2 graphically points out the Slow EMA lag. The Slow EMA greatly smoothes out the actual price fluctuations. It is easy to spot the longer price trend. In essence, the Slow EMA eliminates to a great extent the market noise or price gyrations.

When Fast and Slow EMA lines are plotted together we get what's known as a *crossover* or trading signal. When the Fast EMA (three-minute) line is greater than or above the Slow EMA (nine-minute) line, then stock prices are going up. This is a mathematical truism. The Fast EMA line must be greater than the Slow EMA line in order to pull the slower EMA line to a higher price value.

Conversely, when the Fast EMA line is smaller than or below the Slow EMA line, stock prices are going down. Again, this is a mathematical truism. The Fast EMA line must be smaller than the Slow EMA line in order to pull the slower EMA line to a lower price value. Figure 14.2 illustrates this point.

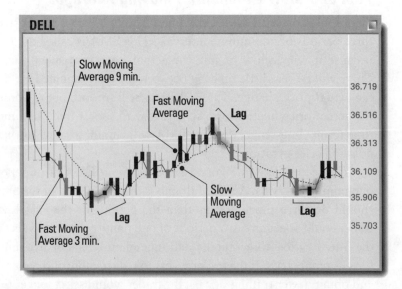

Figure 14.2 *Fast and Slow Exponential Moving Average Lines*

There are three trading signals or crossovers in Figure 14.3. The first signal occurs when the Fast EMA line crosses over and goes above the Slow EMA line. It is a signal that stock prices are going up and is thus a signal to open a long position on that stock. Note that prices were already moving up when the crossover occurred. Again, that illustrates the time lag. Subsequently, a trader following the EMA crossover signals will never pick the stock price at the bottom and at the peak. However, as the trader is plotting the EMA of the three periods of one-minute interval price observations in real time, that time lag is minor.

The second signal occurs when the Fast EMA line crosses and goes below the Slow EMA line. It is a signal that stock prices are already going down and is thus a signal to sell. Note again that prices were already moving down when the crossover occurred, a consequence of the time lag.

After closing the long position, a trader would immediately enter into a second trade and sell the stock short. The short position would be closed when the Fast EMA crosses over and above the Slow EMA. That would constitute a signal to buy the stock and cover the short sale. At the same time, it is a trading signal to open the long position.

Note that the trader is always in the market. There is always a signal to open a long or short position. The danger here is that there is a

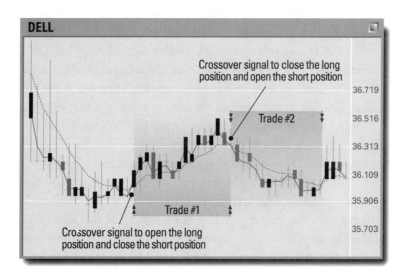

Figure 14.3   *Fast and Slow Exponential Moving Average Lines Crossover*

clear and distinct possibility that the trader will overplay the market. For example, if the market is not trending—that is, if only small, random price gyrations are taking place—then the trader might enter a long position and quickly discover that prices had reverted back. He would end up being whipsawed by the market price gyrations. The stock prices might go up only $\frac{1}{8}$ of a point and then decline, forcing the trader to quickly sell.

To avoid being whipsawed, the trader could increase the number of time intervals in the Slow EMA line from 9 to 12. That would make the Slow EMA slower, and thus it would avoid many crossover buy-or-sell trading signals. However, the slower EMA line would result in an increased lag time.

Moving Average Convergence/Divergence

Another useful technical analysis tool is the *Moving Average Convergence/Divergence* (MACD), which gauges the strength of the upward or downward price movement. MACD lets you measure the extent of the divergence and convergence between the Fast and Slow EMA lines. If the divergence or distance between the Fast and Slow EMA lines is increasing, then the price movement is gaining strength. If the distance between the Fast and Slow EMA lines is decreasing or converging, however, then the price movement is losing strength. This concept is elaborated in MACD analysis.

MACD analysis was developed by Gerald Appel in 1985. MACD is a derivative of two EMA lines, and it is an excellent price-trending indicator. It is also considered to be somewhat of an oscillator tool. An *oscillator* is a line that indicates whether a stock is overbought or oversold. It indicates whether prices have moved too far or too fast in either direction and thus are vulnerable to a reaction or reversal. The best way to explain MACD is to construct it from scratch.

To do so, we begin by subtracting the Fast EMA (three-minute) line from the Slow EMA (nine-minute) line. When the stock prices are increasing, the Fast EMA line is greater than the Slow EMA; thus the MACD line is positive. If stock prices continue to increase at a rapid rate, then the gap between the Fast EMA line and the Slow EMA line will also continue to increase. Thus the MACD line will be positive and continue to grow as well. Figure 14.4 illustrates this point.

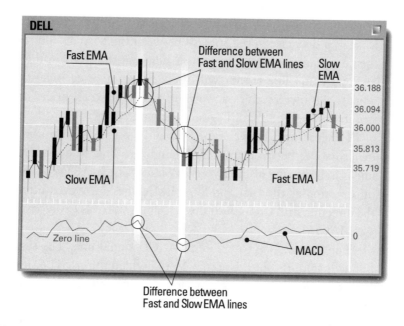

Figure 14.4 *Moving Average Convergence/Divergence (MACD)*

Conversely, when a stock's price decreases, the Fast EMA line is below the Slow EMA line, thus the MACD line is negative. If the stock's price continues to decline, then the gap between the Fast EMA line and the Slow EMA line will continue to increase also, and the MACD line will continue to be negative. In essence, the MACD line will quickly tell the trader if the price trend is up or down and whether that positive or negative price trend is increasing or decreasing.

If the MACD is positive or above the zero line and if there is a divergence (that is, an increase in the spread) between the MACD and zero line, the trader should interpret that as a bullish sign. If the MACD is still positive and there is a convergence (that is, a decrease in the spread) between the MACD and the zero line, the trader need interpret that as a sign that the bulls in the market are losing steam. The trader should expect a price reversal: in essence, she would receive a warning sign that stock prices will probably stop increasing and begin to decline.

By the same token, if the MACD is negative and below the zero line and if there is a divergence (that is, an increase in the spread) between the MACD and the zero line, then the trader should interpret that as a bearish sign. If the MACD is still negative and there is a convergence (that is, a decrease in the spread) between the MACD and the zero line, then the trader interprets that as a sign that the bears in the market are losing steam. The trader will then expect a price reversal. In other words, a trader receives a warning sign that stock prices are likely to stop decreasing and will begin to increase.

The crossover between the Fast and Slow EMA lines corresponds to the crossover between the MACD and zero line. In essence, the MACD line is a derivative of the two EMA lines. The MACD conveys the same information as the Fast and Slow EMA lines. However, information on the direction and strength of the price movement is easily visualized with the MACD line.

The next step is to create a MACD signal line. The signal MACD line will smooth out the actual MACD fluctuations. The signal MACD line is needed in order to get clear buy or sell signals, which are the crossovers between the MACD and signal MACD lines. The MACD signal line is the Exponential Moving Average of the calculated MACD.

For example, the MACD signal line is the EMA of the nine periods of MACD values. These crossovers between the MACD and signal MACD lines are often used as buy or sell signals. In essence, the MACD is the Fast line and the signal MACD is the Slow line. When the MACD crosses over and above the signal MACD line, that is a bullish signal to buy. When MACD crosses below the signal MACD line, that constitutes a bearish signal to sell the stock.

The final step is to plot the MACD histogram. The size and the pattern of the MACD histogram bars act as an oscillator indicator. The MACD histogram is displayed as the difference between the MACD and signal MACD lines. When the MACD crosses over and above the signal MACD line, then the MACD histogram would have positive values. A positive MACD histogram indicates a bullish signal to buy.

The MACD histogram also helps the trader to visualize the level of price divergence or convergence between the MACD and MACD signal lines. The actual absolute price differential between the MACD and signal MACD values is rather small, but the computer program will automatically resize that small value. The key is to visualize whether there is convergence or divergence between the MACD and signal MACD lines. If the MACD histogram is increasing in value, then the bullish sign has intensified. If the MACD histogram is decreasing in value, however, then the bulls are running out of steam.

When the MACD crosses below the signal MACD line, then the MACD histogram has negative values. A negative MACD histogram constitutes a sell signal. The key is to focus and visualize whether there is convergence or divergence between the MACD and signal MACD lines. If the MACD histogram is negative and decreasing in value, then the bearish signal has intensified. If, however, the MACD histogram is negative and decreasing at a diminishing rate, then the bears are running out of steam.

The MA and MACD are the starting points or entry level of computerized technical analysis. I'm not saying that MA and MACD indicators are the *best* computerized technical analysis tools, because there is no one best technical analysis indicator. But despite MA and MACD limitations, they remain the most popular and commonly used computerized technical analysis tools because their underlying foundations are scientifically sound.

15

Price Volatility and Oscillator Indicators

Imagine having a technical tool that tells you the position of a current stock price relative to that stock's most recent high and low prices. Technical analysis tools called *oscillator indicators* were specifically designed to accomplish this objective. Several oscillator indicators are available, but in this chapter I focus on the most relevant and popular oscillators used for short-term stock trading.

An *oscillator* is defined as a line that indicates whether a stock is overbought or oversold. It indicates whether prices have moved too far or too fast in either direction from the stock's average price and thus are vulnerable to a reaction or reversal. In essence, an oscillator indicator monitors the risk of price volatility.

We can differentiate between two measurements of price volatility:

➤ *Absolute price volatility*, which is measured by a standard deviation

➤ *Relative price volatility*, which is measured by a Beta coefficient

Absolute Price Volatility

The simplest method of ascertaining risk is to look at the high and low prices of a stock during a certain period of time, such as over 52 weeks. The range between the high and the low gives us the difference between the two extremes. If that range is substantial, the security carries substantial risk. A smaller range between the high and low prices constitutes a lower risk.

A more useful approach to gauging risk is to plot the distribution of all daily stock prices, from the low to the high price extremes, during a 52-week period. Figure 15.1 depicts a hypothetical price distribution pattern of high and low prices for 250 closing price observations. Assuming normal distribution, which is the most common assumption in statistics, we observe that prices cluster around the mean value, with an equal number of prices higher and lower than the average price.

It is possible for two stocks that have identical average prices for the 52-week period to have different degrees of risk. For instance, one stock (A) might have more extreme high and low price values; thus the distribution tails would spread farther from the mean. Another stock (B) might have prices that gathered closely around the mean, and thus the tails are closer to the average value. Which of these two stocks would have the lower absolute price volatility risk?

The standard deviation from the average price is a measure of the stock's absolute risk. Stock B has a lower price variance from the average price; thus stock B has a lower standard deviation. A lower standard deviation means a smaller variance from the mean value, and thus a smaller risk. Stock A has a greater variance from the average price; consequently it has a higher standard deviation and thus a greater absolute price risk.

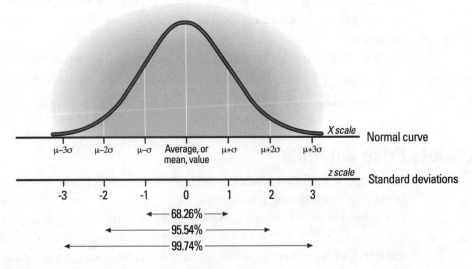

Figure 15.1 *Probability Distribution*

Relative Price Volatility

Suppose that we have collected daily stock price data for a particular stock for a year, and we now have 250 data observations (given 250 trading days in a year). Compare that information to the S&P 500 prices for the same period of time. We measure the daily S&P 500 Index return on a horizontal axis, and the daily stock prices for the stock on a vertical axis. Using a basic econometric regression analysis, we develop a linear line of the best data fit, which has an intercept value (*alpha*) and a slope (*Beta*). The *Beta coefficient* (or the slope coefficient) is a statistical measure of the price volatility of a particular stock in relation to the entire stock market's volatility (that is, the S&P 500 Index). The Beta coefficient provides a measure of the relative market volatility of that security.

The Beta coefficient is a part of any fundamental analysis and can be found on many financial search engines on the Internet, such as on Yahoo! or MSN.com. Figure 15.2 illustrates three hypothetical Beta values with distinctly different relative price volatility measures. If the returns of the S&P 500 Index increase by 10%, then a stock with the Beta value of 0.5 would increase in value only by 5%. If the Beta is 1, the stock return will increase proportionately by 10% as well. Similarly, if the returns of the S&P 500 increase by 10%, then the stock with a Beta value of 2 would increase in value by 20%.

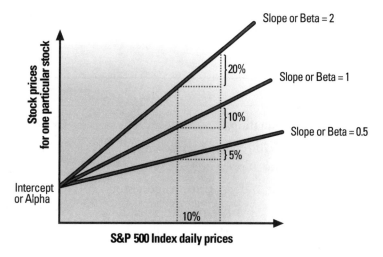

Figure 15.2 *Calculating Beta*

The Beta value can range from zero to a positive number such as 3. Stocks that have a Beta value less than 1 are considered to be stable stocks, as they are less price volatile than the overall S&P 500. If the Beta value is equal to 1, the stock's price volatility is identical to the overall average market volatility. If the stock has a Beta value greater than 1, then that stock is more volatile relative to the entire stock market's volatility. Table 15.1 summarizes all possible Beta values.

My recommendation to day traders is to trade stocks that are volatile and liquid. Look for stocks that have a Beta value greater than 1.5 and have average daily trading volumes greater than 500,000 shares. Another investment strategy is to buy stocks that have a high Beta value (large price volatility) in the bull market and then move to stocks with a low Beta value (low price volatility) in the bear market.

Bollinger Bands

A few years ago I encountered in a book on stock trading an analogy about oscillators that was very instructive. Imagine walking a large dog on a long leash in fresh snow. The dog is pulling you and refuses to walk in a straight line. Instead, he continually bounces from side to side. If the dog strays too far to one side, he feels resistance from the leash and would turn in the opposite direction, or the direction that has the least resistance. Furthermore, every now and then the dog would be so enticed by something (for example, a cat) on the left or right side that he would exert enough force to pull you in that direction.

Table 15.1 *Relative Price Volatility: Beta Values*

Beta Value	Explanation	Example
Negative Beta	S&P 500 Index goes down and the stock price goes up	Gold mining stocks
Beta less than 1	Stable and less price volatile stocks	Utility stocks
Beta equal to 1	Overall market and the stock have the identical price volatility	S&P 500 Index fund
Beta greater than 1	More volatile stocks	Internet stocks

Draw an analogy between the dog's footprints formed in the snow and stock prices. Most of the time, the dog's prints (or the stock prices) stay within the left and right boundaries of the long leash. Imagine that the left- and right-side boundaries of your dog leash are your price support and resistance boundaries. The Bollinger bands indicator is essentially your stock price "leash." Of the available oscillators, the Bollinger bands is my favorite. It is commonly used by day traders and is available in trading software packages.

The Bollinger bands indicator was developed by John Bollinger. This technical tool is an excellent way to determine price support and resistance levels. Price resistance is a price level at which prices have stopped rising and have either moved sideways or reversed direction; it indicates an overbought market. Price support, however, is a price level at which prices have stopped falling and have either moved sideways or reversed direction; it indicates an oversold market. The Bollinger bands oscillator monitors the risk of price fluctuations within price support and resistance levels.

The Bollinger bands indicator is an improvement over the fixed percentage bands that were once commonly used by professional traders. Traders used two bands around a current price as support and resistance levels. A + 10% from the current price would become a price resistance band. A − 10% from the current price would become a price support band. As is apparent, fixed percentage bands were not very flexible; they created two parallel lines that did not change with increased or decreased price volatility.

The Bollinger bands indicator uses standard deviations instead of fixed percentage lines for the support and resistance bands. The standard deviation of the stock price is the measure of the absolute risk arising from the stock's price volatility. The starting assumption is that stock prices during a certain time interval have a normal distribution around the average price. For short-term stock trading, let us use as an example 14 observations of one-minute interval price data. These observations allow us to analyze the absolute price volatility of the stock during the last 14 minutes of trading. Here I assume that the stock prices are normally distributed around the mean price and the prices deviated equally on the plus and minus sides from the existing Moving Average price. Figure 15.1 illustrates such normal (or bell-shaped) price distribution with the average stock price in the middle, and the high and low prices on the ends.

As price volatility increases for a particular stock, the price variance increases as well. The standard deviations automatically adjust for increased or decreased intraday or intraweek price volatility. A higher price variance from the average automatically increases the standard deviation. In times of increased price volatility, the high and low prices are relatively far apart from the average (mean) price, and the standard deviation is large, and the Bollinger bands increase. In times of decreased price volatility, the high and low prices are relatively close to the average price, and the standard deviation is small, and the Bollinger bands decrease.

Statistical theory tells us that 68% of all price observations reside on a +1 standard deviation (+1 St.D.) and a −1 standard deviation (−1 St.D.) from the mean. Furthermore, 95% of all price observations reside on a +2 standard deviation (+2 St.D.) and a −2 standard deviation (−2 St.D.) from the mean. Figure 15.3 selects +1.85 St.D. and −1.85 St.D. for the upper and lower Bollinger bands lines. The upper band of +1.85 St.D. above the Moving Average point constitutes the price resistance level at that point in time; the lower band of −1.85 St.D. below the Moving Average point constitutes the price support level. Statistical theory tells us

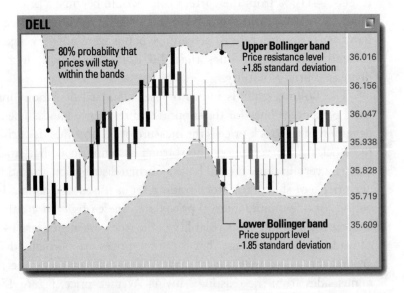

Figure 15.3 *Bollinger Bands*

that there is an approximately 80% probability that all prices would fall within the upper and lower Bollinger bands, and only a 20% probability that actual prices would go above or below the two Bollinger band lines.

With these probabilities in mind, a day trader should always try to stay within the Bollinger bands trading range. When the stock prices approach the upper Bollinger band, the price has reached its price resistance level and the stock is overbought. It would not be a good idea to open a long position (buy the stock) when the prices approach the upper Bollinger band.

Conversely, it is not a good idea to open a short position (sell short the stock) when the price has reached its support level (the lower Bollinger band). When this happens, many traders would believe the stock to be oversold.

Momentum Indicator

The momentum indicator (MOM) is another technical analysis tool that can be useful to day traders. The MOM is an oscillator-type indicator that is used to ascertain whether there is upward or downward price momentum and to determine overbought or oversold markets. It shows visually the pace or strength at which stock prices are moving, and helps ascertain whether the price momentum is gaining or losing steam. In this chapter, the momentum indicator is plotted as a line attached to the main diagram, but in some software packages, the MOM is plotted as a histogram (that is, as bars).

The MOM is calculated by subtracting the current closing price from the closing price of several periods ago. The past period can be any period selected by the trader. My preference is to use the same period that is used for the Slow EMA (discussed in chapter 14). In chapter 14, the Slow EMA was constructed by using the stock closing price of nine one-minute intervals. So, the stock's current MOM value will be calculated by subtracting the current closing price from the closing price nine minutes ago. In other words, $MOM = P(t) - P(t - 9)$. Figure 15.4 displays the momentum indicator.

The MOM oscillates or fluctuates above or below the zero line. If the current closing price is higher than the closing price of nine minutes

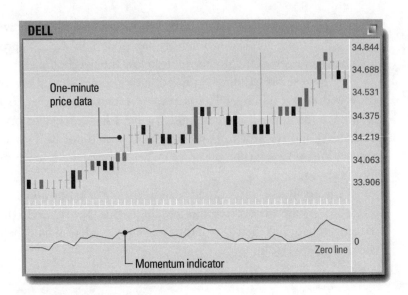

Figure 15.4 *Momentum Indicator*

ago, then the MOM value is positive. Conversely, if the current closing price is lower than the closing price nine minutes ago, then the MOM value is negative. If the current closing price is the same as the closing price nine minutes ago, the MOM value is zero.

If the MOM values are positive and increasing, that constitutes a bullish sign. Conversely, if the MOM values are negative and decreasing, that constitutes a bearish sign. If the MOM systematically fluctuates around the zero line between the positive and negative values, that points to a choppy market. This is important for the trader, because it is difficult to trade stocks that have extremely choppy MOMs.

If the MOM values rise too far above the zero line, that could indicate an overbought market. If the values are positive but the MOM reverses its direction and starts to move down toward the zero line, that could be an early sign that the positive (upward) price momentum is losing its steam. Conversely, if the MOM values fall too far from the zero line, that could indicate an oversold market. If the MOM value are negative but the MOM reverses its direction and starts to move upward toward the zero line, that would be an early sign that the downward price momentum is losing its steam.

Stochastic Oscillator

George Lane developed the stochastic oscillator indicator in the 1970s. It was designed to show when a stock becomes overbought or oversold within a certain trading range. The stochastic oscillator is one of the most popular overbought/oversold indicators available today. Most trading software products incorporate stochastic analysis.

The stochastic indicator refers to the location of a stock's current price in relation to its price range over a specified period of time. The indicator generates readings between 0 and 100. It is commonly accepted that readings over 75 constitute an overbought market. In this situation, it is likely that relatively high prices have attracted sellers who entered the market, sold the stock, and made a profit. It is possible that the price movement will soon reverse its trend. It is a signal (or warning) to traders not to open a long position. In essence, the overbought stochastic market line at 75 constitutes an arbitrary price resistance line.

Conversely, it is commonly accepted that readings under 25 constitute an oversold market. An oversold market exists when stock prices have declined rapidly due to a large influx of sellers. At that time, the relatively low prices would attract buyers who enter the market to pick up a stock at a perceived bargain price. In that case, there is a distinct possibility that the price movement will reverse its trend. It is a warning not to sell short the stock; instead, it signals to traders to look for the possibility of opening a long position if an uptrend emerges. The oversold stochastic market line at 25 would constitute an arbitrary price support line. Figure 15.5 depicts the stochastic oscillator indicator. The chart in Figure 15.5 uses a stochastic oscillator that is based on the 9 one-minute intervals used in other examples.

As you can see from Figure 15.5, the stochastic oscillator fluctuates between the two market extremes. When plotted on the chart, the stochastic indicator has very jagged peaks and troughs. Anything between 25 and 75 indicates a normal trading range.

Fast and Slow Stochastic

The stochastic oscillator, or the *Fast Stochastic* (%K), is defined as the difference between the current stock price and the lowest stock price in the last nine minutes, which is then divided by the difference between the

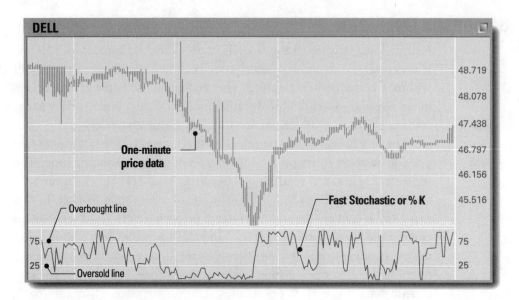

Figure 15.5 *Stochastic Oscillator Indicator*

highest and lowest prices in the last nine periods. In other words, %K is defined as [P(t) – Lowest P(t – 9)] divided by [Highest P(t – 9) – Lowest P(t – 9)] , where the [Highest P(t – 9) – Lowest P(t – 9)] represents the price-trading range in the last nine minutes and the [P(t) – Lowest P(t – 9)] represents the location of a current price in relation to the lowest price in the last nine minutes.

The stochastic indicator chart appears to have very jagged peaks and troughs. Many traders prefer to use *Slow Stochastic* (%D), which is the slower or smoothed-out stochastic oscillator. The Slow Stochastic is basically a Moving Average (MA) of the Fast Stochastic. Therefore, the moving average stochastic line will smooth out some of the jagged peaks and troughs of the Fast Stochastic line.

Some technical analysts plot the Fast Stochastic line next to the Slow Stochastic line. The two lines (%K and %D) would generate many crossovers. The crossovers can be interpreted as buy and sell signals. For example, if the Fast Stochastic crosses over and goes above the Slow Stochastic, that would constitute a buy signal. If the Fast Stochastic crosses and goes under the Slow Stochastic, that would constitute a sell signal. However, my preference is to treat and use the stochastic oscillator indicators strictly as overbought and oversold indicators and not as trading buy and sell signals.

Relative Strength Index

The relative strength index (RSI) was developed by well-known technical analyst J. Welles Wilder in the late 1970s. It is one of the most common oscillator indicators used by swing investors who might be holding the stock for several days, although it is frequently used by day traders as well. Similar to the stochastic indicator, the RSI indicator was designed to show when a stock becomes overbought or oversold within a certain trading range.

The RSI generates readings between 0 and 100. It is commonly accepted that readings over 70 constitute an overbought market. Again, the term *overbought* implies that stock prices went up too fast and too far because of a high influx of buyers, and that sellers will want to sell the stock to make a profit. The RSI reading of 70 is a signal to a trader not to open a long position because the RSI has approached an arbitrary price resistance line. Traders should in this case look for short-selling opportunities.

Conversely, RSI readings under 30 are considered to constitute an oversold market. An *oversold* market is a situation where stock prices have declined rapidly due to a large influx of sellers, which attracts buyers who want to buy the stock at the perceived bargain price. A low RSI reading is not in itself a buy signal. Rather, it is a signal to look for the possibility of opening a long position if a positive trend is ascertained. It is a signal to traders not to short sell the stock.

Finally, an RSI value of 50 can serve as the zero line used by other oscillators.

The calculation for the relative strength index is the following:

$$RSI = 100 - \left\{ \frac{100}{1 + RS} \right\}$$

where RS is the relative strength, or:

$$RS = \frac{\text{(average of net positive closing price changes for the selected time period)}}{\text{(average of net negative closing price changes for the selected time period)}}$$

Suppose we are dealing with daily price data and our selected time period is 14 days, which is the default period for most RSI oscillator software applications. If fewer days, such as a nine-day period, are used to calculate the RSI, the RSI indicator will be more volatile or choppy.

If the closing price in one period, such as one day, is higher than the previous day's closing price, then that day will have a positive net price change. However, the closing price in one period could be lower than the previous day's closing price; then that day will have a negative net price change.

If the positive net price changes are greater on average than the negative net price changes (indicating a bullish market condition), then the numerator will be larger than the denominator and the RSI will increase in value. For instance, imagine that the average of net positive closing-price changes for the selected 14-day period is 80, and suppose that the average of the net negative closing-price changes for the selected 14-day time period is 40. Then, the RS is $^{80}/_{40}$ (or 2), which would result in the following:

$$RS = 2$$
$$RSI = 100 - \left(\frac{100}{1 + 2} \right)$$
$$RSI = 100 - 33.3$$

In this hypothetical example, the RSI is relatively high at 66.6, which indicates that prices are approaching an overbought market level, determined by the RSI benchmark of 70. At that overbought level, a price reversal or price decline is likely. In other words, stock prices had reached such high level to attract profit taking or selling.

If there are more negative net price changes than positive net price changes (indicating a bearish signal), the numerator will be smaller than the denominator and the RSI will decrease in value. Conversely, imagine that the average of the net positive closing-price changes for the selected 14-day time period is only 40, and that the average of the net negative closing-price changes for the selected 14-day time period is 80. Then, the RS is $^{40}/_{80}$ (or $^{1}/_{2}$), which would result in the following:

$$RS = 0.5$$
$$RSI = 100 - \left(\frac{100}{1 + 0.5} \right)$$

$$RSI = 100 - \left(\frac{100}{1.5} \right)$$
$$RSI = 100 - 66.6$$
$$RSI = 33.3$$

Conversely, when the RSI is relatively low at 33.3, it indicates that prices are approaching an oversold market level, as defined by the RSI benchmark of 30. At that oversold price level, a price reversal or price increase is possible. In short, stock prices had reached such low level that they attracted new investors or greater buying.

Figure 15.6 depicts the RSI oscillator for Dell Computer Corporation.

The key to reading the RSI oscillator is to look at these two characteristics:

1. Level of the RSI reading; whether the RSI reading is high or low

2. Direction of the RSI oscillator; whether the RSI reading is going up or down

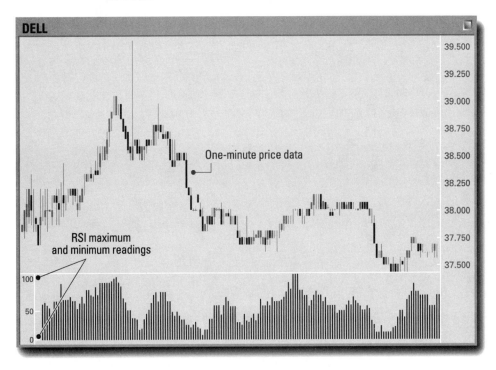

Figure 15.6 *Relative Strength Index (RSI)*

A bullish trading signal would be RSI readings at a low level, such as around 30, along with an increase in each RSI reading. The current RSI reading must be higher than the previous RSI bar reading or the RSI is going up. Conversely, a bearish RSI signal would be RSI readings at a high level such 70, and a continuous decrease in each RSI reading.

In summary, oscillator indicators are technical analysis tools that tell you where a current stock price is relative to its most recent high and low price range. Oscillators help traders avoid buying a stock at the relative high price or short selling a stock when the price is at the relatively low level. They are crucial tools for monitoring the trading risks associated with price volatility.

16

Broad Market Measures and Trading Volume

An old stock market adage states that "a rising tide lifts all boats." And though this is certainly true of boats, it is not always true for the stock market. The rising stock market tide will lift the price of most of the boats, but not all of them. Some boats are beyond hope. Even with a strong rising market tide, there will always be laggards.

Nevertheless, it is important always to monitor the broad stock market. The trader must be aware at all times of the direction and intensity of overall market sentiment. Paying attention to a broad market index can keep you abreast of the current overall price momentum.

Market Indices

The most frequently asked question about the stock market is, "How is the market doing today?" The correct way to answer this question is to give the price change that's quoted in a market index.

A market index reveals the overall market price performance at any point in time. It provides the benchmark used to compare individual stock returns to the overall market. The most commonly quoted market indices are the S&P 500 (SPX), the Dow Jones Industrial Average (DJIA), the NASDAQ Composite (COMP), the NASDAQ 100 (NDX), the NYSE Composite (NYA), the Russell 2000 (RUT), and the Wilshire Small Cap.

Several studies have indicated that there is a relatively high correlation among the major stock indices. Most of the time the market indices move in tandem. When the S&P 500 Index increases in value, most likely the Dow Jones Industrial Average Index also goes up in value. The coefficient of correlation between the S&P 500 and the Dow Jones Industrial Average is approximately 0.96. (A coefficient of correlation of 1 indicates perfect correlation, whereas a coefficient of correlation of zero indicates no correlation.) The high correlation is not surprising. First, the companies that are part of the two indices are operating at the same time in the same economic environment. Second, there is an overlap between the two indices—30 companies in the Dow Jones Industrial Average are also part of the broader S&P 500 Index.

Although market indices tend to move in the same market direction but at a different pace, occasionally market indices might diverge. A recent example of this is the NASDAQ Composite Index and the Dow Jones Industrial Average during the first months of 2000, when the NASDAQ increased approximately 13% and the Dow Jones declined 14% in the same time period. Financial commentators began speculating about a dual stock market. The technology-driven—and, particularly, the Internet growth-driven—NASDAQ stock market seemed to be appreciating in value, while stock prices of old industrial companies were declining because of higher interest rates on future corporate earnings.

Then, in April 2000, a major price correction in the technology sector occurred. On Friday, April 14, 2000, the NASDAQ plunged a record 355 points, or approximately 10%, which was its worst one-day drop in history. All told, April 2000 saw an unprecedented decline in the technology-loaded NASDAQ market, which declined 25% in value during one week of trading. The prices of the NASDAQ and the Dow Jones Industrial Average are now a good deal more balanced.

Index Construction

The important difference among indices is the method of construction. There are basically two issues regarding the development of a market index:

1. Sample size
2. Weighting scheme

The *sample size* is the number of stocks in the index. A large sample size means that the index is designed to monitor a broader stock market. It is a statistical truism that the larger the sample, the more accurately the sample measures broad market performance. For instance, the Standard

& Poor 500 Index, with its sample size of 500 stocks, is a much better indicator of the overall market performance than the Dow Jones Industrial Average, which has a sample of 30 stocks.

There are a number of specialized indices that have, by design, small samples. Such specialized indices are designed to monitor a single industry sector that might have a limited number of firms. For example, the Semiconductor Index (SOX) monitors only a small number of stocks in this industry. The sample is small because the population of the entire industry sector is small.

The second issue is the index weighting scheme, which reveals how much importance is assigned to each stock. There are two main stock-weighting approaches:

1. Market capitalization weighting

2. Price weighting

Market capitalization weighting means that each stock is assigned a weight based on the firm's relative market value or size in the stock market. Large firms, such as Microsoft, Intel, or Dell, carry more relative weight in the index than the firms that have smaller market capitalization. The S&P 500 Index is an example of the market capitalization-weighted index; most market indices are market capitalization-weighted. *Price weighting* means that each stock is assigned a weight based on the firm's relative stock price in the market at that point in time. Companies that exhibit high prices carry more relative weight in the index than do firms that have low prices. The Dow Jones Industrial Average is an example of a price-weighted market index. Table 16.1 illustrates the difference between the two weighting schemes for five hypothetical stocks.

The calculation of the returns for two market indices reveals the dramatic difference in the outcome. The same five stocks display different returns under the two constructions. For example:

$$\text{Return based on the price-weighted index} = \frac{(162 - 149)}{149} = 0.72\%$$

$$\text{Return based on the market capitalization-weighted index} = \left(\frac{200,600,000 - 184,200,000}{18,400,000} \right) = 9.99\%$$

Table 16.1 *Market Index Construction*

Stock	Price at the Beginning Period	Number of Shares	Market Capitalization at the Beginning Period	Price at the End Period	Market Capitalization at the End Period
AAAA	20	1,000,000	20,000,000	22	22,000,000
BBBB	24	1,800,000	43,200,000	29	52,200,000
CCCC	30	1,500,000	45,000,000	32	48,000,000
DDDD	35	800,000	28,000,000	36	28,800,000
EEEE	40	1,200,000	48,000,000	43	51,600,000
Total	149	6,300,000	184,200,000	162	202,600,000

Finally, the computational procedure adds another twist in market index construction. Some indices use a simple arithmetic average in their calculations; other indices use a geometric mean. Different indices also use different methods of adjusting for stock splits, stock dividends, and changes in the number of outstanding shares.

The S&P 500 Index

One way to monitor the broad market is to monitor the Standard & Poor 500 Index (S&P 500), which is the market capitalization weighted index and an indicator of the general stock price movement for the 500 largest companies in the United States. The symbol for the S&P 500 Index is SPX and it can be charted or displayed as if it is a stock.

A good way to understand the S&P 500 Index is to visualize it as a lake filled with 500 stocks. Just like any other lake, this lake has its water inflow and outflow. Membership in the index is based on a company's current market capitalization, which continuously changes with stock prices. There are always companies that are appreciating in value at a much faster pace than the rest of the market, and consequently these stocks will reach the benchmark and qualify to be added to the index first. Inclusion into the index generates an immediate boost in demand for these stocks. Many investors invest in the S&P 500 Index fund on a regular monthly or biweekly basis through investment plans such as 401(k) plans. Thus stocks that are added to that purchase mix will have a continuous built-in demand. Conversely, the stocks that are dropped from the index are subsequently dropped from that purchase mix, so the stock will suffer a decrease in demand.

Many trading software packages allow the trader to overlay a stock index such as the S&P 500 next to any stock prices being monitored. The S&P 500's values are commonly quoted by the stock data feed providers. The software automatically resizes the index next to the prices of a particular stock. If your trading software does not have the overlay feature, my recommendation is to open a separate window and monitor at least one broad market index. It is an easy way to ascertain if prices of a stock are moving in the same direction as the broad market.

Figure 16.1 provides an example of a technical analysis chart that has a broad market overlay. In this example, the stock price of Dell (DELL) was highly correlated at the moment of analysis with the broad stock market as measured by the S&P 500 futures.

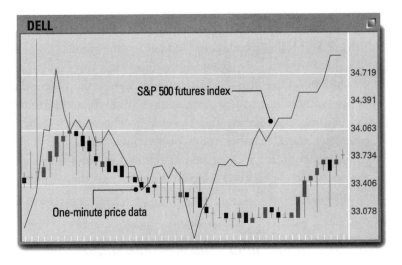

Figure 16.1   *Broad Market Index Overlay*

S&P 500 Futures

Many traders believe that the S&P 500 futures is a leading market indicator. By contrast, a cash index, such as the S&P 500 Index or the Dow Jones Industrial Average Index, is a lagging indicator. For instance, the S&P 500 Index reflects the actual or historical price changes of the underlying stocks that comprise that cash index. On the other hand, the S&P 500 futures price changes reflect the expectations about the overall market condition by market speculators who buy and sell the S&P 500 futures contracts.

The S&P 500 futures are standardized futures contracts with an expiration date; they are being traded on the Chicago Mercantile Exchange. In essence, the S&P 500 futures contract is a financial derivative. The value of the futures contract is tied directly to the underlying cash value of the index. In fact, the delivery of the contract is the cash settlement of the difference between the original transaction price and the final price of the index at the termination of the contract. The price of the index futures will be highly correlated with the value of the corresponding index. The activity of the index arbitrageurs ensures that the deviations between the price of the index futures and the value of the underlying cash index are relatively minor.

The futures index and the prices of the S&P 500 futures contracts reflect to a great extent anticipation by market professionals and speculators about the future of the broad market. Because the futures contract is actively traded, the trader can plot and overlay the price value of the futures contract against the stock price. Instead of plotting the value of the S&P 500 Index (the lagging indicator), the trader can plot the price of the S&P 500 futures index (the leading indicator).

The futures are displayed in different format than the index symbols because futures are contracts that have different expiration months—March, June, September, and December. The codes for March, June, September, and December are respectively H, M, U, and Z. The year of the futures contract is displayed at the end of the futures symbol. For instance, the code for the S&P 500 Index futures that expires in December 2001 is "SPZ1."

The Dow Jones Industrial Average Index

The Dow Jones Industrial Average Index was one of the first published stock market indices and is a price weighted index. Charles Dow, founder and editor of the *Wall Street Journal,* published the index in *The Journal* on July 3, 1884. At that time, the index consisted of only nine stocks, and most of them were railroad companies. Today, the index consists of 30 large and established U.S. industrial companies. In addition, today we have the Dow Jones Transportation Index (TRAN), consisting of 20 large transportation companies, and the Dow Jones Utilities Index (UTIL), consisting of 15 large utility companies. Finally, the Dow Jones Composite Index (COMP) combines the three Dow Jones indices into one merged price index consisting of 65 stocks.

Specialized Indices

Some traders who trade mostly NASDAQ stocks pay much closer attention to narrower market indices, such as the NASDAQ 100. If you prefer to track NASDAQ 100 futures rather than NASDAQ 100 Index, the code for the NASDAQ 100 Index futures that expire in December 2001 is "NDZ1."

Finally, day traders who specialize in a few technology stocks closely monitor certain sector indices, such as an Internet, telecommunications, or software index on an exchange such as the Chicago Board Options Exchange (CBOE).

Market Breadth Indicators

Advance–decline issues, advance/decline ratio, advance–decline line, and TRIN (Trading Index) are some of the indicators measuring broad market breadth that are available on most sophisticated trading software platforms. They all have the same foundation and objective:

➤ They are designed to measure broad market price momentum.

➤ They are based on the difference in the number of advancing and declining issues.

The difference between the advancing and declining stock issues is the starting point of the analysis. There are approximately 3,000 common stocks listed on the NYSE. If the overall market is flat, and one ignores those stocks that are unchanged in price, one can expect that 1,500 stocks would advance in value and 1,500 stocks would decline in value. That would mean that advance–decline issues would be set at zero.

Suppose that 2,000 stocks advance and 1,000 stocks decline in value, which puts the advance–decline issues at +1,000. Any advance–decline issue reading over 1,000 indicates a strongly bullish market sentiment. Conversely, imagine that only 1,000 stocks advance, whereas 2,000 stocks decline in value, which would cause the advance–decline issues to be –1,000. Any negative advance–decline issues reading at –1,000 indicates a strong bearish market sentiment.

To find the advance/decline ratio, we divide the number of advancing issues by the number of declining issues. Using our earlier example, when 2,000 stocks advance and 1,000 stocks decline in value, the advance/decline ratio is 2, which would indicate a strong bullish market sentiment. When the advance/decline ratio is greater than 1, the overall stock market is increasing in value. When only 1,000 stocks advance, while 2,000 stocks decline in value, the advance/decline ratio becomes 0.5, which is a bearish sign. When the advance/decline ratio is less than 1, the stock market is decreasing in value. In essence, the advance/decline ratio is the quick and easy way to quantify the pulse of the broad market.

The next step is to run a cumulative total of all advance–decline issues on the NYSE. If we plot that cumulative total of all advance–decline issues over time in a line format, the result is the advance–decline line, which is one of the most popular market breadth indicators. The actual figure of the cumulative advance–decline line has no practical meaning. The important thing is the direction and slope of the advance–decline line, which reveals the overall trend and the strength of the broad market. A positive and steep line indicates strong bullish market conditions, whereas a positive and relatively small slope indicates a weak bullish market. Conversely, a negative, steep line indicates strong bearish market conditions, whereas a negative and relatively small slope indicates a weak bearish market.

Table 16.2 depicts calculations for different market breadth indicators, using hypothetical daily data for two weeks of trading on the NYSE. The time interval can be adjusted to any time frame, such as minute, hourly, or daily data, to reflect the focus of the analysis.

TRIN was developed by Richard Arms in the late 1960s. *Barron's* weekly business newspaper, which reported it first, called the ratio the "short-term trading index." TRIN is a market breadth indicator that

Table 16.2 *Hypothetical Advance–Decline Issues, Advance/Decline Ratio, and Advance–Decline Line*

Time Interval	Advance Issues	Decline Issues	Advance–Decline Issues	Advance/Decline Ratio	Advance–Decline Line
1	2,000.00	1,000.00	1,000.00	2.00	1,000.00
2	1,600.00	1,400.00	200.00	1.14	1,200.00
3	800.00	2,200.00	−1,400.00	0.36	−200.00
4	1,200.00	1,800.00	−600.00	0.67	−800.00
5	1,100.00	1,900.00	−800.00	0.58	−1,600.00
6	1,000.00	2,000.00	−1,000.00	0.50	−2,600.00
7	1,200.00	1,800.00	−600.00	0.67	−3,200.00
8	1,700.00	1,300.00	400.00	1.31	−2,800.00
9	1,900.00	1,100.00	800.00	1.73	−2,000.00
10	2,000.00	1,000.00	1,000.00	2.00	−1,000.00

expands on the previously mentioned advance–decline issues, advance/decline ratio, and advance–decline line indicators. It is the ratio derived from two independent ratios—advancing/declining issues ratio and advancing/declining volume ratio. In addition to monitoring the number of advancing and declining issues, TRIN adds the measure of trading volume associated with the advancing and declining issues. In other words:

$$\text{TRIN} = \frac{\text{Advancing Issues/Declining Issues}}{\text{Advancing Issues Volume/Declining Issues Volume}}$$

Most traders use TRIN as an overbought and oversold indicator rather than as a broad market price momentum indicator. As a general rule, an overbought market must have a TRIN ratio less than 1; a TRIN ratio reading below 0.8 would constitute a warning to traders that the NYSE is overheating.

The following is an example of hypothetical NYSE trading data:

If Advancing Issues   = 2,000
Declining Issues   = 1,000

Advancing Issues Volume = 750,000,000 shares
Declining Issues Volume = 250,000,000 shares

$$\text{TRIN} = \frac{(2,000/1,000)}{750,000,000/250,000,000} = \frac{2}{3} = 0.66$$

Conversely, an oversold market must have a TRIN ratio greater than 1; a TRIN ratio reading above 1.1 constitutes a warning to traders that the NYSE prices are declining too far too quickly and that a price reversal is a strong possibility.

Suppose the opposite is true:

If Advancing Issues = 1,000
Declining Issues = 2,000
Advancing Issues Volume = 250,000,000 shares
Declining Issues Volume = 750,000,000 shares

$$\text{TRIN} = \frac{(1,000/2,000)}{250,000,000/750,000,000} = \frac{0.5}{.33} = 1.5$$

Trading Volume

Stock price movement is the most important dimension of technical analysis. Although the price is the focus of technical analysis, trading volume is the fuel that generates price change. It would be ideal if we could monitor in real time the money flow for the particular stock. The money flow would be the true indicator of the future price potential. It would tell us if there is more or less "fuel" in the market for that stock. For many technical analysts, the volume is a proxy variable (that is, a substitute variable) of the money flow.

Most actively traded stocks that are commonly traded by day traders have substantial daily trading volume. In other words, the absolute trading volume is always large—millions of shares traded every day. Looking at the raw absolute trading volume does not reveal much. Subsequently, technical analysis focuses on deviation from the normal trading activities. Increasing volume often accompanies higher prices. Conversely, declining volume is an advance warning of a possible price correction. Most traders use trading volume statistics to confirm an existing price movement.

Plotting the raw trading volume in real terms on a chart, however, would reveal only the combined buying and selling size of the trading or total volume, but not its direction, i.e., whether the volume is primarily buying or selling and thus whether it is a possible indicator for advance or decline.

One should keep in mind that volume statistics are always subject to brief distortions. Option expirations and program trading can clearly affect intraday volume without providing any underlying cause for price increase or decrease. In addition, spikes in the trading volume without any gradual increase over several minutes or hours may be the result of news leaks or certain stock analysts' comments.

On-Balance Volume Indicator

One of the simplest volume indicators is the *On-Balance Volume (OBV) indicator*. Joseph Granville developed the OBV indicator in the 1960s. On-balance volume is plotted as a line representing the cumulative total of the trading volume. When the closing price for the one-minute trading interval is higher than the closing price for the previous one-minute trading interval, that trading volume is assigned a plus (+) sign. If the closing price ends up on the up-tick, the OBV indicator assumes that the stock is under accumulation. If the closing price for the one-minute trading interval is lower than the closing price for the previous one-minute trading interval, then that trading volume is assigned a negative (–) sign. In other words, if the closing price ends on the down-tick, then the OBV indicator assumes that the stock is under distribution. The OBV is a simple running cumulative total of the plus and minus (upside and downside) trading volume.

The OBV indicator can be overlaid on price data or plotted in a separate subgraph. The OBV illustrates the trading volume flow in order to determine whether there is buying or selling pressure. Figure 16.2 illustrates the OBV indicator for the intraday one-minute interval prices and volume of Dell (DELL).

A trader would like to see the price and the OBV indicator moving in the same direction. If both the price and OBV are moving up, the trend is considered strong. If the price is going up but the running cumulative OBV line is declining, then divergence exists and there is a possibility of a price reversal. Conversely, if both the stock price and the OBV

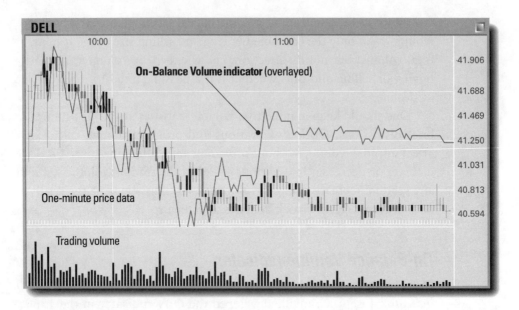

Figure 16.2 *On-Balance Volume Indicator and Trading Volume*

indicator are moving down, the downward trend is considered strong. However, if the stock price is going down but the running cumulative OBV line is increasing, or if the stock price is going up while the running cumulative OBV line is decreasing, a price reversal is likely.

Technical Analysis Chart with Combined Indicators

Finally, traders can combine several technical analysis indicators into a single chart. Figure 16.3 is an example of such a combined effort. The graph is crowded with several technical analysis indicators, including the Fast and Slow EMA lines, Bollinger bands, and the momentum indicator. Sometimes it is difficult to differentiate among the lines on a small chart, but the lines can be color-coded for easier reference.

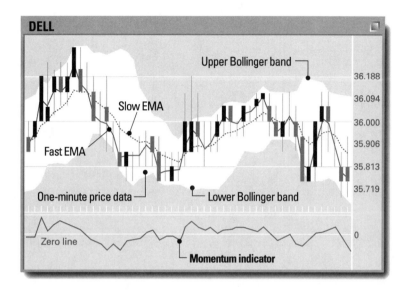

Figure 16.3 *Combined Technical-Analysis Indicators: Fast and Slow EMA Lines, Bollinger Bands, and the Momentum Indicator*

The trader can pack a lot of analysis into a small chart. It is my opinion that more information is preferable to less. However, novice traders usually start with a few basic indicators and then add others as they gain experience. Too much analysis can, at times, cause confusion or can even lead to trading paralysis.

Introduction to Order Executions

In SECTION IV, WE DEFINE, EXPLAIN, AND GRAPHICALLY ILLUSTRATE THE mechanics of day trading. In this trade management section we describe how professional day traders execute their trades efficiently and precisely. The NASDAQ, NYSE, and electronic communication networks (ECNs) order execution platforms are described in great detail.

➤ Different types of trade orders, such as market, limit, stop, and stop-limit orders, are explained. Then order qualifiers such as the day order, good until canceled, all or none, and others are described. Clarification on using limit versus market orders and priority of orders is presented. Trading terms such as bidding, buying, offering, and selling are explained. As well, NASDAQ's Small Order Execution System (SOES) and SelectNet "broadcast" versus "preference" orders are explained in detail, along with an explanation of the SelectNet preference buy and sell order trading strategies.

➤ Island (ISLD) as an ECN is then covered. We explain the concepts of bidding the high BID versus bidding the BID through Island, and offering the low ASK versus offering the ASK through Island. In addition, Island order mechanics and the Island book, which displays every Island buy and sell order, are clarified.

- ➤ Then Instinet (INCA), the largest ECN, is covered, followed by a discussion on private versus public financial markets. At that time, concepts of locked-up markets versus crossed-up markets, and locked-down markets versus crossed-down markets are introduced. Trading strategies using Instinet are discussed, including what constitutes a bullish or bearish signal.
- ➤ Finally, the NYSE, its specialists, and Super DOT are defined and explained. We discuss trading strategies on the NYSE as well as utilizing limit orders on the NYSE.
- ➤ Since short selling is much different than common buying and selling of stocks, we explain in detail the concept of short selling and its order mechanics and in particular trading against the hedge on the NYSE.

17

Trade Orders and NASDAQ's Small Order Execution System

I FIRMLY BELIEVE THAT DAY TRADERS USE THE FASTEST EXECUTION TOOLS available, and thus they obtain better prices and greater liquidity than does the general public. Although one can be an effective trader without using limit orders or cutting the spread, the power of these tools can help you maximize your trading profits. It is always helpful if a novice day trader understands how professional day traders execute their trades. You can learn to drive a fast sports car but elect to drive it slowly. In the end, the decision is yours.

Trading Terminology

Before we proceed, the following four trading terms need defining:

1. *Bidding.* Bidding is passive buying. The trader is a price maker: He is trying to purchase securities at a better or lower price than the inside ASK price. Usually, the trader will bid to purchase the security at the inside BID price, the lowest possible price at which he can buy the stock. If the trader is less aggressive, he can bid the high BID, which is the price higher than the inside BID and lower than the inside ASK. It's probable that the trader will use an electronic communication network (ECN) such as Island to execute those trades, because he would more likely be dealing with other individuals instead of market makers, who are less likely to budge on price.

In either case, the trader needs a seller. There is no guarantee that the trader will find that seller or that the trade will be executed at that price level. The trader's objective is to cut the spread between the BID and ASK prices and buy the stock at the lower price. This is a difficult task if the market is moving up. If the price of the stock has a clear upside momentum, why would anyone sell the stock at the lower price?

2. *Buying.* Buying is aggressive purchasing. The trader is a price taker: He is sending an order to purchase a stock at the posted inside ASK price. The trader is aggressive; he wants this stock badly and quickly because of the upside price momentum. The trader is willing to sacrifice the spread and is taking the stock from someone who is offering it for sale at the inside ASK price through the Small Order Execution System (SOES) or an ECN—either a market maker posting the best inside ASK price within the SOES, or another trader offering to sell the shares at the best inside ASK price through an ECN. Because the purchasing price is the inside ASK price, there is a very good probability that the order will get filled.

3. *Offering.* Offering is passive selling. The trader is a price maker; he is trying to sell securities at a better or higher price than the inside BID price. Usually the trader will offer to sell the security at the inside ASK price, or the highest possible price at which he can sell that stock. If the trader is less aggressive, he can offer the low ASK, which is the price higher than the inside BID and lower than the inside ASK. Again, the trader would use one of the ECNs or SelectNet to execute those trades.

In either case, the trader needs to find a buyer. There is no guarantee that the trader will find that buyer, and no guarantee that the trade will be executed at the desired price level. The trader's objective is to cut the spread between the BID and ASK prices and sell the stock at the higher price. This is a difficult task if the market is moving down. If the price of the stock has a clear downside momentum, the buyer has an incentive to wait for the price to move further down before buying the stock.

4. *Selling.* Selling is aggressive selling. The trader is a price taker in that he is sending an order to sell a stock at the posted inside BID price. The trader is an aggressive seller. He wants to dump the stock quickly because of a downside price momentum. The trader is willing to sacrifice the

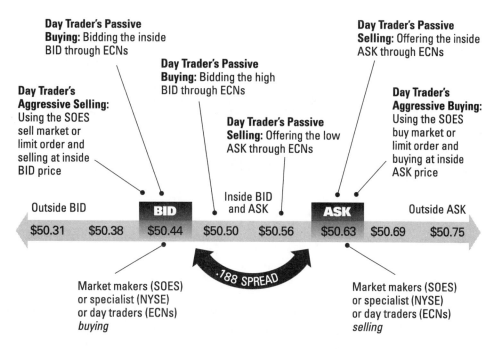

Figure 17.1 *Bidding, Buying, Offering, and Selling*

spread between the inside BID and ASK prices. The trader is giving that stock to someone who is bidding the stock for purchase at the inside BID price through the SOES or ECNs—either a market maker posting the best inside BID price within the SOES or another trader bidding to buy the shares at the inside BID price through an ECN. Because the selling price is the inside BID price, there is a very good probability that the order will get filled. Figure 17.1 helps to illustrate this point.

Types of Orders

Traders can enter a number of different types of orders on the NASDAQ and NYSE. The type of order used is determined mostly by the trader's objectives. Following is a list of trade-execution orders. Figure 17.2 provides additional illustration.

Figure 17.2 *Types of Execution Orders*

1. *Market order.* The most common type of trade order is the *market order.* Although it does not specify a price, it is executed at whatever price is available when the order reaches the exchange floor. A market order will always be executed, but traders or investors cannot be sure of the execution price.

2. *Limit order.* When customers wish to buy or sell a security at a specific price, they enter a *limit order*—an order that can only be executed at the specified price or better. A buy limit can be executed at the limit price or lower; a sell limit can be executed at the limit price or higher. A buy limit order is placed below the current market price of the security, whereas a sell limit order is placed above the current market price. Because a limit order is entered at a price that differs from the current best price, it is unlikely that the order would be executed immediately. Therefore, a limit order is usually given to a NYSE specialist to hold until it can be executed. It is possible that the order may never be executed, because the limit price is not reached or there are other orders at the same price with higher priority.

3. *Stop order.* A stop order becomes a market order to buy or sell securities once a specified price is attained or penetrated. The specific price indicated by the investor is called the *stop price*. Once the order is activated, the investor is guaranteed execution, but there is no guarantee of the execution price. A sell stop order is always placed below the current market price of the security and is typically used to limit a loss or protect a profit on a long stock position. A buy stop order is always placed above the current market price and is used to limit a loss or protect a profit on a short sale.

4. *Stop limit order.* A stop limit order is similar to a stop order in that a stop price will activate the order. However, once activated, the stop limit order becomes a buy limit or sell limit order, and it can only be executed at a specified price or better. Thus, as its name implies, a stop limit order is a combination of a stop order and a limit order. A stop limit order eliminates the risk of a stop order when the investor is not guaranteed an execution price, but exposes the investor to the risk that the order may never be filled. A sell stop limit order is always placed below the current market price of the security; it is used to limit the loss (or protect a profit) on a long position. Once activated, it becomes a sell limit order. A buy stop limit order is always placed above the current market price of the security; it is used to limit the loss (or protect a profit) on a short position. Again, once activated, it becomes a buy limit order.

Order Qualifiers

In addition to the types of orders that an investor may enter, there are various qualifications that may be used to fill an order. The following is a list of the order qualifiers:

1. *Day order.* Every order is a day order unless otherwise specified. If not executed, it is automatically canceled at the end of the day.

2. *Good until canceled* (GTC) *or open order.* This is an order that remains in effect until executed or canceled. The floor broker should periodically update GTC orders.

3. *At the opening.* This is an order to buy or sell at the opening price. If not executed at the opening, it will be canceled.

4. *At the close.* This order is to be executed as close to the closing price as possible. There is no guarantee that the price will be the closing price.

5. *Not held* (NH). This qualification gives the floor broker discretion as to the time and price of an order. If the floor broker does not execute or does not obtain the best price, the broker will not be held responsible. A NYSE specialist cannot accept a not-held order.

6. *All or none* (AON). According to this qualification, the entire order must be filled on the same transaction. The order does not have to be filled immediately; it can be executed during the course of the trading day.

7. *Immediate or cancel* (IOC). This qualifier dictates that as much of the order as possible must be executed immediately. The portion that is not immediately executed is canceled.

8. *Fill or kill* (FOK). This qualification combines the AON and IOC orders. The entire order must be executed immediately or the entire order is canceled.

Limit Versus Market Orders

As a general rule, the trader should use the buy limit order rather than the buy market order, since specifying the buying price is always a good risk-management practice. The trader needs to be in control and buy the stock at the right price. If the market is moving very fast and the trader is using market orders, he might overpay for a security. If the trader uses the buy market order, he is abdicating somewhat the ability to control the price. In other words, the trader is "chasing" the stock.

If the trader has a long stock position and the price is dropping quickly, the trader could use the sell market order rather than the sell limit order. If the trader uses the sell limit order, the order might not get filled, and the trader would miss the market altogether. Because the objective is to minimize the risk and get out of the stock quickly, the trader could use the sell market order. Unfortunately, using the sell market order is an invitation to get a fill at the bottom. A better strategy yet is to try to go out of market. In other words, the trader should try to sell the stock at the outside market and not use the current inside BID price.

For example, if the stock tanks, your best bet is to take out the best Island ECN BID, even if that BID price is outside the market, because the order will be matched directly. Another option is to use NASDAQ SelectNet and preference a market maker who might be a few price notches (or color levels on the Level II screen) below the inside BID price. However, this would not ensure a fill to the same degree that routing an order through an ECN would.

Conversely, if the stock is taking off fast and you desperately want to get in (or get out of) the short position, then your best bet is to take out the best available Island ASK price, even if that ASK price is higher and outside the market. With the NASDAQ stocks, use NASDAQ SelectNet and preference a market maker who might be a few price notches (or color levels on the Level II screen) above the inside ASK price.

The bottom line is that traders should use market orders sparingly. If a stock is appreciating in value and the trader wants to close a profitable long position, she might use the market order. If the trader is selling with the up-tick price or the green BID bar on the trading screen, then a market order is the appropriate choice.

Limit Orders on the NYSE

One important distinction between the NYSE and the NASDAQ is their treatment of limit orders. To protect individual traders and investors, the NYSE enacted rules that assign priority to customers' orders over those of NYSE specialists. In other words, a customer's limit orders, up to 2,100 shares, will be placed in front of a specialist's orders, even if the specialist had been the first in line. Traders trading on the NASDAQ market do not have that protection.

This is a tremendous advantage for NYSE traders. For the limit order to be executed, someone has to be on the other side of the trade buying or selling the stock at the market BID and ASK price through the market orders. Specialists will seldom fill these orders. It is the investors on the NYSE who are sending the market orders that close the trade. In other words, when the trader submits a limit order to buy the stock at the BID price, the investor is selling that stock at the BID price through the market order. Conversely, when the trader submits a limit order to sell the stock at the ASK price, the investor is buying that stock at the ASK price via the market order. That means that traders on the NYSE can trade without paying the BID and ASK spread. The traders, therefore, are making the spread, which is a typical day trading strategy.

Priority of Orders

Because a number of orders can arrive at the exchange floor at approximately the same time, a priority system has been established to determine which order will be executed first. The priority of trade orders is as follows:

1. Price
2. Time
3. Size

The first priority is always price. The highest BID and lowest ASK will always come first. After price, time is the determining factor. If all bidders or offerers are equal in price, then whoever came into the trading crowd first will take preference over later bidders or offerers. If the orders are equal in price and time, then the size of the order is the determining factor. Normally, the larger order will receive priority.

What this all means is that market orders do not have any priority over limit orders. Suppose, for example, that the best BID and ASK prices are 50 and 50.125, and the following is the order sequence received at the trading post:

1. LMT Buy 50.125 300
2. MKT Buy 50.125 1,000
3. MKT Buy 50.125 2,000

If this is the order time sequence, the buy limit order for 300 shares will be executed before the two market orders. The point of this exercise is to show that limit orders do not have any inherent disadvantages over market orders if they are submitted first. Hence, it is better for a trader to be in control of her trading and submit a limit order rather than a market order.

NASDAQ SOES Orders

The NASDAQ's Small Order Execution System (SOES) was designed specifically for the benefit of small investors or traders who are trading on the NASDAQ. Traders or investors always buy the stock at the posted low ASK price or sell the stock at the posted high BID price from the market makers through the SOES. The execution order is routed directly to the NASDAQ market makers. SOES orders at the same price are executed on a first-come, first-served basis. This assures that the traders or investors receive the best posted price.

The second key feature of the SOES is its mandatory nature. The NASD currently requires that all market makers post their BID and ASK prices and subsequently honor those trades. Because SOES orders are mandatory for the market makers and are executed automatically, the SOES is a very powerful trading-execution tool. When stock prices are moving up, the SOES buy order is a good tool for getting into the market quickly at a posted ASK price.

On January 14, 2000, the SEC approved the NASD rule-change proposal to convert and expand the SOES into NASDAQ's primary trading platform, called the NASDAQ National Market System (NNMS), which is sometimes referred to as the SuperSOES. However, the SuperSOES implementation has been postponed several times and it has not been implemented at the time this chapter was written. When implemented, the new SuperSOES, or the NNMS, will be enhanced by an increase in the maximum order size for NASDAQ national market securities (from 1,000 to 9,900 shares), a reduction in the order-execution delay (from 17 to 5 seconds), and an allowance for market makers to execute their proprietary orders, thus eliminating the market makers' exposure to dual liability. Dual liability results if a market maker receives and executes an order through SelectNet and immediately thereafter receives an execution against its quote through SOES.

Market makers are required to post their best BID and ASK price as well as their share size, such as 1,000 shares. This information is displayed to the entire world on the Level II screen. Under the new Super-SOES proposal, market makers would also have an option to indicate a reserve-size share amount at that BID and ASK price, which unfortunately will not be displayed on the Level II screen. However, having the reserve size indicated in the system will improve the efficiency and speed of the automatic electronic execution.

Consider the following scenario: Two market makers, A and B, are ranked in time priority. Both market makers publicly post an inside BID at $20, with a minimum 1,000 shares and a reserve of 2,000 shares. A sell limit order is entered into the NASDAQ system at $20 for 5,000 shares. Obviously, the NNMS will first take out the displayed minimum 1,000 shares each from both market makers. Then, the NNMS will take out 2,000 shares from market maker A, followed by 1,000 shares from market maker B, for a total of 5,000 shares. Under the current system, the order would most likely get partially filled for the posted minimum 1,000 shares from each market maker (A and B).

The speed of the SOES order execution depends on how many market makers are at the inside BID and ASK market and how many other day trading SOES orders are in the computerized queue. The unanswerable question is, How many and how quickly are the market makers refreshing the inside BID and ASK quotes? For instance, the market makers are only required to post 1,000 shares on the Level II screen, and that is exactly what they do. Thus the posted 1,000 shares on the Level II screen may not be the actual trading size. The market makers do not like to disclose to the public the true size or interest of their buying or selling intentions. The "ax" market maker can continue to refresh 1,000 after 1,000 shares of any particular stock at the lowest ASK price (that is, he can continue to sell), and thus effectively stop any price momentum.

Getting in the market with the SOES used to be the most common execution method of day traders. Once traders ascertained an upward price movement, they quickly jumped into the market using an SOES limit order. They bought the stock at the posted inside ASK price rather than bidding into the stock at the inside BID price or higher BID price. The SOES granted them quick execution at the guaranteed best ASK price at that time. The key was to get into the market quickly to pick up that price momentum. Today, the ECNs have assumed the role of preferred order-execution vehicle.

Today, after a trader takes a long position in a stock, and after the stock appreciates in value, the trader commonly tries to get out of that position through an ECN, such as Island. If the BID and ASK prices are 50 and 50.125, for instance, the trader has four options for selling the stock:

1. An SOES, ARCA, or SelectNet sell limit order at the inside BID price of 50.

2. An offer to sell the stock at the current inside ASK price through the ECN at 50.125.

3. An offer to sell the stock at a lower price than the current inside ASK price through the ECN at 50.063.

4. Take out the best Island BID, even if the price is lower than the inside BID.

The probability is high that the trader might use either the second or third option to get a better selling price for the stock. Most likely, the trader would try to cut the spread, sell the stock at 50.063, and earn an additional $\frac{1}{16}$. The additional $\frac{1}{16}$ on a 1,000-share increment block translates into a $62.50 gain.

The SOES treats limit orders priced at the current inside BID and ASK market as market orders that are immediately executed. The SOES orders are unpreferenced orders, which are executed against the market makers in rotation. Currently, the SOES does not execute an unpreferenced order against a single market maker more than once every 17 seconds, although NASDAQ has proposed a change to five seconds. That means the market makers can be "SOESed" by the trader, and the market makers have the option to refresh the same price or back away to the outside BID and ASK market (after the proposed five-second delay).

SOES Mechanics

All NASDAQ stocks have an SOES limit. Most trading stocks currently have a 1,000-share limit, although the limits are proposed to go up to 9,900. Most trading software automatically displays the tier limit under the share amount allowed under the SOES. The trader cannot send out through the SOES an execution order for more than the tier limit. If the market makers are not available at the inside BID or ASK market, then the SOES order will be canceled automatically. If the only party available at the inside BID or ASK market is an ECN, such as Island, the SOES order will be rejected. Certain small capitalization stocks may display a few market makers on the Level II screen, but the stock may not be traded through the SOES. In that case, the trading software would generate this message: "No SOES market maker available."

From the trader's perspective, the maximum SOES order size for a security is either the proposed 9,900, or the current limit of 1,000, or 500, or 200 shares, depending on the price and trading volume of that security. New IPOs have usually 200 or 100 tier limits, although in time the limits might be adjusted to 500 or 1,000 shares. Only public customers' orders that are not larger than the maximum order size may be entered by the SOES order-entry firm (the day trading firm or NASD broker or dealer) into the SOES for execution against the SOES market maker. Orders in excess of the maximum order size may not be divided into smaller parts for purposes of meeting the size requirements for orders entered into SOES. The SOES hours of execution are 9:30 A.M. to 4:00 P.M. Eastern time.

The SOES previously had a five-minute rule, which was modified in the summer of 1998. The old rule stated that if an order was filled through the SOES, the trader could not trade that same stock in the same direction within five minutes. For example, the trader could not buy 1,000 shares of Microsoft and then buy another 1,000 or any other amount of Microsoft within five minutes of buying the original 1,000 shares. Again, that rule has been modified. Now, if the trader can show that each Microsoft order was a separate and individual trading decision, then it is okay to trade the same Microsoft stock in the same direction within five minutes. A trader could buy Microsoft, then buy Yahoo!, and then buy Microsoft again, which would all constitute separate investment decisions. If the price of Microsoft is different for the first and second Microsoft trades, then each order is a separate investment decision.

SOES orders used to be the bread and butter of the day trading business. Unfortunately, NASDAQ market makers and the NASD have instituted myriad small and seemingly innocuous rules that have transformed the SOES into a negligible percentage of the NASDAQ's trading volume today. The NASDAQ market makers pushed for—and NASD passed—several SOES rules that benefit the market makers—such as SOES limit size and the revised five-minute rule—that have made trading with the SOES very difficult. In response to these changes, the traders simply turned their backs on the SOES and opened their arms to ECNs. Simply put, ECNs ultimately provide a faster, cheaper, and friendlier trading environment than do the NASDAQ's SOES or SelectNet. Time will tell whether the proposed changes will make the SuperSOES (or NNMS) and SelectNet the traders' primary trading media once again.

18

NASDAQ SelectNet and Island Orders

Understanding all order-execution methods, including the Small Order Execution System (SOES), SelectNet, and electronic communications networks (ECN) alternatives, is paramount for successful day trading. It is crucial that you fully understand differences among different execution methods before beginning to trade live. In addition to knowing how to open a trade position, it is equally important to know the order-execution exit strategy. In other words, appreciate how you are going to efficiently exit the position before getting into it.

SelectNet is an order-execution service owned and operated by NASDAQ. Whereas the SOES execution service is mandatory for market makers, use of SelectNet is completely voluntary. As the name implies, the trader would select and offer to the market makers a bid to buy or an offer to sell shares of a stock. The submitted order does not have to be filled by the market makers. In other words, there is nobody on the other side of the trade order that is obligated to fill SelectNet orders. The market maker has 15 seconds—which sometimes feels like an eternity to day traders in the fast-moving market—to either fill the SelectNet order or move off the posted price. SelectNet's hours of execution are 9:30 A.M. to 6:30 P.M. Eastern time.

All orders with traditional brokers are currently routed through SelectNet. With the proposed SOES changes, all orders will be routed through the new SuperSOES. SelectNet will be used only for large orders (larger than the posted NNMS-sized orders), to hit ECNs, or to go out of market (outside market). SelectNet will become a completely voluntary and interactive marketplace for oversized orders between the traders on one side and the market makers and ECN market participants on the other. A SelectNet order will get filled only if the market makers perceive that the trader's bid or offer is a good deal. Traders who use trading-execution software that has the SelectNet feature can either broadcast their bids or offers to all market makers, or preference a single market maker or ECN market participant.

SelectNet Broadcast Orders

The first option is to broadcast the bid and offer. Traders can broadcast to all market makers their bid to buy a stock at the current inside BID price. They can also broadcast to all market makers their bid to buy a stock at the higher BID price. The trader's bid would be posted throughout the NASDAQ network to all market makers, but it would not show up on Level II screens. The offer to buy the stock at the inside BID price or higher BID price will be visible only to marker makers.

Why would a trader want to use the SelectNet broadcast as an execution vehicle? If the buy order gets filled, the trader would buy the stock at the inside BID price. At worst, the trader would buy the stock at the higher BID price. Either way, the trader will be better off using the SelectNet broadcast than buying the stock through the SOES at the best ASK price. But isn't it always better to buy at the lower price than the higher price? Well, the trader will be better off buying the stock at the inside BID or higher BID price than at the lowest ASK price. However, the key phrase is "if the bid offer gets filled." There is no guarantee that the market makers will fill the order. The trader only hopes that the order will get filled.

SelectNet Preference Orders

The second option is to preference a single market maker through SelectNet. When the SelectNet preference order is submitted to the market maker, that order will show up on the market maker's computer screen. The market maker would then have 15 seconds either to fill the order or to move off the posted price. In essence, the trader is reminding the market maker that the posted price needs to be honored. The SelectNet preference bid forces the selected market maker to act. If the order is not executed by the market maker and if it is not during a high-volume period, it is a good practice to refresh SelectNet orders after 15 seconds. At high-volume periods, however, SelectNet is extremely slow, and orders can stay open for minutes without the trader being able to cancel or get a confirmation no matter what trading system is used. At such a time the trader also cannot cancel the SelectNet order for ten seconds. So if the market starts to move in the opposite direction, the trader does not have the option to cancel the order. In all probability, the market maker will fill the order during that time. After ten seconds, the trader can manually send a cancel order or the order will be canceled automatically by the software after a user-defined preset time (15 seconds). The trader will then receive a confirmation message on the computer screen that the SelectNet order has been canceled.

SelectNet Order-Execution Mechanics

When using trading software such as CyberTrader or TradeCast, placing a SelectNet order is a relatively simple task. The trader simply types the stock symbol in the appropriate window and presses Enter. Next, the trader holds down the Shift key while pressing the default function key for the SelectNet order-routing action. Figure 18.1 displays an example of the SelectNet window that would open, along with Level II screen information.

Figure 18.1 *SelectNet Order Execution and Level II Screen*

If the asterisk (*) shown in Figure 18.1 is selected, the software will send a SelectNet broadcast order to all market makers. The trader could send out a SelectNet preference order to a particular market maker with a click of the mouse button. In this example, the trader can select one market maker who is advertising to buy Cisco Systems (CSCO) at 64.375: The trader could send his bid to sell CSCO at 64.375 to Goldman Sachs & Co. (GSCO), to Bear Stearns & Co. (BEST), to Smith Barney Shearson (SBSH), to J. P. Morgan Securities Inc. (JPMS), or to Herzog Heine Geduld Inc. (HRZG).

The trader can access any market maker through SelectNet preferencing. He selects a price, and the software will match that price with all the available market makers at the price shown on the Level II screen. In Figure 18.1, clicking the price arrow in the box changes the market-maker window, displaying the market makers and ECNs available at that price.

The trader can use the up and down arrows to the right of the price box to adjust the price. Clicking on these arrow keys or using the keyboard arrow keys will increase or decrease the price by $\frac{1}{16}$. When the trader clicks OK, the order is sent through the NASDAQ SelectNet network. If the trader increases the inside BID price by $\frac{1}{16}$, she is broadcasting to all market makers in the universe that she is bidding to buy the stock at the BID price, which is higher than the current inside BID price.

In essence, traders who want to buy a stock through SelectNet have two alternatives. They can bid to buy the stock at the inside BID price, or as the traders would say, "Bid the BID." Or, they can bid to buy the stock at the price higher than the current inside BID, or "Bid the high BID."

Conversely, traders who want to sell a stock through SelectNet would also have two options. They could offer to sell the stock at the inside ASK price, or "Offer the ASK." Or, the traders could offer to sell the stock at a price lower than the current inside ASK, or "Offer the low ASK."

Unlike with the SOES, there is no tier-size limit on a SelectNet order. The trader can bid to buy or offer to sell in increments of 2,000 or more shares. Because SelectNet is a voluntary order-execution system, no one is forced to honor any trade. The market makers even have the option to execute partial orders through SelectNet at their discretion. In addition to the posted market makers, the trader can also access Instinet (INCA) and other ECNs through the SelectNet order-execution system.

SelectNet Preference Buy-Order Trading Strategy

One common day trading strategy is using the SelectNet preference order to get in or out of a stock when the market is moving quickly. The trader can bid or offer on SelectNet as a way to take advantage of market momentum. Figure 18.2 helps to illustrate this point.

Imagine that the inside market is 50.50 to 50.563 for this stock. Let's assume that the stock has strong upside momentum. The trader eagerly wants to buy 1,000 shares of this stock. There is only one market maker on the Level II screen who is posting the lowest ASK price of 50.563. If the trader decides to utilize the SOES buy limit order at 50.563, he will probably not be the first trader in the computerized queue, and the SOES buy limit order would probably not get filled.

If B. T. Alex Brown Inc. (BTAB) leaves the inside ASK price, the new lowest ASK will become 50.625. At that time, the trader can submit an SOES buy limit order at 50.625. Again, he will be competing with many other traders who are attempting to execute the same SOES buy market or limit orders at that price. If the upside price momentum is strong, the trader might miss the market. There are only two market makers posting 1,000 shares for sale and one advertising 500 shares. Those market makers could refresh the price and sell more than the

Figure 18.2 *SelectNet Preference Buy-Order Routing*

posted 2,500 shares. If the market is moving, it is likely that the best ASK price will go up quickly.

Rather than risking the opportunity altogether to buy a stock that is moving up fast, traders can elect from the beginning to preference the market makers who are on the outside market at that time. Using our example in Figure 18.2, the astute trader could immediately submit the SelectNet preference buy order for 1,000 shares to J. P. Morgan Securities Inc. (JPMS) or Lehman Brothers Inc. (LEHM) for 50.625, although the lowest ASK price at that time is 50.563. In essence, the trader would forgo the best ASK price and pay $\frac{1}{16}$ more. But that would enhance the probability that the trader would end up owning stock that is currently moving up in value.

SelectNet Preference Sell-Order Trading Strategy

Conversely, let's assume that the stock has strong downside momentum. The inside market is 50.563 to 50.625 for this stock. The trader eagerly wants to get out of the long position and sell 1,000 shares. There is only one market maker on the Level II screen who is posting the highest BID price of 50.563. If the trader decides to utilize the SOES sell limit order

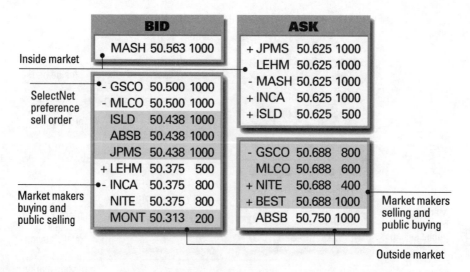

Figure 18.3 *SelectNet Preference Sell-Order Routing*

at 50.563, he will probably not be the first in line in the nation. The probability is that the SOES sell limit order would not get filled.

If Mayer & Schweitzer Inc. (MASH) leaves the inside BID price, the new highest BID would become 50.50. At that time, the trader can submit an SOES sell limit order at 50.50. The trader would compete with many other traders who would attempt to execute the same SOES sell market or sell limit orders at that price. If the downside price momentum is strong, the trader might miss that price as well. There are only two market makers who are each posting 1,000 shares for purchase. Those market makers could refresh the price and buy more than the posted 2,000 shares. However, if the market is moving downward, it's probable that the best BID price will further decrease quickly.

Rather than risking the opportunity to dump a stock that is moving down fast, traders can elect from the beginning to preference the market makers who are on the outside market at that time. Figure 18.3 illustrates this point. The astute trader could immediately submit the SelectNet preference sell order for 1,000 shares to Goldman Sachs & Co. (GSCO) or Merrill Lynch & Co. (MLCO) for 50.50. The trader would forgo the best BID price and sell for $1/16$ less. But that would enhance the probability that the trader would end up dumping a stock that is declining in value.

Island Trade Orders

Island is an ECN with the ticker symbol ISLD. It is owned and developed by Datek Online Holding, and its purpose is to match bids and offers electronically. Orders that are not matched immediately in the Island book will then be displayed on Level II screens if the order is over 100 shares and at the inside BID and ASK. Unlike SOES orders, Island orders do not have tier size limits. Although Island is predominantly used to trade NASDAQ stocks, some NYSE stocks may be traded through Island. Island's hours of execution are 8:00 A.M. to 8:00 P.M. Eastern time.

When a trade order is entered into Island, the Island system directs the order first to an Island server for order matching and then, if it is not immediately filled, to the NASDAQ SelectNet system. Traders can access Island directly or through the SelectNet execution system. Placing Island orders directly to Island, as opposed to preferencing Island via SelectNet, is the faster of the two routes.

The Island Book

The Island book allows a trader to see every Island buy and sell order for a particular stock. The Level II screen allows the trader only to see the Island high BID and low ASK prices, or the inside market. In essence, the Island book displays the "depth" of the Island at different price levels. The Island book shows all bids and offers at every price level, as well as the available quantity of shares. Thus the concept of the Island book is similar to the NASDAQ Level II screen.

However, the fact that the Island book shows actual shares is an important distinction between the Level II screen and the Island book. Market makers are required to post the required minimum stock-share sizes (that is, tier limit) offered for sale or purchase on the Level II screen, and that is exactly what is shown on the Level II screen. The market makers do not wish to show their full hands. For instance, a market maker broadcasts that 1,000 shares of Cisco (CSCO) are offered for sale. In reality, the same market maker might be selling 100,000 shares of CSCO. From the Level II screen, the traders cannot tell the actual size of the CSCO inside or outside market.

The Island book, however, displays the actual size of the inside or outside market for any stock. This is very useful information. Imagine that the trader can see 100,000 shares of CSCO being offered for sale at one price level higher than the inside ASK price. That would indicate that the supply of CSCO is increasing dramatically. There is a distinct possibility that the price of CSCO will decline in the near future. Figure 18.4 demonstrates this situation.

The trader can simply type in a stock symbol (for example, CSCO), and the Island book will display the inside BID and ASK prices and the total number of shares available at that level. In this example, there are 1,000 shares at 50.50 at the Island buys and 800 shares at 50.563 at the Island sells. In addition, the Island book displays all available price levels and share sizes. All actual bids and offers at the same price level are lumped together. For instance, the large 100,000 offer for sale at 50.625 could be possible, as it may be comprised of many smaller orders. The Time and Sales Island window displays the price and share amount of all prints, or actual individual buys and sells. These are commonly color-coded on the computer screen (green for buys and red for sells). In the black and white Figure 18.4, bold lettering represents the red Island sells.

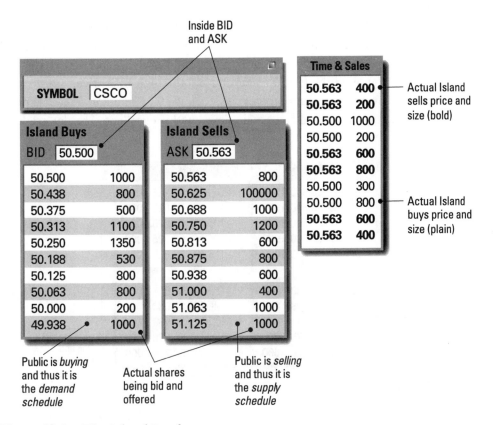

Figure 18.4 *The Island Book*

All Island orders are based on the FIFO system: first in, first out. It is important to know what is being traded on Island. The trader who has access to the Island book can plan an exit strategy. Suppose that the trader has a long position in CSCO. If the trader observes a large 100,000 sell offer at 50.625, she might submit an offer to sell CSCO at 50.594. This would ensure that the offer is first in line for Island execution, unless someone offers stock at a lower price. In addition, that offer would place the trader ahead of the large sell offer of 100,000 at 50.625. In essence, the trader would make sure that she gets out before the anticipated price decline that comes with the large sell offer.

Bidding the High BID

The day trader could bid to buy the stock at the higher BID price than the posted inside BID of 50.50. Suppose that the day trader enters his

Island (ISLD) bid to buy the stock for the higher price of 50.563, which is $\frac{1}{16}$ higher than the inside BID shown in Figure 18.5, which is our starting point. Figure 18.6 displays the Level II screen after the day trader entered the Island order and bid the high BID price.

The new inside market for the stock is 50.563 and 50.625. The probability of this Island order being executed is excellent. The day trader is

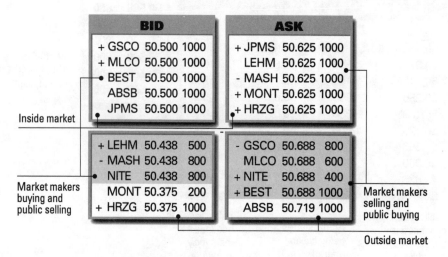

Figure 18.5 *Inside and Outside Market Before the Island Order*

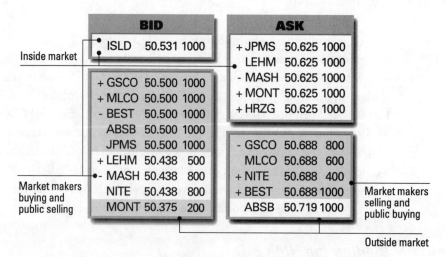

Figure 18.6 *Inside and Outside Market After Bidding the High Bid Through Island*

advertising nationally that he wants the stock and has submitted to pay the best selling price in the nation for it. Other day traders or market makers with access to the Island system and who are selling the stock at this time could accept the trader's bid and sell the stock at 50.563. The probability is great that the order would get filled. The shares of that stock would be sold to the day trader at 50.563 rather than being sold at the lower price of 50.50 to the five listed market makers.

Someone who has access to the Level II screen and Island execution system would have to enter the sell order for 1,000 shares at 50.563. Island would then automatically match the two orders, and both orders would get filled. After the Island system has matched and executed the buy and sell order for 1,000 shares at 50.563, the Island bid will disappear from the Level II screen. The inside market BID and ASK prices will revert back to 50.50 and 50.625. Assuming that there were no other changes, the Level II screen would look again like Figure 18.5.

Bidding the BID

The day trader has the option to attempt to buy the stock at a price lower than 50.563. He can bid the BID which is 50.50. In other words, the day trader can submit the bid through Island to pay the same price for the stock as the other five market makers. Figure 18.7 shows this.

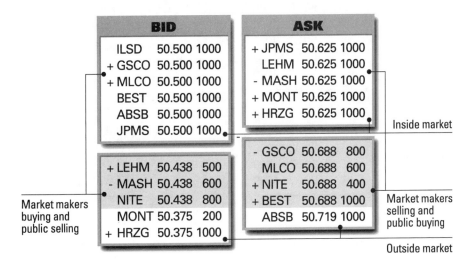

Figure 18.7 *Inside and Outside Market After Bidding the Bid Through Island*

However, the probability is now lower that the order will get filled, because the day trader has the competition of five other market makers who are buying the stock for that same price.

Conversely, suppose that the day trader wants to close an existing long position in that stock. The day trader could use SOES to sell 1,000 shares of that stock to one of the five market makers who posted the lowest BID price of 50.50, as displayed in Figure 18.5. Again, the spread is $\frac{1}{8}$. The day trader could attempt to cut the spread and sell the stock for a better price. The Island order is an excellent vehicle through which to complete this assignment.

Offering the Low ASK

The day trader could offer to sell the stock at the lower ASK price than the posted inside ASK of 50.625. Suppose that the day trader decided to enter the Island offer to sell the stock for the lower price of 50.563, which is $\frac{1}{16}$ lower than the inside ASK in Figure 18.5. Figure 18.8 displays the Level II screen after the day trader entered the Island order and offered the low ASK price.

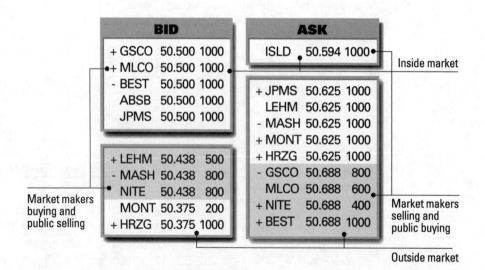

Figure 18.8 *Inside and Outside Market After Offering the Low Ask Through Island*

The new inside market for that stock is now 50.50 and 50.563. The probability of this Island sell order being executed is great. The day trader is broadcasting nationally that he wants to sell the stock and is willing to accept the lowest selling price in the nation for that stock. Other day traders or market makers with access to the Island system and who are buying this stock at this point of time could accept the offer and buy the stock at 50.563. Thus, the probability is great that the sell order will get filled.

The mechanics of the Island order are the following: Someone who has access to the Level II screen and Island execution system would enter the buy order for 1,000 shares at 50.563. The Island would automatically match the two orders, and both orders would get filled. After the Island system has matched and executed the buy and sell order for 1,000 shares at 50.563, the Island offer will disappear from the Level II screen. The inside market BID and ASK prices will revert back to 50.50 and 50.625 as represented in our starting point, Figure 18.5.

Offering the ASK

The day trader also has the option to attempt to sell the stock at a higher price than the 50.563. He can offer the ASK. The day trader can submit the offer through Island to accept the same selling ASK price for the stock as the other five market makers. Figure 18.9 shows this. The day trader can offer through Island the same inside ASK price of 50.625 for the stock. However, the probability is now lower that the order would get filled, since the day trader now has competition.

Island Fills

Island fills are quick and relatively inexpensive. Island trades usually cost $1 more than SOES orders. If the Island system has a better BID or ASK price available than the trader's submitted BID or ASK price, Island will fill the order at that better price. The trader should not use "fill or kill" orders through Island, however, as it is likely that such orders will not get filled. The downside of Island orders is partial fills.

The Island execution system displays the trader's Island order on the Level II screen only if the trader has entered the highest BID or the

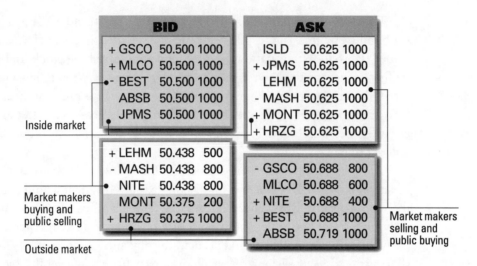

Figure 18.9 *Inside and Outside Market After Offering the Ask Through Island*

lowest ASK. If several traders enter multiple Island orders at the same BID or ASK price, the Island system will simply add up the share sizes to reflect all submitted orders. Island orders must be greater than 100 shares to be displayed on the Level II screen.

CHAPTER

19

Instinet

INSTINET (INCA) IS THE LARGEST ELECTRONIC COMMUNICATION network (ECN). A private corporation headquartered in New York City, it is owned by the Reuters Group PLC. Instinet Corporation is registered with the SEC as a NASD broker/dealer and is a member of all U.S. stock exchanges and other major international stock exchanges. Instinet was created in 1969 to furnish equity transaction services specifically to an international base of institutional investors (that is, fund managers).

As the name implies, Instinet *(www.Instinet.com)* is a trading network of large financial institutions. It does not take the role of a principal: Instinet does not buy or sell securities for its own account. Its only business is to provide 24-hour access to securities brokerage services for the benefit of its institutional customers. As a proprietary ECN, Instinet provides its institutional customers with a vehicle with which to transact their securities trading business among themselves at a lower cost and often at a better price.

All Instinet orders are basically "hit or take" orders. In other words, the order goes directly to the Instinet book, and if there is a price match, the order will be filled electronically. If there is no price match, the order will be cancelled automatically. If the price is matched but there are not enough shares available, then Instinet will provide a partial fill, which is the norm among the ECNs. All Instinet orders are limit orders and the hours of execution are 8:00 A.M. to 6:30 P.M. Eastern time.

The day trader can execute an Instinet order by preferencing INCA through the NASDAQ SelectNet. In addition, many day trading firms have a stand-alone Instinet order-execution computer on the trading floor. However, Instinet plans to set up a retail service to compete with the other ECNs. In other words, traders could open an account with Instinet and thus bypass brokers or middlemen that offer the ECN access, including Instinet. But Instinet is important not only as a vehicle that executes trade orders. Instinet transactions represent activities of large financial institutions. Those transactions can provide insight into the activities of the Wall Street professionals.

There are a few proprietary software packages that track or filter the trading activities on Instinet. First, this software keeps track of the volume of shares of a stock that is being bid and offered by the financial institutions through Instinet. Second, it keeps track of prices that are bid and offered by the financial institutions. Most important, the software will keep a record if and when there is a price differential between the stock prices on the public exchange (that is, NASDAQ) and the private exchange (that is, Instinet). This information can provide insights to the day trader on whether there is the potential for a particular stock price to go up or down.

Locked-Up Markets

Let us suppose that there is a difference in the Cisco (CSCO) stock price and share volume that are bid and offered between the public (NASDAQ) and private (Instinet) markets. Suppose that the NASDAQ ASK price is identical to the Instinet BID price. This would constitute a *locked-up market*. Since prices in the private market are generally higher than prices in the public market, this constitutes a bullish, or buy, sign,

---

Table 19.1 *Locked-Up Markets*

Instinet ASK	>	NASDAQ ASK
Instinet BID	>	NASDAQ BID
Instinet BID	=	NASDAQ ASK

because it is assumed that large financial institutions that trade large sums of money on Instinet know more about the financial markets than the individual investors and traders who trade on NASDAQ. If the Instinet BID and ASK prices are higher than the NASDAQ BID and ASK prices, this constitutes a buy signal. Table 19.1 illustrates this.

In Figure 19.1, the inside BID and ASK prices for CSCO are 50.50 and 50.625. There are three market makers buying on the BID side and two market makers selling CSCO shares on the ASK side. It is impossible to ascertain the actual size of buying and selling by the market makers, because market makers are not required to post the size. They are required only to display the minimum shares that they are willing to buy and sell. In reality, the volume flow can be many times larger than the posted minimum. Therefore, the 3-to-2 ratio of BID to ASK market makers is the only indication of the volume flow in the public market.

On the other hand, the private market (Instinet) has a different price and volume structure for this stock. The high BID and the low ASK price for CSCO on Instinet is 50.625 and 50.75. It is simple to ascertain the size of buying and selling by the financial institutions, because the participating Instinet institutions post the sizes of their bids and offers. Together the institutions are bidding to buy 21,500 shares of CSCO. On the other hand, the institutions are offering to sell only 400 shares of CSCO. Therefore, the ratio of BID to ASK volume is positive ($^{21,500}/_{400}$), and it is an indication of the actual volume flow in the private market.

Figure 19.1 reveals that the NASDAQ and Instinet markets are already locked up: the Instinet BID price and NASDAQ inside ASK prices are the same. Also, look at the buying volume of the Instinet. Once the 400 shares are sold on Instinet, financial institutions that want to purchase CSCO will move to the public market. They would start buying CSCO shares in the public market from the two market makers on the ASK side. That would clearly deplete the existing supply of CSCO shares that are being offered for sale by the two market makers at 50.625. Those market makers would quickly increase the price (due to higher demand), or they would leave the inside ASK price. Later, different market makers would come in with a new higher inside ASK price.

Figure 19.1 also displays the locked-up Instinet and NASDAQ markets with substantial Instinet BID volume. This constitutes a clear buy signal. Sometimes the Instinet and NASDAQ markets can be locked up, with the Instinet volume on the ASK side. Imagine that there are 21,500

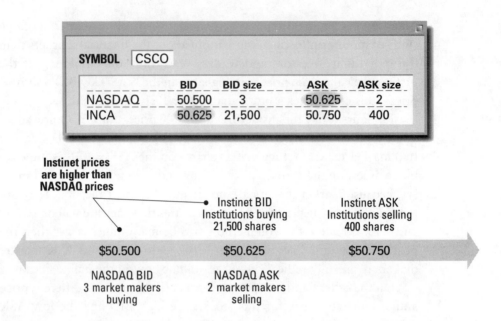

Figure 19.1 *Bullish Signal: Locked-Up Markets with Large BID Volume*

shares in the Instinet BID book and 40,000 shares in the Instinet ASK book. That would mean that there are many more Instinet sellers than there are Instinet buyers. The sheer size of the selling volume would act as a suppressing force on any future price increase.

Crossed-Up Markets

Suppose that there is a major difference in the stock price and share volume that are being bid and offered between the NASDAQ and Instinet markets. This time the NASDAQ ASK price is lower than the Instinet BID price. That would constitute a *crossed-up market*. The crossed-up market also constitutes a very strong bullish or buy signal. Table 19.2 displays the crossed-up markets. Since the prices in the private market are much higher than the prices in the public market, this constitutes a very strong bullish sign.

The difference between the locked-up and crossed-up markets is subtle. In the crossed-up markets, the Instinet BID is even higher than the NASDAQ ASK. This alone will create an arbitrage opportunity.

Table 19.2 *Crossed-Up Markets*

Instinet ASK	>	NASDAQ ASK
Instinet BID	>	NASDAQ BID
Instinet BID	>	NASDAQ ASK

In Figure 19.2, the inside BID and ASK prices for CSCO are 50.375 and 50.50. Again, there are three market makers buying on the BID side and two market makers selling CSCO shares on the ASK side. The 3-to-2 ratio of the BID to ASK market makers is the only indication of the volume flow in the public market. The private market has a dramatically different price and volume structure for this stock. The high BID and the low ASK price for CSCO on Instinet are 50.625 and 50.75. There is a $\frac{1}{8}$ spread between the Instinet BID and NASDAQ inside ASK prices. The institutions are bidding to buy 21,500 shares of CSCO and offering to sell 400 shares of CSCO. Therefore, the ratio of BID to ASK volume is positive (that is, $^{21,500}/_{400}$); it is an indication of the actual volume flow in the private market.

Since there is a major difference in the buying and selling prices of the two markets (the $\frac{1}{8}$ spread), there is potential for a price arbitrage. That means the institutional trader could buy the stock on the NASDAQ at the lower inside ASK price from two market makers, and simultaneously sell it at the higher BID price on the Instinet. This would be a riskless trading transaction. The arbitrage would result in higher demand for CSCO shares in the public market and increased supply of CSCO shares in the private market. The ultimate result would be increased CSCO prices in the public market and lowered CSCO prices in the private market. The $\frac{1}{8}$ spread between the Instinet BID and NASDAQ inside ASK prices would gradually disappear, and the markets would cease to be crossed.

Also, the buying volume on the Instinet indicates a strong potential for the price to increase. Once the 400 shares are sold on the Instinet, financial institutions that want to purchase CSCO will move to the public market. They would again start buying CSCO shares in the public market from the two market makers on the ASK side. That would again deplete the existing supply of CSCO shares that are offered for sale by the two market makers at 50.50. Those market makers would quickly increase the

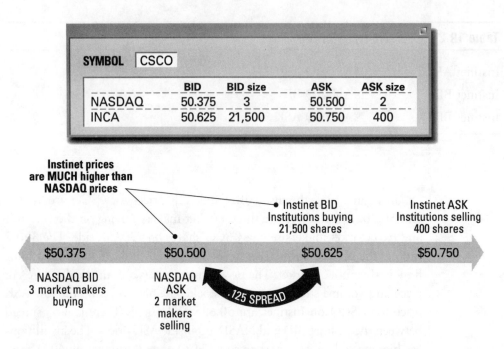

Figure 19.2 *Strong Bullish Signal: Crossed-Up Markets with Large BID Volume*

price (due to higher demand), or they would leave the inside ASK price. Later, different market makers would come in with a new higher inside ASK price. Again, the next inside ASK price would be higher (50.625).

Figure 19.2 displays the crossed-up Instinet and NASDAQ markets with the large Instinet BID volume. That constitutes a strong buy signal. The Instinet and NASDAQ markets can be crossed up, with large Instinet volume on the ASK side. Suppose that there are 21,500 shares in the Instinet BID book and 40,000 shares in the Instinet ASK book. That would mean that there are more Instinet sellers than there are Instinet buyers, and the selling volume would suppress any future price increase.

Locked-Down Markets

Suppose that there is a difference in the CSCO stock price and the share volume that are bid and offered between the public and private markets. Imagine that this time the NASDAQ BID price is same as the Instinet ASK price. That situation would constitute a *locked-down market*. Table 19.3

Table 19.3 *Locked-Down Markets*

Instinet ASK	<	NASDAQ ASK
Instinet BID	<	NASDAQ BID
Instinet ASK	=	NASDAQ BID

displays the locked-down markets. The prices in the private market (Instinet) are generally lower than the prices in the public market (NAS-DAQ), so this would constitute a bearish sign. In Table 19.3, the Instinet BID and ASK prices are lower than the NASDAQ inside BID and ASK prices; this constitutes a sell signal.

The NASDAQ inside BID and ASK prices for CSCO are 50.625 and 50.75. There are three market makers buying on the BID side and two market makers selling CSCO shares on the ASK side. The 3-to-2 ratio of the BID to ASK market makers is the only indication of the volume flow in the public market. On the other hand, the private market has a different price and volume structure for this stock. The high BID and the low ASK price for CSCO on Instinet is 50.50 and 50.625. The institutions are bidding to buy 400 shares of CSCO. Furthermore, the institutions are offering to sell only 21,500 shares of CSCO. Therefore, the ratio of BID to ASK volume is negative ($^{400}/_{21,500}$); it is an indication of the actual volume flow in the private market.

In Figure 19.3, the selling price on the private market is the same as the buying price on the public market. Also, look at the selling volume on Instinet. Once the 400 shares are bought on Instinet, financial institutions that want to sell CSCO will move to the public market. They would start dumping the large volume of CSCO shares in the NASDAQ market. The three market makers on the BID side would most likely stop buying CSCO shares that are being bid for purchase at 50.625. Those market makers would quickly lower the price due to the higher supply of CSCO coming from the institutional investors. In other words, they would leave the inside BID price, so the prices are coming down.

Figure 19.3 also displays a substantial Instinet ASK volume. The locked-down markets and the large Instinet ASK volume constitute a sell signal. Sometimes it is possible to have the Instinet and NASDAQ mar-

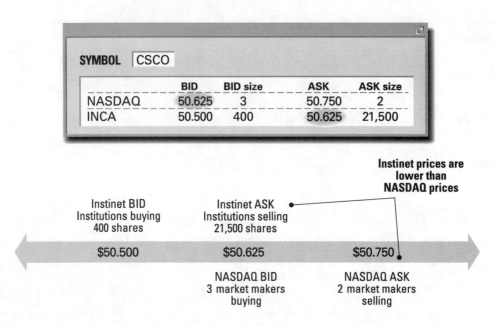

Figure 19.3 *Bearish Signal: Locked-Down Markets with Large ASK Volume*

kets locked down, and the large Instinet volume on the BID side (that is, buying side). Imagine that there are 40,000 shares in the Instinet BID book and 21,500 shares in the Instinet ASK book. That would mean that there are more Instinet buyers than Instinet sellers, and the buying volume would act as a support to any future price decrease.

Crossed-Down Markets

Again, suppose that there is a major difference between the NASDAQ and Instinet markets in the stock price and share volume that are bid and offered. This time the Instinet ASK price is much lower than the NASDAQ BID price. That situation constitutes a *crossed-down market*, as presented in Table 19.4. The crossed-down market constitutes a strong bearish or sell signal.

In the crossed-down market, the Instinet BID and ASK prices are substantially lower than the NASDAQ inside BID and ASK prices. This constitutes a strong sell signal. There is a subtle difference between the locked-down and crossed-down markets. In the crossed-down markets,

Table 19.4 *Crossed-Down Markets*

Instinet ASK	<	NASDAQ ASK
Instinet BID	<	NASDAQ BID
Instinet ASK	<	NASDAQ BID

the Instinet ASK is even lower than the NASDAQ BID. This alone will create an arbitrage opportunity. Figure 19.4 displays the crossed-down markets.

In Figure 19.4, the NASDAQ inside BID and ASK prices for CSCO are 50.625 and 50.75. Again, there are three market makers buying on the BID side and two market makers selling CSCO shares on the ASK side. The 3-to-2 ratio of the BID to ASK market makers is the only indication of the volume flow in the NASDAQ market. The Instinet market

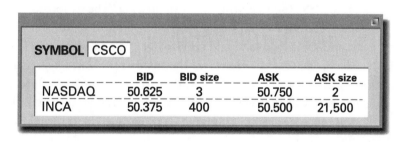

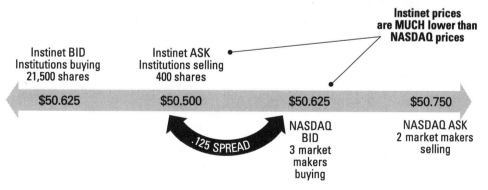

Figure 19.4 *Strong Bearish Signal: Crossed-Down Markets with Large ASK Volume*

has a dramatically different price and volume structure for this stock. The high BID and the low ASK prices for CSCO on Instinet are 50.375 and 50.50. The institutions are bidding to sell 21,500 shares of CSCO and offering to buy only 400 shares of CSCO. Therefore, the ratio of BID to ASK volume is negative ($\frac{400}{21,500}$), which is an indication of the adverse volume flow in the private market.

Both the Instinet BID and ASK prices are lower than the NASDAQ prices. The crossed market exists when the Instinet ASK price is lower than the current NASDAQ inside BID price. In fact, there is a $\frac{1}{8}$ spread between the Instinet ASK and NASDAQ inside BID prices.

Given the major difference in buying and selling prices between the two markets (the $\frac{1}{8}$ spread), there is the potential for a price arbitrage. This gives an institutional trader the chance to buy the stock on Instinet at the lower ASK price and simultaneously sell it at the higher BID price on the NASDAQ. These would be riskless trading transactions. The arbitrage would result in a higher supply of CSCO shares in the public market and increased demand of CSCO shares in the private market. The result would be lowered CSCO prices in the public market and increased CSCO prices in the private market. The $\frac{1}{8}$ spread between the Instinet BID and NASDAQ inside ASK prices would gradually disappear, and the markets would cease to be crossed.

Also, the selling volume on the Instinet indicates a strong potential for a price decrease. Once the 400 shares are bought on Instinet, financial institutions that want to sell CSCO will move to the public market. They would again start selling CSCO shares to the three market makers on the BID side. Those three market makers would quickly lower the price (due to higher selling from the institutional customers). In other words, the three market makers would leave the inside BID price. The next NASDAQ inside BID price would be lower.

Figure 19.4 also displays a large Instinet ASK volume. The crossed-down market and the large Instinet ASK volume constitute a strong sell signal. The Instinet and NASDAQ markets can be crossed down, and the large Instinet volume can be on the BID side or buying side. Suppose that there are 40,000 shares in the Instinet BID book (rather than 400 shares) and 21,500 shares in the Instinet ASK book. That would mean that there are more Instinet buyers than Instinet sellers. The buying volume would act as a support level to any future price decrease.

Basic Trading Strategies Using Instinet

The basic day trading strategy using the Instinet tool is summarized in Table 19.5. The key is to be circumspect (that is, observant) and notice when the NASDAQ and Instinet markets are crossed or locked. However, that is not an easy task. Instinet and NASDAQ price quotes are updated and changed continuously. Crossed and locked markets can disappear in seconds. The trading software that filters the price information between the two markets can provide the color-coded alerts for the crossed and locked markets. That helps a trader visualize the trading opportunities.

As a rule of thumb, the larger the spread in the crossed-up or -down markets, the stronger the trading signal. If the spread between the crossed markets is substantial, many professional traders will take the

Table 19.5 *Instinet and Day Trading Strategies*

Markets	Prices	Volume	Trading Signal
Locked up	NASDAQ ASK = Instinet BID	Large Instinet BID volume	Bullish signal
Locked up	NASDAQ ASK = Instinet BID	Large Instinet ASK volume	Weak bullish signal
Crossed up	NASDAQ ASK < Instinet BID	Large Instinet BID volume	Strong bullish signal
Crossed up	NASDAQ ASK < Instinet BID	Large Instinet ASK volume	Weak bullish signal
Locked down	NASDAQ BID = Instinet ASK	Large Instinet ASK volume	Bearish signal
Locked down	NASDAQ BID = Instinet ASK	Large Instinet BID volume	Weak bearish signal
Crossed down	NASDAQ BID > Instinet ASK	Large Instinet ASK volume	Strong bearish signal
Crossed down	NASDAQ BID > Instinet ASK	Large Instinet BID volume	Weak bearish signal

opportunity to profit from price arbitrage. Traders need to pay close attention to the actual volume being offered on the Instinet BID and ASK side. A large Instinet BID volume by itself is always a positive or bullish indicator. Conversely, a large Instinet ASK volume is always a negative or bearish indicator.

Again, using the Instinet indicator is an advanced trading strategy. First, the day trader must have access to the Instinet market data or the software that would filter and process that information. Second, it is difficult to monitor trading activities on two different markets. The opportunities to observe the price differentials between the two markets are short lived. Day traders must continuously be alert to these opportunities.

20

NYSE Orders

Every listed stock that trades on the NYSE floor is assigned a specialist, the NYSE member firm that may handle one or more stocks traded at the same trading post. The role of the specialist is to maintain a fair and orderly market in specific securities. The specialist may act in a principal capacity (as a dealer) when trading for her own accounts or may act in an agent capacity (as a broker) when executing orders for the NYSE commission house brokers.

Most likely, the specialist will remain as an agent or broker between the buyer and the seller. The specialist will seldom take on the role of the principal or dealer. The specialist will do that only in order to maintain marketability and to counter temporary imbalances in the supply and demand of a security. In other words, the specialist must maintain a continuous market by standing ready to buy when there are no bidders (buyers) or sell when there are no offerers (sellers) at the trading post. By doing so, the specialist is said to maintain a market in the security. In essence, the specialist is the only "market maker" available for that security. There is no competition among different Wall Street firms to provide liquidity for that stock. A specialist is a monopolist.

When entering the trading crowd, a broker may ask the specialist for the "size of the markets." This information will tell the broker the current prices for the highest buyer and the lowest seller. The specialist is the only person who has the complete picture regarding the demand and supply of that stock. The specialist will enter all buy and sell orders in his order book. He would then match buyers with sellers and thus maintain a fair and orderly market in that stock. The specialist may never compete with the public orders, but he can bid higher or offer lower in order to reduce the spread between the bid and offer price.

Since there is only one "market maker" for NYSE securities, there is no Level II screen information available for these securities. A day trader who does not have a seat on the exchange will not know the depth of the market at any point of time—this information is available only to the specialist on the exchange floor. Thus, day traders on the NYSE deal with a very limited set of stock information. Figure 20.1 displays what NYSE traders can observe on their screens.

The first box is essentially the Level I screen information. There is very little difference in the Level I information between the NYSE-listed

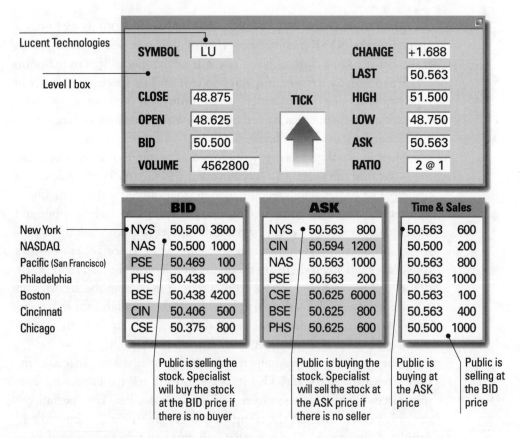

Figure 20.1 *NYSE Trading Information*

securities and the NASDAQ's over-the-counter (OTC) stocks. The only difference between the listed securities and OTC stocks is the *ratio* field. The ratio field for the OTC stocks displays the number of marker makers on the inside BID and ASK side. In this example, with Lucent Technologies (LU), there is always only one specialist. However, there are several regional exchanges, in addition to the NYSE, that trade listed securities. In Figure 20.1, there are two exchanges that furnish the highest BID or the best selling price for Lucent. On the other side, only the NYSE has the lowest ASK or the best buying price. Thus the ratio field states that there are two exchanges with the best selling price and only one exchange with the best buying price. The probability is great that the NYSE will provide the best prices for the listed stocks among different regional exchanges.

Another important distinction between the NASDAQ Level II screen and the NYSE screen is the ability to view the actual size of the inside market. In this example, the NYSE specialist has sell orders for 3,600 shares of Lucent. On the other hand, the NYSE specialist has buy orders for only 800 shares of Lucent. The day trader can deduce that there are more sellers than buyers for the stock at this price level. That could indicate a potential for the price to decrease. In this case, the ratio of selling to buying is relatively small ($^{3,600}/_{800}$), so the downward pressure is relatively small. But, imagine if there is an order to sell 36,000 shares rather than 3,600 shares. That ratio alone would indicate a large potential for the price to decline in the near future. Many day traders state that this is why they decided to trade mostly NYSE stocks—there is less information to look at and they have the ability to see the true BID and ASK size.

The NASDAQ Level II screen does not show actual shares. Market makers are required to post only the absolute minimum of shares that they are willing to buy or sell. Consequently, a bid for 1,000 shares by the market maker (on the inside BID) is misleading. The same market maker could be "sitting" on the inside BID refreshing the inside BID price and buying, for example, 100,000 shares. However, the NASDAQ Level II screen does show the depth of the market. It displays how many other market makers are willing to pay for the stock at different price ranges. The NYSE screen does not show any of that information. Day traders on the NYSE do not have access to market depth information.

The other useful information is the actual buy and sell orders that are being filled. That information is available in the Time and Sales window, which is also displayed in Figure 20.1. The day trader can see in real time whether the sales are being executed at the BID or the ASK price. The large number and size of executed sales at the ASK side would indicate a buying pattern. That would constitute a bullish sign. The large number and size of executed sales at the BID side would indicate a selling pattern; that would constitute a bearish sign. Occasionally, the Time and Sales window will display prices that are not the inside BID and ASK prices. The different prices might be old prices that are being reported with delay or the preferenced trade orders.

Therefore, there is no real Level II screen information for the listed stocks of the NYSE screen. The different exchanges are color-coded at the same price level, similar to the NASDAQ Level II screen. However, the probability is that day traders can only directly access the NYSE. The NYSE uses a system called Designated Order Turnaround (DOT and Super DOT). The DOT system allows orders to be entered by day traders from the day trading firm's trading floor directly into the NYSE computer execution system. The order bypasses the floor broker and goes directly to the NYSE specialist for execution. Therefore, even if other exchanges have better prices than the NYSE, it is impossible to route that order electronically to different exchanges.

The day trader may enter a number of different order types on the NYSE, such as market orders, limit orders, or stop orders. There are several order qualifiers that can be input by the day trader. Table 20.1 summarizes those order qualifiers. For instance, the limit orders can be limit on price (LMT), limit on close (LMT CLO), limit or better (LMT OB), stop (STOP), and stop-limit (LMT STP). Furthermore, the market orders can be current market price (MKT), market on close (MKT CLO), and market price or better (MKT OB). The following time qualifiers apply to both the limit and market orders: good until canceled (GTC), opening (OPG), fill or kill (FOK), immediate or cancel (IOC), good through date (GTD), and day order (DAY).

Most trading software recognizes immediately when a listed stock order is being sent out to the NYSE. At that time, the NYSE order execution window will appear. The day trader can then select trade order qualifiers. Most of the time, day traders are inputting simple price limit orders. Since all trading software packages have user-friendly and simple command keys to cancel an existing open order, canceling an open listed order on the Super DOT is a simple task. The NYSE hours of execution are 9:30 A.M. to 4:00 P.M. Eastern time.

Table 20.1 *NYSE Trade Order Qualifiers*

Order Qualifier	Order Description
LMT CLO	Limit order can be filled at the close of the market
LMT OB	Limit order that gives the specialist the authority to try to get the trader a better price, at his discretion
STOP	Specialist does not execute the order until it reaches a specified price and the order becomes the market order
LMT STP	Specialist will execute the order at a specified price and will cancel it if the price changes
DAY	Specialist will cancel at the end of the day
GTC	Order is good until it is canceled
GTX	Order is good until it is executed
OPG	Specialist will send out the order at the open of the next day
FOK	If the quantity of shares requested is not available in the books at the time, the order will be canceled
IOC	Trader requests an immediate fill even though it could be a partial fill
GTD	Trader can specify a certain date when order can be canceled
AON	All or None: Fill the entire order at once or reject the order

Limit Orders Strategy on the NYSE

One important distinction between the NYSE and NASDAQ is the treatment of limit orders. In order to protect individual traders and investors, the NYSE enacted rules that assign priority to customer orders over those of the specialist. In other words, the customer's limit orders will be placed in front of the specialist's orders, even if the specialist was the first in line. The day traders trading on the NASDAQ market do not have that protection.

This feature affords many trading opportunities to day traders. The day traders can continuously buy the stock on the BID and sell it on the ASK, which is a tremendous advantage. In order for a limit order to be executed, someone has to be there on the other side of the trade buying or selling the stock at the market BID and ASK price through the market orders. Specialists seldom fill these orders. It is the investors on the NYSE who are sending the market orders closing the trade. In other words, when a day trader submits a limit order to buy a stock at the BID price, the investor is selling that stock at the BID price through the market order. Conversely, when a day trader submits a limit order to sell a stock at the ASK price, the investor is buying that stock at the ASK price via the market order.

This means that the day traders on the NYSE can trade without paying the BID and ASK spread. In fact, the day traders are making the spread. On slow moving NYSE stocks with substantial trading volume, day traders can buy the stock at the BID price and sell it a few minutes later at the ASK price. Since the NYSE rule grants the day trader's limit orders preference over the specialist's orders, there is a good possibility that the order will get filled.

Trading Against the Hedge Box

NASD, which governs NASDAQ, ruled in the summer of 1998 that the NASDAQ market would no longer allow trading against the *hedge box*. However, the NYSE does not have any rules prohibiting this practice. The NYSE is an independent and self-regulated organization, which never officially adopted the NASDAQ rule prohibiting trading against the hedge box. Until the NYSE adopts that rule, grading against the hedge box is legal on NYSE.

Until the summer of 1998, trading against the hedge box was a widespread practice among professional day traders on the NASDAQ. It was a clever tool used to bypass the NASD short selling up-tick rule, which stipulated that a legal short sell must occur on the last up-tick price. The NASD stipulated that an investor or trader can short sell a stock only when the BID price bar on the software screen is green, which indicates that the last price tick is higher than the previous tick.

Unfortunately, that is the most difficult part of short selling. The day trader must bet on the stock price going down even though the last price information shows the opposite—a price increase. Wouldn't it be a lot easier if the day trader could short sell that stock on a down-tick, when the price is already declining? Fortunately, this can be accomplished on the NYSE by trading against the hedge box.

There are three types of trading accounts:

1. The Type I account, which is a cash account;

2. The Type II account, which is a margin account; and

3. The Type III account, which is a hedge account.

Most day traders will open a Type II account and trade using money deposited in that margin account. Most likely, the established margin account will be in the name of the day trader and will carry his social security number as a tax identification number.

In addition to a margin account, the day trader will need another account, which will be the Type III account or hedge account. However, the Type III account must be in the name of another person and must carry a different social security number as a tax identification number. Most likely, the day trader will use the name and social security number of his spouse or parent. Finally, the two accounts will be linked, or as securities industry folks would say, "cross-guaranteed." Equity from one account will be used to offset equity in the other account.

To create a hedge box, the day trader needs to complete two separate trading transactions. Suppose that Lucent Technologies (LU) is trading on the NYSE at 49.938 and 50. The first transaction would be to open 1,000 shares in a long position in LU at the ASK price of 50. The second transaction would be to short sell the LU stock. To sell short the stock, the day trader must ensure that:

1. LU is on the broker's short list (that is, the shortable stocks that can be borrowed from the broker); and

2. The short sell must be legal, or the last BID price must be on the up-tick (suppose that 49.938 was an up-tick and thus had a green BID price).

Figure 20.2 depicts that starting point.

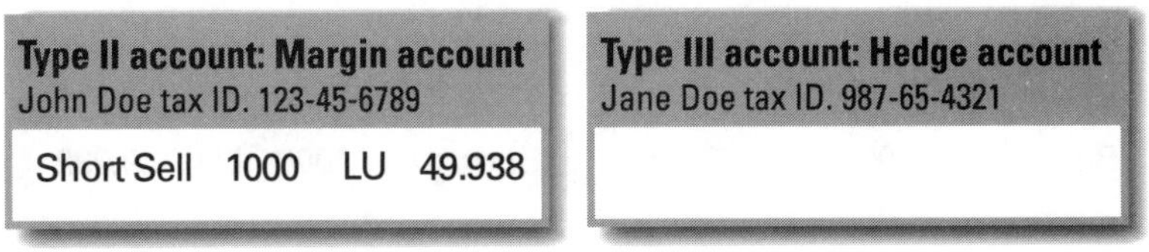

Type II account: Margin account	Type III account: Hedge account
John Doe tax ID. 123-45-6789	Jane Doe tax ID. 987-65-4321
Short Sell 1000 LU 49.938	

Figure 20.2 *Creating the Hedge Box: Step #1*

The second step is to journal (transfer) the short sell trade (1,000 LU @ 49.938) from the margin account into the hedge account. This is a relatively simple process. The day trader tells the day trading firm's office manager to journal the short sell trade from the Type II account to the Type III account. Since both accounts are linked (cross-guaranteed) and serviced (or cleared) by the same broker, this is an easy and cost-free accounting procedure. Figure 20.3 depicts this step.

The hedge box is now complete. The position in the margin account is 100% hedged, or covered, by the equivalent and opposite position in the hedge account. The day trader has two opposite open positions in two separate linked accounts:

1. The margin account has one open long position for 1,000 shares of LU; and

2. The hedge account has one short position for 1,000 shares of LU.

If the stock declines in price by 1 point, this would mean a $1,000 loss in the margin account and a $1,000 gain in the hedge account. Conversely, if the stock price goes up by 1 point, there would be a $1,000 gain in the margin account and a $1,000 loss in the hedge account. Either way, the day trader is 100% covered or hedged. The trader will not make or lose any money by keeping the equivalent long position in the margin account and short sell position in the hedge account.

If the day trader decides one day to close the hedge box, the trader would instruct the office manager to journal back the short-sell position from the hedge account into the margin account and close both positions. The short-sell position is essentially a sell position that will close the equivalent long position. In essence, the trader bought LU at 50 and sold it at 49.938, thus losing $\frac{1}{16}$ ($62.50) on that trade. When the transaction cost (the commission) is taken into account, the trader lost approximately $100 in creating this hedge box.

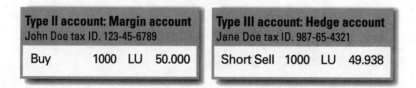

Figure 20.3   *Creating the Hedge Box: Step #2*

The NASD recognizes that the day trader's long position is 100% covered with the equivalent and opposite position in the hedge account, and thus the margin maintenance requirement is only 5% of the value of the long position and not the 50% margin requirement for Regulation T. To clarify, *Regulation T* is the federal decree governing the amount of credit that may be advanced by the NASD brokers or dealers to customers for the purchase of securities. In other words, the day trader will lose 5% of the purchasing power or approximately $2,500 by establishing this hedge box. If there are no opportunity costs for creating hedge boxes, such as the 5% loss in purchasing power, a day trader could establish hundreds of different hedge boxes. In other words, the day trader can open the maximum of 20 hedge boxes. The 5% loss in the purchasing power is the opportunity cost for opening the hedge box. In essence, the 5% of the purchasing power could have been used to purchase more stocks. Finally, professional day trading software packages are capable of monitoring hedge boxes and reminding (or informing) the day trader if a particular stock is hedged.

What is the benefit of creating a hedge box? Assume that the stock market is facing a major correction, and that most stocks, including Lucent Technologies, are declining in value. The only way a day trader can make money in a down market is to short sell. Since stock prices tend to fall at a faster pace than they tend to increase, a day trader can earn substantial sums of money in a short period of time by taking short-sell positions. However, it is difficult to make a legal short sell if prices are continuously on a down-tick (a red BID price). If the day trader submits a short-sell order on a down-tick, the specialist will hold the order until the stock up-ticks. But if the day trader has created a hedge box, the trader does not have to wait for an up-tick to make the short sell. Figure 20.4 depicts how this is done.

Since the margin account has only one long position, the day trader is allowed to close the long position and sell the stock at any time. The day trading software will recognize that the trader has a 1,000 long position in LU, and it will process the sell order for 1,000 shares of LU at 49.875. In essence, the day trader does not need to short sell the stock, but rather only to sell the stock. The day trader can simply sell the Lucent stock on a down-tick and then a few hours (or minutes) later purchase the same stock at the lower price (48.875). Selling a stock at 49.875 and then buying it at 48 will constitute one round-trip trade

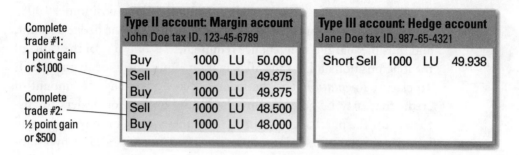

Complete trade #1: 1 point gain or $1,000

Complete trade #2: ½ point gain or $500

Type II account: Margin account			
John Doe tax ID. 123-45-6789			
Buy	1000	LU	50.000
Sell	1000	LU	49.875
Buy	1000	LU	49.875
Sell	1000	LU	48.500
Buy	1000	LU	48.000

Type III account: Hedge account			
Jane Doe tax ID. 987-65-4321			
Short Sell	1000	LU	49.938

Figure 20.4   *Trading Against the Hedge Box: Final Step*

(trade 1). In essence, the day trader earned 1 point by selling the stock at 49.875 and later buying it at 48.

Suppose that the price decline for LU continues. With the completed trade 1, the margin account shows again a 1,000-share long position in LU. Again, the day trader does not have to wait for an up-tick to short sell Lucent. The day trader can sell LU at 48.502 and then buy it a few minutes or hours later at the lower price of 48. That would constitute the second complete trade (trade 2), and this time the trader earned ½ point or $500. At the end of the trading day, the hedge box for LU will look exactly the same as it did in Figure 20.3: 1,000 shares long position in the margin account and 1,000 shares short sell position in the hedge account. When the NYSE opens for trading on the next day, the day trader is free to pursue this trading strategy again and again.

V

Day Trading Techniques

Do you remember ever seeing the warning sign, "**DANGER, HIGH VOLTAGE**," on an electrical transformer or a high-voltage power line? It dawned on me that a similar sign, "**DANGER, HIGH VOLATILITY**," could be placed on any computer that is used for day trading. In section V, we describe the tools, concepts, and trading techniques that are used by successful day traders to manage high price volatility.

➤ We begin with an overall strategy for day trading, followed by general suggestions for successful day trading. Chapter 21 will summarize all the signals that indicate the potential for price increases and decreases, as well as the indicators for overbought and oversold markets.

➤ Chapter 22 explains risk management skills and tools for day traders, which is crucial information for this business. We suggest several alternative approaches to day trading: slow, intermediate, and fast trading. We also explain in section V how day traders deal with losing streaks.

➤ Next we identify and differentiate among several day trading styles: specialist, scalper, market maker, and position trader.

➤ The psychology of day trading and the psychological characteristics of day traders is the last topic of this section. Emphasized is the need to develop a day trading plan and the ability to visualize trading. In addition, the topic of stress associated with day trading is introduced, as well as the potential stress reducers.

21

Day Trading Strategies

I**N MY OPINION, IT IS MORE IMPORTANT TO DO THE RIGHT TRADES THAN TO**
do the trades right. Many traders become preoccupied with trade-order
execution mechanics. They become very proficient in understanding the
NASDAQ and NYSE market order-execution systems. They have
learned the rules of trading and they have mastered trading-execution
software. They know how to enter and exit trades efficiently, but these
skills alone do not make them good day traders.

The most important piece of the equation is the ability to pick the
right trades. A day trader could master an order-execution system and
still lose money day trading. If the day trader consistently has a majority of losing trades, then he probably won't be in the business very long.
It is possible to be a profitable day trader even with a majority of losing
trades, but one would need to limit losses and maximize profits, which
requires a great deal of trading discipline.

The Overall Strategy

Day trading success ultimately depends on the overall impact of two
trading factors:

1. In general, a profitable day trader must have a higher percentage of
winning trades than losing trades. Let us assume that the ratio of winning to losing trades is 60% to 40%, which is a realistic assumption
given the quality and quantity of financial information available to day

traders. The long-term objective is to improve that winning percentage through time and experience.

2. The day trader must maximize the financial value or benefits derived from her winning trades and minimize the financial cost of losing trades. In other words, the dollar value from the 60% winning trades should be substantially higher than the dollar value derived from the 40% losing trades. This is when risk management becomes a crucial skill.

To improve the overall percentage of winning trades, the day trader should trade only when the odds of winning are in the day trader's favor, or when the probability of winning has increased. It is my opinion that the probability of winning increases when the following events occur:

The day trader trades on the same side of the stock trend. As day traders often state, "Trend is a friend." Again, a day trader does not need to anticipate or predict the future market trend. All she needs to do is react to existing and observable price trends. The trend can be seen on the Level II screen and on real-time technical analysis charts. There is no need to time the market turns perfectly and buy at the bottom and sell at the peak of the cycle. Also, the trader does not need to be contrarian and buy a stock when everyone else is selling it, or short the stock when everyone else is going long. That is one investment strategy, but it is not day trading.

The day trader trades on the same side of the market as the Wall Street professionals. The probability is greater that the market makers can predict future market prices more accurately than can the average day traders. If key market makers are accumulating a stock, the probability is that the stock will increase in value. Conversely, if key market makers are disposing of a stock from their inventory, the probability is that the stock will decrease in value. A common expression among day traders is, "Shadow the ax." Again, this action can be observed on the Level II screen.

The day trader does not buy overbought stocks or short the oversold stocks. He is always cognizant about a stock's intraday price resistance and support levels. That information is observable on technical analysis charts such as the Bollinger bands. (This does not preclude buying the 52-week high and short selling the 52-week low. This can be a profitable trading strategy—many good day traders simply buy higher the 52-week high and short sell lower the 52-week low.)

The day trader attempts to buy the stock at the BID price and sell at the ASK price, which is the basic trading strategy of the Wall Street professionals (the market makers and specialists). By cutting or eliminating the BID and ASK spread, the trader's profitability of the trades will increase by the amount of the eliminated spread.

The day trader should take a trading position only after observing a clear trading signal to buy or short sell the stock. Without such a clear signal, the trader is gambling.

Trading Recommendations

The following suggestions are based on the author's personal opinions. Day trading is not an exact science, and there is no bulletproof trading method or strategy that can sustain scientific scrutiny. The recommendations are presented as a list, not necessarily in order of relative ranking. Readers might disagree with one or more suggestions, and that is okay. Every trader develops her own style.

The author is not advocating that a novice trader incorporate all of the following recommendations immediately. Only experienced day traders should utilize some of the recommendations, such as the recommendation to trade expensive and volatile NASDAQ stocks in increments of 1,000 shares. Chapter 22, on risk management, elaborates further on how the novice trader should move along the ubiquitous learning curve. All of these suggestions have been mentioned previously throughout the book; the list can serve as a summary of day trading recommendations.

Day traders should consider the following:

1. *Consider trading relatively volatile stocks.* The stock's relative volatility is measured by the Beta coefficient, which tells how much a stock moves in relation to the S&P 500 Index. A stock with a Beta value of 1.5 or higher (that is, the stock is 50% more price volatile than the S&P 500 Index) would be a good start. Technology stocks usually fit this requirement. Appendix 4 lists the 100 NASDAQ and NYSE stocks that have high price volatility and daily trading liquidity. Many traders attempt to trade stocks that are not volatile, but it is difficult to make money day trading if the trading stocks are not moving, and there is no point in monitoring stocks tick by tick if prices are historically stable.

2. *Consider trading stocks that have high absolute price volatility*: stocks with a daily price range of at least 2 points. The difference between the intraday high and low stock prices should be 2 points or higher. That is how day traders make their money—through high absolute intraday price movement. It is possible to have high relative price volatility (high Beta) and low absolute volatility (low intraday price range) if a stock is inexpensive. Again, technology stocks tend to be expensive and volatile; thus they have both high relative and absolute volatility.

3. *Consider trading stocks that have high absolute liquidity.* A stock's liquidity is measured by the average daily trading volume statistics, which tell how many shares are traded on average every day. The daily trading volume should be at least 500,000 shares. It is crucial to have many buyers and sellers for a stock. If there is no liquidity (if fewer than 500,000 shares are traded daily), traders could have a difficult time getting out of the trade at the desired price. For instance, the price could drop very quickly, and the trader might simply get stuck in a long and losing position.

4. *Consider trading stocks in the right size.* Traders should start day trading with 100-share increments, but eventually they need to graduate to trading in increments of 1,000 shares. Ultimately, the objective of day trading is to trade the NASDAQ and NYSE stocks in increments of 1,000 shares and to profit from the small intraday price movement. A small relative gain of $\frac{1}{8}$ (12.5 cents) per share would result in a large absolute profit of $125 if 1,000 shares were purchased in that single trade. If the trader were to purchase only 100 shares, the profit would be only $12.50. That would not even cover the transaction cost.

5. *Trade stocks that are expensive.* Again, the objective of day trading is to profit substantially in absolute dollar terms from relatively small intraday price movements. For an expensive stock ($100 or more per share), a small relative change of 1% is 1 point, which would constitute $1,000 potential profit if 1,000 shares were purchased that day. And this is quite common and feasible. Stocks move up or down easily 1% during the trading day. On the other hand, for an inexpensive stock ($10 per share), a 1-point price change would be a large relative change of 10%. If 1,000 shares were purchased, the stock price would need to change up or down 10% to earn $1,000 potential profit. This, on the other hand, does not happen very often.

6. *Trade stocks that have a small spread*. If the trader is looking for quick order execution and a guaranteed price (for example, using SOES), then he would buy the stock from the market makers at the higher ASK price and sell the stock to the market makers at the lower BID price. If the spread is small, such as $\frac{1}{16}$, the day trader does not have to wait long for a $\frac{1}{16}$ price movement just to break even. A day trader needs to detect a small price movement, wait for the price to go up $\frac{1}{16}$, and the trader is already in the money. On the other hand, if the spread is large, such as $\frac{1}{2}$, the day trader must wait for a $\frac{1}{2}$ price movement just to break even. And that can be a long and risky wait. The only exception is if the day trader employs a specific strategy to cut the spread (for example, buy and sell in between the BID and ASK prices) through execution on the ECNs; then the stock must have a large spread.

7. *Trade stocks that have substantial depth on the BID and ASK side on the Level II screen*. The stock should have several market makers on both the BID and ASK sides. There should be many buyers and sellers for that stock to promote and ensure an easy entry and exit for that particular trade.

8. *Have a reason to trade that particular stock at that particular point in time*. Day traders should observe trading signals to buy or sell a stock. A trading signal could be a combination of several events occurring simultaneously: some would be observed on the Level II screen, and some are technical analysis indicators.

9. *Trade stocks that have a momentum or price trend*. Do not purchase or sell short a stock that is not moving at that point in time. Otherwise, you are just hoping for an appropriate outcome. The day trader would have only 50% probability of guessing and making a winning trade if there is no observable price momentum or direction. Before a day trader takes a long or short stock position, he needs to observe a series of up-ticks or down-ticks that would indicate or prove a price trend. Day traders do not need to be proactive and anticipate a price movement; they need only be reactive and follow the observable price movement.

10. *Take the stock position (long or short) that coincides with the broad market price movement (for example, S&P 500 Index) or the industry sector market movement (such as the Semiconductor Index)*. At the least, a day trader should be cognizant of the S&P 500 Index or the NASDAQ 100 Index price movement. It would be difficult to expect that one stock would appreciate in value if there were a broad stock market sell-off. The probability of making a winning trade declines if the day trader takes a position against the broad market.

11. *Be cognizant of the stock's intraday price support and resistance levels before entering the trade.* The Bollinger bands indicator is an excellent and dynamic technical analysis tool that shows real-time intraday price support and resistance levels. The problem is that day traders often enter long or short trading positions too late. The price was already at the upper or lower Bollinger band level (at the intraday support or resistance level) when the day trader decided to open the position. A trader should not purchase a stock if the stock is at the price resistance level or at the upper Bollinger band at that point in time; this is the time to seek short-selling opportunities. Conversely, the day trader should not sell short a stock if the stock is at the price support level or at the lower Bollinger band; instead, the day trader should look for buying opportunities.

12. *Be cognizant of the stock's intraday price support and resistance levels when preparing to exit the trade.* Again, some day traders often wait too long to exit or close their long or short trading positions. For example, the price may have already peaked and started to decline when the trader decided to exit the long position. By then, it could be too late. The price could be declining too fast, and a small profit could turn into a small loss. It is always better and easier to sell at the price strength, when the price is still increasing or stable and not declining. Day traders should look to exit their short positions when the price is at the price support level or the lower Bollinger band level. Conversely, day traders should seek to close their long positions when the price is at the upper Bollinger band or the price resistance level.

13. *Consider using predominately limit buy orders rather than market buy orders,* thus controlling the entry price. In addition, limit orders will help the trader obtain a better price by attempting to buy at the BID price and sell at the ASK price.

14. *Consider using the ECNs rather than SOES when trading on the NASDAQ.* That would help in buying the stock at the BID price and selling it at the ASK price.

I have mentioned before that the day trader must first observe a signal to buy or sell a stock before executing a trade. Too many times, a day trader enters a trade based on a gut feeling. Gut feeling is not good enough. Since there is no such thing as a crystal ball to predict future outcomes, the next best device would be a signal that indicates a potential for price movement. Some trading signals are observable on the Level II screen, and some are derived from technical analysis indicators.

All signals need not occur simultaneously to generate a clear buy or sell signal. The trading universe does not have to be lined up perfectly for the day trader to decide to buy or sell a security. However, the day trader must be able to recognize and understand the majority of listed signals in order to detect the price trend.

Potential for Price Increase

Following is a summary of observable events that characterize potential for price increase for a particular stock. They are the buy signals to open a long position and close a short position. If the list refers to Level II information and market makers, the listed events apply to NASDAQ stocks. When there is no reference to the Level II screen or to market makers, the event can be applied to the NYSE as well.

1. A series of green or up-tick BID and ASK prices showing on the Market Ticker window for a particular stock. That is the alert that prices are moving up.

2. Counterclockwise movement on the Level II screen as more market makers leave the inside ASK and join the inside BID. For example, a day trader should be able to detect on the Level II screen any price quote that is moving up from the bottom of the ASK side to the top of the ASK side. Then, that price quote would jump over from the ASK side to the top of the BID side, and eventually move down to the bottom of the BID side.

3. The first market maker enters a new high BID price. That would create a new higher BID price. That would clearly state that one market maker is willing to pay more for that security than the other market makers.

4. The last market maker leaves the inside ASK price. Thus the higher ASK becomes the new inside ASK price. The new higher inside ASK price becomes the best selling price, which would mean that the public is buying and the market makers are selling at the higher price.

5. An "ax" or a key market maker has joined the inside BID price on the Level II screen. That would mean that the ax is buying the stock.

6. An ax or a key market maker has refreshed the inside BID price on the Level II screen. That would mean that the ax continues to buy that stock. After being hit for the order, the market maker chooses to maintain the same inside BID price.

7. An ax or a key market maker has left the inside ASK price on the Level II screen. That would mean that ax has stopped selling that stock. After being hit for the order, the market maker chooses not to maintain the same inside ASK price.

8. A market maker simultaneously leaves the inside ASK and joins the inside BID price. That would mean that the market maker has stopped selling the stock and has instead become the buyer of that stock.

9. The buying trades are going off at ASK price on the Time and Sales window. That would indicate that the public is buying the stock.

10. The buying trades are going off at 500 or 1,000 shares of volume on the Time and Sales window. That would indicate substantial acquisition volume. In other words, it would indicate that the public is buying a substantial quantity of shares.

11. There is a crossover between the Fast Exponential Moving Average (Fast EMA) line and the Slow Exponential Moving Average line. In other words, the Fast EMA, which in our earlier example consisted of three observations of one-minute interval data, has crossed over and above the Slow EMA line, which in our earlier example was built from nine observations of one-minute interval data.

12. The MACD line is positive and is increasing at an increasing rate. That would indicate divergence between the Fast and Slow EMA lines. In other words, the Fast EMA is increasing at a faster rate than the Slow EMA line. Bulls in the stock market are getting stronger.

13. The price has reached the lower Bollinger band, which constitutes the intraday price support level.

14. The momentum indicator (MOM) is positive and is increasing at an increasing rate. That would mean that there is a price increase momentum at this point in time. From the earlier example, the current stock price is higher now than the stock price nine minutes ago.

15. The price and On-Balance Volume (OBV) indicator move in the same direction. If both the price and OBV are moving up, the trend is considered strong. However, if the current price is going up and the running cumulative OBV line is declining, then divergence exists, and there is a distinct possibility of price reversal.

Figure 21.1 summarizes and displays graphically the information on a Level II screen that would characterize potential for a price increase for a particular stock. Figure 21.2 displays graphically the information available on technical analysis screens that would characterize potential for a price increase for a particular stock.

Potential for Price Decrease

The following list is a summary of observable events that characterize the potential for a price decrease for a NASDAQ stock. These are the sell signals to open a short position and close a long position.

1. There are a series of red or down-tick BID and ASK prices showing on the Market Ticker window for a particular stock. Prices are going down.

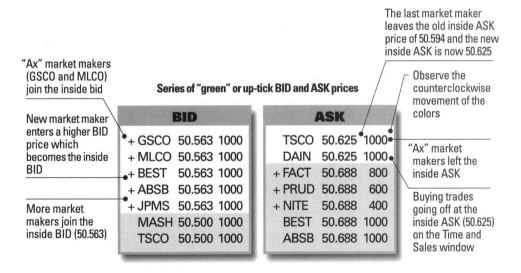

Figure 21.1   *Level II Information That Indicates Potential for Price Increase*

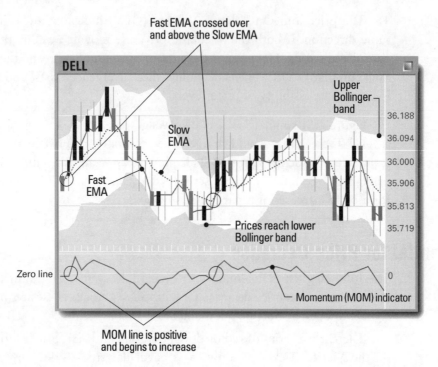

Figure 21.2 *Technical Analysis Information That Indicates Potential for Price Increase*

2. The day trader should be able to observe the clockwise movement on the Level II screen as more market makers leave the inside BID and join the inside ASK price. For example, a day trader should be able to detect on the Level II screen any price quote that is moving up from the bottom of the BID side to the top of the BID side. Then, that price quote would jump over from the BID side to the top of the ASK side, and eventually move down to the bottom of the ASK side.

3. The first market maker enters a new lower ASK price, to create a new lower ASK price, and would clearly indicate that one market maker is willing to sell that security for less than the other market makers.

4. The last market maker leaves the inside BID price. Thus the lower BID becomes the new inside BID price. The new lower inside BID price becomes the best buying price, which would mean that the public is selling and market makers are buying at the lower price.

5. An ax or key market maker has joined the inside ASK price on the Level II screen. That would mean that the ax is selling the stock.

6. An ax or key market maker has refreshed the inside ASK price on the Level II screen. That would mean that the ax continues to sell that stock. After being hit for the order, the market maker chooses to maintain the same inside ASK price.

7. An ax or key market maker has left the inside BID price on the Level II screen. That would mean that the ax has stopped buying that stock. After being hit for the order, the market maker chooses not to maintain the same inside BID price.

8. A market maker simultaneously leaves the inside BID and joins the inside ASK price. That would mean that the market maker has stopped buying the stock and has instead become the seller of that stock.

9. The selling trades are going off at the BID price on the Time and Sales window. That would indicate that the public is selling the stock.

10. The selling trades are going off at 500 or 1,000 shares of volume on the Time and Sales window. This would indicate substantial stock distribution volume. In other words, it would indicate that the public is selling a substantial quantity of shares.

11. There is a crossover between the Fast Exponential Moving Average (Fast EMA) line and the Slow Exponential Moving Average line (Slow EMA). In other words, the Fast EMA has crossed over and below the Slow EMA line.

12. The MACD line is negative and is decreasing at an increasing rate. This would indicate divergence between the Fast and Slow EMA lines. In other words, the Fast EMA is decreasing at a faster rate than the Slow EMA line. Bears in the stock market are getting stronger.

13. The price has reached the upper Bollinger band, which constitutes the intraday price resistance level.

14. The day trader should be able to observe that the momentum indicator (MOM) is negative and is decreasing at an increasing rate. That means that there is a price decrease momentum at this point in time.

15. Finally, the day trader would like to observe that the price and On-Balance Volume (OBV) indicator are moving in the same direction. If both the price and OBV are moving down, then the downward trend is considered strong. However, if the current price is going down and the

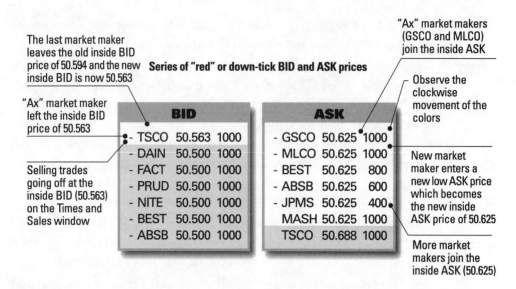

The last market maker leaves the old inside BID price of 50.594 and the new inside BID is now 50.563

Series of "red" or down-tick BID and ASK prices

"Ax" market makers (GSCO and MLCO) join the inside ASK

Observe the clockwise movement of the colors

"Ax" market maker left the inside BID price of 50.563

Selling trades going off at the inside BID (50.563) on the Times and Sales window

New market maker enters a new low ASK price which becomes the new inside ASK price of 50.625

More market makers join the inside ASK (50.625)

BID		
- TSCO	50.563	1000
- DAIN	50.500	1000
- FACT	50.500	1000
- PRUD	50.500	1000
- NITE	50.500	1000
- BEST	50.500	1000
- ABSB	50.500	1000

ASK		
- GSCO	50.625	1000
- MLCO	50.625	1000
- BEST	50.625	800
- ABSB	50.625	600
- JPMS	50.625	400
MASH	50.625	1000
TSCO	50.688	1000

Figure 21.3 *Level II Information That Indicates Potential for Price Decrease*

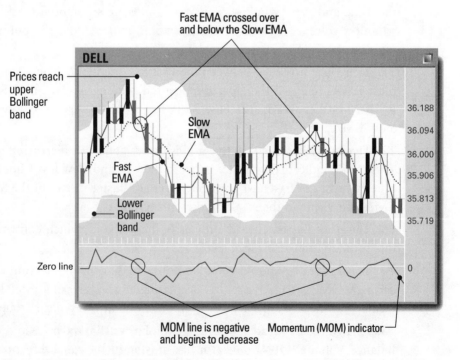

Fast EMA crossed over and below the Slow EMA

Prices reach upper Bollinger band

Slow EMA

Fast EMA

Lower Bollinger band

Zero line

MOM line is negative and begins to decrease

Momentum (MOM) indicator

Figure 21.4 *Technical Analysis Information That Indicates Potential for Price Decrease*

running cumulative OBV line is increasing, then divergence exists, and there is a distinct possibility of a price reversal.

Figure 21.3 summarizes and displays graphically the information on a Level II screen that would characterize potential for a price decrease for a particular stock. Figure 21.4 displays graphically the information on a technical analysis screen that would characterize potential for a price decrease for a particular stock.

Overbought and Oversold Indicators

The following are alerts for overbought and oversold markets. An over-bought market means that prices have risen too steeply and too fast; an oversold market means that prices have fallen too steeply and too fast. The two overbought and oversold indicators are the MACD and stochastic indicators. They show when prices have moved too far and too fast in either direction and thus are vulnerable to a reaction.

When the MACD line is negative and moving up toward the zero line, that indicates convergence between the Fast and Slow EMA lines. In other words, the Fast EMA is decreasing at a slower rate than the Slow EMA line. It is an indicator of an oversold market; bears in the stock market are losing steam. The oversold indicator occurs when the Fast Stochastic (%K) line has reached 25 or goes below 25.

Conversely, an overbought indicator would be a positive MACD line that is decreasing and moving down toward the zero line, indicating convergence between the Fast and Slow EMA lines. In other words, the Fast EMA is increasing at a slower rate than the Slow EMA line. Bulls in the stock market are losing steam. An indicator of the overbought market occurs when the Fast Stochastic (%K) line has reached 75 or goes above 75. An additional indicator of the overbought market occurs when the RSI has reached 70 or goes above 70.

22

Risk Management

To SURVIVE AND PROSPER IN THE DAY TRADING BUSINESS THE MOST important ingredients for success are risk management, risk management, and risk management. This is probably the most important topic of this book. The day trader's risk management skills will make the difference in whether she succeeds or fails in this business. And those skills are particularly relevant for new day traders.

In my opinion, the mission for new day traders is not to make money initially. In fact, the novice day trader should expect to lose money at the beginning. The learning curve for the day trading profession is steep and expensive. The day trader's objective should be long-term survival. If a novice day trader stays in the business six months from the opening of a trading account, it is probable that the day trader is making a profit. If the novice day trader stays in this business after one year from the opening of the trading account, then there is a strong probability that the day trader is making a six-figure annual income.

It is easy to lose money day trading. Day traders commonly trade the most volatile and expensive high-tech NASDAQ stocks in increments of 1,000 shares. A 1-point loss when trading 1,000 shares of a volatile Internet stock translates into a $1,000 loss. Before one is ready to trade these stocks in large increments, one has to go up the learning curve, and that learning curve is steep. However, the learning curve does not have to be expensive. It is my opinion that most people lose money day trading because they start live day trading before they are ready. Furthermore, when they do start day trading, they start trading volatile and expensive stocks in large increments. That is a recipe for losing a lot of money quickly.

The key to survival is to start slowly, and gradually move up. A child has to learn to crawl before he can walk. Only after the child has mastered walking can he attempt to run. I remember how long it took my son to learn to hold a pencil properly. For years, he would hold a pencil as a stick. It took three years or so for him to master a skill that seems by adult standards to be notably elementary. The same analogy can be applied to day trading. What seems simple and obvious to experienced day traders is obscure and complex for the novice trader. It takes time to pick up those trading skills.

Starting slowly is the paramount consideration. It is the best way to ensure that the novice day trader does not "blow up" in the first few months of day trading. It is very easy to blow up at the beginning, when the novice day trader will make many errors and mistakes. Those mistakes could be inputting order errors (pressing the wrong key) or misreading the market direction (making the wrong trade). The novice day trader cannot possibly eliminate all errors and mistakes; mistakes are part of the learning process. The first objective is to minimize the number of mistakes. The second objective is to minimize the cost of those mistakes and to learn from them. Those mistakes do not need to be expensive.

The Slow Trading Approach

The slow day trading approach is the conservative approach. This slow approach provides an opportunity to learn the business gradually without losing a lot of money. The first step is to select slow stocks—stocks that do not move very fast. They tend to be relatively stable and do not move very much or fast in either price direction, so the reaction time is much longer, thus the novice day trader has plenty of time to react to the price movement and to get the order executed.

The color-coded price levels on the Level II screen for slow stocks do not "fly" as fast as those of more volatile stocks. BID and ASK prices move at a slower pace, so the novice day trader can visualize the price movement. She can see and interpret the price movement on the Level II screen. It is possible to visualize and determine who among the market makers is buying and selling a particular stock, and once the price trend is ascertained, the novice day trader has time to react and execute an order before the price moves away.

On the other hand, "fast" stocks such as expensive Internet stocks simply move too fast. The day trader does not have time to react. At one moment the price is going up, and a few moments later the price is going down. It is difficult to ascertain a trend. A good analogy would be that the day trader is surrounded by trees (the real-time stock price ticks) and cannot see the forest (the stock price trend). Furthermore, since the price is moving fast, it is difficult to get the order filled at the desired price level. A novice day trader may submit a limit buy order, but by the time the trader gets the time and courage to press the correct execution key, the stock price has already moved up, and the order does not get filled.

Slow stocks tend to be inexpensive stocks with a price less than $20 and more than $5 per share (there is no point in day trading penny stocks, stocks valued at $5 or less). Because they are relatively inexpensive, the stocks do not move a lot in absolute dollar terms. However, the slow stocks might be as volatile as the fast stocks in relative (that is, percentage change) terms, and may have a high Beta, just like the fast stocks, so the relative volatility might be the same. Although the slow stocks' prices might move with the same percentage magnitude as the fast stocks, it is the absolute dollar change that counts. The 5% price change for the $20 stock is only 1 point. On the other hand, a 5% price change for a $100 stock is 5 points. For the novice day trader, it is easier to follow stocks that move 1 point in a day than those that move 5 points in a day.

A price movement of $\frac{1}{4}$ or $\frac{1}{2}$ is a real price trend for a slow stock because it represents a relatively high percentage change in price. That is a real price movement, so it is possible to observe the market forces of supply and demand that generated the price movement. For example, one could observe a buildup of market makers on the inside BID side and a reduction in the number of the market makers on the inside ASK.

On the other hand, the $\frac{1}{4}$ or $\frac{1}{2}$ is a relatively small percentage change in price for fast, expensive stocks, such as Internet stocks. That is noise in the market and is not a real price movement. It is more difficult to detect the market forces of supply and demand that generate price movement for fast stocks. The fast stocks can continuously gyrate up and down without any discernible price pattern. Thus it is easy to get "jiggled out" when trading the fast stocks.

For example, a novice day trader opens a long stock position after observing on the computer screen a few price up-ticks and anticipating continued price increase momentum. A few minutes (or seconds) after the order confirmation, the trader observes a few price down-ticks on the screen. She quickly gets out of the long position at a small loss, but a loss nevertheless. She then decides to open a short position, anticipating a continued downward price movement. After the short-sale order confirmation has been received, the novice trader discovers a few price up-ticks on the screen for that stock. In order to minimize the loss, the trader quickly gets out of the short position at a small loss. Two trades later the novice trader is down a few hundred dollars. The trader was jiggled out of a few hundred dollars by the market makers.

The slow approach, which consists of trading slow, inexpensive stocks, assures that the novice day trader will not get easily jiggled out by market gyrations. The trader would be able to ascertain or visualize real price movement. At that time, the novice day trader would go with the trend.

In addition, trading slow stocks would also limit the initial number of trading transactions. Fewer transactions limit the number of possible mistakes, which further enhances the probability of long-term survival. Fewer transactions, of course, also limits the potential to make money. However, the objective of the novice day trader is not to make money initially, but to learn to day trade. The focus is on long-term trading continuation. In order to make money day trading in the long run, the novice day trader must survive in the short run.

The most important step that the novice day trader can undertake initially is to start day trading in increments of 100 shares. Trading slow stocks will minimize the total number of losing trades. Trading in increments of 100 shares will minimize the cost of those mistakes. The novice day trader cannot avoid making losing trades. It is realistic to expect that a novice day trader will have two-thirds winning trades and one-third losing trades. With time and experience, the percentage of winning trades should increase. If the novice trader starts day trading in increments of 1,000 shares, then one small trading mistake with a price change of $\frac{1}{8}$ would translate into a $125 loss. It is easy to make a $\frac{1}{8}$ mistake, and $125 mistakes can quickly add up.

It is much preferred to trade in increments of 100 shares. Then one small trading mistake with a price change of $\frac{1}{8}$ would translate into only a $12.50 loss, which the novice day trader can afford to absorb. The novice trader can afford to make many small mistakes (that is, $\frac{1}{8}$ price change mistakes), learn something from each mistake, and still be as well off as with one $\frac{1}{8}$ small mistake when trading in 1,000 share blocks. It is my firm advice to all new day traders to start trading in increments of 100 shares.

However, it is true that it is very difficult to make money day trading if one trades in increments of 100 shares. If the round-trip trading transaction cost (commission) is $37.50, and if the day trader is trading in increment of 100 shares, then the stock price needs to go up (or down for the short sell) $\frac{3}{8}$ just to break even on that trade. The price movement of $\frac{3}{8}$ is substantial and indicates real price movement for the inexpensive, slow stocks. But remember, the objective of the novice day trader is not to make money initially, but to learn to day trade. Again, the focus is on long-term day trading existence.

Therefore, it is my recommendation that a novice day trader start with 100 shares and increase the trading allotment 100 shares each week. With each passing day, the novice day trader should learn something from past mistakes. Trading in allotments of 100 shares ensures that mistakes are not expensive, and that trading capital is preserved. The second week, the novice day trader can increase the allotment from 100 shares to 200 shares. That is my recipe for minimizing the overall cost of learning the day trading business.

The Intermediate Trading Approach

The intermediate trading approach is somewhere in between the slow and fast approaches. It is risky to jump from the slow to the fast approach overnight. However, the intermediate trading approach provides a soft landing. The first step is to select intermediate stocks, which do not move as fast as some of the expensive Internet stocks. Such stocks tend to be somewhat stable and do not move extremely fast in either price direction, so the trader's reaction time is somewhat manageable. Thus the intermediate day trader has sufficient time to react to the price movement and to get the trade order executed.

Intermediate stocks—stocks with prices between $20 and $50—are more expensive than slow stocks. They might be just as volatile as the fast stocks in relative percentage change terms. The intermediate stocks might have a high Beta value, but it is the absolute dollar change that counts. A 5% price change for a $50 stock is 2.5 points. On the other hand, a 5% price change for a $100 stock is 5 points. The intermediate day trader would have an easier time following stocks that move 2.5 points in a day than those that move 5 points in a day.

Since the intermediate stocks are more expensive, the $\frac{1}{4}$ point is a relatively small percentage change in price. The $\frac{1}{4}$ price movement is a noise in the market. It is not a real price trend. My point is that the $50 stocks continuously gyrate up and down without any discernible price pattern, and it is easy to get jiggled out when trading those stocks. Day traders should always be aware of that danger.

The next step that the intermediate day trader can undertake is to trade in increments of 500 shares. This will somewhat limit the cost of wrong trades. If the day trader trades in increments of 500 shares, one small trading mistake with a price change of $\frac{1}{8}$ would translate into only a $62.50 loss. It is better to lose $62.50 than $125.

It is also possible to make money day trading if the day trader trades in increments of 500 shares. If the round-trip trading transaction cost is approximately $32, and if the day trader is trading in increments of 500 shares, then the stock price needs to go up or down only $\frac{1}{16}$ to break even on that trade. A price movement of approximately $\frac{1}{16}$ is immaterial and quite common. Trading in allotments of 500 shares would ensure that mistakes do not add up quickly into an enormous loss.

The Fast Trading Approach

The fast trading approach is the domain of experienced day traders. It is an aggressive trading approach. The focus of attention is on fast stocks: those stocks whose prices move extremely fast. The stocks tend to be the expensive (greater than $50 per share) and volatile Internet and high-technology stocks. They are extremely volatile and move notably fast in either price direction. Consequently, the trader's reaction time is very short. The fast day trader does not have much time to react to the price movement and to get the order executed.

Again it is the absolute dollar price change that counts. A 5% price change for a $150 stock is 7.5 points. The fast day trader must be attentive throughout the day in order to follow the stock that moves 7.5 points in a day. A $\frac{1}{2}$ point is a relatively small percentage change in price for stocks priced at $150. It is a noise in the market and not a real price trend. The $150 stock would continuously gyrate up and down without any discernible price pattern, and it is very easy to get jiggled out when trading those stocks.

The fast day trader usually trades in increments of 1,000 shares. Trading in increments of 1,000 shares exposes the day trader to substantial loss due to bad trades. But, high risk is associated with high returns. Day trading in increments of 1,000 shares is the best way to make a lot of money. If the round-trip trading transaction cost is approximately $32, and if the day trader is trading in increments of 1,000 shares, then the stock price needs to go up or down only $\frac{1}{32}$ to break even on that trade. Again, the price movement of approximately $\frac{1}{32}$ is immaterial and common. It happens all the time. However, a $\frac{1}{32}$ price movement can go in the wrong direction as well. Trading in an allotment of 1,000 shares guarantees that trading mistakes are expensive.

Losing Money

Why have so many people failed with day trading? Why is it that so many people have lost money when, on the surface, day trading is deceptively simple? The answer, my friends, lies in the size of the trading transaction. The core of day trading is to trade in increments of 1,000 shares or more and to exploit the frequent short-term price volatility of stocks and earn small incremental profits. Trading in 1,000-share increments is a double-edged sword. On the upside, a day trader can quickly earn $125 profit if the price goes in the favorable direction by a single $\frac{1}{8}$ of a point. Conversely, the day trader can quickly lose $125 if the price goes in the opposite direction by $\frac{1}{8}$ of a point.

This is where the trader's discipline comes in! The key is to minimize or control the losses. If $\frac{1}{8}$ is your loss limit, then do not lose more than $125 on a trade. If $\frac{1}{4}$ is your loss limit, then do not lose more than $250 on a trade. Either way, stick with your self-imposed loss limit. For instance, if a price drops $\frac{1}{4}$ of a point, get out of the trade. Do not wait for your $250 loss to turn into a higher loss! Minimize the downside, and maximize the upside. That is the secret to success. However, many new day traders do not have the required discipline. They allow a small loss to turn into a large loss. They wait too long, so that an initial $\frac{1}{8}$ or $\frac{1}{4}$ loss turns into a $\frac{3}{8}$ or $\frac{1}{2}$ loss or an even larger loss.

Know your exit price points in advance for your losing trades (as well as your winning trades). Visualize your trade before you make it. If the trade is a winning trade, plan your exit price. More important, if the trade is a losing trade, stick to your loss limit strategy.

In addition, all accounts are margin accounts. So there is an issue of 2-to-1 financial leverage (the 50% Regulation T margin requirement). For instance, a $10,000 initial deposit creates $20,000 buying power. However, leverage works in both directions. Positive leverage happens when a day trader quickly picks up $\frac{1}{4}$ point or a $250 gain on a relatively small initial investment (the initial account deposit).

Conversely, negative leverage occurs when a day trader quickly loses a $\frac{1}{4}$ or a $250 loss. If the day trader lost only $250 every trading day, the entire equity would be wiped out in two months. Because of 2-to-1 leverage, it is possible to lose more money than one's initial account deposit.

Risk Management Tools

The following six measures are the day trading risk management tools. All day traders, regardless of their relative experience, can easily apply them. These measures are my suggestions, and they will only limit risk exposure, not eliminate all day trading risk. Furthermore, the measures will not guarantee that a day trader will be successful. The risk management measures are ranked in order, although the ranking is only my personal opinion.

1. The first and foremost risk management measure is to go flat at the end of the trading day. The day trader should close all of her open positions at the close of the market. There are many reasons for doing so. First, this eliminates any overnight risk exposure, since the market forces of supply and demand remain active after market close. Institutional investors and traders continue to trade after the market hours through Instinet. Corporations wait for the market to close to announce corporate news. The federal government issues economic reports at 8:00 A.M.

Eastern time. There are many exogenous reasons that can influence a stock to open with a price gap.

By keeping an overnight position, the day trader risks a lot to save a little. All the day trader could possibly save is the commission cost. And since the commissions are deeply discounted, the day trader is not saving a lot. If the day trader believes that the stock will continue to appreciate in value, the trader always has an option to buy the same stock when the market opens. If the stock opens with the gap up, the day trader is also forgoing the value of that upward gap. But that is a big *if*. The potential reward of earning additional money from the gap does not justify the substantial risk that comes with overnight long or short positions.

One of the most important advantages that day traders have is the ability to be in control of the trading portfolio. Day traders can observe price momentum tick by tick, and if the traders are wrong they can get out of that position quickly. The day trader is always in full control. If the day trader keeps an overnight long or short position, the trader has abdicated that trading control. He has to wait for the next day to resume control over his money.

In essence, if you are a day trader, do not let yourself become an investor.

2. The second crucial risk management tool is to get out of losing trades. The day trader must react to the market activity. If the price is going up, the day trader should open the long position. Suppose that the day trader is wrong. The long position is losing money. The price of the stock has reversed its trend, and now it is going down. The day trader has received a clear signal to get out. In fact, every down-tick is a signal to the day trader to get out. The day trader then has two choices: (1) Get out of the stock immediately and minimize the loss, or (2) hold on to the long position and hope for a price reversal.

Hope is a four-letter word. It is not good to hope. A day trader who hopes that the open stock position will turn around has abdicated control over her trading money. Yes, it is possible that the position could reverse and the stock price might bounce back. Yes, it is even possible that the losing position could turn into a profitable trade. Yes, everything is possible. But how likely is that to occur? What is the probability that the stock will bounce back? If a day trader can't logically ascertain the probability of a price reversal occurring, the day trader should close that position immediately. It is the only prudent thing to do.

The day trader should not wait for a small loss to turn into a bigger loss. The trader needs to get out of that losing long position as quickly as possible. How many price signals (price down-ticks) does it take to convince that trader that he was wrong on that trade? Is it $\frac{1}{8}$ or $\frac{1}{4}$ or $\frac{3}{8}$? If he is trading in 1,000-share blocks, does the trader need to lose $125 or $250 or $375 before admitting that he was wrong?

My advice is not to "marry" the losers. In other words, do not get attached to losing stock trades. The stock price is going in a different direction than anticipated. Listen to the market. See the obvious. Do not fight the ticker tape. Get out of that position! New day traders must learn to admit they were wrong—and that is the key—admitting that your trade was wrong and moving on to the next trade.

3. The day trader must set loss limits. The levels of loss limits will vary among day traders. The loss limit depends on the day trader's trading style, the amount of trading capital available, the level of day trading experience, and individual willingness to assume risk. Nevertheless, the day trader must retain those self-imposed loss limits throughout the trading day. The loss limit could be $\frac{1}{4}$ or $\frac{3}{8}$ or $\frac{1}{2}$ of a point, or even higher, such as 1 point, if the trader has a large account. However, 1 point should be the maximum loss that a day trader would lose on a single trade.

The circumstance that the day traders can control in their day trading endeavor is the amount of their losses. They can somewhat influence the profits or the upside aspects of the day trading business. They can decide whether to enter a stock position or not. They can decide when to close an open a position so they have control over the exit strategy. But the day trader does not know how much money she will make on any position. If prices are going up, the day trader will continue holding that position. The amount of profit will depend on the strength of that price increase momentum. However, day traders must manage their losses, or the downside aspect of the business. That is the key to trading success: Use control to minimize the downside, and try to maximize the upside.

Another loss limit device is to set an absolute dollar amount that the day trader is willing to lose for one day of trading. As stated, the absolute dollar loss amount will vary among day traders; it will depend on the day trader's available trading capital and individual willingness to assume risk. The amount could be $500 or $800 or $1,000 or higher. Everyone will have bad trading days. The key is to contain how expensive the bad trading days are. They do not have to be expensive. If trading is not going in the right direction one day, close your open positions and go home to reenergize. The next day might be different. There is always the next day.

Furthermore, the day trader should also set an absolute dollar amount that he would be willing to lose for one week of trading. That amount should be higher than the loss limit imposed for the day losses. However, it should not be proportionately higher (for example, five times higher). It would be unrealistic to expect that the day trader will lose the maximum loss amount every single day. If that is the case, the day trader does not know what he is doing. Go back to the drawing board. The day trader should reassess his entire day trading strategy and ultimately appraise whether day trading is a suitable business.

4. If the stock price is moving quickly against the trader's position, the trader should get out of that position quickly. Too often, the day trader admits that a trade was bad and decides to get out, but instead of getting out in the fastest possible way, which is through the SOES market order, the trader tries to extract a better price. Instead of selling the stock at the best BID price via the SOES market order, the trader attempts to submit an offer to sell at the inside ASK or lower ASK price (that is, $\frac{1}{16}$ lower ASK) through an ECN such as Island.

Since the stock price is dropping fast, the probability is low that the offer to sell at the ASK will get filled. At that time, the trader will attempt to resubmit a new offer to sell at the new ASK, which is lower than the previous ASK price. Again, the probability is low that the offer to sell will get filled, because the stock price is falling quickly. By the time the trader drops the idea of offering the stock for sale through the ECNs and executes the SOES market order at the inside BID price, the BID price is already down. The trader has lost money trying to pick up a $\frac{1}{16}$ higher selling price. The inside BID price is now lower than it was a few moments ago.

5. Another common risk exposure is to pyramid the stock position. The day trader starts with a 1,000-share long or short position. Then the trader quickly adds a few thousand more shares to the existing open position. (Obviously, that is subject to availability of trading funds.) If the stock price quickly reverses its course, the trader would have trouble selling several thousand shares quickly. The day trader eventually sells all the shares, and it is likely that the obtained average selling price is lower than the price obtained if the block had only been 1,000 shares.

6. Another risk exposure is to open multiple stock positions. The day trader starts with a 1,000-share long or short position, and then adds several other different stocks to the existing open position. (Again, that is all subject to availability of trading funds.) It is not a simple task to monitor numerous open positions. Experienced traders can do it because they have been doing it for a long time. Inexperienced traders have a difficult time doing it. The probability is that they will miss several opportunities to close the open positions at a better price. They might miss the trading signals. They might miss the price reversals. It is my opinion that new day traders should stick with only one open position at a time. With time and experience, day traders can add one or two more open positions.

The Losing Streak

Every day trader will sooner or later face a losing streak. Sometimes that losing streak can be so pronounced and severe that it challenges the trader's confidence. The question is not whether the losing streak will happen, but what to do when it does happen. So what can be done?

1. My advice would be to stop losing money. At first sight, this advice seems comical. But bear with me. If the losing streak is pronounced, stop trading for a few days. Take a break. Take time off and recharge your batteries. The market will be there when you come back. With a fresh, reenergized mind, you might find the trading outcome to be different. The point is that you have stopped losing money. During the time off from day trading, take a look at your losing trades. Print a price chart of the stocks that are responsible for the losing streak that day, and mark all of your buy and sell points. Examine the buying and selling decisions. Try to understand why those trades were bad. Try to learn from your mistakes.

2. Also, go back to the basics. Reexamine and reevaluate your trading style. Keep a trading diary. Write down the reasons for entering the trades. See whether those reasons passed the reality test. Write down the reasons for exiting the trades. See whether the exit strategies are efficient. Look for your individual trading patterns. The worst option is to blame something or someone else for the losses. Do not blame the losses on bad luck. Luck has nothing to do with the recurring losses. Traders are individually responsible for their own losses.

3. When the day trader comes back to trade reenergized, the key is to reverse the losing streak. The objective is to score profitable trades, regardless of how small the profit is. In other words, place anything green on the board. If it is a $\frac{1}{16}$ gain, take it. Sell it for the small gain. The focus is to rebuild confidence. Again, the objective is to stop bleeding, or stop losing money. Any trading gain is a step in the right direction.

4. Reduce the trading share size. If the day trader is commonly trading in increments of 1,000 shares, then drop the size to 500 shares. That would alleviate some of the pressure of losing a lot of money. If there is a loss, it is not dramatic. Again, the focus is to stop losing money. If the trader is losing money, it is not a lot of money lost. With a few profitable days, the trader's confidence will be regained. At that time the day trader can resume trading the normal lot size of 1,000 shares.

5. Do not double the risk exposure. The worst thing a day trader can do is to double the money in order to recover losses quickly. Do not start pyramiding trading positions and trading in increments of 2,000 shares. Adding additional shares will only add additional psychological pressure. Also, the loss potential is now much greater. Doubling the shares will not stop the losses. Instead, the day trader has increased exposure to potentially higher losses. How would an additional large trading loss help the day trader to regain lost confidence?

CHAPTER

23

Day Trading Styles

EVERY DAY TRADER EVENTUALLY DEVELOPS A TRADING STYLE THAT REFLECTS her risk tolerance and individual personality. Many different trading techniques can be generalized into four distinct day trading styles. Those styles are the specialist, the scalper, the market maker, and the position day trader.

In reality, many day traders use hybrids of different styles. During any portion of the trading day, a day trader could be a specialist. But when the opportunity arrives, the trader can quickly become a scalper, taking advantage of a price jump for a stock that is suddenly moving up due to some exceptional good news. Yes, day traders are opportunists. A day traders can start the day trading business with one style and discover quickly, after losing some money, that the style is not working for her and try another trading style. Day traders are continuously in the process of evolving and modifying their approaches.

The Specialist Day Trader

This type of day trader specializes in a few NASDAQ or NYSE stocks that are actively traded and have substantial intraday price volatility. Those stocks are usually well-known stocks such as Dell, Intel, Microsoft, Cisco, or similar high-technology stocks. Some day traders specialize in one or two stocks from each technology industry sector, such as semiconductors, networks, Internet, software, hardware, and database providers. Since those high-tech stocks and industry sectors have significant intraday price volatility, there are plenty of opportunities to day trade. Even if nothing is happening in one industry sector, other sectors might be active and volatile.

A *specialist* day trader would select five or ten stocks and input the symbols of those stocks into the Market Ticker window. Then he would watch for price momentum. The moment the day trader is alerted to any kind of price movement on the Market Ticker window, he would input that stock symbol into the Level II, Time and Sales, and the technical analysis chart windows. The trader would start to analyze that stock closely, in essence, looking for a trading signal that tells him to open a long or short position.

Because specialist day traders focus on just a few stocks, they develop a very good feel for these securities. They monitor the stocks' performance continually, and thus know about the stocks' monthly, weekly, and intraday price data. For instance, they develop a good feel for the stocks' intraday price support and resistance levels. In addition, specialists read and monitor everything written or published in the mass media or Internet on their stocks. For example, the specialist day trader would know when the companies he monitors plan to announce earnings reports.

Because of their intense concentration on only a few stocks, specialists are willing to take on additional risk. If the stock price momentum is there, they are willing to purchase or short sell additional shares—to pyramid or increase their position from 1,000 shares to several thousand shares. Specialists believe that the additional risk associated with the higher number of shares is a calculated risk. A stock could reverse its trend $\frac{1}{2}$ point or higher, and the specialist day trader would hold onto the position. He would be willing to absorb a $\frac{1}{2}$-point loss and wait for the stock to reverse a losing trend because he feels confident that he knows the stock behavior well. Specialists develop a higher tolerance for risk than scalper day trader.

Being a specialist day trader has its advantages. Specialists develop a great deal of knowledge about their stocks, so they tend to have a greater percentage of winning trades than scalper day traders. They occasionally hold overnight positions, justifying the additional exposure risk with the explanation that they know the stock well. Since they monitor only a few stocks, specialists tend to make fewer trades and thus they save on commission costs.

It is my opinion that specialists assume lower risks. They make fewer trades each day, and when they do trade, they take positions in the stocks that they know well. On the other hand, they have lower profit potential. Since the specialists monitor only a few stocks, they miss many opportunities elsewhere in the market, where stock prices could be extremely volatile. Consequently, specialists seldom have "fabulous" trading days. They assume lower risk and thus the potential for a lower rate of return.

The Scalper Day Trader

Day traders who are known as *scalpers* are the original Harvey Houtkin's "SOES bandits." Harvey Houtkin is a pioneer of the day trading business who coined the unfortunate term "SOES bandit" to depict an anti-establishment image of day trading. The term *bandit* connotes that day traders are somehow taking something that does not belong to them. That is untrue. Day traders take risks like any other professional stock trader. When and if they earn money trading stocks, they earn it because they are smart, quick, and efficient. They are not bandits.

Scalping is the most common day trading style. As the word implies, the scalper monitors a great number of volatile stocks that have decent daily trading volume (at least 500,000 shares per day). They sift through a sea of financial information to pick up on any stock that is moving up or down. They watch CNBC reports and observe the real-time and dynamically updated Top NASDAQ and NYSE Advances and Declines reports and the 52-Week High and Low price breakouts window.

In addition, scalpers often spend many hours on the Internet, searching and sifting through financial information Web sites. They look for clues about any stocks that might be in play the following trading day to obtain early insights about which stocks might be volatile.

The Internet has several chat rooms designed specifically for day traders. Those Internet chat rooms offer rumors, tips, and advice. Beware of the quality of information available in those chat rooms. They are often the source of pump-and-dump stock schemes. Unscrupulous stock promoters and manipulators use Internet chat rooms to talk up a stock's price and then sell or "dump" the stock at an inflated price. The author's advice is *caveat emptor*—buyer beware!

Day trading stocks on news can be extremely lucrative. There are numerous events, such as stock upgrades or downgrades, mergers and acquisitions reports, or stock splits that can cause an immediate public reaction in the price of a stock. Most likely, the market (that is, the public) will overreact, and the stock price will move greatly. A word of caution: The day trader should avoid submitting a market buy order during a time when the market is absorbing positive news, because the order could get filled near the stock's high intraday price. The ensuing profit taking (that is, selling) could quickly lower the price of that stock. The day trader could end up selling the stock at a loss. (It is always a good idea to utilize a limit buy order.)

When a stock price has upward momentum, the most common execution strategy employed by scalpers is to buy the stock at the inside ASK price via SOES. There is no point in submitting an offer to buy a stock at the inside BID, or to try to cut the spread (by submitting the high bid). The market makers and other day traders would not be interested in selling a stock with a positive (upward) momentum at a lower price than the ASK price. Once the day trader owns the stock (that is, has a long stock position) and after the price increases, if there is still a positive price momentum, the day trader can attempt to sell the stock by offering to sell it at the inside ASK or near the inside ASK price.

If the scalpers believe that particular stocks have the potential to move up or down that day, they will add these stocks into the Market Ticker window. From that time on, they monitor these stocks for any price momentum. If there is no price movement that day or that week, the day trader simply deletes that stock symbol from the Market Ticker. If price movement is detected, scalpers input that stock symbol in the Level II, Time and Sales, and technical analysis chart windows, and quickly analyze the stock to determine whether to buy it or sell it short.

Because scalper day traders do not specialize in trading any particular stock, they do not develop a good feel for any securities. They do not closely and continuously monitor all stocks' performances, and thus they do not form a strong opinion about the stocks' intraday price support and resistance levels. As a rule, scalpers do not have a high tolerance for loss. They get in and out of trading positions quickly. If they are right about a stock, they will stay in that trading position long enough to pick up $\frac{1}{4}$ or higher profit. If the scalpers are wrong, they will quickly leave with a minimal loss of $\frac{1}{8}$ or $\frac{1}{4}$.

Scalpers are not willing to absorb higher risk. They do not want to hold and wait for a stock to reverse a losing trend, because they do not feel confident that they know the behavior of that stock that well. A scalper seldom holds an overnight position. That is not their style. Because they don't focus on any particular stock, scalpers are not willing to take any additional risks. They seldom pyramid or increase their position from 1,000 shares to several thousand shares.

Scalpers tend to make a lot of trades. Sometimes, the trades are only a few minutes long. It is not uncommon to find scalpers who make 100 trades per day. Sometimes, a winning trade of $\frac{1}{16}$ would suffice. That is $62.50 gross profit on a trade of 1,000 shares. A day trader is scalping $\frac{1}{16}$, $\frac{1}{8}$, or $\frac{1}{4}$ from the existing price momentum. Since this style generates many trading transactions, $\frac{1}{16}$ and $\frac{1}{8}$ and $\frac{1}{4}$ could add up to a substantial sum at the end of the trading day.

Since scalpers do not acquire a great deal of knowledge about any particular stock, they tend to have a lower percentage of winning trades. They simply surf the NASDAQ and NYSE markets looking for intraday price volatility. If a stock is moving up, a scalper buys that stock. He sometimes takes a position in a stock that he knows nothing about. In my opinion, scalpers assume greater risk than specialists. However, since scalpers monitor many stocks, they have more opportunities to score "home runs." A home run would be a winning trade with 1 point or more. On 1,000 shares traded, that would translate into $1,000 profit or higher. Consequently, scalpers have the potential to enjoy fabulous trading days. Since scalpers monitor a great number of stocks and they tend to make many trades, they pay a lot in commissions. Day trading shops love to have successful scalpers in their trading rooms. They are simply good for business. In summary, scalpers assume higher risk and thus higher potential for profitability.

The Market Maker Day Trader

This group of day traders tries to exploit the large spread between the BID and ASK prices. The spread varies from stock to stock. It depends mostly on trading volume. Thinly traded stocks always have a larger spread than the actively traded stocks. First of all, there are few NASDAQ market makers making the market for inactive stocks. That means lower competition. There is also little inflow and outflow of funds (that is, order flow) for those stocks. Thus it is difficult to ascertain any visible supply and demand. Consequently, thinly traded stocks carry substantially larger trading risk. The large spread is the compensation to NASDAQ market makers for providing liquidity for those illiquid stocks.

Most day traders, whether they subscribe to any of the following styles—specialist, scalper, market maker, or position day trader, do not trade thinly traded stocks. These stocks are simply too risky. Upward price movement can be quickly reversed; prices could start declining sharply, and the trader could have a hard time getting out. Since there is little liquidity (that is, few buyers entering the market for that stock), the trader would have to sell the stock to the few existing market makers for that stock who are buying the stock for their own portfolios. But the NASDAQ market makers have already adjusted the price to a lower level. The trader would end up selling the stock at a loss.

On the other hand, actively traded stocks such as Dell, Intel, Microsoft, or Cisco have very small spreads. There are plenty of market makers making the market for those stocks. There is a substantial inflow and outflow of funds. In essence, there is visible supply and demand. It is easier and safer to trade such liquid stocks. The spread tends to be narrow ($\frac{1}{16}$ or $\frac{1}{8}$) for actively traded stocks.

For expensive stocks that trade in the $100-plus range, the spread tends to be larger ($\frac{1}{4}$ or $\frac{3}{8}$). However, the value of a $\frac{1}{4}$ spread for a $100 stock is smaller in relative terms than the value of a $\frac{1}{8}$ spread for a $20 stock. For example, a $\frac{1}{4}$ spread for $100 constitutes $\frac{1}{4}$ of 1% of the stock price, or 0.25%. On the other hand, a $\frac{1}{8}$ spread for a $20 stock constitutes $\frac{5}{8}$ of 1% of the stock price, or 0.63%. In essence, a $\frac{1}{4}$ spread for the expensive stocks is a smaller spread in relative terms than a $\frac{1}{8}$ spread for the inexpensive stocks.

The level of spread depends on the forces of supply and demand for that stock. Often during the trading day that spread widens. The spread can go up to $\frac{1}{2}$ to $\frac{5}{8}$ for expensive stocks such as Yahoo! (YHOO) and Amazon.com (AMZN). An astute day trader can decide at that time whether to play the market maker's game. Figure 23.1 illustrates this point.

NASDAQ market makers buy stocks from the public at the lower BID price and sell the same stock to the public at the higher ASK price, and thus earn the spread. In the example in Figure 23.1, that spread of $\frac{5}{16}$ is substantial. Perhaps the spread widened at that point because all market makers (sellers) left the lower ASK price of $150\frac{5}{8}$, and thus the

Figure 23.1 *Day Trader Acting as Market Maker*

higher ASK price of $150^{11}/_{16}$ became the best ASK price. Conversely, the spread could also be widened if all market makers (buyers) left the previously highest BID price of $150^{3}/_{8}$, and the lower BID price of $150^{5}/_{16}$ became the best BID price. The bottom line is that the spread for a variety of supply and demand conditions had widened to $^{5}/_{16}$.

The astute day trader acting as *market maker* would notice that development. She would then offer to buy that stock at a price higher than the current best BID price, and submit a "High Bid on Island for $150^{3}/_{8}$." The day trader would submit a bid through an ECN such as Island to buy the stock for the higher price of $150^{3}/_{8}$. The $150^{3}/_{8}$ bid would be posted electronically through the Island system nationwide. That price would constitute the best BID price in the nation at that point in time. The chances are that the bid would get filled. If one were selling that stock, one would rather sell the stock for the higher price of $150^{3}/_{8}$ than the lower price of $150^{5}/_{16}$.

After the bid has been accepted and the buy trade confirmed, the day trader acting as the market maker would immediately offer to sell that stock at the price lower than the current best ASK price. The day trader would submit a "Low Offer on Island for $150^{5}/_{8}$." In other words, the day trader would submit through an ECN such as Island an offer to sell the stock for the lower price of $150^{5}/_{8}$. The $150^{5}/_{8}$ offer would be posted electronically through the Island system nationwide. That price would constitute the best ASK price in the nation at that point of time. Again, chances are that the offer would get filled. If the public were buying that stock, then the public would rather buy that stock for the lower price of $150^{5}/_{8}$ than the higher price of $150^{11}/_{16}$.

The day trader may be rewarded handsomely for this activity. In the example from Figure 23.1, if the day trader were trading in 1,000-share increments, the gross profit would be $\frac{1}{4}$ or $250. Also, the net result would be that the spread would be reduced from $\frac{5}{16}$ to $\frac{1}{4}$. If the spread remains at $\frac{5}{16}$, many more day traders would be attracted to this opportunity. A large spread such as $\frac{5}{16}$ attracts many day traders who would continuously attempt to bid and offer at a better price. They would repeat this process again and again. The ultimate result is a cut in the spread.

This strategy can work if the spread is large or wide. If the spread is small, such as $\frac{1}{16}$, there is little potential for cutting the spread—to offer to purchase the stock at any price higher than the current best BID price. The day trader could submit an offer to buy the stock at the current BID price through an ECN such as Island. However, there is no guarantee that the order would get filled. At that time, the day trader would be competing with other market makers to purchase the same stock at the same quoted price as other market makers.

Cutting the spread would be an example of a day trader doing something that is "socially redeeming." That does not mean that day traders are an especially benevolent group of people; they are pursuing their own self-interest, which is to make as much money as possible. However, the ability to submit better BID and ASK prices through the ECNs would end up generating a socially beneficial result: a lower spread between the BID and ASK price.

It is not surprising that NASDAQ market makers and the Wall Street establishment do not like day traders who act as market makers. Cutting the spread cuts into market-making profitability. However, this type of day trading has generated favorable media attention. Several reporters have portrayed it as a story of "David versus Goliath" or a story of small day traders wrestling with the established NASDAQ market makers.

The Position Day Trader

This style of day traders is a hybrid between the aggressive investor and the passive day trader. The *position* trader pays close attention to technical analysis indicators and studies a stock closely before opening a position. If the trader is right, she keeps that position open for a longer period of time than usual. The time frame of analysis of a position trader is much longer than that of the typical day trader. Sometimes that time frame is one day, and sometimes it is a few days. Position traders often keep overnight positions. They tend to make fewer trades and keep those trades open for a longer period of time. They also seek higher price movement than the typical day trader. They wait for the stock to move a few points higher before closing a position.

Position traders tend to have trading accounts with high capital. Subsequently, they can afford to purchase more than 1,000 shares at a time and often pyramid their trading positions. They might start with 1,000 shares, and if the market moves in the right direction, they would take an additional 1,000 shares or more. In contrast, 1,000-share increments tend to be a norm and a limit for traditional day traders. Position day traders usually have extensive experience in stock investments. They tend to be savvy stock market participants. They also tend to watch the NYSE market closely.

Position traders often take multiple stock positions. Given a large trading account, the position trader could purchase several stocks and monitor his performance simultaneously. Sometimes, position traders create a "basket" of stocks (for example, Internet stocks) and do a basket trade. Several day trading software packages have the capability of creating a basket of stocks for quick execution. If the position trader believes that the Internet sector has the potential to go up, the trader might execute a basket order.

With the click of the mouse, the position trader would send a simultaneous order to buy several Internet stocks in 1,000-share increments. From that point on, the position trader would closely monitor the performance of all stocks in the basket. If any stock is not performing as expected (the price is not moving up or decreasing in value), the trader would quickly sell that stock. The trader would continue to monitor the other stocks in that basket, and as long as those stocks are performing as expected (the price is increasing), the position trader would keep them. In essence, the position trader keeps the winners and sheds the losers.

This overview of the four kinds of day trading styles is an oversimplification of the day trading business. The purpose is only to illustrate different trading styles and to provide information on general day trading standards. Eventually, all day traders develop their own trading styles and philosophies that might incorporate features of any of the four day trading styles mentioned here.

The Psychology of Trading

CONFIDENCE BREEDS SUCCESS! OR IS IT THAT SUCCESS BREEDS CONFIDENCE? What comes first? It is the eternal "chicken or the egg?" question. If I must choose between the two, confidence wins. A day trader must be confident to succeed in this business. If a novice day trader starts to trade live with any lingering doubts about the future outcome, the trader is likely to fail. The doubts become self-fulfilling prophecies. It is my opinion that the day trader's beliefs and actions must be congruent. It is crucial that the day trader believe in herself; the belief that one can be a successful trader is essential in reaching that goal.

Visualization

The novice day trader must be able to visualize himself as a successful and profitable day trader. The visualization of the day trading process is crucial. The new trader must be able to state clearly what an experienced and successful day trader would do under various trading circumstances. A good day trader visualizes his trade before making that trade. He knows at what price he is willing to buy a stock, how the stock might react while the position is open, and at what circumstances and price he is willing to sell.

For instance, if the trading loss were _ of a point, the experienced day trader would exit that position immediately. The novice day trader should be able to visualize himself performing the very same action: exit the trade at the time. When such circumstances arrive, and they will, the novice day trader knows exactly what to do. If the trader has an open position a few minutes before the market close, he knows that a successful day trader would close that open position immediately regardless of his profit and loss status.

The Trading Plan

The novice day trader should have a trading plan that clearly spells out what she will do under different trading scenarios. It is easier to visualize day trading activities with a defined trading plan or "trading map" in place. The trading plan should address the following questions:

1. Why do I want to day trade?

   This is an important question. The new day trader should understand her underlying motivation for day trading. What is the attraction? Is it the lure of quick and easy money or the potential to make a lot of money? Is it the ability to be self-employed, or is there a passion and sincere interest in the stock market? Understanding one's own motivation is an important ingredient to success.

2. What is my time frame for reaching profitability? When do I become profitable?

   The trading plan should state that the novice day trader expects to lose up to a specific amount at the beginning, and that it may take six months to become profitable. When such losses come at the beginning, and they will, the novice day trader will not panic. The losses are part of the plan. He can continue with the plan and move up the learning curve.

3. What do I trade (what stocks and how many shares) in the first month, the second month, and so on?

   The trading plan should call for the novice day trader to trade slow stocks (relatively inexpensive NASDAQ stocks that do not move rapidly) in the beginning. If the trading plan requires the novice day trader to trade slow stocks in increments of 100 shares for the first week (and then increase the trading amount each week by an additional 100 shares), the novice day trader should follow that plan.

4. What should my trading style and philosophy be at the beginning? What trading style better fits my personality? How much risk am I willing to tolerate?

   If I start and continue as a specialist day trader (specializing in a few NASDAQ or NYSE stocks) then the risk will be lower, as well as the profit opportunities. If I adopt a scalper's method (seeking price momentum anywhere on the NASDAQ or NYSE) then the risk will be higher, as well as the profit opportunities.

5. How do I prepare for the next trading day?

   The day trading plan should state how the day trader would prepare for each trading day. Does the day trader plan to read the *Investor's Business Daily* before coming to the day trading shop? Does he plan to watch CNBC early every morning to ascertain the public's market sentiment?

6. How do I trade at the opening of the market?

   The day trading plan should specify how the trader would react at the market open. Will the day trader sit and watch the first 10 or 20 minutes of trading to ascertain the trend for that day, or will the trader jump into the market at the opening?

7. What do I do when a trade goes against me?

   This answer should be the most prominent part of the trading plan. In other words, what is my loss limit for one trade? Do I lose $\frac{1}{4}$ or $\frac{3}{8}$ or $\frac{1}{2}$ or higher before getting out of the trade?

8. What do I do when several trades go against me in one day?

   In other words, what is the maximum loss I would accept in a given day? If the loss exceeds the maximum, then trader should stop trading for that day.

9. What are my stock buying and selling signals?

   The trading plan must be very specific about trading signals. The new day trader must know exactly what signs or signals she is waiting to receive from the stock market. For example, is it:

   A movement in the Level II screen?

   The crossover between the Fast and Slow Exponential Moving Averages?

The price approaching the intraday support or resistance levels (upper or lower Bollinger bands)?

10. What are my exit points or exit signals?

In addition to being specific and stating when the trader will enter the market (that is, take a long or short position), the plan should also state when to exit the position. In other words, what is the trading signal to close a profitable position? Is it:

A movement in the Level II screen?

The crossover between the Fast and Slow Exponential Moving Averages?

The price approaching the intraday support or resistance levels (upper or lower Bollinger bands)?

A specific price increase (for example, $\frac{1}{2}$ point)?

11. What do I do at the close of the market?

The trading plan should state what the trader would do at the end of the trading day. Does the day trader plan to review the trades from that day and ascertain what trades were losers and why? How many trades had winning percentages? The key is to create a daily routine to evaluate (analyze) the trading actions and to learn from the trades, and particularly to learn from mistakes. If the trader was trading Dell that day, she would print the entire Dell intraday price chart and locate on the chart the entry and exit points for that day. Are the entry and exit points at the optimum? (The probability is great that they are not.) Learning something new about day trading every day will eventually translate into successful trading in the long run.

Most novice day traders do not plan to fail in their day trading businesses. They simply fail to plan. The new trader will find it easier to visualize the day trading process if she invests time in writing a trading plan. The trading plan must be specific. For instance, it should state,

The following are my buy or sell signals: _____.

The following are my risk management tools: _____.

Finally, I, the day trader, will follow my own day trading rules.

How to Write an Effective Day Trading Plan

To write an effective day trading plan, one must be able to visualize the trading process. One also must know the technical side of the day trading business. How does one obtain technical knowledge of or expertise in day trading? Reading day trading books is a step in the right direction. My recommendation is to read all of the available books on the topic of day trading, of which there are many. Buying and reading these books is the most economical way to educate oneself.

In addition, the novice day trader should spend a few weeks paper trading or simulation trading. Most day trading software packages have a demo mode. Finally, spend some time in the day trading shop in your town, if there is one, behind a successful trader, if possible, and see for yourself whether the day trading business can be profitable. Knowledge is the key.

Psychological Characteristics of the Successful Trader

In addition to possessing a technical knowledge of day trading, day traders must have a certain psychological makeup. Possessing adequate knowledge of the technical aspects of day trading is important, but it is not an absolute guarantee of success. Many highly knowledgeable traders have lost money day trading. To be a success in this risky endeavor, the day trader must be a disciplined risk taker. Not every aspiring trader has those two key psychological components: discipline and the ability to assume risk.

Day trading activities involve the making and losing of money, and that provokes strong and varied emotions. The range of human emotions present during day trading is significant. At times, the day trader can expect to experience happiness, disappointment, excitement, fear, panic, anxiety, and thrill. Different people are predisposed to deal with such emotions differently.

Traders have well-defined psychological characteristics or traits that permeate their daily trading activities. Let us call these traits a *trading temperament,* where temperament is defined to be a "constitution of peculiar or distinguishing mental characteristics." So what are the traders' peculiar or distinguishing mental characteristics?

It is my opinion that the two most important psychological characteristics for day traders are

1. Self-discipline, and

2. Ability to assume risk.

Self-discipline is the first, and the most important, characteristic. Day traders must exercise self-discipline at all times. The disciplined day traders know ahead of time what they will do under certain trading circumstances. As mentioned previously on numerous occasions, the day trader must be disciplined enough to accept the fact that his trading decision is wrong. Once he recognizes that a particular trade went bad, the trader must quickly get out of that trade with a minimal loss. This is the core of risk management. This is also easier said than done. Day traders, like most people, are often reluctant to admit they have made an error. They are simply unwilling to take a small loss and move on to other trading opportunities. Instead, undisciplined traders hope that their losing stock position will reverse its trend. That is when small losses can turn into large losses.

In addition, the day trader must be disciplined enough to wait patiently for a trading signal to buy or sell a stock. That trading signal can be a technical analysis signal, such as the crossover between the Fast and Slow Moving Average lines, or it could be a movement in the NASDAQ Level II screen. The disciplined day trader will not enter a trade without a clear reason to enter. Otherwise day trading becomes gambling.

The ability to assume risk is the second important characteristic of the trading temperament. A day trader must have the courage to take a trade position and assume the associated financial risk. Day traders have to make trading decisions quickly. As mentioned previously, the objective of day trading is to exploit short-term daily price volatility, with the key words in this statement being *short-term*. Trading opportunities will come, but they are short-lived. The day trader must be able to recognize a short-term price movement and act upon it. There is little time to complete a time-consuming comprehensive analysis. The day trader must have the psychological courage to pull the trigger without the benefit of a comprehensive analysis. Otherwise, if the trader waits too long, the trading opportunity will disappear.

Stress Reducers

Trading is a stressful business. The day trader is in and out of the market constantly, continuously processing market information and taking risks. She is continuously looking for trading opportunities, and when an opportunity is recognized, must quickly decide whether to enter the trade. Consequently, stress is always present, with some days being more stressful than others. Following is a list of proven and generic stress reducers:

➤ Get at least seven or eight hours of sleep daily.

➤ Exercise for quick relief from stress. Try to maintain a regular exercise routine.

➤ Eat well-balanced meals daily. Avoid skipping meals.

➤ Foster a meaningful emotional life. Make the principle of love a motivating force in your family life.

➤ Foster meaningful social relationships. Talk out your problems with your trusted friends.

➤ Set goals in your life. Having a purpose in life will keep your life happier.

➤ Avoid excessive amounts of change in your life at one time. Change is good. Too much change is not.

➤ Arrange for personal time off, and engage in activities that are relaxing.

➤ Learn to say "No" to additional projects and responsibilities for which you have no time or energy.

Dealing with Trading Stress

Yes, losing money in this business is a real possibility. The fear of losing money is at the heart of most day trader's stress. Take away the fear of losing money, and the stress disappears. I have never met anyone who was stressing out over paper trading losses. My recommendation to everyone is to start day trading only with money that you can afford to lose. Do not trade money that you cannot afford to lose.

Also, the day trader should always keep in mind that the one and only item she can control is the amount of her loss. Day traders cannot control the amount of profit from each trade, since they cannot influence a stock's price movement. Price is a function of the market supply and demand forces. However, the trader can determine her loss. Practicing risk management skills (for example, minimizing trade losses to $\frac{1}{4}$ of a point) rigidly is the most important step in reducing a trader's stress level and promoting the trader's long-term survival.

The other condition that generates anxiety is the general uncertainty that is associated with stock trading. Day trading is not an exact science. There are no guarantees that the price of a stock will continue to go in a certain direction, despite the existence of certain market signals. Every day trader must accept and deal with uncertainty. If you are looking for certainty and guarantees, then day trading is not for you.

In my opinion, day trading is an art that is based on a set of clearly defined trading rules and risk management applications. All day trading decisions should be based on the trading rules as defined in the individual trader's trading plan. Consequently, every trade should be within the limits of the self-imposed risk management parameters. Practicing the risk management steps daily is the best way to manage stress and the only way for the day trader to ensure long-term survival in this business.

Day trading is a competitive business. When the day trader is buying and selling stocks to make money, he is continuously competing against professional NASDAQ market makers, NYSE specialists, and other day traders who are also in business to make money. The results of the trading competition are evident immediately. The trading "score" is always visible on the trader's computer screen. The day trader knows at all times whether he is making money or not. Consequently, there are plenty of emotional ups and downs that come with that competition.

A good day trader will try to detach herself from that emotional roller coaster. She avoids any emotional attachment to a given stock or position. Buy and sell decisions should be entered unemotionally, if that is possible. A good day trader treats trading as a business. If the successful trader makes a wrong trade decision, then she simply closes that position with a loss, without blaming herself mentally, and moves on to the next trading opportunity. If the trader makes a winning trade, she simply looks for the next trading opportunity without celebration.

My father used to tell me that there are two important strategies for dealing with stress, and I have heard the same two principles several times from other people. In fact, Richard Carlson wrote a book whose title states these two rules:

1. Don't sweat the small stuff.

2. It is all small stuff.

If the novice day trader is prepared to lose $15,000 trying to learn and start a new business, and if he does ultimately lose that $15,000, then losing a predetermined and accepted dollar amount constitutes small stuff.

SECTION

VI

Introduction to Day Trading Brokers

➤ In section VI, the question of where to day trade is addressed. We begin in chapter 25 by distinguishing between the two types of electronic brokers: (1) direct-access brokers, and (2) Internet-based brokers. We further differentiate between the two choices: (1) trading from the office of a direct-access broker; or (2) trading at home using the services of either an Internet-based broker or a direct-access broker. Recommendations for selecting an appropriate day trading broker are offered.

➤ Additional topics related to the selection of a broker are covered as well: trading remotely with a day trading firm, and how firms gauge an individual's suitability for day trading. Chapter 25 includes a description of the features of the trading software used by most day trading firms and informs readers how these trades are cleared. The Securities Investor Protection Corporation (SIPC) is discussed in chapter 26.

➤ Finally, in the appendixes, we discuss some of the finer points of day trading. Since almost all day traders open margin accounts, Regulation T and long, short, and combined margin accounts are described in detail in Appendix 2. In addition, restricted margin accounts, margin maintenance requirements, and intraday margin calls are explained.

➤ In addition to dealing with price volatility, day traders must also deal with the IRS. The good news is that the probability of being audited by the IRS is very low. Several tax issues are briefly discussed in Appendix 3, such as defining tax rates, income, capital gains and losses, trading expenses, and the three IRS tax classifications for traders: market maker, investor, and trader.

25

Direct-Access Brokers

ALL ELECTRONIC STOCKBROKERS MUST DELIVER TO TRADERS THREE elements:

1. Data or stock quotes, whether the quotes are delivered in real time or delayed;
2. Tools for data analysis, whether they are technical charts or Level I or II screen information;
3. A platform from which to execute your trade orders electronically.

Not all electronic brokers deliver the required trading ingredients in the same fashion. In short, not all electronic stockbrokers are created equally.

The most common type of brokers we discuss are the traditional online discount brokers, such as Charles Schwab, E*Trade, or Waterhouse. These brokers are truly Internet-based because they use Web browsers like Microsoft's Internet Explorer or Netscape's Communicator to automate the interface between the traders and brokers. The traders simply e-mail trade orders to the brokers, who then route the orders electronically to the NASDAQ market makers or NYSE specialists. The major and crucial distinction becomes where the trade orders are routed for execution after the broker receives the order. Subsequently, the issue of payment for order flow emerges, which is discussed in great detail in the next chapter. Online brokers account for the great majority of NASDAQ or NYSE electronic trading executions, and they account for more than 14 million customer accounts. Due to their sheer market size and relevance, these brokers are covered in great detail in chapter 26.

The second type and most relevant to day traders are direct-access brokers. As the name implies, these brokers offer day traders direct access to NASDAQ market makers, NYSE specialists, and ECNs. Day traders can preference one market maker and send an order for execution directly to that market maker at price levels that might be different from the current inside BID and ASK prices. In addition, these brokers present to day traders sophisticated trading platforms that offer real-time data feed, real-time data analysis, and direct real-time order routing and execution to the NASDAQ SOES and SelectNet, the NYSE DOT, and many ECNs, such as Island or Archipelago.

Finally, most of these direct-access brokers offer the latest in order-execution technology—intelligent order routing. These brokers provide to traders sophisticated trading software packages that are downloaded from a broker's servers. Subsequently, the software packages reside on the trader's PC. This decentralized software architecture provides to day traders the capability to quickly and easily make optimum trade order routing decisions. With the press of a function key on the keyboard, the intelligent routing software will process the order efficiently, resulting in faster trade execution and a better price. In a few milliseconds the intelligent routing software scans all ECNs as well as the NASDAQ SOES and SelectNet for the best price at that point in time and then routes or forwards the trader's limit order.

Direct-access brokers come in two versions: home-based and office-based. A new trader will determine whether to trade on-site, from the trading floor of a day trading firm's branch office, or from home via an Internet brokerage firm. In fact, the first decision a new trader will make is deciding where to trade. Whatever the decision, the trader obtains the direct access to the stock market. There are advantages to both options.

Trading from the Office of a Direct-Access Day Trading Firm

One day trader in Sacramento told me that he clearly prefers trading at the office because trading at home has a distressing feel of being unemployed. The option to trade in the office of a specialized electronic direct-access day trading firm that has branch offices all over the United States has historically been the first choice for most day traders. The direct-access day trading firms cater only to professional traders who demand instantaneous Level I and II quotes and fast, sophisticated real-time analysis tools, as well as direct access to SOES, SelectNet, and ECNs, and most important, reliable and cheap trade executions. These day trading firms specialize in electronic day trading only. There are no IRAs accounts, checking accounts, financial planning services, or option trading opportunities offered. Table 25.1 lists the larger firms.

The direct-access day trading firms tend to be new and small firms. Often, the day trading branch office is one large room (the trading floor) packed with several computers (with large, 21-inch-screen monitors)

Table 25.1 *Day Trading Firms (in alphabetical order)*

Firm's Name	Internet Address
All-Tech Investment Group	www.attain.com
Andover Trading	www.andovertrading.com
Bright Trading	www.stocktrading.com
Broadway Trading	www.broadwaytrading.com
Castle Online	www.castleonline.com
DirecTrade	www.d-trade.com
Investors Street	www.investors-street.com
Momentum Securities	www.soes.com
Navillus Securities	www.navillus.com
NDX Trading	www.NDXtrade.com
On-Line Investment Services	www.onli.com
ProTrader	www.protrader.com
Self Trading	www.selftrading.com
Summit Trading	www.summittrading.com
Tiger Investment Group	www.tigerinvestment.com
Van Buren Securities	www.vbsecurities.com
Yamner & Co.	www.yamner.com
YourTrade	www.YourTrade.com

connected to the firm's servers, which are connected to the NASDAQ, NYSE, and ECNs' computer systems. Day traders can execute trades themselves, without using a middleman—a brokerage firm. The largest direct-access day trading firm that subscribes to the branch offices approach is the Austin-based ProTrader (formerly known as Cornerstone Securities). ProTrader, which was founded in 1993, carries accounts for more than 650 active day traders who are trading in one of 19 branch offices in the United States.

Although staying home to trade is clearly convenient, going to the office to trade seems to be the preferred, more professional option. First, there are fewer distractions, such as family members stepping in with questions or requests, when traders trade together on the trading floor. There is also a synergy among the traders on the floor.

That synergy is visible in most day trading shops. The traders communicate among themselves throughout the day and call out the stocks that are moving at that moment. This is an enormous help. Multiple sets of eyes can see more than one pair of eyes can. A single trader cannot possibly monitor the entire universe of NASDAQ and NYSE stocks. Also, it is in the trader's own interest to talk out his relative position. If a trade position is long, the trader has a vested interest in broadcasting that trade, so that other people in the shop might join in on the same side of the trade and buy that stock (and increase demand). If it were a winning trade, then they all profit. If it were a losing trade, then they all share the pain.

Some professional day trading firms have created their own proprietary "squawk boxes," or broadcasting systems. One day trading firm, Bright Trading, broadcasts live audio from the Chicago S&P 500 Futures floor. The futures market theoretically represents a leading indicator of the broad stock market for a few short seconds. According to many day traders, a few seconds' head start is a tremendous help.

Other day trading firms have hired research assistants who sit in front of computer monitors and sift through the sea of real-time financial data provided by Wall Street news service organizations, such as Bloomberg. These research assistants continuously review and analyze all available data. Often the research assistants learn about the news before it is publicly disseminated over CNBC. When they encounter news (for example, company earnings or stock-split reports) that can move stock prices, the research assistants broadcast that news immediately to all branch offices. Every office has a speaker in the background that transmits this information. Some traders choose to ignore the squawk box, and focus and specialize on only a few stocks. But for many traders who surf the market and actively seek any stock that is moving, the squawk box is an extremely valuable tool.

To stay in business and to compete against the Internet brokers, professional day trading firms must keep investing money in the best available trading technology. Day trading firms must maintain a competitive edge by differentiating their services from electronic trading that can be practiced at home via the Internet. In addition to providing direct access to NASDAQ SOES and SelectNet and NYSE DOT, professional day trading firms must at least offer direct access to Island (ISLD) ECN. Some firms offer direct access to other ECNs in addition to Island, such as Instinet (INCA), Archipelago (ARCA), Terranova (TNTO), or Bloomberg Tradebook (BTRD).

Professional day trading firms must also provide their customers with a choice of trading platforms or trading software packages, such as CyberTrader, TradeCast, or RealTick III. These are truly sophisticated and completely integrated stock trading packages. A good financial software package will provide more than just Level I or II screen information, which is readily available elsewhere. Even the point-and-click order execution interface is a common software feature. The following trading instruments are standard features in these financial software packages:

➤ "Smart" or "hot" function keys for trade executions that quickly route trade orders in the most efficient manner for the best possible price. The smart order routing systems ensures the optimum price execution, and it is not available if you are trading with an online broker;

➤ Different types of sophisticated market alerts, such as alerts for crossed and locked markets;

➤ Information on market-makers' movements within the inside and outside BID and ASK quotes;

➤ An "account manager" that tracks, in real time, the trader's pending and open trade positions, purchasing power, and current profit and loss situations.

In addition to its sophisticated computer and networking technology, every day trading branch office must have staff members who are computer experts to provide on-site technical support to all traders in a timely manner. If the network is down, the staff must be able to reboot the servers and reestablish the trading environment quickly. If traders have questions regarding the software, the tech staff must have the answers. Downtime, which inevitably occurs in this electronic trading environment, will thus be kept at a minimum. The expertise of the day trading firm's staff provides an edge over trading from home, where traders have to deal with technology issues on their own.

Choosing a Day Trading Office

Traders investigating a branch office should take a look at the branch's computer equipment. They should consider what equipment traders use at their workstations. How fast are the computer processors? Each trader should have at least one 21-inch monitor, if not two linked 21-inch monitors. There is so much data in this business, the monitor screen becomes the trader's "real estate." The larger the monitor screen, the more information can be displayed.

Another important advantage to trading on-site is being able to learn from a group of experienced and profitable traders. My recommendation to the novice trader is to look for a firm that has successful full-time traders in place. Many successful traders do not mind passing along their knowledge and experience, as long it does not interfere with their individual trading. However, remember that successful full-time traders are a rare breed. The probability is high that there will be more part-time traders than full-time traders on the floor. At some point, however, part-time traders might graduate to full-time trading.

Many day trading firms provide structured training programs, with several levels of training. The first level might be an introduction to day trading. For newcomers, that introduction is the starting point. The second level might consist of detailed coverage of different and specific topics, such as trade execution, technical analysis, trading strategies, or the psychology of trading. The third level of training might include a few weeks of simulations or demo paper trading. The final step might be to trade live next to an experienced and successful trader who acts as a mentor. Be sure to ask the branch manager of any office that you are considering about the firm's training program and the cost of that program. Day trading firms routinely charge for training to cover expenses and also to screen potential traders. If a person is not willing to pay for training, that person will probably not open an account and trade in that office.

In addition, go to the branch office during trading hours and test the overall atmosphere. Is it friendly? Is the office staff pleasant and helpful? What kind of support and service does the branch provide to its traders? Talk to other traders in the office and ask them if they like trading there. Is the firm competitive in terms of cost? How does it calculate its commission costs? How does it charge for split orders? How does it charge for ECNs and NYSE orders? Finally, if there is more than one day trading firm in town, shop around.

Trading with a Non-Retail Day Trading Firm

Most day trading firms with a local branch office (that is, trading floor) are essentially following a traditional day trading retail business model. These firms continuously seek and recruit new retail customers. These retail customers put their own money at risk without any supervision from the broker. This business model requires a continuous inflow of fresh blood, since there is considerable turnover and attrition among retail clients. The great majority of new retail accounts will close within the next 12 months.

The less common alternative is to open an account with a day trading firm that does not seek retail customers. One such day trading firm is Las Vegas-based Bright Trading, with offices in 35 locations by the end of 2000. Bright Trading day traders are independent contractors who lease the electronic trading stations for $600 per month and deposit a $25,000 performance bond. All of their initial loses will come out of the performance bond. After completing the firm's one-week training program, which has a $1,000 fee, traders can start trading only NYSE stocks with the company's capital. At first, traders start trading stocks in increments of 100 shares, and after displaying competence, Bright Trading management will increase the allotment to 400 shares. Eventually, when the traders prove to management a certain degree of trading proficiency, the trading allotment goes up to 1,000 or 2,000 shares. In addition, traders give up 25% of their profit, which will be returned to the traders at the end of the year as a performance bonus, which becomes an incentive to stay and trade with the firm. The firm makes money by charging a standard commission, which is approximately $10 to $12 per ticket.

Trading from Home Using the Office of a Direct-Access Day Trading Firm

Some traders are able to trade from their homes using remote trading capabilities provided by a local day trading firm, even though the firm has a branch office. Instead of sitting in the firm's branch office in front of a trading monitor, the trader works at home, electronically connected to the local branch office. The trader's home workstation receives the same information as the branch office workstations. At home, the traders have an electronic router or modem and a dedicated and fast telephone line with a large data bandwidth (DSL or ISDN line) that quickly transmits data. Traders receive live price quotes from their NASD broker/dealer's quote server and send their execution orders to their NASD broker/dealer's execution server.

Not all local day trading firms provide the option of trading from home. DSL or the virtual private networks (VPNs) are not available everywhere in the country. (Although a DSL connection is generally more expensive than a standard phone-line connection, it does provide superior speed and reliability.) The average monthly cost for DSL or cable data service is about $40. Also, the day trading firm must set up for a sophisticated data network: Both DSL and VPN are expensive to set up. Because remote traders are not as active as on-site traders, the cost of setting up that additional service is often not justified. The business of remote trading is also technologically labor-intensive. There are always networking issues. Therefore, it is not surprising that some day trading firms do not want to provide this option.

Trading at Home with a Direct-Access Broker via the Internet

There are a few direct-access brokers, such as the Austin-based CyBer-Corp *(www.cybercorp.com)*, Houston-based TradeCast *(www.tradecast.com)*, New York City-based TradeScape *(www.tradescape.com)*, and Los Angeles-based MB Trading *(www.MBtrading.com)*. In my opinion, these brokers have successfully bridged the gap between the trading tools available historically only to Wall Street professionals and those that have been available to amateur traders at home. These newcomers on the brokerage scene cater specifically to active traders who wish to trade from their homes.

All four companies have deep roots in the day trading business. In the mid-1990s, Philip Berber (CyBerCorp), with Jim Howell and Bobby Earthman (TradeCast), started out with software development companies that produced the two software trading platforms that are the current industry standards for day trading shops. In 1999, CyBerCorp and TradeCast have taken giant leaps into the cyberspace brokerage business. They have modified or stripped their sophisticated day trading platforms that were leased to a few day trading firms for the mass Internet market. In 1997, Omar Amanat (TradeScape) created a sophisticated direct-access trading platform for the mass market via the Internet called Electronic Communications Portal (ECP). Also, MB Trading is a branch of Terra Nova Trading, one of the nine ECNs currently present in the marketplace. Also, MB Trading is using Townsend Analytics trading platform called RealTick III *(www.realtick.com),* which provides sophisticated real-time data analysis and trade execution. Like Cyber-Trader or TradeCast, both the TradeScape's ECP and MB Trading Real Tick III provide to day traders the direct-access technology as well as intelligent order routing for executing trades at the best available price.

CyBerCorp, TradeCast, MB Trading, and TradeScape charge a monthly fee for real-time streaming data of Level I and II information and a commission that varies from $15 to $20 per 1,000 shares. These brokerage services are designed specifically for day traders and hyperactive investors. To active traders trading from their homes, these companies provide direct access or routing to all of the ECNs, NASDAQ market makers, and NYSE specialists. Critics point out that these brokerage services are simply stripped-down trading machines in your home. There is very little guidance, support, or hand-holding. In other words, you should know a lot about trading—day trading in particular—before attempting to take full advantage of this type of Internet brokerage service.

Other lesser known direct-access brokers that aim their services at active day traders via the Internet are On-Site Trading *(www .OnSiteTrading.com),* TradePortal *(www.TradePortal.com),* EXP Trader *(www.EXPtrader.com),* Interactive Brokers *(www.InteractiveBrokers .com),* Edge Trade *(www.EdgeTrade.com),* and TradeStation Pro *(www.TradeStation.com).*

Staying home to trade, whether using the services of online brokers or the remote trading capabilities of direct-access brokers, has its disadvantages. The trader is alone. There is very little personal interaction between the trader and the outside world. There may be no one outside of immediate family to speak to and to share the daily trading experience with. There is no one to turn to and ask a question. Some people have a hard time dealing with that kind of professional isolation.

Trading Software

Many successful traders began with one of the Internet brokers, such as E*Trade, and then graduated to a specialized direct-access day trading firm that provides faster execution and better prices as well as better real-time stock information (through more sophisticated trading analysis software programs). It is no secret that day trading software packages (such as CyBerTrader, Real Tick III, TradeScape's ECP, and TradeCast) are a world apart from any trading software packages used by online brokers. These packages are sophisticated professional trading platforms developed by young, aggressive software development firms for the young and aggressive day trading environment.

I believe that day trading firms have much better trading tools than do mainstream Internet brokers. I find it ironic that the same Wall Street firms that once vilified day traders as "SOES bandits" are now actively buying or looking to buy the software firms that provided day trading technology. Today Wall Street perceives emerging day trading technology as the next generation of trading technology. I would even venture to argue that the day trading software is often better and faster than the trading systems used by some of the institutional Wall Street brokerage firms.

It is not surprising that Charles Schwab paid an astonishing sum of $400 million to purchase CyBerCorp, the developer of CyBerTrader software. Schwab paid such a high price because Internet brokers are now targeting active, or swing, traders who are in search of that illusive comparative advantage in the business of stock trading and who are requesting the bells and whistles of the latest trading software. In recent years, Internet brokers, with their huge war chests, have tried to close the software gap. In addition to purchasing CyBerCorp, Schwab also created the higher-end trading platform called Velocity, and E*Trade created its high-end trading system called Power E*Trade. Internet brokers are now offering software features that have been the norm in the day trading business, such as the dynamic Level II screen, basket-trade orders (multiple stocks and simultaneous order entries), and elimination of the order preview screening process.

However, it is my opinion that there is a structural limit to how far Internet or online brokers can go to bridge the technology gap between the online and direct-access trading. First of all, the technology must be standardized to fit the Internet browser architecture. Second, Internet brokers must standardize their order entry window and data display screens further because they are catering to millions of customers with different investment objectives and levels of sophistication and trading skill. And, because the trading software resides on the Internet brokers' servers, even if you have a fast DSL Internet connection plugged into your home PC, your trade still must wait in queue with the other thousands of investors. You must wait for your Internet pages to be assembled on the server for downloading.

On the other hand, the architecture of the direct-access day trading software is fully decentralized. The actual trading software resides on each trader's workstation. CyBerCorp, TradeCast, MB Trading, and TradeScape trading software programs are initially downloaded to the traders' machines. The price quotes and news stream directly in real time from the stock market through the data feed provider in raw form via a broadband connection or satellite dish. Charts and Level I and II displays are processed quickly through the fast processor right on the trader's workstation. Thus the information comes up much faster on the computer screen than it does for those traders working at home.

In addition, direct-access traders in the office or at home use all that decentralized computer power to keep many windows open on their screens simultaneously. Many day trading shops place two or more 21-inch monitors on each trader's desktop. Day trading software packages further accommodate traders by allowing users to customize the displays—from the color of their Level I and II screens to a choice of several trading alerts, to technical analysis charting and preprogrammed executions.

Trading depends on the speed and control of the trade-order execution. One reason that successful traders prefer to trade through the direct-access day trading firms rather than through online brokers is the ability to execute trades quickly. All direct-access day trading firms use advanced trading software packages that create sophisticated trading environments. Some software vendors provide trading software that uses macro keys or smart function keys to automate the trade-execution orders. This type of sophisticated trading software is simply not available for traders who use online brokers. Consequently, traders using the software packages at the direct-access day trading firms are one step ahead of traders using Internet brokers. Please note that these advanced features are available to day traders in the offices of the direct-access day trading firms, as well as in a streamlined or down-sized version for home-based traders who trade through direct-access brokers such as CyBerCorp, TradeCast, MB Trading, and TradeScape.

Clearing Trades

Most Internet-based brokers, and particularly day trading firms, are not self-clearing brokerage firms. Some are relatively small brokerage firms without the necessary financial and staffing resources to process, record, and administer several thousand trades every day in a hundred, and sometimes a thousand, different customer accounts.

Consequently, trading firms must use or hire some other NASD broker or dealer firm to clear or process their trades. *Clearing firms* are specialized Wall Street firms that have the financial resources, such as the fidelity bonding requirements, and the staffing and computer-data management expertise to process many thousands of trades every day.

There are only a few securities clearing firms (for example, Southwest Securities and Penson Securities) that are specialized to handle day trading requirements. Traditional investors are satisfied if the trade settlement date is three days after the trade date, but that time frame is unacceptable for the trader. Therefore, clearing firms will settle all trades on the same day that they are placed.

All money goes through the clearing firm as well. When a new trader opens a trading account with a trading firm, the trader issues a check in the name of the clearing firm. The clearing firm keeps track of all trades done by all traders in that trading firm. The clearing firm then calculates the profit or loss from each trade and deducts the commission cost. When the trader closes the account, the clearing firm will cut the check or transfer the money to another account. At the end of the month, the clearing firm will send a check to the trading brokerage firm for the portion of the trader's commission, which becomes the brokerage firm's income.

Day Trading Suitability

To the day trading firm, the first and most important issue regarding the opening of a trading account is the customer's suitability for the trading business. Trading is not for everyone. It is a risky endeavor. It is an unfortunate fact that many individuals have opened trading accounts with day trading firms or Internet brokers without fully understanding the skill set required in this business and the associated risks. It is important that the risks are clearly disclosed up front. The risk associated with trading is usually disclosed somewhat more adequately if the account is opened with a branch office of a day trading firm. At least the new trader has the opportunity to talk to a live person and ask questions. On the Internet, however, a new trader can open a trading account without ever talking to a live human being.

The first question regarding an individual's suitability to be a trader involves technical competence. Many new traders are lured to this career by media coverage that glamorizes and romanticizes trading, and few have any experience in trading securities or commodities. At best they might have an investment account with a discount brokerage firm. It would not take much time for a branch manager to ascertain such a lack of technical experience. Consequently, these individuals will need to spend time learning new terminology and skills. Before approving the new account, a branch manager should urge prospective traders to complete all of the firm's training courses (or any other available trading training).

The second issue regarding an individual's suitability involves financial competence. It is important to understand from the outset that traders place their money at substantial risk at all times. Thus new traders must understand that they will use only their speculative money for this endeavor. The intent is to trade money that the trader can afford to lose. The prospective trader's net worth and liquid net worth status would quickly reveal whether she could absorb the financial losses. For instance, a liquid net worth of $100,000 would indicate that the prospective trader could afford to lose $15,000 or $20,000 before becoming a proficient trader.

There might be other considerations that would point to an individual's suitability for trading. For example, there might be questions regarding future expectations: Does the prospective trader have unrealistic views on trading? Does the new trader need to earn money trading immediately to support himself? Does the prospective trader have several dependents in the family? What is the source of the start-up money?

Finally, the prospective trader must sign the required forms and risk-disclosure statements to acknowledge that all risk always resides with the trader. The trading firm will not assume or accept any risk or liability. The trader is responsible for any action regarding the trading account. The associated market risk that comes with the buying and selling of securities is just common sense—it always goes with the trader. In addition, the trader will also always assume the accompanied technology risk (for example, computer or network breakdowns).

CHAPTER
26

Online Brokers

All firms—whether online, discount or full service—have an obligation to ensure the best execution of their customers' orders. That's not just good business practice; it's a legal obligation. Firms have this same duty to their customers to find the best prices—whether they charge $10 per trade or $100 per trade. . . . I urge all firms now to review their practices to ensure they're doing right by their customers.

> *Arthur Levitt*
> *Chairman*
> *U.S. Securities and Exchange Commission*
> *May 1999*

IN ESSENCE, THERE ARE TWO TYPES OF BROKERS THAT PROVIDE SERVICE VIA the Internet: direct-access brokers, such as CyBerCorp or TradeCast, and generic online brokerage firms, such as Charles Schwab or E*Trade. Either way, you are connected to the Internet and trade from home. The key difference is their order execution of trade orders.

Using a direct-access broker, you as a trader are in control of your execution price. A trader can route (preference) a trade order for execution directly to any NASDAQ market maker or ECN using the SelectNet preferencing mechanism. When you are using the services of an online broker you do not have this execution control. More important, more than half of the online brokers end up routing customers' orders to the "corresponding" wholesaler market makers for the payment for the order flow.

The Securities and Exchange Commission (SEC) reported in 2000 that 17 of 29 online brokerage firms were not meeting their obligation to provide the best execution for their customers' trades in 1999. According to the study, more than half of the Internet brokers "improperly emphasized payment for order flow in deciding where to send orders." In other words, the reason that a majority of customers did not receive the best execution price is that most online firms have other market makers complete their customers' trades in exchange for payments of as much as 2 cents a share.

These *payments for the order flow*, which are currently legal, determine where a customer's order is sent. The SEC ruled in the early 1990's that this practice is allowed as long as brokers disclose it to their retail clients. However, the controversy remains over the payment for order flow. Even if another market maker or trader on the ECN is offering a better price, the online broker will send the customer's market order to the corresponding market maker to be filled at a worse price. For instance, a day trader would receive $1/16$ ($62.50) less than the prevailing market price at that point in time on a typical 1,000-share transaction. Even worse, in the fast-moving market, corresponding market makers have incentive to sit on an order for a few seconds longer and let the price go up further before executing the order, and to fill them from their own inventories, thus increasing the market maker's profitability at the trader's expense.

Payments for order flow have been declining in recent years, mostly because market spreads between the BID and ASK prices have been declining as well. The largest NASDAQ market-maker wholesaler, Knight/Trimark Group (NITE), which accounts for approximately 15% of NASDAQ market-making activity, routinely pays order flow to E*Trade, Waterhouse, and Ameritrade brokers. In addition, E*Trade, Waterhouse, and Ameritrade brokers have equity stake in Knight/Trimark. The largest online broker, Charles Schwab, does not accept the payment for order flow, but it sends almost all of its market orders to its wholly owned subsidiary, Mayer & Schweitzer (MASH), which is one of the largest and most influential market makers. The net impact is the same—traders potentially do not receive the best price execution for their market orders.

Many traders do not pay attention to this common practice. However, it is important that all traders understand that payment for order flow is corrupting trade executions. It is equally important that traders understand that payment for order flow costs money. Traders are often more focused on a low trade commission cost, although the practice of payment for order flow will cost them more than the discounted $7 commission. From the trader's perspective, there is a clear trade-off between low-cost commissions for the market order and the best price execution. Brokers use the payments for order flow from the corresponding market makers to subsidized the low commissions. It is my opinion that traders ultimately end up paying more for the subsidized low commissions, and my experience that serious day traders would routinely select the better price execution as the more cost-effective method for trading stocks.

Online Brokers

The pioneer of the online brokerage business was the discount brokerage arm of the investment banking firm Donaldson, Lufkin & Jenrette. In 1987, the Internet service provider Prodigy asked Donaldson, Lufkin & Jenrette—after being rejected by Schwab, Fidelity, and Dean Witter—to set up an online brokerage business for Prodigy. That marked the beginning of the Financial Network, which later transformed into DLJ Direct. The firm's start was very slow and modest, with the light volume of a dozen trades per day. In 1999, DLJ Direct opened 700,000 online accounts and was doing 20,000 trades per day.

Success breeds imitation, or in other words, success breeds competition. Twelve years later, DLJ Direct has lost its leadership role. In terms of volume, it ranked seventh among the online brokers in 1999. Table 26.1 depicts the online trading volume leaders in 1999.

All online brokers are not created equally. There are some dramatic differences among them, because they are all trying to differentiate and tailor their services to specific market segments. A one-size-fits-all approach to online trading does not work. In addition, the field of the online brokerage firms is in a constant state of motion. Internet brokers are continuously upgrading and improving their services and lowering prices. My advice is to do your research, obtain current information, and determine which broker meets your particular needs as a trader.

Table 26.1 *Top 10 Online Brokers in 1999 (by Volume Market Share)*

Broker	Internet Address	Market Share
Charles Schwab	www.schwab.com	25
E*Trade	www.etrade.com	14
Fidelity Investments	www.fidelity.com	12
Waterhouse Securities	www.waterhouse.com	12
Datek	www.datek.com	11
Ameritrade	www.ameritrade.com	9
DLJ Direct	www.dljdirect.com	4
SureTrade	www.suretrade.com	2
Discover Brokerage	www.discoverbrokerage.com	2
National Discount Brokers	www.ndb.com	1

Some Internet brokers, such as Schwab *(www.schwab.com),* E*Trade *(www.etrade.com),* or DLJ Direct *(www.DLJdirect.com),* try to provide "one stop shopping" by offering, in one seamless trading environment, the full menu of securities services: stocks, options, bonds, mutual funds, IRAs, research, charting, and trade execution. Then there are the online brokers that compete specifically by the lowest possible commissions, often at less than $10 per trade, such as FirstTrade ($6.95), SureTrade ($7.95), Wang Investments ($8), A. B. Watley ($9.95), Trading Direct ($9.95), and Datek ($9.99). These commissions are most likely based on market orders. The cost of the limit orders would probably be $5 more.

A new twist to the Internet-brokerage price competition is the emergence of commission-free trades. The biggest name brokerage entry in this field was American Express *(www.AmericanExpress.com),* which offered a free limit, market, and stop-order service to its wealthier customers who maintain accounts of $100,000 or more. American Express clients with a minimum of $25,000 in their accounts can buy stock online free of any commissions, but the sell orders cost $14.95. However, American Express changed its mind by the end of 2000 and it currently offers only 10 free market order trades if the account exceeds $100,000. If the account is less than $100,000 traders now get only three free market order trades. In addition, the commission cost went up to $19.95.

Another variation on zero-commission trades is available from Free-Trade.com *(www.FreeTrade.com)*, which offers experienced online traders who have a minimum of two years' online trading experience free buy and sell market orders; all limit orders are $5 each. Finally, a new entry in this field is San Francisco-based The Financial Café *(www .TheFinancialCafe.com)*, which charges no commissions on market orders and $16.95 for limit or stop orders.

Other online brokers, such as Datek, E*Trade, and Schwab, offer after-hours trading. Datek, which owns Island ECN, provides after-hours trading from 8:00 A.M. to 8:00 P.M. EST through Island. Schwab provides after-hours trading services through the REDIbook ECN, and E*Trade routes its after-hours trades through Instinet ECN. Be aware that the volume of after-hours trading is extremely thin, so trading is difficult. Because of lower trading volume, the spread between the BID and ASK is somewhat larger than during the regular market hours from 9:30 A.M. to 4:00 P.M. EST. In other words, due to the larger spread, the actual cost of trading during the extra hours is higher.

Online brokers such as Discover *(www.DiscoverBrokerage.com)*, Fidelity *(www.fidelity.com)*, Schwab, DLJ Direct, and E*Trade advertise the ability to acquire IPOs. These brokers can make such claims because they are owned by or affiliated with the large investment banks. For instance, the investment bank Donaldson, Lufkin & Jenrette owns DLJ Direct; Morgan Stanley owns Discover. Fidelity has partnered with the investment bank Lehman Brothers, and E*Trade has an alliance with Robertson Stephens and Goldman Sachs & Co. Schwab has a corresponding relationship with Credit Suisse First Boston, J. P. Morgan, and Chase Manhattan Hambrecht & Quist. However, the IPO allotment given to the online brokers has been extremely small, ranging from 1 to 10%. I believe that online brokerage firms use and advertise the potential for purchasing IPOs as an enticement to traders to open accounts with their firm. In all probability, it is extremely unlikely that investors would receive any shares of a hot IPO from any of the online brokers.

Some online brokers provide Level II quote screens for an additional monthly fee. This is an important tool for short-term day traders. Most Internet brokers today do not provide such information at all. Those that do provide such information free of charge are A. B. Watley *(www.abwatley.com)*, Firstrade *(www.firstrade.com)*, Scottsdale Securities *(www.scottrade.com)*, Wang Investments *(www.wangvest.com)*,

Web Street Securities *(www.webstreet.com)*, Freeman Welwood *(www.FreemanWelwood.com)*, and CompuTEL Securities *(www.computel.com)*. As an absolute minimum, the trader should look for an Internet broker that provides on-screen trade confirmations. There is no worse feeling than sending an online buy order and then not knowing whether you have the stock or not.

Full-service Wall Street brokers are the latest entry into the increasingly crowded field of online brokerage business, resulting in a blurring of the lines of demarcation between full-service and discount brokers. Merrill Lynch, Morgan Stanley, Paine Webber, and Salomon Smith Barney have unveiled fee-based online brokerage services that are extremely competitive. The Wall Street firms charge a large flat annual fee, such as $1,500 for Merrill Lynch or $1,000 for Morgan Stanley, for unlimited trading and free proprietary financial research and advice. For an active day trader who makes approximately 50 trades a year, this is comparable in terms of cost to 50 trades with Charles Schwab (at $29.95) or 100 trades with E*Trade (at $14.95), which do not offer any significant in-house research capabilities.

Online-Broker Issues

Recently, the General Accounting Office (GAO) collected data from 12 online brokerage firms which accounted for almost 90% of online trading in 1999. The GAO identified "trade delays and trade breakdowns" to be a big problem. In fact, so common were trade delays and trade breakdowns at one firm that the firm's management did not track them. In addition, GAO reported that online firms provided customers with little information on the risks of margin trading. Nearly half the online brokerage companies did not detail the risks to their customers for opening margin accounts. Only a third of the online brokerage firms posted stock margin information on their Internet sites, such as a list of stocks the firm will not allow customers to buy on margin.

When considering online brokers, you should always look into the level of technical support the broker offers. Will the level of support be significant for your needs? For instance, many Internet brokerage firms are not geared toward servicing the accounts of active day traders, who might enter several dozen orders each day. The day trader's account is one among many thousands of accounts, most of which belong to investors who are only managing their own portfolios and perhaps submitting a few trades per month. The investors, regardless of how active they might be, are not day traders and thus their needs are different.

There are other issues associated with online brokers: How fast is the data feed? Is the data feed delayed or real-time? How fast and reliable is the trade execution? Does the online broker route the order to a wholesaler for the order-flow payment? Do you get the best price? Do you have access to ECNs? Trading access to ECNs is crucial for active traders. How quickly does the day trader receive trade confirmation? What software does the online broker use for executing the trades? What other features are included in the trading software offered to the trader? What is the commission cost?

It is also extremely important that the trading firm or Internet-based broker that holds the customer's trading accounts is a member of the Securities Investor Protection Corporation (SIPC). SIPC is the product of the Securities Investor Protection Act, which was passed by Congress to safeguard customers' funds and securities in the event that the NASD broker/dealer becomes insolvent. Branch offices of trading firms make sure that the SIPC label is displayed prominently somewhere on the trading floor. The SIPC provides insurance coverage up to a maximum of $500,000, of which no more than $100,000 may be for cash losses.

There are many questions to ask when looking for an online broker, and each online broker has different answers. Because the electronic brokerage business has mushroomed in the United States during the past few years, it pays to research your online broker. Gómez *(www.gomez.com)* currently ranks 55 brokerage firms that offer online stock-trading brokerage services. Similarly, Internet Investing *(www.internetinvesting.com)*, ConsumerSearch *(www.ConsumerSearch.com)*, Xolia *(www.Xolia.com)*, SmartMoney *(www.SmartMoney.com)*, Money *(www.Money.com)*, and Wall Street Online *(www.wallstonline.com)* provide reference lists and screening of the online brokers.

I personally like Gómez's scoring methodology. The ranking assists traders who want to do business on the Internet in identifying brokers whose online offerings best meet their needs. Gómez ranks the online brokers by how well they serve traders in each of 100 or more objective criteria categories. Table 26.2 displays the overall scores for the top 20 online brokers. The highest score is 10; the lowest is 0. Thus if the brokerage firm earns an overall score of 10, then the firm provides the best services at the lowest cost.

Finally, Gómez rolls up the criteria into customer profiles. It weighs the individual criteria by customer profile according to the importance of that criteria to a particular customer profile. For instance, Gómez looks at four standard customer profiles: Hyperactive Trader, Serious Investor, Life-Goal Planner, and One-Stop Shopper. Traders should pay

Table 26.2 *Gómez's Top 20 Internet Brokers*

Rank	Internet Broker	Overall Score
1.	E*Trade	7.66
2.	Charles Schwab	7.39
3.	Fidelity Investments	7.37
4.	DLJ Direct	6.84
5.	TD Waterhouse	6.43
6.	NDB	6.32
7.	My Discount Broker	6.24
8.	A. B. Watley	6.13
9.	Morgan Stanley Dean Witter Online	6.08
10.	Suretrade	6.06
11.	Ameritrade	6.05
12.	Siebert	5.99
13.	Web Street	5.95
14.	WingspanBank.com	5.90
15.	Quick & Reilly	5.81
16.	Datek	5.77
17.	WallStreet Electronica	5.72
18.	Empire	5.7219
19.	American Express Brokerage	5.71
20.	Freeman Welwood	5.64

Source: Ranked by Gómez.com

close attention to the customer-profile rankings, because not all firms cater to every profile. In addition, the best firm overall may not be the best firm for a given trader and his or her unique trading style, needs, or intentions. For each customer profile, a different set of criteria is more important and therefore weighted more heavily.

Table 26.3 shows the overall score for the top 20 Internet brokers for the most active traders, such as swing traders or day traders. The

Table 26.3 *Top 20 Internet Brokers for Active Traders*

Rank	Internet Broker	Overall Score
1.	E*Trade	7.54
2.	A. B. Watley	6.86
3.	Firstrade	6.67
4.	Web Street	6.64
5.	Suretrade	6.63
6.	Empire	6.60
7.	TD Waterhouse	6.60
8.	My Discount Broker	6.39
9.	America First Trader	6.37
10.	KeyTrade Online	6.33
11.	Scottrade	6.31
12.	Wang Investments	6.31
13.	Fidelity Investments	6.30
14.	Ameritrade	6.30
15.	Datek	6.28
16.	Trading Direct	6.18
17.	DLJ Direct	6.12
18.	NDB	6.03
19.	Brown	5.89
20.	WallStreet Electronica	5.88

Source: Ranked by Gómez.com

most important factors for day traders are low-cost trading, a simple interface, charting, online confirmations, and fast execution.

Experts estimate that 15,000 online brokerage accounts are opened every day, which puts tremendous technological strains on online brokers. Due to the large amount of traffic on the Internet in general and large trading volumes by online brokers, system performance is sometimes slow. Real-time stock quotes become delayed quotes. Order confirmations are slow, often leaving the online trader in the dark. Traders sometimes wonder if they actually own the stock and whether they can now sell it.

Therefore, the reliability of online trading becomes an important issue. The online trader depends on the performance of several electronic service vendors: the Internet service provider (ISP), the data feed provider, and the brokerage computer system. Most Internet brokers now offer Secure Socket Layer (SSL) Java script routing of trade orders through the brokerage firms' host servers instead of relying on slow and unprotected e-mail servers. Nevertheless, serious Internet traders will build their own system redundancy, such as maintaining two trading accounts at different brokerage firms and having two different ISPs for their Internet access.

Wireless Trading

Another new twist is the emergence of wireless-trading technology. Many brokerage firms in the United States are actively and aggressively offering wireless-trading options to their wealthy or more active trading clients in order to differentiate their trading services. The wireless trading option is attractive to many active traders whose busy lifestyles are such that they spend a lot of time away from their desks and computers, either traveling or shuttling between meetings. Wireless trading is conducted via digital cell phones, two-way pagers, or handheld computers. The cost of such equipment ranges from $200 for a cell phone with the Internet access to $450 for a handheld computer organizer, such as a Palm Pilot.

However, at this point, the level of received information is rather limited. It is impossible to compress the typical stock market data found on 17- or 20-inch computer monitors on a four-line cell phone display. It is impossible to get real-time streaming price quotes or NASDAQ Level II information or interactive real-time technical analysis charting.

Nevertheless, a four-line display is adequate to check account balances, access market-price data (Level I quotes), receive certain trade alerts or news, and execute electronically buy or sell orders. The trades are executed electronically, just as if the trade order was submitted electronically through your PC via the Internet. Keep in mind that wireless-trading technology is still in its infancy, and at present a wireless network can be a rather unreliable trading medium.

27

Summary

NATURA NON FACIT SALTUM. THIS IS LATIN FOR "NATURE DOES NOT make leaps." A century ago, the famous economist Alfred Marshall began his *Principles of Economics* textbook with that statement. His point was that any progress or change is always small and gradual. I would like to close this book with the same reminder. Success in the day trading business does not come overnight, easily, or with any degree of certainty. Day trading is neither a "Get Rich Quick" nor a "Get Rich Click" scheme. It is not fast or easy money, and certainly, there are no guarantees in this business.

Most important, it takes many months and many good and bad trades to get there. And the majority of new day traders will never get there. So start slowly. Start trading slowly with slow stocks that do not move dramatically, and trade in increments of 100 shares. Then gradually move up. Increase the number of shares by 100 each week. After a few weeks of live trading experience, consider trading more volatile stocks.

It takes time to become a proficient day trader. Experienced traders estimate that it takes three to six months of live trading before one matures into an accomplished day trader. Add to that the time required to acquire the basic day trading skill set. Before making a single trade, a new day trader invests many hours reading and researching about day trading. In addition, the new day trader will allocate several weeks to paper trading to become comfortable with trading software and its execution system.

It is also extremely unrealistic to expect that anyone will start making money immediately. In fact, expect to lose money at the beginning. The learning curve is steep, and it does not need to be expensive, though losses at the beginning are inevitable. It will take several thousand dollars of losing trades before one graduates into a profitable day trading business. Losses can be $15,000 or higher before a novice day trader turns the corner. The level of losses depends on the trader's discipline and risk management skills. My advice is to have minimal expectations at the beginning.

It is also important that a new day trader trade only the money that he can afford to lose. If you cannot afford to absorb the loss, then please do not even start the business of day trading. As a day trader, one continuously makes trading decisions on whether the price of a stock will move in a certain direction. Critics of day trading state that this activity constitutes speculation. If speculating means buying and selling stocks in expectation of profiting from market fluctuations, then all day traders are short-term speculators. All of us would agree that any speculative endeavor assumes a substantial risk of losing money. If you cannot assume that risk, then do not trade.

Starting a day trading venture is very much comparable to starting a new business. After investing the time to learn the basic skills and investing the start-up capital to open a trading account, the new day trader is finally in business. Each trading decision is a business decision that translates immediately into a profit or loss. Is it realistic to expect that every new business will take off immediately? Is it realistic to expect that everyone who has started a new business will succeed?

If the business of day trading were that simple, lucrative, and low risk, then everyone would be day trading. Why would anyone bother to work and commute to a nine-to-five job? Why not simply sit in front of a computer monitor at a day trading branch office or at home via an Internet connection and make a living trading stocks? If this new business of day trading were that easy, there would be a line of people eager to get in the business in front of every day trading firm's branch office. Well, there are no such waiting lines. This business looks deceptively easy to start; yet it is very difficult to master and profit from.

Why have so many people failed in the day trading business? Sometimes I believe that the day trading success fits the infamous "80–20 rule." Eighty percent of the profit goes to 20% of day traders.

Conversely, 80% of the day traders fight over the remaining 20% of the profits.

Why is it that so many traders have lost money day trading? The answer to this question lies in the core of this deceptively simple trading practice. The nature of day trading is to exploit short-term price volatility and earn small incremental profits by trading in increments of 1,000 shares. The rewards and risks of this business rest in the fact that 1,000 shares are always at risk. Trading a large block of shares is a double-edged sword. The day trader can quickly earn $250 profit if the price goes in a favorable direction by $\frac{1}{4}$ of a point; conversely, the day trader can quickly lose the same amount if the price goes in an unfavorable direction.

This is where the trader's discipline comes in. The key is to minimize losses and maximize the upside potential. If $\frac{1}{4}$ is the day trader's loss limit, then he should not lose more than $250 on that trade. However, many new day traders do not have the discipline necessary to control their losses. They allow a small loss to turn into a large loss. They wait too long, so that an initial $\frac{1}{4}$ loss turns into $\frac{3}{8}$ or $\frac{1}{2}$ or an even larger loss.

Another common and costly mistake is that many day traders force their trades. They enter a trade position without receiving a clear buy or sell signal. The day trader does not need to anticipate price momentum; there is no obligation to be proactive and forecast or time the market's next peak or valley. All day traders need to do is to be reactive (and not proactive) and recognize an existing or observable price momentum.

Treat day trading as a real business. If trading is treated as a hobby, it will evolve into a very expensive hobby. So, be focused and keep a daily log of your trades. Review your trades and learn from your mistakes. Appendix 6 is a simple true-or-false quiz that will test your general understanding of basic day trading principles. Take the quiz and see if you know this business.

Success in day trading comes with acquired knowledge of trading, invested time and effort, and continuous and disciplined practice of risk management skills. Since there are few home runs in this kind of trading, the trading success appears in small and incremental profits with numerous successful trades. Finally, when you lose money on a bad trade, don't lose the lesson.

1

Electronic and Print Stock Trading Information

A FEW YEARS AGO, MOST STOCK MARKET INFORMATION WAS PROPRIETARY and costly. Investors and traders had to subscribe to and pay financial information companies dearly for real-time quotes, news, and research. Even the delivery of that information was cumbersome and expensive. Investors and traders had to lease or purchase satellite dishes, computers, and software to process this continuous flow of data. The Internet has transformed the way stock information is delivered.

The Web

Today, all of the financial information companies have Web sites, where they post the same quality of financial information free of charge. Although some sites charge a nominal monthly fee, investors and traders can still research a stock on demand at their convenience at any time of day—all at a fraction of what it would have cost fewer than five years ago.

Because the Internet phenomenon is truly an information revolution, these financial information sites are extremely dynamic. The content and format of these sites tend to change frequently, and new sites from new companies emerge continuously.

There are many day trading Internet sites available today, and more are being designed. Most of the sites require a paid subscription for "premium" service, although all of them offer some free access or a free trial subscription. Internet resources have been mentioned throughout this book, but, I offer here a brief list of my favorite sites, all of which provide useful and educational information in attractive and easy-to-use formats:

Trading Markets (*www.tradingmarkets.com*)

TraderBot (*www.TraderBot.com*)

The Fly on the Wall (*www.theflyonthewall.com*)

The Intelligent Speculator (*www.IntelligentSpeculator.com*)

Pristine Day Trader (*www.Pristine.com*)

Day Trading Stocks (*www.DayTradingStocks.com*)

Trading Tactics (*www.TradingTactics.com*)

The First News (*www.TheFirstNews.com*)

Falcon Eye (*www.FalconEye.com*)

For novice day traders, I recommend The Rookie Day Trader *(www.RookieDayTrader.com)*, and for day trading tax information, I suggest Traders Accounting *(www.TradersAccounting.com)*.

My favorite general financial directory and reference Internet sites are Yahoo! Finance *(www.finance.yahoo.com)* and Microsoft Network MoneyCentral *(www.moneycentral.MSN.com)*. These two sites deserve special mention because they are complete and they are absolutely free. At these sites, investors and traders can review stock quotes, charts, company fundamentals, news, and discussion boards.

Other free general financial sites worth your time:

Invest-O-Rama (*www.investorama.com*)

Online Investor Magazine (www.onlineinvestor.com)

Thomson Financial Network (*www.thomsoninvest.net*)

INVEStools (*www.investools.com*)

Among the sites that charge a nominal fee but provide a great deal of value is Wall Street City *(www.WallStreetCity.com)*.

In addition to sites that offer general stock market information, there are several specialized and focused Internet sites. For fundamental stock research, I suggest Zacks Investment Research *(www.zacks.com)*, Multex Investor Network *(www.multexinvestor.com)*, and BestCalls *(www.BestCalls.com)*.

Among the fundamental research sites that charge a nominal fee, I like Hoover's Online *(www.Hoovers.com)*.

For technical stock analysis, I recommend:

BigCharts (*www.BigCharts.com*)

BigEasy (*www.BigEasyInvestor.com*)

FreeRealTime (*www.FreeRealTime.com*)

ClearStation (*www.ClearStation.com*)

For stock market news analysis, I like

CBS MarketWatch (*www.CBSMarketWatch.com*)

CNN Finance Network (*www.CNNfn.com*)

CNBC (*www.CNBC.com*)

Reuters MoneyNet (*www.moneynet.com*)

Among the news sites that charge a nominal fee but provide a great deal of value are *The Wall Street Journal (www.wsj.com),* The Street *(www.TheStreet.com),* and Briefing.com *(www.Briefing.com).*

For an education in general stock investing and trading, I suggest the Internet sites from the American Association of Individual Investors *(www.AAII.com),* The Investment FAQ *(www.invest-faq.com),* and Armchair Millionaire *(www.armchairmillionaire.com).*

For anyone interested in chat rooms for investors and traders, Silicon Investor *(www.siliconinvestor.com)* and Raging Bull *(www.RagingBull.com)* have some good resources. In addition, the Web site for the Federal government's Securities and Exchange Commission *(www.sec.gov),* as well as those for the NYSE *(www.NYSE.com)* and NASDAQ *(www.NASDAQ.com)* stock exchanges, provide useful information. FreeEDGAR *(www.freeEDGAR.com)* is an Internet site that compiles and provides a ton of free fundamental stock research data from the SEC EDGAR database.

Stock traders and investors who trade electronically have an opportunity to eavesdrop electronically on conference calls between corporate management and Wall Street analysts. Several Internet sites broadcast corporate earnings conference calls:

Best Calls (*www.BestCalls.com*)

Street Events (*www.StreetEvents.com*)

Street Fusion (*www.StreetFusion.com*)

VCall (*www.Vcall.com*)

Keep in mind that it is very difficult to sort through the wealth of information transmitted during long conference calls and to pick up on the fine points.

There are several Internet-based data feed providers that provide delayed and real-time stock quotes and news for a fee or sometimes free of charge:

Standard & Poor's ComStock *(www.spcomstock.com)*

PCQuote *(www.Pcquote.com)*

Quote *(www.Quote.com)*

Bloomberg *(www.Bloomberg.com)*

eSignal *(www.esignal.com)*

Data Broadcasting Corporation *(www.DBC.com)*

Print Media

I believe strongly that reading books on stock investing and trading, such as this book and many other similar titles, is the most cost-effective way to acquire the required knowledge of the stock market. Investors and traders can pick up a great deal of concise information in a single book.

In addition to books, there is a new kid on the block: *Active Trader* ($4.95 per issue), a monthly magazine *(www.ActiveTraderMag.com)* designed specifically for swing and day traders. Also, the *Online Investor (www.OnlineInvestor.com)* is a monthly magazine ($24.95 for annual subscription) that provides timely and quality electronic trading information.

There are also several time-tested sources of printed stock market information. *The Wall Street Journal* and *Investor's Business Daily* are standard daily reading fare for most professional investors and traders. Finally, many daily newspapers in America provide summaries of financial data in their finance sections.

Another form of print media includes market newsletters, which contain buy or sell stock recommendations. A typical newsletter contains a brief analysis of a particular stock, along with a recommendation. Potential subscribers should ascertain whether the newsletter is appropriate in terms of the following:

➤ Does the newsletter cover the appropriate financial product?

➤ Does the newsletter cover the appropriate trading or investment strategy?

➤ Does the newsletter cover the appropriate time holding strategy?

➤ Is the delivery mechanism appropriate in terms of time (e-mail, fax, or mail)?

➤ What is the newsletter writer's reputation or track record, if there is any?

➤ Do you agree with the newsletter writer's reasoning and logic?

There are several Internet sites devoted exclusively to market newsletters. These sites provide quick comparisons among several newsletter categories, such as product, strategy, rates, and frequency of publication, as well as links to the publishers' Internet sites. The sites are: INVEStools *(www.investools.com)*, Newsletter Network *(www.margin.com)*, and the Hulbert Financial Digest *(www.hulbertdigest.com)*.

My personal feeling about the overall value of newsletters is one of healthy skepticism. If there is a Holy Grail to stock trading and investing, and in my opinion there is no such thing, why would anyone disclose it for a minor subscription fee? If you are thinking of subscribing to a market newsletter, my recommendation is to ask for a free examination copy or a free trial subscription.

Other Resources

Finally, consider attending a stock trading conference, such as the Online Trading Expo (go to *www.OnlineTradingExpo.com* for dates and locations), that are being organized throughout the year in major U.S. cities. Also, consider enrolling in a trading seminar, such as the Online Trading Academy (visit *www.OnlineTradingAcademy.com* for more information). The price range for the seminars varies from a few hundred to a few thousand dollars. Just as you would when purchasing any product or service for the first time, do the research and check the offering company's references and credentials—before you sign up for the seminars.

Day Traders and Margin Accounts

ALL DAY TRADERS OPEN MARGIN ACCOUNTS FOR THEIR TRADING transactions. They receive from the clearing firm daily margin account activity statements. Day traders must know how to read and understand these statements. Following is a brief explanation of margin account terminology.

The Federal Reserve Board, under Regulation T (Reg. T) of the Securities and Exchange Commission Act of 1934, regulates the extension of credit by NASD broker/dealers to traders and investors. The Reg. T is expressed as a percentage of the total purchase price. The current Reg. T margin requirement is 50% for long and short securities transactions. Only *marginable* securities, which include all stocks on the NYSE and NASDAQ national market system, may be purchased on margin.

When the NASD broker or dealer extends a credit to a day trader who wants to trade securities, the trading transactions must be executed in a *margin account*. Opening a margin account requires that the day trader sign a margin agreement, which specifies the following:

➤ The day trader agrees to pledge the securities in the margin account to the NASD broker/dealer as collateral for the loan.

➤ The day trader grants permission to the NASD broker/dealer to repledge (that is, "rehypothecate") the same securities at the bank as collateral for the loan. The bank will issue a loan to the NASD broker/dealer at a specific interest rate, which is called in the industry the *brokers' call rate*.

➤ The day trader also grants permission to the NASD broker/dealer to lend the same security to other brokers' customers who sold short that particular security.

The entire hypothecation process has four distinct steps:

1. The day trader pledges or hypothecates securities to the NASD broker/dealer.

2. The NASD broker/dealer rehypothecates the same securities that were used as collateral for the loan to the bank.

3. The bank lends to the NASD broker/dealer money at the brokers' call rate.

4. The NASD broker/dealer lends to the day trader at the margin interest rate, which is a bit higher than the broker's call rate.

The Long Margin Account

Figure A2.1 shows what happens when a day trader purchases a security on margin. The long market value will fluctuate with the price of the security throughout the day. Suppose that the day trader has purchased 1,000 shares of a stock that is priced at that time at $40. The long market value is $40,000. The debit balance represents the amount that was borrowed by the day trader and is owed to the NASD broker/dealer firm. In this example, given the 50% Reg. T requirement, the maximum amount that the trader can borrow is $20,000. That is the base amount that will be used to calculate the interest charges paid by the customer. The annual interest rate charged is usually in the range of 8% to 9%. The customer will deposit $20,000 in the margin account. The equity is the customer's deposited money. The equity can be also calculated by subtracting the amount owed from the current market value of the stock position. Figure A2.1 illustrates this point.

If the security appreciates in value, the long market value will increase. Since the borrowed amount remains the same (the debit balance remains at $20,000), the trader's equity increases as well. When the equity in the account exceeds the Reg. T requirement of 50%, the day trader has excess equity in the account. Figure A2.2 elaborates further on this point.

Suppose that the stock price increases from $40 to $60. The long market value is now $60,000. Since the borrowed amount or the debit

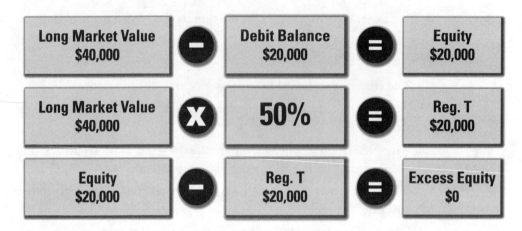

Figure A2.1 *Long Margin Account*

balance remains the same at $20,000, the trader's equity increases to $40,000. The Reg. T 50% requirement on the $60,000 current market value is $30,000. That means that the day trader has excess equity of $10,000 in the account.

The excess equity in a margin account is referred to in the industry as the *special memorandum account* (SMA). In this example, the trader can use the $10,000 SMA to purchase additional securities or to withdraw cash. In fact, the trader can purchase $20,000 worth of securities

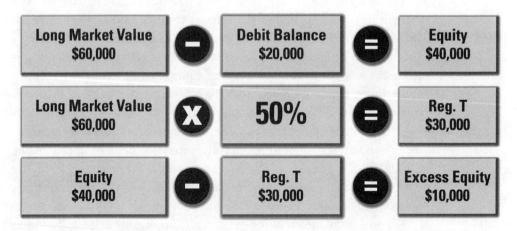

Figure A2.2 *Long Margin Account with Stock Price Appreciation*

with the $10,000 SMA. The trader has higher buying power because the excess equity or SMA can be used to buy additional securities. The quickest way to calculate buying power is to divide the SMA by the Reg. T requirement. The formula for buying power is the following:

$$\text{Buying Power} = \frac{\text{SMA}}{\text{Reg. T}}$$

While the higher price results in excess equity, a decline in stock value might cause a long margin account to become *restricted*. A margin account becomes a restricted account if the equity falls below the Reg. T 50% requirement. Figure A2.3 illustrates this point.

Now, let us suppose that the stock price has decreased from the initial price of $40 to $30. The long market value is now $30,000. Since the initial borrowed amount or the debit balance remained the same at $20,000, the trader's equity decreased to $10,000. The Reg. T 50% requirement on the $30,000 current market value is $15,000. That means that the day trader now has negative excess equity in the account of minus $5,000. The account is now restricted.

If a margin account is restricted, the day trader can continue making additional purchases by meeting the Reg. T requirement on a particular additional purchase. It is not mandatory to deposit additional money to bring the entire account up to the Reg. T requirement. With a restricted margin account, 100% of any sale proceeds will be used to

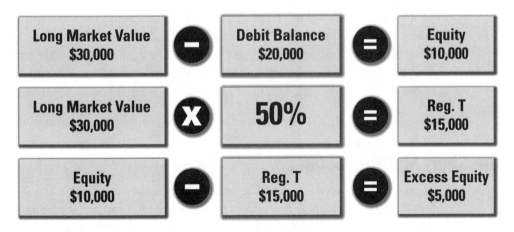

Figure A2.3 *Restricted Margin Account*

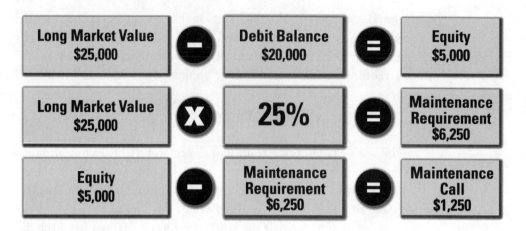

Figure A2.4 *Margin Maintenance Requirement*

reduce the debit balance in the margin account. If the price drops dramatically, the day trader will receive a margin maintenance call from the broker. The NASD requires that all customers maintain at least 25% equity of the current market value in their accounts. Figure A2.4 illustrates this point.

Now, let us suppose that the stock price decreased dramatically from the initial price of $40 to $25. The long market value is now $25,000. Since the initial borrowed amount or the debit balance remains the same at $20,000, the trader's equity has decreased to $5,000. The NASD and NYSE minimum maintenance requirement is 25%; that 25% requirement on a $25,000 current market value is $6,250. That means that the day trader's equity in the account is below the minimum maintenance requirement. The day trader will receive a maintenance call from the broker. The broker will require that the day trader deposit $1,250 into the account.

The Short Margin Account

When a day trader sells short a security in her margin account, the day trader has established a *credit balance* in the margin account. Figure A2.5 shows what happens when the day trader sells short a security on margin. First, the short-sale value will fluctuate with the price of the

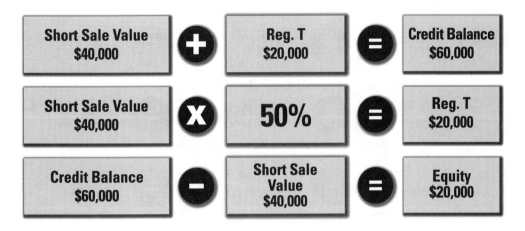

Figure A2.5 *Short Margin Account*

security. Suppose that the day trader has sold short 1,000 shares of a stock that is priced at $40. The short sale value is $40,000.

The credit balance represents the total short sale proceeds and the Reg. T margin requirement on the short sale value. In this example, given the 50% Reg. T requirement, the maximum amount that the trader can borrow for the short sale is $20,000. That is also the base amount that will be used to calculate the interest charges paid by the customer. The customer had to deposit $20,000 in the short margin account. The equity is the customer's deposited money. Equity can be calculated by subtracting the credit balance from the current short market value of the security that was initially sold.

The day trader anticipates that the security will decrease in value, so she has opened a short position. If the price were to decrease, the short market value would decrease. Since the borrowed amount remains the same (the credit balance remained the same at $60,000), the trader's equity has increased. When the equity in the account exceeds the Reg. T requirement of 50%, the day trader has excess equity in the short margin account. Figure A2.6 elaborates on this point.

For example, suppose that the stock price decreased from $40 to $30. The short market value is now $30,000. Since the borrowed amount or the credit balance remained the same at $60,000, the trader's equity increased from $20,000 to $30,000. The Reg. T 50% requirement on the

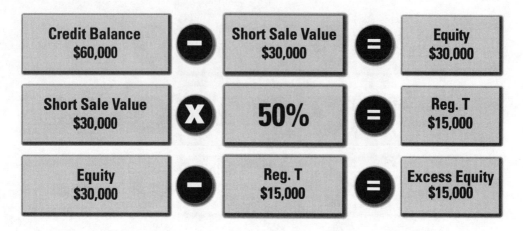

Figure A2.6 *Short Margin Account with Stock Price Depreciation*

$30,000 current short market value is $15,000. That means that the day trader has excess equity in the account of $15,000. In this example, the trader can use the $15,000 excess equity to purchase or short sell additional securities or to withdraw cash. In fact, the trader can purchase $30,000 worth of securities with the $15,000 excess equity.

The NASD and NYSE minimum maintenance requirement for stocks in a short margin account and selling for more than $5 per share is 30%. The brokerage firm will regard the long and short margin accounts as one margin account. The combined equity for the long and short margin accounts is displayed in Figure A2.7.

If a day trader has an overnight position, he must be able to understand how the total equity and interest charges on his margin activity statement are being calculated. After all, the total equity, buying power, and margin interest charged to the trader is the trader's money.

Figure A2.7 *Combined Equity for Long and Short Margin Accounts*

Intraday Margin Call

If a day trader always closes his open positions before the close of the market, he does not need to worry about margin interest charges or maintenance calls. (Some clearing firms, however, do charge margin interest for intraday trading, even if all positions are closed at the close of market. The day trader should definitely ask about margin interest charges when opening an account.) However, a day trader should worry about *intraday margin calls*. It is very common for a day trader to exceed his buying power sometime during the trading day. Day traders transact so many trades during the day that it is quite possible to lose track of one's daily purchasing power. Even if the day trading software has an account manager feature, which dynamically updates the trader's buying power, it is still easy to exceed one's buying power. Also, it must be acknowledged that day traders commonly try to maximize their leverage. In doing so, they sometimes push the envelope too far and exceed their purchasing power.

For example, if a day trader deposited $20,000 into his or her account, given the Reg. T requirement, the trader's buying power is $40,000. Suppose that day trader makes only one trade that day. The trader purchased and sold 1,000 shares of a stock that was priced at the point of the purchase and sale at $44. After the closing sale, the day trader is flat. He did not even make any money on this trade. (In fact, the trader lost money if the cost of the trade transactions is taken into account, but let us ignore that.) Nevertheless, the day trader purchased $44,000 worth of the stock even though the trader had only $40,000 in buying power.

The day trader will receive an intraday margin call for $2,000 from the clearing firm. The clearing firm will ask that the day trader deposit into the account an additional $2,000 within the next five trading days. That is because the trader purchased stocks with credit the trader did not have. The trader needs to bring his account purchasing power to $44,000. Even though the day trader is flat (having no long positions) in the stock, the trader would still need to come up with the extra cash. Given the 50% Reg. T credit requirement, a $2,000 deposit would increase the purchasing power to $4,000, and the total purchasing power would be $44,000.

A $2,000 intraday margin call should not be difficult to meet. But suppose that the intraday margin call is for $20,000 rather than $2,000. If the trader has net worth liquidity, then the $20,000 intraday margin call would not be an issue. However, if the trader does not have $20,000 and the intraday margin call is not met in the next five trading days, the clearing firm will most likely close his account. Then, if the day trader wants to continue trading in that branch, he would have to open another account under a different tax identification number. This is not that simple. The day trader would need to establish a legal entity (that is, a General Partnership or Limited Liability Company) and ask the IRS for a new tax identification number, which takes time and effort.

It is easier to meet the intraday margin call and deposit $20,000 within the next five trading days. Day trader A can ask one of his fellow traders in the office, such as trader B, for an intraday margin call loan of $20,000 for a 24-hour period. This procedure is relatively simple and risk-free. Both traders A and B have accounts with the same clearing firm. Day trader A is flat. In other words, that stock position is already closed. There is no market risk for trader B.

The two traders need to sign and fax to the clearing firm's margin desk a one-page document with their instructions. The trading colleague (trader B) who is providing the loan would simply ask the clearing firm to *journal in* $20,000 from his account to trader A's account to meet that intraday margin call. At the same time, the signed document will request that on the next day the clearing firm *journal out* $20,100 back into trader B's account from trader A's account. Note that a $100 fee is attached to the original $20,000 loan balance.

Since both day traders A and B have signed this faxed document, the clearing firm will honor this request. The journal entry would have satisfied the intraday margin call for day trader A, and trader B would have received $100 compensation for this risk-free service. However, day trader B will have $20,000 less cash or $40,000 less purchasing power for that trading day (24 hours). If trader B has an account with a large trading capital, the lower purchasing power should not be an issue. This loan procedure becomes an easy and risk-free way to pick up an additional $100 for one day. Again, however, such a transaction is between two private individuals. A day trading firm will not facilitate this intraday margin call loan, although the firm would be the indirect beneficiary of this common practice. Both traders would continue to trade with the firm and thus continue to generate the commission income.

3

Day Traders and Taxes

IT IS AXIOMATIC THAT DEATH AND TAXES ARE UNAVOIDABLE. THIS BOOK would be incomplete without a discussion of the topic of trader's tax issues. Here I attempt to cover this complex issue briefly. This appendix is not designed to be an authoritative source on traders' tax issues, because I am not a tax attorney or tax accountant. There are only a few books that deal specifically with the tax issues that stock investors and traders face, and I strongly encourage you to do your own research on this topic. One good reference is Ted Tesser's *The Trader's Tax Survival Guide*.

Tax Rates

Because this is not a tax book, we cover only the basic tax concepts. I would like to reiterate that *cash basis accounting*—a method of reporting income when it is received and expenses when they are incurred—is the foundation of the trader's tax return. All income is subject to progressive or graduated federal tax. In other words, as the individual's income increases, the average and marginal tax rate increase as well. There are five marginal tax rates, or tax brackets, in the United States; they vary from 15% to 39.6%. Table A3.1 shows the 2000 tax rate schedule for taxpayers who are filing returns as single or married and filing jointly.

According to Table A3.1, if your filing status is single, you pay a 15% tax rate on the first $26,250 and a 28% tax rate on income higher than $26,250 and lower than $63,550.

Table A3.1   *2000 Tax Rate Schedule*

Single Filing Status			Married Filing Jointly Status	
Taxable Income Over	Taxable Income Under	Marginal Tax Rate	Taxable Income Over	Taxable Income Under
$0	$26,250	15%	$0	$43,850
$26,250	$63,550	28%	$48,050	$105,950
$63,550	$132,600	31%	$105,950	$161,450
$132,600	$288,350	36%	$161,450	$288,350
$288,350	N/A	39.6	$288,350	N/A

In addition to paying taxes to the federal government, individuals also pay income taxes to the states in which they live. However, there are a few states, such as Florida and Nevada, that do not have a state income tax.

Income

The next step is to define income. The federal tax law defines *income* as any acquisition of wealth that excludes gifts and inheritances. In other words, income may be defined as any gain derived from capital and labor. In fact, the Internal Revenue Service (IRS) defines the following fourteen specific categories of income:

1. Compensation for services
2. Income from business
3. Gains from dealings in property
4. Interest
5. Rents
6. Royalties
7. Dividends

8. Annuities

9. Income from life insurance policies

10. Pensions

11. Partnership income

12. Income from ownership interest in an estate or trust

13. Income from discharge of debt

14. Alimony payments

Traders and stock investors need to know what is specifically excluded from the definition of income:

1. The return of capital or return of an original investment, such as the cost of stocks;

2. Unrealized stock gain or appreciation, meaning that the investor is not liable for stock appreciation until the stock is sold

The U.S. Tax Reform Act of 1986 also differentiates between three different types of income:

1. Earned income

2. Investment income

3. Passive income

The different types of income are taxed at the same rate as regular income, with the exception of long-term capital gains. This income differentiation becomes important when determining which losses can be deducted on tax returns. The IRS tax code has always had earned income and investment income categories. But, in 1986, the U.S. Congress created for the first time a new type of income—*passive income*. Passive income comes from passive activities. A passive activity is one in which the taxpayer is not directly and materially involved. This definition covers all rental income and the income from limited partnerships in which limited partners do not participate in management decisions.

Earned income is compensation received for providing goods or services. *Investment income* is portfolio income that includes interest, dividends, royalties, and annuities, as well as gains or losses from the disposition of an investment. Earned and investment incomes are considered ordinary incomes and are taxed at the individual tax rate.

Capital Gains and Losses

The other important tax issue is the concept of capital gains and losses. *Capital gain* (or *loss*) is defined as a gain (or loss) that comes from the sale of capital assets. The IRS defines a capital asset to be any business or non-business property. The exceptions are inventories, accounts receivable, and properties that are held for sale in the normal course of trading. Securities are considered to be capital assets. If a capital asset such as stock is sold for less than its cost, the IRS considers this to be a capital loss. If the capital asset is sold for more than its cost, the IRS considers this to be a capital gain.

Capital losses may be used to offset capital gains. Furthermore, within certain IRS limits, capital losses may be used to offset ordinary income. The IRS also differentiates whether capital gains are short term or long term. The holding period starts on the day the buy order was executed, or in other words, on the trade date. Conversely, the holding period ends on the day the sell order was executed. All capital gains or losses are considered short term if the holding period is less than one year, and long term if the holding period is more than one year.

Another tax concept is the issue of the stock cost basis. The *cost basis* of a security is the total price paid for the stock, including the commission cost. The cost basis will be adjusted periodically for any stock dividends and stock splits. A *stock split* occurs when a company decides to divide its share in two, three, four, or more. In the event of a 2-to-1 stock split, the stockholders will have twice as many shares, but each share will be worth half as much. Since nothing else about the company has changed, shareholders aren't better or worse off. All capital gains or losses are realized or recognized in the tax year of the trade date on which the security has been sold.

The final step is to determine the net impact of the capital gains and losses. Given the stock cost basis, the holding period, and the final stock selling price (including the cost of the commission, which would be deducted from the proceeds), the trader or investor can determine the level of short-term and long-term capital gains and losses. The trader would net the short-term losses against the short-term gains, and the long-term losses against the long-term gains.

If the trader or investor has had a poor year and the net result is both short-term and long-term losses, the net losses are combined and deducted from ordinary income, up to a $3,000 maximum. If the net losses exceed $3,000, the unused portion can be carried forward and used to offset ordinary income for the next tax year. The losses can be carried forward indefinitely. This is an apparent double standard. There is no limit on capital gain that is subject to federal taxation. If you made money, the federal government wants a percentage cut of that entire gain.

If a trader or investor has a mixed performance and the net result is a short-term gain and long-term loss, the long-term loss can be used to offset the short-term gain. If the net is positive, the net gain is added to ordinary income and taxed at the ordinary tax rate based on the progressive tax schedule.

If the trader or investor has an overall positive performance and the net result is both short-term and long-term gains, the positive short-term net gain is added to ordinary income and is taxed at the ordinary tax rate. The positive long-term net gain is taxed at the ordinary tax rate, up to a maximum of 28%, even if the taxpayer's other ordinary income is taxed at the higher rate.

Expenses

The first half of the tax equation is income; the second half is expense. The IRS looks keenly at what expenses can be deducted from income. The IRS test on whether expenses are allowed has four questions:

1. Is the expense necessary to produce that income?
2. Is the expense ordinary and common in conducting that type of business activity?
3. Is the expense reasonable with regard to the level of the generated income?
4. Is the expense allowed or legal under the existing federal tax code?

Whether expenses incurred in trading are necessary, ordinary, and reasonable is clearly subjective. Because each tax return is unique, the answers to these questions will vary from one trader to another. This variety means that traders have the ability or potential to interpret what constitutes necessary, ordinary, and reasonable expenses. A word of caution—there are many self-employed individuals who are clashing with the IRS over business expenses that they think are necessary, ordinary, and reasonable.

The best tax preparation strategy is to be prepared to document and explain to the IRS why certain trading expenses are claimed to be necessary, ordinary, and reasonable. The trader who might someday be audited must be prepared to back up (with supporting documents) and substantiate his trading expense claims.

Ted Tesser's tax book for traders lists several trading expenses that are commonly accepted by the IRS, including the following:

➤ Computer and software expenses, if trading from the home

➤ Real-time data feed cost

➤ Brokerage fees

➤ Margin interest expense

➤ Cost of books, seminars, and other educational tools on trading

➤ Subscriptions to professional magazines, papers, and publications

➤ Tax advice

➤ Trading advice

➤ Legal fees

➤ Accounting fees

➤ Safe deposit box fees for the storage of trading documents

➤ Portion of home expenses that qualify as home office deductions, if trading from the home

The IRS code also differentiates among three classes of investors: market maker, investor, and trader.

Market Maker

The definition of market maker, for tax purposes, is clear. The *market maker* is the NASD broker or dealer who is a merchant of securities. The NASD broker/dealer might be an individual, a partnership, or a corporation. The market maker has an established place of business and regularly buys and sells securities in the ordinary course of business. Securities are the market maker's inventory; they are not capital assets.

All of the income made by the market maker is automatically considered to be ordinary income. There are no short-term capital gains or losses. The market maker can claim an unlimited amount of losses. Because the market maker is a business, a self-employment tax must be paid. All expenses, such as interest charges, are treated as business-related expenses.

Investor

The IRS defines an *investor* as an individual who buys and sells securities for her own account. All expenses incurred in investment activities are considered to be investment expenses, and not business expenses. Therefore these expenses are deducted as miscellaneous itemized deductions on Schedule A of the investor's tax return. Investment expenses are subject to a 2% limitation. All income is treated as investment income, not ordinary income. Finally, the maximum net loss that can be used to offset ordinary income is $3,000.

Trader

For the IRS, the *trader* is clearly a hybrid between the investor and the market maker. The U.S. courts have always recognized this tax classification, although the tax forms do not specifically list this category. In addition, in 1997, Congress recognized that "traders are taxpayers who are in the business of actively buying, selling, or exchanging securities or commodities in the market." Congress also stated that market makers are the securities dealers who deal directly with the customers. In other words, traders are actively involved in the exchange of securities on the market, rather than in the exchange of securities directly to the customer—a fine distinction that has significant tax implications.

And what separates the traders from investors? The IRS does not have a hard number or a specific test that will differentiate investors from traders. In general, the IRS looks at the following in order to consider whether a taxpayer is a trader rather than an investor:

➤ Regular, continuous, and frequent trading

➤ Substantial number of trades

➤ Short-term trading style

➤ Small, if any, income derived from dividends

➤ Expenses declared on Schedule C

Traders buy and sell securities for their own accounts, just as investors do. Unlike the investor, however, the trader's level of trading activity is dramatically higher. The IRS looks at the frequency of the trades, the length of the holding period, and the source of profit. A typical day trader makes several dozen trades every day, while holding the stock for only a few minutes or a few hours. He profits from the daily short-term price fluctuations. On the other hand, the investor holds the securities for a longer period of time (sometimes more than one year), performs fewer securities transactions, and earns profit from dividends as well as from capital appreciation.

Tax Treatment

One of the main points of this book is that trading is a business. The trader must treat this business seriously if she has any hope of being successful. It is a business that requires time commitment, dedication, and hard work. Thus, it is not surprising that the IRS treats equities trading as a business. A day trader makes many trades every day while holding the stock for a few minutes or hours and profits from short-term price fluctuations. A swing trader makes several trades every week while holding the stock for a few days. It is clear that day trading is not investing. It is also my opinion that swing trading is a business as well as day trading.

All trading expenses are considered to be business-related expenses and are 100% deductible on Schedule C of the individual's tax return. However, trading income is considered to be short-term capital gains, and thus must be reported on Schedule D. Recall that there is a $3,000 limit on the amount of short-term losses that can be applied on Schedule D to offset ordinary income for that year.

However, this $3,000 limit can be avoided if the trader elects to mark-to-market his position under IRS section 475. According to mark-to-market accounting rules, traders can put all of their trading income and losses on Schedule C, and thus not carry anything into the next year. In essence, Congress allows traders to use section 475 to show all income or expenses on Schedule C and yet not be subject to self-employment tax. There is no self-employment tax because the trader's income is considered to be a short-term capital gain and not ordinary income. There is no box on the tax form to select section 475; it must be noted on Schedule C. (My advice is to hire a tax accountant to prepare the trader's tax return properly.)

Traders must use two forms to report income and expenses from trading activities. They report the trading income as investment income (short-term capital gains) on Schedule D, and trading expenses as ordinary business expenses on Schedule C. In terms of tax liability, one can argue that traders are better off than market makers. Both market makers and traders can claim trading expenses. However, market makers are subject to self-employment tax, whereas traders are not—one of the few times that market makers do not have an advantage over traders.

Because the IRS treats traders as a hybrid between investors and market makers, there are certain tax advantages available to traders that are not available to investors. For example, for traders:

➤ Itemized deductions are not necessary to claim and deduct trading expenses. Traders can take the standard deduction and still take additional expense deductions on Schedule C.

➤ All trading educational seminars are tax-deductible business expenses.

➤ All investment interest expense (that is, the margin interest expense) is considered trading expense and is allowed as a normal business expense.

➤ The home office expense is routinely allowed as a business expense if the trader trades from home.

➤ All trading business expenses are not subject to any floor or minimum value, such as the 2% to 3% floor on Schedule A that investors must pay.

Table A3.2 summarizes the IRS tax treatment for the three classifications.

IRS Tax Audits

It is always a good practice to expect the best and be prepared for the worst. There is always a possibility that the IRS will audit a trader. This section covers that worst case scenario—the IRS tax audit.

First of all, to be classified as a trader, it is not necessary to create a separate legal entity. An individual is entitled to achieve trader status simply by being a trader. However, many tax accountants, including Ted Tesser, argue that Limited Liability Partnership, Limited Liability

Table A3.2 *IRS Tax Classification Summary*

Tax Issue	Market Makers	Traders	Investors
Profits treated as	Earned income	Short-term capital gains or losses within investment income and reported on Schedule D [with 475 exception noted, gains and losses reported on Schedule C]	Short-term capital gains or losses within investment income and reported on Schedule D
Loss limits applied against earned income	No limits	$3,000 limit per year with carry forward to next year [with 475 exception noted]	$3,000 limit per year with carry forward to next year
Subject to self-employment tax	Yes	No, even if trading is your only source of income	No
Expenses treated as	Business expenses	Business-related expenses with 100% deductible and reported on Schedule C	Investment-related expenses itemized and reported on Schedule A

Company, or Corporations Subchapter C or S entity forms are preferred legal vehicles for stock trading. In general, these forms can offer more tax, retirement, and estate planning options to traders than the individual entity structure can.

In his book, Ted Tesser argues that there is no such thing as a one-size-fits-all entity structure that is the most preferred. In some cases, multiple ownership structures might be created to maximize benefits. Tax attorneys and accountants call this *tax planning* and, as with anything else, tax planning can be as complicated or as simple as you wish it to be.

We all have an interest in minimizing our tax liabilities. None of us wants to pay more to the government than is necessary. In fact, most Americans believe, rationally or irrationally, that we already pay too much in taxes. Minimizing taxes does not mean cheating on your tax returns. That is clearly illegal. It also does not mean finding tax loopholes in the IRS code and exploiting them. Minimizing taxes legally means obtaining knowledge of the IRS code (as applied to your individual tax circumstances) and using current allowable deductions and exemptions to the fullest advantage.

Investors and traders often push the envelope of IRS code interpretation on their tax returns. Consequently, their returns are selected for IRS audits. It is always important to keep good records of your trading transactions and expenses. In the event that the IRS audits your return, these records can substantiate your deductions and expense claims.

It is also preferred that these records be in an electronic format. Because day traders may conduct thousands of trades in a single year (for swing traders, this number is lower), it can be difficult to provide a quick summary of all trades. Trading software often has the capability to export, or copy, daily trade activity records onto a disk. This copy can then be imported at a later date into any spreadsheet program.

The Probability of Being Audited

The good news is that the odds are in your favor that you will not get audited. The IRS simply has a colossal task. Every year the IRS collects more than $1.5 trillion to fund the U.S. government. It processes more than 200 million tax returns from more than 110 million U.S. taxpayers. It issues over 80 million refunds and distributes over one billion forms and publications. In addition, the IRS must enforce the tax laws of this country and ensure that the taxpaying public pays the proper amount of tax. As you can see, the IRS is overwhelmed. Consequently, only a small portion of the 110 million taxpayers will ever be subject to an IRS audit. The IRS audits approximately only 3 million tax returns annually.

The news gets even better. The first target of the IRS audit is the known criminal (let us hope that this does not apply to you). The next targets are certain highly paid professionals. The IRS customarily targets doctors, dentists, lawyers, and CPAs because of their relative high-income levels and their propensity for practicing creative accounting. The next groups of targeted individuals are salespeople, airline pilots, flight attendants, and business executives, because they tend to have unusually high expense deductions relative to their income. Often these expenses are poorly documented. If you are not in any of these listed professions, your chances of being audited are often fewer than 1%.

The process of selecting individual tax returns for an audit is highly computerized. The IRS computer program selects tax returns that do not comply with the IRS code or that have certain discrepancies between the reported incomes as being reported by the taxpayer and other businesses that issue the W-2 or 1099 forms. Therefore, you must make sure that all income is reported.

It is also important that tax returns are clean and fully completed. All questions must be answered completely. Avoid including large sums of money under the "Miscellaneous Income" or "Miscellaneous Expenses" sections. It is always better to be specific. Avoid making sloppy or careless mathematical mistakes. There are several computerized tax preparation software packages on the market that will ensure that your completed tax return is clean, complete, and mathematically correct.

Avoid using certain deductions that customarily trigger the IRS audits. The home office deduction is one item that commonly raises IRS scrutiny. But if you are an Internet trader, this home expense is legal and allowed. Avoid using rounded-off expense deductions, as they indicate guessing. It is always a good idea to work with a professional and capable tax accountant. If the IRS suspects that a tax accountant is too aggressive or unscrupulous, it can trigger IRS audits for the accountant's entire client base. The IRS will notice if an individual reports millions of dollars of gross sales from trades. However, the same trading activity will not raise any IRS flags if the legal entity doing the trading is a corporation or limited partnership. The IRS is very accustomed to seeing large dollar figures on corporate or limited liability partnership returns.

Unfortunately, a small number of IRS audits are randomly selected. The IRS uses this type of random selection to ascertain the overall taxpayers' compliance with the tax laws. In addition, each IRS district office has a different percentage of returns audited. Some districts are more aggressive (or efficient) and therefore perform substantially more audits, while some districts are more relaxed. The bottom line here is that the probability is great that you will not be audited.

APPENDIX 4

Good Trading Stocks for 2001

Large Relative Volatility and Daily Trading Volume

Symbol	Company Name	Rank	Beta	Avg. Daily Volume	Exchange	52-Week Low	52-Week High
SGNT	Sagent Technology, Inc.	1	6.42	915,500	NASDAQ	45.38	2.25
NTRO	Netro Corp.	2	6.41	951,400	NASDAQ	119.63	19.94
ISLD	Digital Island, Inc.	3	5.62	2,352,700	NASDAQ	156.94	11.13
AIPN	American International Petroleum Corp.	4	5.17	1,838,400	NASDAQ	2.06	0.34
ASKJ	Ask Jeeves, Inc.	5	5.14	720,500	NASDAQ	190.5	9.75
ICGE	Internet Capital Group, Inc.	6	5.1	4,198,300	NASDAQ	212	9
TFSM	24/7 Media, Inc.	7	4.86	681,500	NASDAQ	65.25	3.94
CPTH	Critical Path, Inc.	8	4.62	997,400	NASDAQ	119.5	26
NITE	Knight Trading Group, Inc.	9	4.61	4,426,200	NASDAQ	60.06	23.5
FDRY	Foundry Networks, Inc.	10	4.37	1,804,100	NASDAQ	212	50.5
ALLR	Allaire Corp.	11	4.35	912,800	NASDAQ	94.13	5.75

ITRA	Intraware, Inc.	12	4.24	534,900	NASDAQ	99	4.25
IDCC	InterDigital Communications Corp.	13	4.19	1,091,600	NASDAQ	82	5.31
BBSW	Broadbase Software, Inc.	14	4.08	942,200	NASDAQ	86	8.47
DRIV	Digital River, Inc.	15	4.07	511,800	NASDAQ	43.63	3.25
DCLK	DoubleClick, Inc.	16	4.04	4,617,900	NASDAQ	135.25	8.75
VERT	VerticalNet, Inc.	17	4.01	3,153,100	NASDAQ	148.38	19.5
PCLN	Priceline.com Inc.	18	4	3,835,200	NASDAQ	104.25	4.13
JWEB	Juno Online Services, Inc.	19	3.97	753,400	NASDAQ	87	2.19
BEOS	Be Inc.	20	3.83	706,400	NASDAQ	39.56	2.28
LBRT	Liberate Technologies	21	3.78	1,402,300	NASDAQ	148.5	16
INSP	InfoSpace, Inc.	22	3.64	5,596,900	NASDAQ	138.5	11.59
EXDS	Exodus Communications, Inc.	23	3.63	11,483,300	NASDAQ	89.81	18.47
FFIV	F5 Networks, Inc.	24	3.62	999,000	NASDAQ	160.5	22.38
AGIL	Agile Software Corp.	25	3.55	634,800	NASDAQ	112.5	18.31
BWEB	BackWeb Technologies Ltd.	26	3.5	584,700	NASDAQ	59.13	5.25
CMGI	CMGI, Inc.	27	3.45	7,674,400	NASDAQ	163.5	12.88
VIGN	Vignette Corp.	28	3.42	5,067,600	NASDAQ	100.57	18.38
BVEW	BindView Development Corp.	29	3.41	716,700	NASDAQ	45.75	4.5
EGRP	E*TRADE Group, Inc.	30	3.38	6,136,400	NASDAQ	40	10.56
YHOO	Yahoo! Inc.	31	3.38	11,993,400	NASDAQ	250.06	45.06
ENTU	Entrust Technologies Inc.	32	3.28	1,349,800	NASDAQ	150	20.31
EBAY	eBay Inc.	33	3.25	5,603,600	NASDAQ	127.5	43.5
TRAC	Track Data Corp.	34	3.22	1,285,900	NASDAQ	12.25	0.94
SWCM	Software.com, Inc.	35	3.21	546,000	NASDAQ	200	59.5
SCNT	Scient Corp.	36	3.13	1,013,400	NASDAQ	133.75	11.38
EXAP	Exchange Applications, Inc.	37	3.09	655,900	NASDAQ	74.75	2.38

INAP	InterNAP Network Services Corp.	38	3.07	853,400	NASDAQ	111	13
NETP	Net Perceptions, Inc.	39	3.04	664,100	NASDAQ	66.5	4.13
USIX	USinternetworking, Inc.	40	3.02	1,635,700	NASDAQ	71.7	2.97
NTBK	Net.B@nk, Inc.	41	3.01	509,400	NASDAQ	34.38	8.13
EPNY	E.piphany, Inc.	42	2.99	631,500	NASDAQ	324.88	43
MPWR	Mpower Communications Corp.	43	2.99	776,900	NASDAQ	52.03	4.88
GTS	Global TeleSystems, Inc.	44	2.97	2,129,100	NYSE	36.5	1.94
VITR	Vitria Technology, Inc.	45	2.9	1,176,200	NASDAQ	106	13
DIGX	Digex, Inc.	46	2.89	829,200	NASDAQ	184	24.75
LCOS	Lycos, Inc.	47	2.88	3,101,900	NASDAQ	93.63	32.06
BYND	Beyond.com Corp.	48	2.86	1,098,700	NASDAQ	13.5	0.75
ASYT	Asyst Technologies, Inc.	49	2.83	923,100	NASDAQ	67	13.88
MFNX	Metromedia Fiber Network, Inc.	50	2.81	4,733,100	NASDAQ	51.88	15.25
AMZN	Amazon.com, Inc.	51	2.79	9,085,300	NASDAQ	113	19.38
BRCM	Broadcom Corp.	52	2.78	4,606,400	NASDAQ	274.75	54.28
LRCX	Lam Research Corp.	53	2.77	4,455,100	NASDAQ	56.81	13.94
PRTL	Primus Telecommunications Group, Inc.	54	2.77	528,600	NASDAQ	52	4.31
SCI	SCI Systems, Inc.	55	2.77	1,393,200	NYSE	65.13	19.53
OMKT	Open Market, Inc.	56	2.76	1,436,800	NASDAQ	66	2.31
RNWK	RealNetworks, Inc.	57	2.76	3,195,700	NASDAQ	96	10.13
ISSX	Internet Security Systems, Inc.	58	2.72	656,800	NASDAQ	141	34.5
ARBA	Ariba, Inc.	59	2.69	6,933,700	NASDAQ	242	36.5
RHAT	Red Hat, Inc.	60	2.69	2,951,300	NASDAQ	151	10.63
CLS	Celestica, Inc.	61	2.67	1,009,200	NYSE	87	26.75

MPPP	MP3.com, Inc.	62	2.66	897,700	NASDAQ	64.63	2.5
PAP	Asia Pulp & Paper Company Ltd.	63	2.64	529,800	NYSE	8.81	1
AMES	Ames Department Stores, Inc.	64	2.62	757,700	NASDAQ	35.25	3.63
INKT	Inktomi Corp.	65	2.62	3,140,100	NASDAQ	241.5	46.91
MUSE	Micromuse, Inc.	66	2.62	604,600	NASDAQ	210	43.53
PRGN	Peregrine Systems, Inc.	67	2.62	1,997,600	NASDAQ	80.63	15.31
TWE	TD Waterhouse Group, Inc.	68	2.62	554,700	NYSE	27	11.5
ALGX	Allegiance Telecom, Inc.	69	2.6	769,300	NASDAQ	110.14	22
ITWO	i2 Technologies, Inc.	70	2.58	3,624,900	NASDAQ	223.5	29.63
TWRS	Crown Castle International Corp.	71	2.58	1,211,300	NASDAQ	44.75	17.88
CLST	CellStar Corp.	72	2.56	523,500	NASDAQ	13.13	2
VYTL	Viatel, Inc.	73	2.56	1,056,200	NASDAQ	75.38	6.75
IFMX	Informix Corp.	74	2.55	5,811,600	NASDAQ	21.25	3.63
WCII	Winstar Communications, Inc.	75	2.55	1,727,800	NASDAQ	66.5	14
GSTRF	Globalstar Telecommunications Ltd.	76	2.54	3,513,000	NASDAQ	53.75	5.5
STRX	STAR Telecommunications, Inc.	77	2.53	687,400	NASDAQ	9.5	1
FLEX	Flextronics International Ltd.	78	2.49	5,950,300	NASDAQ	44.91	16.81
AOL	America Online, Inc.	79	2.48	19,374,100	NYSE	95.81	37
ARTG	Art Technology Group, Inc.	80	2.47	1,240,600	NASDAQ	126.88	24.19
ATHM	At Home Corp.	81	2.47	6,449,400	NASDAQ	59.75	8.13
GBLX	Global Crossing Ltd.	82	2.46	11,378,800	NASDAQ	62	20.13
ATML	Atmel Corp.	83	2.45	11,473,600	NASDAQ	30.69	8.63

GS	Goldman Sachs Group, Inc.	84	2.45	1,564,100	NYSE	133.63	61.81
KLAC	KLA-Tencor Corp.	85	2.44	5,069,000	NASDAQ	98.5	25.5
KMAG	Komag, Inc.	86	2.44	796,800	NASDAQ	5.31	1.13
ICGX	ICG Communications, Inc.	87	2.43	1,871,500	NASDAQ	39.25	0.19
RDRT	Read-Rite Corp.	88	2.42	2,229,600	NASDAQ	12.38	1.84
STXN	DMC Stratex Networks, Inc.	89	2.42	1,164,800	NASDAQ	49	12.69
WAXS	World Access, Inc.	90	2.42	640,600	NASDAQ	27.5	3.31
INCX	InfoCure Corp.	91	2.41	646,000	NASDAQ	37.38	3.5
TZA	TV Azteca S.A. de C.V.	92	2.41	599,800	NYSE	17.75	3.75
GWRX	Geoworks Corp.	93	2.4	1,002,400	NASDAQ	54.88	2.47
IMMU	Immunomedics, Inc.	94	2.4	731,700	NASDAQ	41.13	1.06
LEH	Lehman Brothers Holdings, Inc.	95	2.4	1,284,000	NYSE	161	60.63
PRIA	PRI Automation, Inc.	96	2.4	575,200	NASDAQ	94.5	13.25
PUMA	Puma Technology, Inc.	97	2.4	1,392,500	NASDAQ	102.44	11.75
PPRO	PurchasePro.com, Inc.	98	2.37	2,845,000	NASDAQ	87.5	9.19
DVNT	Diversinet Corp.	99	2.36	1,063,200	NASDAQ	49.88	4.38
RSAS	RSA Security Inc.	100	2.36	696,400	NASDAQ	93.06	31.5

5

Key NASDAQ Market Makers

Symbol	Market Maker Name
ABSA	Alex Brown & Sons, Inc.
AGIS	Aegis Capital Corp.
BEST	Bear Stearns & Co., Inc.
BTSC	BT Securities
CANT	Cantor Fitzgerald & Co., Inc.
CHGO	Chicago Corp.
CJDB	CJ Lawrence Deutsche Bank
COST	Coastal Securities
COWN	Cowen & Co.
DAIN	Dain Bosworth, Inc.
DEAN	Dean Witter
DLJP	Donaldson Lufkin & Jenrette
DOMS	Domestic Securities
EXPO	Exponential Capital Markets
FACT	First Albany Corp.
FAHN	Fahnestock & Co.
FBCO	First Boston Corp.
FPKI	Fox-Pitt, Kelton, Inc.

GRUN	Gruntal & Co., Inc.
GSCO	Goldman Sachs & Co.
GVRC	Gvr Co.
HMQT	Hambrecht & Quist, Inc.
HRZG	Herzog Heine Geduld, Inc.
JEFF	Jefferies Co., Inc.
JPMS	J. P. Morgan
KEMP	Kemper Securities, Inc.
LEHM	Lehman Brothers
MADF	Bernard Madoff
MASH	Mayer & Schweitzer, Inc. (Charles Schwab)
MHMY	M. H. Meyerson & Co., Inc.
MLCO	Merrill Lynch & Co.
MONT	Montgomery Securities
MSCO	Morgan Stanley & Co., Inc.
MSWE	Midwest Stock Exchange
NAWE	Nash Weiss & Co.
NEED	Needham & Co.
NMRA	Nomura Securities Intl., Inc.
OLDE	Olde Discount Corp.
OPCO	Oppenheimer & Co.
PERT	Pershing Trading Co.
PIPR	Piper Jaffray
PRUS	Prudential Securities, Inc.
PUNK	Punk Siegel & Knoell, Inc.
PWJC	Paine Webber, Inc.
RAGN	Ragen McKenzie, Inc.
RPSC	Rauscher Pierce Refsnes, Inc.
RBSF	Robertson Stephens & Co., Lp
SALB	Salomon Brothers
SBNY	Sands Brothers & Co., Ltd.

SBSH	Smith Barney Shearson, Inc.
SELZ	Furman Selz, Inc.
SHWD	Sherwood Securities Corp.
SNDV	Soundview Financial Group, Inc.
SWST	Southwest Securities, Inc.
TSCO	Troster Singer Corp. (Spear Leads)
TUCK	Tucker Anthony, Inc.
TVAN	Teevan & Co., Inc.
UBSS	UBS Securities
VOLP	Volpe Weity & Co.
WARB	S. G. Warburg & Co., Inc.
WBLR	William Blair & Co.
WEAT	Wheat First Securities, Inc.
WEDB	Wedbrush Morgan Securities
WEED	Weeden & Co., Lp
WERT	Wertheim Schroder & Co., Inc.
WSEI	Wall Street Equities, Inc.
WSLS	Wessels, Arnold & Henderson

APPENDIX

6

Day Trading Quiz

SOME TIME AGO, THE AUTHOR OF THIS BOOK TAUGHT UNDERGRADUATE and graduate level university courses and presented to students many quizzes and exams. Giving quizzes is a bad habit. So here we go. This simple "True or False" quiz will test the reader's general understanding of basic electronic day trading principles. Simply note next to each statement whether the statement is true or false. The correct answers are on a page following this quiz.

1. Counterclockwise movement on the Level II screen as more market makers are leaving the inside ASK and joining the inside BID means that the stock price is going up.

2. A series of red or down-tick BID and ASK prices showing on the Market Ticker window for a particular stock means that prices are going down.

3. An "ax" or key market maker joining the inside BID on the Level II screen means that stock is going down.

4. Trades going off at the ASK price on the Time and Sales window indicate that the public is buying.

5. An "ax" or key market maker simultaneously leaving the inside BID and joining the inside ASK means that the stock is going up.

6. When the Fast Exponential Moving Average (Fast EMA) line has crossed over and above the Slow Exponential Moving Average (Slow EMA) line, this would be a buy signal.

7. The MACD line is positive and is increasing at an increasing rate; this indicates that the Fast EMA is increasing at a faster rate than the Slow EMA line, and the bulls in the stock market are getting stronger.

8. When the price reaches the lower Bollinger band, that constitutes the intraday price support level at that point in time.

9. When the momentum indicator (MOM) is positive and is increasing at an increasing rate, this means that there is price increase momentum at this point in time.

10. If both the price and the On-Balance Volume (OBV) indicator are moving up, there is a distinct possibility of price reversal.

11. An indicator of an overbought market would be a Fast Stochastic (%K) line that has reached 75 or goes above 75.

12. The first and foremost risk management measure for most day traders is to go flat at the end of the trading day.

13. Another common risk management measure for most day traders is to pyramid or double or triple the shares position to recover previous losses.

14. When day traders wish to buy or sell securities at a specific price, they enter SOES market orders.

15. As a general rule, day traders customarily use the buy limit order rather than the buy market order.

16. The maximum SOES order size for a security is 1,000, 500, or 200 shares, depending on the price and trading volume of that NASDAQ security.

17. SelectNet is an order-execution service owned and operated by NASDAQ, and its execution is mandatory for market makers.

18. The day trader can bid to buy or offer to sell orders through SelectNet that are greater than the SOES tier-size limit.

19. Bidding is passive buying when the day trader is trying to purchase securities at a better or lower price than the inside ASK price.

20. Offering is passive selling when the day trader is trying to sell securities at a better or higher price than the inside BID price.

21. An SOES buy limit order is aggressive purchasing, because the day trader is sending an order to purchase a stock at the posted or advertised inside ASK price.

22. An SOES sell limit order is aggressive selling, because the day trader is sending an order to sell a stock at the posted or advertised inside BID price.

23. An ECN or electronic communication network is a proprietary electronic execution system that widely disseminates to the public all trade orders entered by day traders, market makers, or specialists.

24. The Island ECN execution system will display the day trader's Island order on the Level II screen only if the day trader entered the highest BID or the lowest ASK.

25. The day trader cannot bid to buy a stock through Island ECN at a higher BID price than the posted inside BID.

26. The day trader cannot offer to sell a stock at a lower ASK price than the posted inside ASK.

27. The Island book allows the day trader to see the price and size of every Island buy and sell order for a particular stock.

28. The day traders can use Island order execution and short sell a stock on a down-tick by offering to sell the stock $\frac{1}{16}$ higher than the current inside BID price.

29. When the NASDAQ ASK price is identical to the Instinet BID price, this would constitute locked-up markets and a buy signal.

30. When the Instinet BID and ASK prices are substantially higher than the NASDAQ BID and ASK prices, and the Instinet BID is greater than the NASDAQ ASK, this constitutes a very strong buy signal.

31. The larger the spread in the crossed-up or -down markets between the Instinet and NASDAQ, the weaker the trading signal.

32. The NYSE specialist is the only market maker available for that security.

33. The specialist will never take on the role of the principal in order to counter temporary imbalances in the supply and demand of a security.

34. The SIPC provides insurance coverage to the NASD broker/dealer customers' accounts to a maximum of $500,000 of which no more than $100,000 may be for cash losses.

35. The Federal Reserve Board under Regulation T (Reg. T) of the Securities and Exchange Commission Act of 1934 regulates the extension of credit by the NASD broker/dealers to traders and investors; the current Reg. T margin requirement is 50% for long and short securities transactions.

36. When the equity in a margin account exceeds the Reg. T requirement of 50%, the trader has excess equity in the account, which can be used to purchase additional securities.

37. The quickest way to calculate a trader's buying power is to divide the SMA or excess equity by the Reg. T requirement.

38. If day traders always close their open positions before the close of the market, they do not need to worry about margin interest charges or maintenance calls, but they need to worry about intraday margin calls.

39. The novice day trader should have a trading plan that spells out clearly and exactly what she will do under different trading scenarios.

40. The level of losses depends on the day trader's discipline and risk management skills, and losses can be as high as $15,000 dollars or higher before a novice day trader can turn the corner.

Answers

1.	True	21.	True
2.	True	22.	True
3.	False	23.	True
4.	True	24.	True
5.	False	25.	False
6.	True	26.	False
7.	True	27.	True
8.	True	28.	True
9.	True	29.	True
10.	False	30.	True
11.	True	31.	False
12.	True	32.	True
13.	False	33.	False
14.	False	34.	True
15.	True	35.	True
16.	True	36.	True
17.	False	37.	True
18.	True	38.	True
19.	True	39.	True
20.	True	40.	True

Trading Fractions

0.031	1⁄32	0.281	9⁄32	0.531	17⁄32	0.781	25⁄32
0.063	1⁄16	0.313	5⁄16	0.563	9⁄16	0.813	13⁄16
0.094	3⁄32	0.344	11⁄32	0.594	19⁄32	0.844	27⁄32
0.125	**1⁄8**	0.375	**3⁄8**	0.625	**5⁄8**	0.875	**7⁄8**
0.156	5⁄32	0.406	13⁄32	0.656	21⁄32	0.906	29⁄32
0.188	3⁄16	0.438	7⁄16	0.688	11⁄16	0.938	15⁄16
0.219	7⁄32	0.469	15⁄32	0.719	23⁄32	0.969	31⁄32
0.250	**1⁄4**	0.500	**1⁄2**	0.750	**3⁄4**	1.000	**1**

Factor: 0.031 x 1,000 shares = $31

Glossary

absolute liquidity   Total number of shares being traded on an exchange in a day.

absolute price volatility   Total dollar change in the price of the stock.

accumulation   Addition to a trader's original market position; first of three distinct phases in a major trend in which investors are buying. Compare with **distribution.**

Advance–decline   Each day's number of declining issues is subtracted from the number of advancing issues. The net difference is added to a running sum if the difference is positive, or subtracted if the difference is negative.

aftermarket IPO performance   Used to describe how the stock of a newly public company has performed, with the offering price as the typical benchmark.

arbitrage   Simultaneous purchase and sale of two different and closely related securities to take advantage of a disparity in their prices.

ASK   The price at which a holder of a security is willing to sell (as opposed to BID, which is what someone is willing to pay). The asked price is the price paid when a security is bought. It is usually lower than the bid. In over-the-counter trading, securities dealers or market makers profit from the spread between BID and ASK so much that they are often willing to pay discount brokers for order flow.

ASK size   Number of shares associated with the current ASK price or the number of shares the seller(s) is (are) offering for sale at the ask price.

auditor   Firm of certified public accountants that a company hires as an independent third party to review its financial information. Main purpose is to make sure the statements of earnings, financial position, and cash flows fairly present the company's financial condition.

average daily volume   Number of shares traded in a given number of days, divided by that number of days. Useful for judging how liquid a stock is (thinly traded issues are riskier) and whether any one day's volume marks a sharp departure from the norm. The latter usually indicates some news or change of circumstances that could be relevant to shareholders.

bar chart   Displays a security's open, high, low, and close prices using one vertical line for each time period, whether it is for a day, week, month, or so forth. Most popular type of security chart. Left side of the bar is a tick that indicates the opening price. The tick on the right side of the bar is the closing price. The vertical length of the bar shows the price range.

basket trades   Large transactions made up of a number of different stocks.

bear or bearish market   When stocks trend downward for a long period of time. The term comes from the fact that when bears attack, they strike downward with their paws.

Beta   A regression of the estimated coefficient that belongs to a particular variable.

Beta coefficient   A measure of the market/nondiversifiable risk associated with any given security in the market. A ratio of an individual's historical stock returns to the historical returns of the stock market. If a stock increased in value by 12% while the market increased by 10%, the stock's Beta would be 1.2.

BID   Price at which market maker is willing to buy a security from investor. The BID price is the price received when a security is sold by investor.

bidding   Act of buying securities at the posted BID price.

BID size   Number of shares associated with the current BID price or the number of shares the buyer(s) is (are) offering to buy at the posted BID price.

Bollinger band   John Bollinger created a trading band (upper and lower boundary lines) plotted at standard deviation levels above and below a moving average. Because standard deviation measures volatility, the bands widen during volatile markets and contract during calmer periods.

breakout   If a stock has traded in a narrow range for some time (in other words, built a base) and then advances above the resistance level, this is said to be an upside breakout. Breakouts are suspect if they do not occur on high volume (compared with average daily volume). Some traders use a buy stop, which calls for purchase when a stock rises above a certain price.

bull/bear ratio   Market sentiment indicator based on a weekly poll of investment advisors as to whether they are bullish, bearish, or neutral on the stock market. Published by Investor's Intelligence of New Rochelle, New York. Extreme optimism on the part of the public and even professionals almost always coincides with market tops. Extreme pessimism almost always coincides with market bottoms. Historically, readings above 60% have indicated extreme optimism (bearish for the market). Readings below 40% have indicated extreme pessimism (bullish for the markets).

bull, or bullish market   When stock prices have risen steadily over several months. Word comes from the way the animal attacks: When a bull rushes forward, it holds its head low and then gores upward with its horns.

buy on margin   Practice of buying stock with money borrowed from a broker. The loan is collateralized by the security purchased, which is held in a margin account. The broker charges interest, but the rate is usually attractive compared with other forms of debt, as it is secured by an easily marketable stock.

candlestick chart   Chart that displays the open, high, low, and close prices of a security for each time period and illustrates the relationship among these prices. The chart elements look like a candlestick with wicks at both ends. The actual candle portion is called the real body and is determined by the day's open and close prices. The wicks, called shadows, show the price range for the day. When the close is higher than the open, the body is green (if color is available).

change   Dollar difference between the preceding day's closing price and the most recent price. (Prices are delayed by at least twenty minutes.)

close   Final trading price for a security at the end of the most recent trading day.

closed trades   Positions that have been liquidated.

commission   Fee that brokers charge for executing a transaction. Amount is usually based on number of shares or the total dollar amount of the trade.

common stock   Ownership stake in a company. Holders of common stock shares are last in line in terms of their claim to dividends and assets.

confirmation   Indication that at least two indexes—in the case of Dow theory, the industrials and the transportation—corroborate a market trend or turning point.

correction   Sharp, short drop in stock prices, after which the market resumes an upward climb. Of course, when the correction is happening, it's hard to distinguish it from the beginnings of a bear market. Any price reaction within the market leading to an adjustment by as much as one-third to two-thirds of the previous gain.

current offer   Price at which the owner of a security offers to sell it at the posted ASK price.

daily range   Intraday price volatility, or the difference between the high and low price during one trading day.

daily volume (13-week average)   Average number of shares of a company's stock traded daily over the previous 13-week period. Daily volume is one indicator of how liquid a security is. A low daily volume could imply low interest in a stock, a limited float (number of shares outstanding), and/or a highly volatile share price, since even relatively small trades will have an exaggerated effect. Low-volume stocks, also known as thinly traded, are usually seen as riskier than more heavily traded shares.

day order   Trade order to buy or sell a security during the market hours in a trading day.

day trader   Person who buys and sells stocks rapidly during the day to exploit the stocks' intraday price volatility.

day's high   Highest price of the security during the current day's trading. By comparing with day's low, traders can get an idea of how much the stock is fluctuating.

day's low   Lowest price of the security during the current day's trading. By comparing with the day's high, traders can get an idea of how much the stock is fluctuating.

derivatives   Financial contracts the value of which depend on the value of the underlying instrument commodity, bond, equity, currency, or a combination.

distribution   Any set of related values described by an average (mean), which identifies its midpoint, a measure of spread (standard distribution), and a measure of its shape (skew or kurtosis). Also, the act of selling stocks. Or when the traders or investors use the current rally to liquidate old positions in the face of good news. Compare with **accumulation**.

divergence   Two or more averages or indices that fail to show confirming trends.

diversification   Investing strategy that seeks to minimize risk by diversifying among many types of investments. Diversification and risk are directly related. The more diversified a portfolio is, the less risk there is.

dividends   Cash or stock payments from a company's profits distributed to stockholders, an equal amount for each share of stock owned. Listed as dividends on the statement of stockholder's equity.

Dow Jones Industrial Average   Probably the most widely watched indicator of American stock market movements. More than 100 years old, it is well known. By including only 30 stocks, it is manageable. These stocks tend to be those of the largest, most established firms and represent a range of industries. Unfortunately, there are only 30 of them, and they are not always an ideal proxy for the thousands of stocks that make up the market as a whole. Broader indexes such as the Standard & Poor's 500 (for large companies), the Russell 2000 (for smaller companies), and the Wilshire 5000 (for an especially broad measure) have gained popularity.

down-tick   Indicates that the current BID price is lower than the previous BID.

drawdown   Reduction in account equity as a result of a bad trade or series of bad trades.

dynamic data updates   Ability to update an application automatically from within another application.

earn the spread   Act of buying a stock at the BID price and selling a stock at the ASK price, thus earning the difference between the BID and ASK prices.

earnings   Profit, or net income; in this case the sum of the trailing four quarters' net income from continuing operations and discontinued operations.

earnings per share (EPS)   Net income divided by common shares outstanding. A company that earns $1 million for the year and has a million shares outstanding has an EPS of $1. This EPS figure, which represents how much of earnings each share is entitled to, is important as the basis for various calculations an investor might make in assessing a stock's price.

earnings surprise   Difference between what analysts expected a company to earn and what was actually earned. Earnings estimates have gained importance in recent years, and companies that don't measure up often find their shares hammered. (The difference can also be expressed as a percentage.)

electronic communication networks (ECNs)   Allow market makers and any traders to post and display BID and ASK prices on a national system, so that others can fill these orders. Most often the ECN buy or sell orders would become the best buy and sell prices for the security. All ECNs are proprietary systems. To participate in the marketplace, they must be registered with the NASDAQ and NASD. To date, there were eight ECNs on the NASDAQ system: Instinet Corporation (INCA), Island ECN (ISLD), Archipelago (ARCA), Bloomberg Tradebook (BTRD), Spear Leeds & Kellogg (REDI), Attain (ATTN), BRASS Utility (BRUT), and Strike Technologies (STRK).

equilibrium market   Price region that represents a balance between demand and supply.

equity   The part of a company's assets that belongs to the stockholders. In other words, the amount that would remain if a company sold all of its assets and paid off all of its liabilities. Listed as stockholder's equity on the statement of financial position and on the statement of stockholder's equity.

exchange   Organization that provides for trading of a listed security. The biggest, most established companies usually trade on the New York

Stock Exchange (NYSE), but many giants in technology and other newer companies trade on The Nasdaq Stock Market (NASDAQ).

expenses   Costs such as salaries, rent, office supplies, advertising, and taxes. Listed in the operating expenses category on the statement of earnings.

Exponential Moving Average (EMA)   Mathematical-statistical method of forecasting that assumes future price action is a weighted average of past periods. Mathematics series in which greater weight is given to more recent price action.

extreme   Highest or lowest price during any time period; a price extreme.

fade   Act of selling a stock at the rising price or buying a stock at the falling price.

fast market   Declaration that market conditions in the trading pit are so temporarily disorderly with prices moving rapidly that floor brokers are not held responsible for the execution of orders.

52-week high   Highest price for a security or fund during the past 52 weeks, or one year.

52-week low   Lowest price for a security or fund during the past 52 weeks, or one year.

fill   Executed order; sometimes refers to the price at which an order is executed.

fill order   Trade order that must be filled immediately on the floor or immediately canceled.

filter   Device or program that separates data, signal, or information in accordance with specified criteria. Moving Average line is considered to be a filter.

flipping IPO   Buying an IPO at the offering price and then selling the stock soon after it starts trading on the open market. Greatly discouraged by underwriters, especially if done by individual investors.

floor brokers   Employees of brokerage firms working on exchange trading floors.

fundamental analysis   Analytical method by which only the sales, earnings, and value of a given tradeable's assets may be considered. The analysis holds that stock market activity may be predicted by looking at the relative company performance data, as well as at the management of the company in question.

futures Contracts to make or accept delivery of a given commodity on a given date at a prearranged price. Traded on all sorts of things, including corn, pork bellies, S&P 500 Index and U.S. Treasury securities. However, hardly anyone actually delivers (or accepts) all the bacon implied by a futures contract on pork bellies. Investors simply settle up with money. Futures (in the case of S&P 500 Index futures) are a legal way to bet on the direction of a broad stock market, or (in the case of U.S. Treasury securities) on the direction of interest rates.

gap Day in which the daily range is completely above or below the previous day's daily range.

head and shoulders For technicians or chartists, a chart pattern indicating a peak, a decline, a second even higher peak, a decline, a rebound to the level of the first peak, and yet another decline. A head and shoulders pattern is supposed to be bad news, indicating the stock is headed downward.

historical data Series of past daily, weekly, or monthly market prices (open, high, low, close, and volume).

income taxes Fees placed by federal, state, local, and foreign governments on a company's earnings. Listed on the statement of earnings.

in play Stock that is the focus of a public bidding contest, as in a takeover.

index Composite of securities that serves as a barometer for the overall market or some segment of it. The best known of these are the Dow Jones Industrial Average and the Standard & Poor's 500, both of which reflect the performance of large American companies. Other indexes include the Russell 2000, which is an index of smaller stocks. Many indexes are much more specific.

initial public offering (IPO) First stock sold by a company when going public. A feature of runaway bull markets, as there is proven demand for stock and it makes sense to sell shares when they are likely to bring the highest prices. The hottest IPOs can make their purchasers a quick profit by soaring soon after trading begins.

IPO premium Difference between the offering price and opening price. Also called an *IPO's pop*.

insider trading   Buying and selling by a company's own officers and directors for their personal accounts. When investors buy or sell based on material nonpublic information, they are engaged in illegal insider trading.

Instinet   Established in 1969 to serve large institutional investors. Offers to participating institutions the ability to trade NASDAQ and NYSE stocks among themselves 24 hours a day. A private market with often better prices.

institutional ownership   Percentage of a company's shares owned by banks, mutual funds, pension funds, insurance companies, and other institutions, all of them characterized by a propensity to buy and sell in bulk. Big institutional trades are having an increasing impact on the securities markets, as the institutional share of savings increases.

interest-sensitive stock   Stock whose price is very much affected by rising or falling interest rates. Auto makers, home builders, mortgage lenders, financial institutions, and others find that when rates soar, their business dries up. But some stocks can show rate sensitivity because these are stocks that pay hefty dividends. When rates fall, this dividend looks even better. But when rates rise, this dividend is less appealing compared to U.S. Treasury securities and other riskless investments.

investments   Company's equity ownership in unconsolidated subsidiaries and affiliates. Listed in the category of assets on the statement of financial position.

Island   Established in 1996. The fastest-growing ECN. Increasingly more popular trading platform among day traders because it is fast, reliable, and relatively inexpensive.

lag   Number of data points that a filter, such as a Moving Average, follows or trails the input price data.

last price   Current trading price of one unit of a particular security.

last trade size   Most recent number of shares traded of the security.

lead IPO underwriter   Investment bank in charge of setting the offering price of an IPO and allocating shares to other members of the syndicate. Also called *lead manager*.

leverage   Use of debt to increase returns. Investors also use leverage when buying stocks on margin. Associated with risk: An investor who buys stock on margin may run into trouble if the stock falls, leaving the loan insufficiently collateralized.

limit order   Order to buy or sell when a price is fixed. When traders or investors instruct a broker to buy shares at or below a certain price, or sell shares at or above a certain price, they've entered a limit order. These reduce the risk that an order will be filled at a price the traders or investors don't like. The downside is that by waiting for that particular stock price, the stock you want may get away from you, or the stock you want to unload just keeps falling in price.

line chart   Displays only the closing price for a security for each time period. A line connects closing values from each period. Often used for plotting mutual funds, which typically have only a daily close value. Over time, these points present a telling performance history for the security.

liquidity   Ability to quickly convert or sell an asset, such as a stock, into cash.

lockup period for IPO   Time period after an IPO when insiders at the newly public company are restricted by the lead underwriter from selling their shares. Usually lasts 180 days.

long   Establishing ownership of the responsibilities of a buyer of a tradable; holding securities in anticipation of a price increase in that security.

margin account   In stock trading, an account in which purchase of stock may be financed with borrowed money. This amount varies daily and is settled in cash. In essence, a brokerage account that lets an investor or trader buy securities on credit or borrow against securities held in the account. Interest is charged on such borrowing, but usually at attractive rates compared with other forms of debt. Trading on margin can enhance investment returns considerably, but like all leveraged activities, can also backfire. The federal government limits the extent to which margin can be used in equities trading.

margin call   Request for additional capital to bolster the equity in an investor's or trader's margin account. If the trader or investor cannot provide additional cash or securities, the broker will sell the shares.

market maker   Broker or bank continually prepared to make a two-way price to purchase or sell for a security or currency.

market on close   Order specification that requires the broker to get the best price available on the close of trading, usually during the last five minutes of trading.

market order   Instructions to the broker to immediately sell to the best available bid or to buy from the best available offer.

market risk   Uncertainty of returns attributable to fluctuation of the entire market.

market sentiment   Crowd psychology; typically a measurement of bullish or bearish attitudes among investors and traders.

market timing   Using analytical tools to devise entry and exit methods. Technique used by traders or investors who believe they can predict when the market will change course. If the traders or investors can time the market correctly, then they could make huge profits.

market value   Company value determined by investors, obtained by multiplying the current price of company stock by the common shares outstanding.

marketable securities   Financial assets, such as stocks and bonds, that companies can convert to cash. Listed as assets on the statement of financial position.

mean   Result of dividing the sum of the values by the number of observations.

momentum   Time series that represents change of today's price from some fixed number of days back in history.

momentum indicator (MOM)   Market indicator that uses price and volume statistics for predicting the strength or weakness of a current market and any overbought or oversold conditions, and to note turning points within the market.

money flow   Technical indicator that keeps a running total of the money flowing into and out of a security. Money flow is calculated daily by multiplying the number of shares traded by the change in closing price. If prices close higher, the money flow is a positive number. If prices close lower, the money flow is a negative number. A running total is kept by adding or subtracting the current result from the previous total.

most-active list   Stocks with the highest trading volume on a given day.

Moving Average   Mathematical procedure to smooth or eliminate the fluctuations in data and to assist in determining when to buy and sell. Moving Averages emphasize the direction of a trend, confirm trend reversals, and smooth out price and volume fluctuations, or "noise," that can confuse interpretation of the market. The sum of a value plus a selected number of previous values divided by the total number of values.

Moving Average crossover   Point at which the various Moving Average lines intersect each other or the price line on a Moving Average price bar chart. Technicians use crossovers to signal price-based buy and sell opportunities.

Moving Average Convergence/Divergence (MACD)   Crossing of two exponentially smoothed Moving Averages that are plotted above and below a zero line. The crossover, movement through the zero line, and divergences generate buy and sell signals.

moving window   Snapshot of a portion of a time series at an instant in time. The window is moved along the time series at a constant rate. For instance, a three-minute Moving Average line takes into account continuously the observation of the last three minutes.

narrow range day   Trading day with a smaller price range relative to the previous day's price range. In other words, the stock prices were stable during that day.

National Association of Securities Dealers (NASD)   Industry organization that regulates the behavior of member securities dealers. Owns and operates NASDAQ, the automated quotation system for over-the-counter trading. Derives its authority from the federal government. Every securities dealer in the country is required by law to be a member.

Nasdaq Stock Market (NASDAQ), formerly the National Association of Securities Dealers Automated Quotation system   Electronic stock exchange run by the NASD for over-the-counter trading. Established in 1971, it is America's fastest growing stock market and is a leader in trading technology shares. Has more listed companies than the New York Stock Exchange, and handles more than half the stock trading that occurs in the United States.

negative divergence   Two or more averages, indices, or indicators that fail to show confirming trends.

net earnings   Company's total revenue less total expenses, showing what a company earned (or if lost, called *net loss*) for a set period, usually one year. Listed often literally as the bottom line on the statement of earnings. Also called *net income* and *net profit*.

noise   Price and volume fluctuations that can confuse interpretation of market direction.

nontrend day   Narrow range day lacking any discernible movement in either direction.

normal distribution   For the purposes of statistical testing, simulated net returns are assumed to be drawn from a particular distribution. If net returns are drawn from a normal distribution, low and high returns are equally likely, and the most likely net return in a quarter is the average net return.

New York Stock Exchange (NYSE)   America's biggest and oldest securities exchange. Has the most stringent requirements for being listed. The place where most of the nation's largest and best-established companies are listed. Although computers are used, the NYSE remains old-fashioned in that buyers and sellers (representing investors all over the globe) shout orders at one another face to face. In fact, the NYSE's auction system, in which buyers and sellers meet in the open market, usually produces fair market pricing. To maintain an orderly market, specialists on the trading floor manage buying and selling of assigned stocks and have the responsibility of buying when no one else will.

odd lot   Order to buy or sell fewer than 100 shares of stock.

offering   Act of trying to sell a stock at the posted ASK price.

offering price for IPO   Price that investors must pay for allocated shares in an IPO. Not the same as the opening price, which is the first trade price of a new stock.

opening price for IPO   Price at which a new stock starts trading. Also called the *first trade price*.

On-Balance Volume (OBV)   Plotted as a line representing the cumulative total of volume. Volume from a day's trading with a higher close compared with the previous day is assigned a positive value, whereas volume on a lower close from the previous day is assigned a negative value. Traders look for a confirmation of a trend in OBV with the market or a divergence between the two as an indication of a potential reversal.

open   Price paid in a security's first transaction of the current trading day.

open trades   Current trades that are still held active in the customer's account.

opening range   Range of prices that occur during the first thirty seconds to five minutes of trading, depending on the preference of the individual analyst.

operating expenses   Costs related to a company's operations; for example salaries, advertising, sales commissions, travel, and entertainment. Listed on the statement of earnings.

operating income (or loss)   Result of deducting the cost of all sales and operating expenses from a company's net sales. Listed on the statement of earnings.

opportunity cost   Income foregone by the commitment of resources to another use.

oscillator   Technical indicator used to identify overbought and oversold price regions; an indicator that trends data, such as price.

overbought market   Market prices that have risen too steeply and too quickly.

overbought or oversold indicator   Attempts to define when prices have moved too far and too fast in either direction and thus are vulnerable to a reaction.

oversold market   Market prices that have declined too steeply and too quickly.

oversubscribed IPO   Deal in which investors apply for more shares than are available. Usually a sign that an IPO is a hot deal and will open at a substantial premium.

preferred stock   Stock that acts much like a bond but that confers an ownership stake in the company. Preferred shares typically pay a fixed dividend and give their holder a claim to earnings and assets prior to that bestowed by common stock. In general, the higher the preferred yield, the greater the risk. Preferred stock often comes with a conversion clause permitting it to be traded in for common shares.

previous close   Price of the security at the end of the previous day's trading session.

price Current market price of a security or the amount paid to buy one unit of a security.

price/earnings ratio Stock price divided by annual earnings per share. Also known as the P/E multiple. P/E is the single most widely used factor in assessing whether a stock is pricey or cheap. In general, fast-growing technology companies have high P/Es, because the stock price is taking account of anticipated growth as well as current earnings.

program trading Trades based on signals from computer programs, usually entered directly from the trader's computer into the market's computer system.

prospectus Document, included in a company's S-1 registration statement, that explains all aspects of a company's business, including financial results, growth strategy, and risk factors. The preliminary prospectus is also called a red herring because of the red ink used on the front page, which indicates that some information—such as the price and share amounts—is subject to change.

proxy Written authorization from a shareholder for another person to represent him or her at a shareholders' meeting and to exercise voting rights.

put/call ratio Volume of put options divided by the volume in call options. A high ratio (put volume much higher than call volume) is considered by technical analysts a sign of bearish sentiment, indicating the market is headed south.

pyramid To increase holdings by using the most buying power available in a margin account with paper and real profits.

quiet period for IPO Time in which companies in registration are forbidden by the Securities and Exchange Commission to say anything not included in their prospectus, which could be interpreted as hyping an offering. Starts the day a company files an S-1 registration statement and lasts until 25 days after a stock starts trading. The intent and effect of the quiet period have been hotly debated.

range Difference between the high and low price during a given period, such as one day.

ratio Relation that one quantity bears to another of the same kind, with respect to magnitude or numerical value.

reaction Short-term decline in price.

relative strength   Comparison of the price performance of a stock to a market index, such as Standard & Poor's 500 stock index.

resistance   Price level at which rising prices have stopped rising and have either moved sideways or reversed direction; usually seen as a price chart pattern.

retracement   Price movement in the opposite direction of the previous trend.

revenue   Total flow of funds into a company, mostly for sales of its goods or services. Listed as the first category on the statement of earnings.

risk   Chance that something bad (a loss) will happen. Risk in the context of trading and investing simply refers to the variability of returns.

risk tolerance   Amount of psychological pain the trader or investor is willing to suffer from the investments.

road show for IPO   Tour taken by a company preparing for an IPO in order to attract interest in the deal. Attended by institutional investors, analysts, and money managers by invitation only. Members of the media are forbidden.

round trip   Buying and selling the same stock or opening and closing the trade position, especially in a relatively brief period.

running market   Market wherein prices are changing rapidly in one direction with very few or no price changes in the opposite direction.

screening stocks   Practice, abetted by computers, whereby investors or traders search for all stocks meeting a given set of criterion. For instance, traders can screen for all NASDAQ companies with market capitalization above $500 million, daily trading volume 500,000 shares, and Beta value greater than 1.5.

S-1   Document filed with the Securities and Exchange Commission announcing a company's intent to go public. Includes the prospectus. Also called the *registration statement*.

Securities and Exchange Commission (SEC)   Federal agency charged with regulating the securities markets.

securities   Investments, including stocks and bonds. Listed as assets on the statement of financial position.

SelectNet   Introduced in 1990 and designed so that market makers could communicate and execute trades electronically among themselves.

Orders are broadcast to NASDAQ market makers only. Provides day traders with a tool to electronically submit orders directly to the market makers at a better price than the posted best BID and ASK prices. Not a mandatory system for market makers. Market makers have the option to accept or to ignore that offer; a SelectNet order is filled only if the market maker chooses to execute that order.

selling short   Selling a security and then borrowing the security for delivery with the intent of replacing the security at a lower price.

selling stockholders for IPO   Investors in a company who sell part or all of their stake as part of that company's IPO. Usually considered a bad sign if a large portion of shares offered in an IPO comes from selling stockholders.

settlement   Price at which all outstanding positions in a stock or commodity are marked to market; typically, the closing price.

share   Certificate of ownership in a company. Also called *stock*.

short covering   Process of buying back stock that has already been sold short.

short interest   Shares that have been sold short but not yet repurchased; shares sold short divided by average daily volume.

short interest ratio   Indicates the number of trading days required to repurchase all of the shares that have been sold short. A short interest ratio of 2.50 indicates that, based on the current volume of trading, it will take two and a half days' volume to cover all shorts.

signal   In the context of stock or commodity time series historical data, usually daily or weekly prices.

signal line   In Moving Average jargon, the first Moving Average, such as the Fast Moving Average line of three-minute data, is smoothed by a second Moving Average, such as the Slow Moving Average line of nine-minute data. The second Moving Average is the signal line.

Simple Moving Average   Arithmetic mean, or average, of a series of prices over a period of time. The longer the period of time studied (that is, the larger the denominator of the average), the less impact an individual data point has on the average.

slippage   Difference between estimated transaction costs and actual transaction costs.

smoothing   Mathematical technique that removes excess data variability while maintaining a correct appraisal of the underlying trend.

specialist   Trader on the market floor assigned to fill bids or orders in a specific stock out of his own account when the order has no competing bid or order, to ensure a fair and orderly market.

spike   Sharp rise in price in a single day or two; may be as great as 15 to 30 percent, indicating the time for an immediate sale.

spinning IPO   Practice by investment banks of distributing IPO shares to certain clients, such as venture capitalists and executives, in hopes of getting their business in the future. Outlawed at many banks.

split   Occurs when a company decides to divide its shares into two, three, four, or more. Thus a stock worth $100 might be the subject of a 2-for-1 split, resulting in a share price of $50. Holders in this case get twice as many shares, but each is worth half as much as before, and since nothing else about the company has changed, shareholders aren't better or worse off. Traditionally seen as a good sign; companies split their shares when the price of each share is considered high enough to discourage ownership.

spread   Trade in which two related contracts/stocks/bonds/options are traded to exploit the relative differences in price change between the two.

Standard & Poor's 500   Widely followed benchmark of stock market performance. Includes 400 industrial firms, 40 financial stocks, 40 utilities, and 20 transportation stocks. All the firms are large. Also the basis of a large amount of index investing. Inclusion in the index usually causes a stock to rise.

standard deviation   Positive square root of the expected value of the square of the difference between a random variable and its mean; a measure of the fluctuation in a stock's monthly return over the preceding year.

stochastic   Literally means "random."

stochastics oscillator   Overbought/oversold indicator that compares today's price with a preset window of high and low prices. These data are transformed into a range between zero and 100 and then smoothed.

stock   Certificate of ownership in a company. Also called *share*.

stock symbol   Unique, market-approved code that identifies a particular security on an exchange. Generally reflects the name of the security. Also called the *ticker symbol*.

stockbroker   Individual registered with the National Association of Securities Dealers (NASD) who is authorized to buy and sell securities for her customers.

stockholder   Owner of part of a company. Also called a *shareholder*.

stock index futures   Futures contract traded that uses a market index, such as the S&P 500 Index, as the underlying instrument. The delivery mechanism is usually cash settlement.

stops   Buy stops are orders placed at a predetermined price over the current price of the market. They become "Buy at the market" orders if the market is at or above the price of the stop order. Sell stops are orders placed with a predetermined price below the current price. They become "Sell at the market" orders if the market trades at or below the price of the stop order.

stop loss   Risk management technique in which the trade is liquidated to halt any further decline in value.

street name   Name under which a brokerage firm holds the securities of its customers. Most brokerage companies hold their customers' securities in the firm's street name rather than in the name of each customer. By using its street name rather than an individual's name, the brokerage firm can process trades faster.

support   Historical price level at which falling prices have stopped falling and either moved sideways or reversed direction; usually seen as a price chart pattern.

syndicate   Group of investment banks that buy shares in an IPO to sell to the public. Headed by the lead manager and disbanded as soon as the IPO is completed.

target price   Price that investors or traders hope a given security will reach within certain period of time.

technical analysis   Form of market analysis that studies supply and demand for securities and commodities based on trading volume and price studies. Using charts and modeling techniques, technicians attempt to identify price trends in a market.

technology sector   Category that includes computer hardware, software, electronics, electrical equipment, and wireless communications companies.

tick   Last reported stock transaction. Is reported in increments of $\frac{1}{8}$, $\frac{1}{16}$, or $\frac{1}{32}$.

tick indicator   Number of stocks whose last trade was an up-tick or a down-tick.

ticker tape or screen   Real-time report that states the last price and the unique, market-approved code that identifies a particular security on an exchange.

time series   Collection of observations made sequentially in time and indexed by time. All stock price data is the time series data.

trading bands   Lines plotted in and around the price structure to form an envelope or a band, answering whether prices are high or low on a relative basis and forewarning whether to buy or sell by using indicators to confirm price action. *Bollinger bands* are example of trading bands.

trading range   Difference between the high and low prices traded during a period of time.

trailing stop   Stop-loss order that follows the prevailing price trend.

trend   General drift, tendency, or bent of a set of statistical data as related to time.

trend following   Moving in the direction of the prevailing price movement.

trending market   Price moves in a single direction.

trendless   Price movement that vacillates to the degree that a clear trend cannot be identified.

trendline   Line drawn that connects either a series of highs or lows in a trend. Can represent either support, as in an uptrend line, or resistance, as in a downtrend line. Consolidations are marked by horizontal trendlines.

triple witching hour   Last hour of trading on the third Friday of March, June, September, and December, when investors rush to unwind their positions in index options and futures, all of which are expiring on the same day. Triple witching hour has produced some major price swings as investors buy and sell both the derivatives and the underlying securities.

turning point Approximate time at which there is a change in trend.

up-tick Indicates that the current BID price is higher than the previous BID.

value stock Stock that is undervalued by the current stock market. Can be identified on the most basic level simply by examining the key ratios.

venture capital Funding acquired during the pre-IPO process of raising money for companies. Done only by accredited investors.

volatility Measure of a stock's tendency to move up and down in price, based on its daily price history over the latest twelve months.

volume Total units of a security traded on the most recent trading day. An unusually high volume means that important news has just come out, or will come out soon. Rising volume coupled with a rising share price is considered a bullish indicator for a stock, while the opposite is considered a bearish indicator. Technical analysts also track a volume price trend to relate volume and price. Technical analysts believe that the biggest price gains are associated with the heaviest volume trading.

whiplash or whipsaw Alternating buy and sell signals that result in losses; an investment or trade where the price goes in the opposite direction from that which was anticipated right after the transaction was made. A trade is made based on a buy signal generated by a technical indicator. Then, shortly thereafter, the price moves in the opposite direction giving a sell signal. Results frequently in a trading loss. Can also substantially increase the trading commission cost.

Index